Great Britain

in the World Economy

Great Britain
in the World Economy

By ALFRED E. KAHN

COLUMBIA UNIVERSITY PRESS

NEW YORK *1946*

First printing January, 1946
Second printing August, 1946

COPYRIGHT, 1946, BY COLUMBIA UNIVERSITY PRESS

MANUFACTURED IN THE UNITED STATES OF AMERICA

To My Father

Preface

IT MIGHT BE POLITIC to conceal the fact that this text was originally a doctoral dissertation, entitled "The Position of Great Britain in the World Economy, 1919 to 1939, a Study in Equilibrium in Transition." Possibly the reader would have guessed it anyhow. However, if this lowly origin did not daunt the Columbia University Press, I do not see any need to apologize for it. A dissertation is usually the author's first book; well, if there are to be any, there must be a first. Dissertations, and this one was no exception, are often wordy and excessively detailed and footnoted; I have tried to remove such defects by a thorough rewriting, while also bringing the book up to date, since submitting it to Yale in 1942. At least many words have been removed. In this, Professor Howard Ellis and Hannah Kahn Barsky have given invaluable editorial assistance, which I gratefully acknowledge.

However, I have made no effort to remove the book's use of and frequent allusion to economic theory. Contrary to popular supposition, nothing is more "practical" and realistic than theory. There is no way of interpreting economic facts or understanding the problems of the past and the future except in terms of some conception of the nature of the economic process—which *is* economic theory.

There is a long list of people who have, directly or indirectly, made this book possible. This preface affords me one very inadequate means of acknowledging my debt to them. I want to express my sincere gratitude to two men in particular: to Professor Joseph A. Schumpeter for an ideal teacher's kindly and patient advice, criticism, and comfort and to Professor Myron W. Watkins, who first taught me economics, and still does today. There have been other teachers whom I would like to mention: Professors Gustavus Tuckerman, Jr., Harry G. Brown, Elmer Wood, Karl Bopp, Ray Westerfield, and the late James Harvey Rogers. At various times Yale University and Brookings Institution have assisted me financially, for which I give thanks, and the librarians of the Library of Congress, Brookings Institution, and Sterling Library at Yale have helped me more than they may remember. Finally I want to thank those many friends who have seen me through the tedious last stages of checking, revising, and proofreading the dissertation and the book—

among them Virginia Duncan, Ruth Blaisdell, Arthur J. Barsky, Jr., Barbara Kahn, James Gray, Richard Gray, Jr., Hilary Dirlam, Deborah Miller—and my wife, Mary.

ALFRED E. KAHN

New York
July, 1945

Contents

INTRODUCTION   xv

PART ONE

The Balance of Payments and the
Theory of International Equilibrium

I. THE BALANCE OF PAYMENTS   1
The Inevitable Balance   3
The Current and Capital Balances   4

II. THE THEORY OF INTERNATIONAL EQUILIBRIUM   9
The Purchasing Power Shifts   11
Exchange Rates, Gold Flows, and Proximate Adjustments under the Old
    Gold Standard   16
Definitive Re-equilibration   19

III. THE NEED FOR AN ORGANIC THEORY   27
Case Studies: Canada, 1900–1913, and German Reparations   34

PART TWO

Great Britain's Position
in a Changing World

IV. BRITAIN'S PROBLEMS IN A CHANGING WORLD ECONOMY   41
The Changing Institutional Framework and Mechanism of Adjustment   41
Britain's Changing Real Position   51

V. THE DETERIORATING POSITION OF BRITISH INDUSTRY   65
The Staple Industries   65
Underlying Explanations   72
British Inadaptability   78

VI. THE DECLINE AND ADJUSTMENTS OF THE STAPLE TRADES   84
Coal   84
Iron and Steel   88
Cotton Textiles   92
Other Staple Trades   100

VII. THE EXPANDING INDUSTRIES   105
    The New Industries   105
    Automobiles   110
    The Electrical Industries   113
    Rayon   120
    The Building Industries   121

PART THREE

The British Balance of International Payments

VIII. BASIC TRENDS IN THE BRITISH BALANCE OF PAYMENTS   125
    Before 1914   125
    Post-War Years; the Trade Aspect   131
    Post-War Years; the Capital Aspect   137
    The Terms of Trade   144
    The Problems of Adjustment, 1919–39   152

IX. PROBLEMS OF EQUILIBRIUM AND ADJUSTMENTS OF
    POLICY, 1924–31   158
    The Current Balance   158
    Long-Term Lending   161
    Gold, Short-Term Capital, Bank Policy, and the Problems of Equilibrium 164

X. PROBLEMS OF EQUILIBRIUM AND ADJUSTMENTS OF
    POLICY, 1932–39   179
    The Current Balance   179
    Long-Term Lending   188
    Gold, Short-Term Capital Movements, Monetary Policy, and the Problems of Equilibrium 195

PART FOUR

The Shifting Geographical Patterns of Great Britain's International Economic Transactions

XI. SHIFTING GEOGRAPHICAL PATTERNS OF BRITISH EXPORTS
    AND IMPORTS, 1815–1939   208
    Merchandise Exports   208
    Merchandise Imports   214

XII. THE PATTERN IN EQUILIBRIUM, 1929   219
    The Major Triangle: The Great Britain–Empire Side   221
    The Empire–"Foreign" Side   228
    The Great Britain–"Foreign" Aspect   230
    Filling in the Pattern   232

XIII. THE PATTERN IN TRANSITION   236
    Gradual Change, 1900–1929   236
    Rapid Change, 1929–38   239
    The Pattern in 1937   247

CONCLUSION

XIV. THE BRITISH ECONOMY IN TRANSITION   257

XV. THE POSITION OF BRITAIN IN THE POST-WAR WORLD   269

APPENDIX

THE BRITISH BALANCE OF PAYMENTS; METHODOLOGY AND
    DEFINITIONS   293
    Gold Coin and Bullion   294
    Long-Term Capital Movements   296
    Short-Term Capital Movements   297

SELECTED BIBLIOGRAPHY   301

INDEX   309

Tables

1. QUANTUM INDEXES OF PRODUCTION AND TRADE   63

2. GROSS OUTPUT AND EXPORTS IN SELECTED UNITED KINGDOM INDUSTRIES, 1907 AND 1930   68

3. UNITED KINGDOM PRODUCTION AND EXPORTS OF COAL   85

4. IRON AND STEEL PRODUCTION AND TRADE OF THE UNITED KINGDOM   89

5. UNITED KINGDOM COTTON TEXTILE INDUSTRY PRODUCTION, EXPORTS, RAW COTTON IMPORTS   93

6. RELATIVE IMPORTANCE OF THE BRITISH COTTON INDUSTRY   95

7. THE RISE OF NEW INDUSTRIES IN THE UNITED KINGDOM   106

8. THE NEW INDUSTRIES AS EXPORTERS AND IMPORTERS   109

9. AUTOMOBILE PRICES, PRODUCTION, AND TRADE IN THE UNITED KINGDOM   111

10. EXPORTS OF PRIVATE AND COMMERCIAL AUTOMOBILES BY LEADING COUNTRIES   112

11. GROSS OUTPUT AND TRADE IN ELECTRICAL GOODS IN THE UNITED KINGDOM   117

12. NUMBERS OF INSURED WORKERS IN THE BUILDING INDUSTRIES   122

13. BALANCE OF INTERNATIONAL PAYMENTS OF THE UNITED KINGDOM, 1924–38   126

14. UNITED KINGDOM BALANCE ON CURRENT ACCOUNT   127

15. ANNUAL AVERAGES OF UNITED KINGDOM BALANCES OF PAYMENT, CURRENT ACCOUNT   128

16. VOLUME OF UNITED KINGDOM TRADE: AVERAGE ANNUAL RATE OF GROWTH IN PERCENT   131

17. U.K. CURRENT BALANCES OF INTERNATIONAL PAYMENTS, 1907–38 ANNUAL AVERAGES, PEAK YEARS   132

18. UNITED KINGDOM AND WORLD EXPORTS AND IMPORTS 132

19. INDEXES OF EXPORT VOLUME, UNITED KINGDOM PROD-
     UCTS, 1924–37   133

20. INDEXES OF VOLUME OF UNITED KINGDOM RETAINED
     IMPORTS   136

21. ANNUAL AVERAGES OF NEW ISSUES IN LONDON   139

22. INDEXES OF THE UNITED KINGDOM BARTER TERMS OF
     TRADE   144

23. INDEXES OF UNITED KINGDOM TERMS OF TRADE, 1913–38 153

24. INDEXES OF AVERAGE VALUE AND VOLUME, UNITED
     KINGDOM TRADE   180

25. INCOME FROM UNITED KINGDOM OVERSEAS INVEST-
     MENTS   187

26. NEW CAPITAL ISSUES IN THE UNITED KINGDOM AND
     OFFSETTING REPAYMENTS, 1929–38   191

27. RELATIVE SHARES OF THE EMPIRE AND THE UNITED
     KINGDOM IN THE TOTAL FOREIGN TRADE OF EACH
     OTHER   225

28. LEADING EXPORTS OF BRITISH EMPIRE COUNTRIES IN
     1929   229

29. INDIAN BALANCES OF PRIVATE, SEA-BORNE MERCHANDISE
     TRADE   250

30. ANGLO-AMERICAN BALANCE OF PAYMENTS, 1928, 1936,
     AND 1937   252

31. ESTIMATED BRITISH DEALINGS IN EXISTING SECURITIES,
     SUBSCRIPTION TO ISSUES ON FOREIGN MARKETS, AND
     DIRECT INVESTMENTS   298

Introduction

GREAT BRITAIN's economic greatness, far more than that of any other country, has been based upon her international trade, her merchant marine, her foreign investments, and her international banking business. The growth and economic progress of the British people have been grounded largely upon importation of foreign food and raw materials and exportation of manufactures and services, hence upon the evolution of an extremely specialized international position. Their own very sustenance and that of their industry, indeed, are provided in large measure by imported commodities.

The peculiar international economic position of Britain has also determined to an extreme degree the economic structure and operation of the entire world. It was Great Britain who took the lead in that gigantic development of commerce and industry which created the modern world. And her central position before 1914, her supremacy as exporter, shipper, middleman, banker, and her great open commodity markets unified and facilitated the functioning of a truly global economy. That complex of policies, practices, and institutions known as the international gold standard functioned as it did in large measure because it centered about a single financial nucleus located in London.[1] The accelerated changes in Britain's international position in the period 1919 to 1939 have therefore not only seriously affected her own economy. They have also involved a disruption of certain basic patterns of the world economic process, creating flaws and maladjustments which contributed in no small degree to its eventual disintegration and collapse.

It is our intention to study these changes in Great Britain's international economic position with the aid of the theory of international equilibrium. This theory, which purports to explain the functioning of the world economy, is introduced not only because it may prove useful in this study; in view of Britain's focal importance, it is anticipated also that the British experience will be peculiarly illuminating in evaluating the validity and usefulness of the theory itself. Our first chapters, accord-

[1] This is the central thesis of W. A. Brown, Jr., *The International Gold Standard Reinterpreted, 1914–34* (hereinafter, *The Int. Gold Stand.*). Hence, the disintegration of the gold standard is attributed in large measure to the disappearance of Britain's financial supremacy, and to the consequent dissolution of that single unifying nucleus.

ingly, are concerned with the exposition and development of this instrument of analysis.

The British balance of payments charts the changes in her international economic position in a changing world. No economic change of the period is alien to it. The bulk of our study therefore consists of an investigation into the British balance of payments and into the numerous factors determining it and determined by it. In such a study it soon becomes clear that the internal and the international are completely and inextricably linked in mutual causal relationship. Together they form the pattern of the British economy, and no balanced judgment of one is possible without survey of the other. Although our major emphasis is upon the international phase of the British economy, an attempt is made throughout this work to relate this aspect to the broader local and universal economic processes of which it is an inherent part.

The "international economic position" of a country may mean many things. It may mean its economic power in relation to the economic power of other countries. It may mean the material well-being of the people who happen to live within its geographic borders. It may mean the way in which those people, as an economic group and as a mere chance aggregation of individuals, fit into world processes of production, exchange, and consumption.

Our interest is primarily in the latter two: in economic processes and material welfare. Nevertheless, in evaluating economic change and government policy, the first criterion, that is, the power of the corporate political group facing the world as a coherent entity, may also be an essential consideration—particularly during a period of resurgent economic nationalism. Although the ways in which the national interest and the sum total of individual economic interests coincide are probably more important than the ways in which they diverge, such divergence is possible. Economic power is relative; acts which may enhance it, and hence, perhaps, contribute to the "general welfare" (e.g., preference to potential allies, tariffs for self-sufficiency), may indeed be to the economic detriment of the people in absolute terms of real income. This possible divergence in interest, and hence in possible goals of national policy, in large measure explains the differences between the doctrines of the mercantilists of the sixteenth century to the eighteenth and the classical economists of the eighteenth and nineteenth centuries. The former, living in a period of newly emergent national states, sought to magnify national power, even at the cost of—indeed, according to some, by means of—keeping the bulk of the population in poverty.[2] The latter, who were of the age of Locke, Rousseau, and Jefferson, made fewer concessions to any distinct interest of the group as a whole, arguing, instead, that the increased absolute wealth of the individuals within the country rather than the increase of relative national power should be the major preoccupation of national policy. It is clear that "the *tragedy* of the pound," "the *evil* effects of foreign lending," and "the *weak* position of Britain" are meaningless expressions unless the criteria upon which they are based are explicitly stated. In general, unless other considerations are relevant, our concern is with the material welfare of the British people.

[2] Edgar S. Furniss, *The Position of the Laborer in a System of Nationalism*, Boston, Houghton Mifflin, 1920, chap. vi.

Part One
The Balance of Payments and the Theory of International Equilibrium

———— ❧ ————

I. THE BALANCE OF PAYMENTS

THE BALANCE OF PAYMENTS concerns only those economic activities of a country and its people which overflow national boundaries and enter the realm of international transactions. The distinction between these and "internal" transactions is essentially arbitrary. Purchases, sales, loans, and gifts result in either case from similar habits and motivations. All are effected in one great market, still essentially a world market, in which buyers, sellers, lenders, borrowers of all nationalities meet. To a great extent, therefore, it is of little consequence whether transactions happen to be between people living in different countries or those living in the same country.

However, these distinctions are far from meaningless. Politically, they are real lines which cut across the face of world society; and from this alone they obtain economic significance. The psychological fact of national consciousness influences economic choices between foreign and domestic goods and services (the preference may be either way) by consumers, investors, and governments; even the philanthropist considers where, precisely, charity ought to begin. The enormous active influence of the state upon economic life likewise usually operates so as to distinguish internal from external transactions. The mere fact of separate and internally uniform monetary and financial systems creates a greater possibility of divergencies in currency and credit policies and conditions between different countries than within any individual country. And there is no limit to the way in which conscious political policies may create further distinctions between internal and international transactions. Tariffs and trade treaties, competitive currency depreciations, controls of foreign investment, immigration restrictions, and manifold other forms of discrimination strengthen the economic lines cutting across the map of the world economy.

British labor is, after all, quite literally British labor, not simply an arbitrarily delineated segment of the world labor pool; so, indeed, is British capital precisely British, despite its obvious international character; and British land is of course by definition British, not merely part of the world's pool of resources. There is a relative lack of mobility of productive elements between countries, partly because of the factors and controls already mentioned. Therefore, while British standards of living show obvious discrepancies, nevertheless, they do, as a whole, differ from the standards of other countries. In a world of growing nationalism, of increasingly restricted international movements of labor and capital, these differences will be sharpened. The vicissitudes of international competition become vitally significant not merely to separate individuals but to a whole country, not merely in a period of transition and of temporary maladjustment, but permanently.

For these many reasons Britain is in a real sense an economic entity with distinguishing economic characteristics. And British people, although they trade and transact individually, form in a sense a distinguishable group. The economic history of such a group, treated as a group, becomes, then, a suitable subject for study.

A country's balance of international payments is a summation of all the transactions between it (and its nationals) and the rest of the world wherein it receives or expends cash.[1] All international transfers of purchasing power are included, whether or not for current or future *quid pro quo*, whether the cash moving as a result is actually converted into the national currency of the recipient or remains in the form of claims upon the paying country. It represents thus a summation of a country's current demand and supply of the claims on foreign currencies and of foreign claims on its currency, i.e., for the foreign exchange whereby these payments are effected.

For anything more than a single transacting unit, an individual or business, the balance of payments is a statistical fiction. A national balance of payments is an arbitrary aggregation of those disparate transac-

---

[1] Whether transactions which do not involve the intermediation of money ought to be included, whether in fact they may be called transactions at all, depends entirely upon one's definitions. It need only be noted that on the international plane, as internally, such "noncash transactions" do exist, but that their exclusion or inclusion in the balance of payments is a matter of theoretical indifference from the viewpoint of international equilibrium.

tions by separate individuals which happen to cross national boundaries. These transactions are not in most cases made by the country acting as a self-conscious trading unit. The resulting statement has nothing to do with profit or loss, for either the nation or the separate individuals engaged in the transactions included.

Nevertheless, there is, as we have seen, particular cogency in the study of the national balance, an interest which increases with the growth of economic nationalistic differentiation.[2] The balance of payments is thus one extremely useful instrument for analyzing a country's position—but it cannot be used *in vacuo;* its limitations must be recognized.

The Inevitable Balance

It is elementary accounting procedure to conceive of all transactions as two-sided phenomena, involving an equal credit and debit aspect. Every outpayment includes a debit, the cause of the outpayment, and a credit, the reduction of an asset or increase of a liability whereby the outpayment is effected. Similarly, each inpayment involves a credit, the cause of the receipt, and a debit, the means of receipt.

On the international plane cash payments are made with claims on domestic or foreign currencies. The equal and opposite credit involved in every single outpayment (debit), and the debit involved in each inpayment (credit), consists thus in opposite flows of these claims, i.e., of short-term capital. Each export of goods, a credit, involves in the receipt of payment therefor either a decrease in the short-term liabilities of a country's banks to foreigners or an increase in their short-term foreign assets, in either case an outflow of short-term capital (a debit). Every import of goods or other debit involves an opposite inflow of short-term credits (a credit), a drawing down of claims on other countries or an increase of the latters' claims on the outpaying country.

If we include in the compilation of transactions these reverse movements through the reservoirs of foreign exchange, it is obvious that the

---

[2] See Salter, *World Trade and Its Future,* p. 4; F. W. Paish, "Banking Policy and the Balance of International Payments," *Economica,* n.s., III (1936), 404–7. In the converse of this will be recognized the classical truism, so convincingly argued by Sir Norman Angell, that given liberal economic policy the political nationality of any territory will not make the slightest economic difference to anyone. Given illiberal economic policies, or simply relative immobility of factors of production over national boundaries, political nationality becomes potentially of great economic significance. It follows that balances can be constructed for other groups as well, regional or occupational, which will be illuminating in so far as there is justification for the grouping—such justification as we have already found for the national grouping.

resultant balance of payments, the sum of the individual debits and credits, must represent an exact equality, just as does every individual transaction. Most of the short-term credit flows, by which payments are made, will of course balance out over anything more than an infinitesimal period of time. Supply and demand of foreign exchange are continuous; the claims are book transfers which are canceled against each other, leaving the net short-term credit position at any time much the same as before.

This inherent inevitability of balance is merely a restatement of an obvious truism: no country (or individual) can buy, give, or lend more or less than it receives by sale, gift, or loan from all the rest of the world, except in so far as it draws upon or increases its accumulated claims on the rest of the world or increases or decreases its debts. To the extent that purchases and other remittances do not equal sales and other remittances, clearly a country is engaging in some capital transaction, borrowing or lending on long or short term to precisely the same extent.[3] It is of the essence of the transactions themselves that this equation should persist.

THE CURRENT AND CAPITAL BALANCES

The total balance of payments is customarily broken down into two sections, the current balance and the capital balance, with gold coin and bullion taken separately. This is often a summary procedure, and theoretical consistency must frequently be sacrificed to statistical expediency. Nevertheless the division is a useful one. There is considerable variation in opinion and practice in making this distinction between current and capital transactions. Some economists try to draw the line on the basis of whether an immediate *quid pro quo* is involved, thus reserving to the capital account all unilateral transfers, loans, gifts, and tribute.[4] Others seek to distinguish according to the regularity or normal predictability of the payments, thus including regular amortization receipts in the current account.[5] Almost all seek to apply to the current account the economic concept of income, reserving thus for the capital account various capital flows and unusual transfers.[6] The official British current balance,

[3] Canada, Dominion Bureau of Statistics, *The Canadian Balance of International Payments* (hereinafter cited by title only), pp. 15–17; Lewis, *The International Accounts*, pp. 1–2; Aftalion, *L'Equilibre dans les relations économiques internationales*, p. 9.
[4] Heilperin, *International Monetary Economics*, chap. v; Iversen, *Aspects of the Theory of International Capital Movements*, pp. 35–36.
[5] As in Aftalion's "balance of accounts," *L'Equilibre dans les relations économiques internationales*, p. 6.
[6] See Aftalion's "*balance des revenus*," *ibid.*, pp. 9–12, and Viner's "balance of indebted-

which we must use in any event, may not be rationalized along any of the various lines suggested with complete consistency. It simply includes all but capital flows and gold. Thus, it excludes "normal" capital repayments, while including items which may in many cases be far more erratic. It cuts across the classification based upon whether payments are for a *quid pro quo*, immediate or deferred. It is primarily an income account; yet it is by no means clear whether all the unilateral transfers of purchasing power included may be regarded as income.

Net current and capital balances must be equal and opposite, since together they constitute the total balance of payments (including gold in the current balance, for convenience). Each is a mirror and measure of the other.

The theory of international equilibrium is very largely concerned with the causal relationship between the two balances. It is often stated, popularly, that the net capital movement is what is left over after the computation of the current balance, with the clear implication that the first is the result of and is determined by the second.[7] Such a direct relationship is, of course, impossible, since the men who do the lending and the borrowing do so for purely private reasons, as do those whose transactions constitute the current balance. The connections are more subtle, so subtle, indeed, that they have been the subject of endless economic controversy.

Much of this controversy, seeking to establish which of the two balances is usually causal, which usually adaptive, has been fruitless, in our judgment. Every transaction in the balance of payments is bound inextricably with every other, in an intricate network of cause and effect which encompasses not only them but also all the factors which in turn affect them: prices, sectional and general, interest rates, cost and demand curves, bank and fiscal policy, cyclical fluctuations, etc. Any one of these determinants might conceivably at one time or another be the initial disturbing factor. While it is true that some items in the balance of payments are less sensitive than others to such disturbances, it is difficult to

ness," *Canada's Balance of International Indebtedness, 1900–1913* (hereinafter, *Canada's Balance*), pp. 21–22.

[7] The "capital transactions . . . show the amount by which net foreign assets or liabilities have increased or decreased during a period. The income account . . . explains this change." Lewis, *The International Accounts*, p. 67. Here is the result of the misleading analogy to corporate accounts: the income account creates the change in the "net worth"; a balance of trade "deficit" causes an increase in debt. See Iversen, *Aspects of the Theory of International Capital Movements*, p. 66.

generalize from historical experience that the changes in either the trade or the capital balance usually bring about adjustments in the other. In general, just as good a case can be made for the causal influence of trade over capital movements as the reverse—and just as bad. Either would be inadequate.

Capital movements undoubtedly do call forth adjustments in the current balance. But what is it that makes such movements possible in the first place? Clearly, not every country can simply start to export capital and expect the trade balance to adjust automatically. Investment necessitates a surplus of output over current consumption; foreign investment necessitates a surplus of goods or services which are required abroad. Only those countries which have been able to produce and sell such a surplus—and have therefore been in a strong current position to begin with—have been in the long run capable of exporting capital, which is precisely this surplus of exports. It is clearly the productive power of the country, operating first upon its trade balance, which controls in the long run the need for foreign capital and the supply of domestic capital. There are numerous examples of much clearer and more direct connection with change in the current balance, actual or prospective, as cause and capital movements as effect. America's loans to her allies during the first World War were a refunding of obligations incurred in huge previous commodity imports. The belligerents' need for imports necessitated controls of capital flows and liquidation of foreign assets, a conscious adaptation of capital to current balance characteristic of more recent exchange controls. Totalitarian economies lend and borrow almost entirely in order to sell or buy goods. Finally, younger countries have often floated loans in order to buy needed machinery or raw materials from the lending country.[8]

On the other hand, there is abundant evidence of the startling adaptability of commodity trade to changes originating more or less independently in the capital balance. The great influx of capital into Canada from 1900 to 1913,[9] the payment of the Franco-Prussian War indemnity between 1870 and 1876,[10] the sharp decline in Britain's capital exports in the early 1890's after a period of great overlending,[11] and the abrupt

[8] See Aftalion, *L'Equilibre dans les relations économiques internationales*, p. 315; White, *The French International Accounts, 1880–1913*, pp. 214–16.

[9] See Viner, *Canada's Balance, passim*.

[10] Von Haberler, *The Theory of International Trade*, pp. 92–96.

[11] Hobson, *International Trade*, pp. 108–10.

cessation and reversal of capital import into Germany between 1928 and 1931 were all accompanied by amazingly rapid alterations in current balances. However, although in these cases the changes in capital flow must have been the relatively more causative factors, even here the causation was not entirely one-sided. Indeed, as we shall argue below, if the changes in both current and capital balances be considered in terms of the complex pattern of antecedent and concomitant factors of which they are an intimate part, the impossibility of singling out one as initial cause, the other as effect, would be quite clear.

Most economic theory seems to favor the view, expounded mainly by Professors Ohlin and Iversen, that capital movements far more often bring adjustments in commodity trade than vice versa.[12] Taussig, White, and Viner, in their case studies, customarily treat the capital flow as the "disturbing" factor, the trade balance as the "adjusting" factor. The following explanation occurs to the author. There has been little attempt traditionally to analyze the cyclical fluctuations of the balance of payments; most of the theory of international equilibrium assumes, unconsciously or consciously, a static situation of full employment. Now, the possible disrupting factors may be said to fall under two heads: changes in demand and supply dispositions, operating initially upon the current balance, and changes in those factors giving rise to unilateral transfers, capital flows, indemnities, etc. Assuming away cyclical variations leaves little reason for expecting initial changes of the former kind in the short run. Authors have, therefore, customarily studied the more striking changes of the second category, unilateral transfers, and the theory of international equilibrium has as a result become almost synonymous with the "theory of transfers." The origin of such transfers may also be cyclical, but this is usually ignored, except in a brief initial explanation. Beyond that point, they are treated as shifts of claims over a fixed world output from B to A. Under these assumptions, B simply takes a slice of pie smaller than it has earned, A a larger slice, and the trade balance adjusts automatically.

Were it realized, however, that cyclical fluctuations of employment, output, and income are an inherent part of the economic process, not

[12] Ohlin, *Interregional and International Trade*, pp. 383–84, 445; Iversen, *Aspects of the Theory of International Capital Movements*, p. 66. Lord Keynes has taken the opposite view, "The German Transfer Problem," *Economic Journal* (hereinafter *Econ. Jour.*), XXXIX (1929), 6, and Professor Viner takes a middle position, *Studies in the Theory of International Trade* (hereinafter *Studies in Theory*), p. 364.

merely an independent external disturbance,[13] this form of myopia would disappear. The cyclical factors which influence flows of capital at the same time affect trade balances. In the ebb and flow of economic activity, demand and supply dispositions are constantly shifting, for other reasons than inflow and outflow of capital. They are as mobile as capital, and hence an equal potential source of disequilibrium in balances of payments in a world in constant process of movement and change.[14]

[13] Divergent national price movements, caused by the failure of business fluctuations to occur simultaneously, have received some consideration, but only as another possible external disequilibrating factor.

[14] See Chapter III, below.

II. THE THEORY OF INTERNATIONAL EQUILIBRIUM

THE INEVITABLE EQUALITY of balance-of-payments debits and credits is not highly significant. If transactions are being effected, whether easily or with difficulty, the balance will continue. And if a country is bankrupt, if it has neither gold nor foreign assets, if foreigners will not accept its currency, and transactions are therefore not effected, debits will still equal credits. The fact of continuous balance thus offers not the slightest presumption of stability in a given situation and no means of evaluating that situation. Behind its façade may lurk all degrees of instability or breakdown.

A distinction must be drawn between such a superficial technical equality and "equilibrium" of the balance of payments, the latter implying a more enduring adjustment of out- and inpayments and a greater chance for maintaining an optimum level of international economic activity. We shall use the expression "equilibrium" in a country's balance of payments to denote a situation in which over a period of time long enough to exclude seasonal and minor discrepancies the total supply and demand for means of foreign payment are equated, without continuous short-term capital or gold movements in one direction, or sizable fluctuations in the external value of currencies, or default, or measures of control employed to maintain this equality. Such equilibrium requires that all money transfers for goods, services, long period claims, and in satisfaction of obligations be on balance real transfers—of goods, services, satisfactions of obligations, and evidences of debt of longer maturity than international money itself.

This is an arbitrary definition and suffers from the arbitrariness of all definitions. Certain net movements of short-term capital need not be inconsistent with equilibrium. On the other hand, a balance may, even though it fulfills the requirements of the definition, be inherently unstable. A country may be lending or borrowing more on long term or selling or buying more on balance than it can continue to do without eventual readjustment too drastic to be accomplished without serious economic dislocation. Without its qualifications as to stable currencies, the absence of transfer defaults and of government controls, the concept would still amount to little more than the axiom that a country cannot for any length of time buy, lend, or give more than it sells, receives, or borrows on relatively long term. Even as it stands, equilibrium conditions may still conceal enormous instability and be consistent with fluctuations in international economic activity, employment, and real incomes. Usually the conditions which cause such fluctuations are, however, also disruptive of equilibrium, as defined. Equilibrium conditions are certainly more conducive to, and are more likely to be associated with, relative stability and an optimum degree of international economic activity than are conditions of disequilibrium, as defined.

The possible disturbances to such a pre-existing balance, creating a need for adjustment somewhere if equilibrium is to be maintained, may arise from any of the infinite number of causes and effects whose interplay determines every transaction in the balance of payments. Any change —psychological, physical, political, or economic, seasonal, cyclical, or secular, regular and predictable or random, bad harvests, successful advertising campaigns, and wars—all may and do demand continuous adjustment of the whole.

To some disturbances the "adjustment" of the first level is sufficient. In the short run, inpayments and outpayments, excluding cash, cannot possibly be absolutely equal. International short-term balances exist, and gold flows occur, precisely in order to smooth out temporary discrepancies between demand and supply. But enduring equilibrium requires that these flows of short-term credits and gold, however great in gross, tend to a net value of zero.[1]

---

[1] See James W. Angell, *The Theory of International Prices*, pp. 400, 416–17; Kindleberger, *International Short-Term Capital Movements*, pp. 102–3; Bryce, "A Note on Banking Policy and the Exchanges," *Review of Economic Studies* (hereinafter, *Rev. Econ. Studies*), IV (1937), 240–41.

The definition of the text is by no means generally accepted. Viner and Aftalion speak of equilibrium as if it were the same as equality of the current balance and therefore upset by the mere existence of a long-term capital flow. Viner, *Canada's Balance*, pp. 147–48; Aftalion, *L'Equilibre dans les relations économiques internationales*, pp. 5, 97.

There is often more than a hint in such a definition that equality of the current balance is "normal." This idea is fairly explicit in the definition of Marco Fanno, who seems also to imply, quite fallaciously, that equilibrium also requires that the bilateral current balances between any two individual countries must balance: "If the aggregate value of commodities and services exchanged between countries and that of the unilateral economic payments of an income character which are owed by one country to another are equal as between the two countries involved . . . the balance of international payments of the countries in question will be in equilibrium, and all debtor and creditor relations between them will cancel each other completely." *Normal and Abnormal International Capital Transfers*, p. 2. Disequilibrium may be offset by a capital flow, continues Fanno,

The transactions summarized in the balance of payments are for the most part not transactions between states operating as units, but between a host of individuals, private and corporate, motivated by a multiplicity of factors. Hence, in the absence of government controls, it is apparent that equilibrium can be maintained only by an automatic change developing out of the state of disequilibrium itself, a change in the objective economic factors which influence the decisions of these individuals so as to cause them to alter their transactions to the extent and in the manner required. This is the essence of the problem of international economic order, and of the operation of the more or less automatic system which has fulfilled this essential function in the past.

THE PURCHASING POWER SHIFTS

Every transaction, domestic or international, involves an immediate shift of purchasing power, from remitter to recipient.[2] When a national of country B makes a payment to a national of country A, transfer is effected by B's banks either (1) drawing down their foreign balances to supply the needed exchange, or (2) accepting added claims upon themselves by foreign banks. In case 1 the banks of the remitting country, B, lose an equivalent amount of deposits and foreign assets, since the remitters draw checks upon them to pay for the foreign bills. A's banks may or may not experience an equivalent increase of deposits and reserves. They will not if B pays with claims on A, thereby extinguishing a short-term credit to them, A's exporters thus simply taking over the deposits previously owned by B's banks. They will if B pays instead with claims on a

---

but "the disequilibrium, although it is eliminated for the moment, is not cured definitively, and the securities of the debtor country are therefore only an instrument by which it is able to effect a provisional settlement." *ibid.*, p. 3.

Dr. Fanno has a right to frame such definitions as he pleases, but he must realize that such equilibrium as he describes has never existed except by sheer accident. Even in the long run, international trade is not mere barter, because most international, as well as internal, debt is never repaid on balance. Whenever a country does finally repay its foreign debts on balance, the repayment is incident to secular economic development, not to re-equilibrating tendencies, and usually leads then to a capital outflow, and hence rather creates new "disequilibria" than solves old. See Aftalion, *L'Equilibre dans les relations économiques internationales*, Book I, chap. i. Capital movements are just as normal as changes in the trade balance; hence an "unbalanced" current account is just as normal as a "balanced" one, and just as compatible with equilibrium, by any useful definition of the term.

[2] See the lucid accounts of James W. Angell, *The Theory of International Prices*, p. 403 ff., and his section in *Explorations in Economics*, pp. 15–18; also Kindleberger, *International Short-Term Capital Movements*, chaps. ii–iii.

third country, C or D. In any event, at least B's purchasing power will decline.

In case 2, also, there will be a net change in purchasing power, but never on more than one side. B can have no net decline in demand deposits or reserves, because credit is now being extended to her; her remitters' deposits are merely transferred to the ownership of foreign banks. But in A there will be a net rise in demand deposits and in bank reserves held abroad. In both cases, then, there will be an immediate and automatic shift in buying power, either a decrease in the remitting country or a rise in the receiving country, or, in some circumstances, both.

The immediate shift of buying power *in the hands of the nationals of the countries concerned* will, however, always be two-sided. Total buying power in B may be spared primary deflation because her banks borrow abroad on short term (case 2), but domestically owned deposits in B will still be reduced. Total deposits in A may be held constant because B's banks withdraw their balances (case 1), but A's domestically owned deposits will rise. Deposits owned by foreign banks (increase or decrease of which prevents the two-sided purchasing power shift) do not represent as direct a potential demand for foreign goods, services, or securities as do the deposits owned by nationals. They operate upon that potential demand only by entering the money markets, by extensions of credit. Therefore every transaction does cause an immediate change in effective purchasing power simultaneously in B and A.

Since each international transaction involves such an automatic change, any balance-of-payments disequilibrium, any excess of outpayments or inpayments, will immediately entail net purchasing power movements from one country to another, even though total debits and credits be inevitably equated by reverse flows of short credits.[3]

---

[3] Thus, it is sometimes said that an inflow of short-term capital may be deflationary and an outflow inflationary. See Whale, "International Short-Term Capital Movements," *Economica*, n.s. VI (1939), 30–39; International Labour Office (I.L.O.), *Employment, Wages, and International Trade* (Studies and Reports, Series B, No. 32), pp. 29–34. The flows referred to are precisely these movements of the means of payment. In the above case, B "imports" and A "exports" short-term capital. Obviously, however, the factor inflating A's buying power and deflating B's is not the flow of credits, but the transactions paid for by these credits. Such reasoning is therefore deceptive. The I.L.O. report speaks at times as if all short-term capital inflows are deflationary (pp. 40–41). Elsewhere it speaks of the deflationary effects on the world of the United States' heavy short-term capital outflow of 1930 (p. 45), when obviously what was deflationary was the United States' heavy active balance of payments on other accounts. Had the United States taken home its receipts in gold, had it not permitted its foreign balances to accumulate, the deflationary influence upon the world would have been far greater. As we have seen, such a reverse

Every international transaction also entails two secondary purchasing power consequences, which tend to magnify the primary consequences. These consequences are related: an automatic multiplier effect,[4] and an effect upon the expansion or contraction of bank credit.[5] The ultimate alteration in a country's income as a result of a rise or fall of the money stream is a multiple of the original change by the income velocity of money. While the latter is conditioned in large measure by bank policy, this multiplier exists independently of any change in the volume of bank credit. It is a function of many other variables, notably the marginal propensities to save and to import.

The causal relations between these variables are reciprocal. One factor, conditioning both the ease of balance-of-payments adjustment (through the shift in buying power) and the multiplier, tends to regulate the size of the secondary as well as of the primary income effect in accordance with the necessity for such magnification. This is the marginal propensity to import out of the increments or decrements to income resulting from the initial disequilibrium. The reduction of B's incomes by a reduction of A's demand for her goods (or any other similar change on current account) [6] and the increase in A's incomes will both be multiplied less or more, other factors being assumed constant, and the balance of payments more or less quickly adjusted, both directly in proportion (and as a result) as the propensity to import out of that decrement or increment to income is great or small, respectively. The total primary and secondary income effects will thus tend as a result of this factor alone to be great or small as the need is great or small. If the propensity to import is high, on the one hand, the balance of payment adjustment will be rapid, and, on the other, the multiplier will be small. If greater income shifts are necessary, i.e., if the marginal propensity to import is weak, both the primary and secondary income effects will be great and persistent until equilibrium is re-established (the primary because of continued disequilibrium; the secondary because the multiplier is great).

The balance-of-payments adjustment is a function as well of all the

---

flow of short-term credits (case 2) prevents the primary deflation from being greater than it would otherwise be. As we shall see, it thereby alleviates secondary deflation as well.

[4] See Machlup, *International Trade and the National Income Multiplier*.

[5] See F. W. Paish, "Banking Policy and the Balance of International Payments," *Economica*, n.s., III (1936), 407-9.

[6] The transactions of the capital account may not properly be said to have primary *income* effects subject to multiplication.

other factors which condition the multiplier. If, for example, B's nationals maintain their consumption by a reduction of savings, and A's do the same by increasing savings, both actions decreasing the respective downward and upward multiplier effects, the balance-of-payments adjustment will be less readily effected. Other things being equal, the greater the multiplier effect, the easier the balance-of-payments adjustment on this account alone.[7]

The primary and secondary changes in levels of purchasing power thus far discussed occur in both the remitting and the receiving countries, since the domestically owned deposits of both change equivalently and simultaneously in opposite directions. When we come to secondary effects via credit expansion and contraction, however, we find that the shifts of credits between the banking systems of A and B, whereby payments are made, prevent complete reciprocal adjustments. Either (case 1) B's bank reserves, held abroad, are reduced, or (case 2) A's bank reserves, held abroad, are increased, with a resultant tendency toward contraction of credit and hence of money in B or expansion in A. This secondary magnification will occur in both countries simultaneously only if payments are made by claims on other countries, C or D, or if the banks of A and B hold greater reserves against foreign than against domestic deposits, as they should.[8] In the latter event, the shift in ownership of deposits from B's banks to A exporters (case 1) or from B importers to A's banks (case 2) will tend to induce secondary inflation in A or deflation in B, even though there has been no primary change in the total deposits and reserves in either country.[9]

[7] See Machlup, *International Trade and the National Income Multiplier*, pp. 38–42, 57, 84–87, and chap. x. Changes in the volume of savings can permanently prevent readjustment of the trade balance, as Machlup argues, but only if one excludes, as he does by assumption, the possibilities of induced alterations in price levels, bank policy, interest rates, and domestic investment activity. See also Hawtrey, whose terminology is slightly different, but whose concepts are similar, *Currency and Credit*, pp. 76–83; also Harrod, *International Economics*, pp. 107–11, 115–17.

[8] Keynes shows that a country ought to regard an outflow of short-term capital, resulting from a weak balance of payments, in the same light as a gold outflow, and conversely with a credit inflow. In fact, however, it seems to have been a major defect of the gold exchange standard system that it lacked this two-way operation, banks ignoring shifts in the ownership of their deposits between domestic and foreign owners, since their reserves remained unchanged. *A Treatise on Money*, I, 350–56; Heilperin, *International Monetary Economics*, pp. 212–14.

[9] It is often maintained that regardless of whether banks consciously follow such a policy, there will be an effective change in purchasing power on both sides, merely because foreign balances are more likely to be invested in short-term loans on the money or

A third and final way in which purchasing power levels in the respective countries may tend to shift autonomously is through a possible resultant change in the demand for credit. Balance-of-payments transactions may alter the prospective marginal efficiencies of capital in A and B., and hence, by changing respective demands for credit, alter the income velocity of money in each. If B's exports are lagging behind her imports, her exporters will probably tend to curtail their borrowing, with a consequent further tendency to contraction of credit; the opposite tendency may occur in A.[10]

These shifts in purchasing power, which result from each international transaction, operate in large measure through their effect on interest rates. Since each transaction alters the supply of means of payment and banking reserves, it involves a relative upward pressure on interest rates in the remitting and/or a relative downward pressure in the receiving country. Such pressure becomes fully reciprocal, as we shall see, only when short-term credits cease to ease the transfer, and payments are effected by gold flows. Interest rates may be prevented from changing by

---

security markets, with relatively lower income velocity than domestic deposits. Hence the shift of A's deposits from foreign to domestic ownership (case 1) will release funds from "financial" to "industrial" circulation, i.e., for extension to domestic industry, with inflationary secondary consequences. Or the opposite will occur in B (case 2). James W. Angell, in *Explorations in Economics*, pp. 16–17; Kindleberger, *International Short-Term Capital Movements*, pp. 23–25; Keynes, *A Treatise on Money*, I, 243; F. W. Paish, "Banking Policy and the Balance of International Payments," *Economica*, n.s., III (1936), 416–18.

This proposition, ·as stated, is of dubious validity. Foreign funds lent on the money market or disbursed for securities also go into industry, directly or indirectly. Their effect on interest rates is similar to that of domestic deposits. It is true that they need not go into industry; they may, for example, remain idle. So, however, may the funds of businesses. Besides, the balance of payments is the summation of all sorts of transactions other than trade, involving among others increase and decrease of deposits in the hands of investors, banks, insurance companies, which may or may not have a greater "industrial circulation" than foreign bank deposits. In such cases a flow of purchasing power can scarcely be deemed inflationary because it involves a movement from financial to industrial circulation. These shifts will mean necessarily only that in both cases B's domestically owned deposits will decline and A's will rise. The crucial difference between the two types of deposits is, then, in their ownership, rather than any tenuous distinction of their types of "circulation." This has nothing to do with their respective velocities of circulation, but results simply from the fact that domestic deposits are directly available for balance of payments adjustment, those owned by foreign banks only indirectly.
[10] Whale, "The Working of the Pre-War Gold Standard," *Economica*, n.s., IV (1937), 24–25; Gilbert, "The Mechanism of Interregional Redistributions of Money," *Rev. Econ. Studies*, V (1938), 190–91; Walker, "The Working of the Pre-War Gold Standard," *Rev. Econ. Studies*, I (1934), 203.

the above-mentioned possibility, a change in the demand for credit in the same direction as the supply. If so, the change in rates may be considered unnecessary. If on the other hand the changed demand is not enough to offset the changed supply, an alteration in interest rates, which is therefore made necessary, will further reinforce the re-equilibrating secondary income shifts and thus contribute to an enduring readjustment of the balance of payments in a manner to be described below.

EXCHANGE RATES, GOLD FLOWS, AND PROXIMATE ADJUSTMENTS UNDER THE OLD GOLD STANDARD

Every international transaction helps to determine the price of the foreign exchange with which payment is made. Every disequilibrium of the balance of payments will therefore affect not only interest rates but also exchange rates, and the resultant fluctuations will set in motion equilibrative tendencies of varying permanency and strength.

If a country's currency seems not to be basically threatened, temporary small or predictable (e.g., seasonal) pressure on its balance of payments and hence on its currency will normally induce speculative purchases of the weak currency in anticipation of a return movement. Higher short-term interest rates in the weaker country may help make such arbitrage transactions attractive. These semi-automatic equilibrating inflows of short-term capital may be sufficient to check the exchange pressure and tide over temporary or minor weaknesses. If pressure persists, and exchange rates diverge enough to compensate for the costs of getting commodities from one market to another, arbitrage transactions in various internationally traded goods will be encouraged. Under the gold standard, gold will probably be the most sensitive of these commodities; the willingness and ability of a country to supply gold (or, indeed, any other good) at a fixed price sets a limit to the depreciation of its exchange, for gold sales automatically fill the gap in the foreign exchange supply, once local currency has declined to its gold export point.

With gold flows we enter a secondary range of equilibrating tendencies. Short-term credit movements are ineffective in the face of continuing disequilibrium. For one thing, they cannot continue indefinitely. A speculative flow is dependent upon an assurance that currency pressure is temporary, and the slightest exchange risk negates the gains of interest arbitrage.[11] The foreign line of credit available to a country's banks is

---

[11] This was true even under the gold standard. See Hawtrey, "The Gold Standard and the Balance of Payments," *Econ. Jour.*, XXXVI (1926), 64–65. See also the interesting

limited, especially if the currency is persistently weak. Moreover, these flows, as we have seen, mitigate the two-sided effect of the purchasing power flow and hence retard more radical correctives. The initial effects of gold flows are the same: they simply help fill the need for exchange. In their primary and secondary purchasing power effects, however, gold flows have additional equilibrating powers. Here gold sales by producers and hoarders and purchases by actual consumers (and industry) may be excluded, as they are precisely the same in effect as ordinary commodity trade. Our interest is in gold arbitrage.

If gold is exported by B's banks in an arbitrage transaction, their deposits and reserves are unchanged, reserves of foreign balances being substituted for gold. If the proceeds are now supplied to B importers of goods, B's banks will in the end show a net decline in deposits and reserves. A's banks, which buy the gold, experience an increase of both reserves (gold) and deposits, the latter owned in the first instance by B's banks, and later by A exporters. Whereas thus in the balance of payments B's gold exports and commodity imports balance, and A's gold imports and commodity exports balance, purchasing power effects do not cancel out, and in fact are complete and two-sided. A's deposits and reserves have increased and B's have decreased.[12] Were the commodity transactions effected and balanced by short-term credit shifts, on the contrary, the purchasing power effects would be, as we have seen, only one-sided in many respects, all the more since banking systems tend to react less readily to a short-term credit inflow than to gold outflow, even though both may reveal the same weakness. Gold flows are in a sense alternatives to the continued flow of short-term credits. They are also extensions of the equilibrating process, a more drastic second step; since one country can no longer borrow from the other and must pay in cash, the shift of purchasing power is made complete.

Exchange rate effects go one step farther. If disequilibrium persists and gold supplies are exhausted, or if countries no longer adhere to the gold standard, exchange fluctuations will not be restrained by the redeemability of currencies in gold. The various import and export points of other commodities with an international market are reached. Eventu-

---

formulation of this process by Joan Robinson, whose discussion, however, shows a propensity for jumping to conclusions of fact from a highly oversimplified theoretical argument based on rigid assumptions. "Banking Policy and the Exchanges," *Rev. Econ. Studies*, III (1936), 226–29. Also Bryce, "A Note on Banking Policy and the Exchanges," *Rev. Econ. Studies*, IV (June, 1937), 240–43.

[12] See W. A. Brown, Jr., *The Int. Gold Stand.*, I, 87–91.

ally, if adjustment is attained short of defaults and breakdown, it will come in large measure through increased visible and invisible exports from the weak country and decreased imports into it, as the relative external purchasing power of its currency declines. If deflation of incomes and terms of trade (the latter merely by fluctuation of domestic prices) do not serve to keep a country from buying and lending more than is consistent with equilibrium, deflation of its buying power by exchange depreciation must serve. The short-run success of this process is by no means certain. Under conditions of great weakness it may intensify capital flight, leaving defaults and direct controls as the sole means of restoring "equilibrium." In these circumstances high interest rates may have the same effect; they may be taken as an evidence of serious instability and may hence repel, rather than attract, capital, even to the extent of precipitating a breakdown.

It was at one time commonly believed that virtually all balance-of-payments disequilibria were adjusted regularly by gold flows, operating, in causal sequence, upon bank reserves, interest rates, the volume of credit, relative price levels (the terms of trade), and the balance of trade. It was recognized that there might be lags and frictions all along the line, but gold would continue to flow, it was held, until either adjustment or breakdown occurred.[13] This theory is especially inadequate as an explanation of the short-run adjustments of the balance of payments. Such rapid, easy, and continuous adjustments as national balances of payments made under the gold standard would have been impossible under such a slow and cumbersome process.

In fact, the initial adjustments between well-developed international money markets occurred on much the same level as between different regions of one country, using one currency. Seasonal pressures upon bank reserves and balances of international, as of interregional, payments did not regularly cause gold drains, differential bank policies, and shifting terms of trade, in that sequence. The extreme mobility of short-term funds filled the gap, preventing severe inflation and deflation and price disturbances in individual regions except in extreme cases. Relative price level changes seem thus to have been of minor importance both as a means of adjustment [14] (at least in the case of regular seasonal and even

---

[13] For example, Taussig, *International Trade*, chaps. xi–xii, xvii, *passim*.

[14] The classical gold-flow theory considered these price changes the essential means of adjustment; see p. 19, below. See also Beach, *British International Gold Movements and Banking Policy, 1881–1913*, pp. 9, 172; Heilperin, *International Monetary Economics*, p. 169.

cyclical disequilibria) and also as a cause of disequilibrium.[15] Gold flows were not caused primarily by balance of payments disequilibria; instead, they were usually induced by movements in the same direction of short-term capital, attracted by differential interest rates. Thus, differences in interest rates usually caused gold flows, rather than the reverse; and these differential rates were usually the result of heavy seasonal and cyclical demand for credit or currency in one area.[16]

The importance of international movements of short-term credits can therefore scarcely be overestimated. Without them, and above all without the willingness of receiving countries temporarily to accept claims on the remitters in time of stress, thus often obviating the need for gold flows and preventing drastic deflation in the latter, the operation of the international gold standard would undoubtedly have involved far greater hardships, and the system might therefore have held together much less firmly than it did.

Nevertheless, in the case of greater disequilibria, induced short-term capital movements were not and are not adequate substitutes for a more enduring re-equilibration. They may actually hinder that final adjustment by relieving the weak country of pressure in the manner indicated —by precluding gold flows and by removing the full two-sided impact of the buying power shift. Nevertheless, as long as disequilibrium persists, there will also exist continuous influences upon relative levels of purchasing power and upon interest and exchange rates,[17] giving rise to forces which tend toward more definitive solution.

Definitive Re-equilibration

According to the traditional theory, final adjustments of balance of payments disequilibria under the gold standard could occur only as a result of flows of gold from countries with a weak balance to countries with a strong balance, causing shifts in terms of trade against the former and in favor of the latter countries.[18] This theory is no longer acceptable.

[15] The major cyclical cause of gold flows as traditionally envisioned was a price level in one country lagging behind or preceding the rise of world prices. Beach, *ibid.*, 170–73.
[16] *Ibid., passim;* J. C. Gilbert, "The Mechanism of Interregional Redistributions of Money," *Rev. Econ. Studies,* V (1937–38), 187–94, *passim;* Whale, "The Working of the Pre-War Gold Standard," *Economica,* n.s., IV (1937), 21, 25–27.
[17] The flows of short-term capital cannot entirely destroy the interest or exchange rate differentials which give rise to them or their *raison d'être* would disappear and the flow would be reversed.
[18] For one unequivocal statement of this view see Taussig, *International Trade,* pp. 117, 124.

There have been too many instances where the gold flows accompanying huge and comparatively rapid adjustments seem to have been too small and too long delayed to account for those adjustments; in some cases, indeed, the gold flowed in the wrong direction.[19] Moreover, the effect of gold flows upon price levels is uncertain and slow. Even before 1914 central banks by no means consistently adjusted their rates so that a gold inflow increased, and an outflow reduced the volume of credit.[20] And even when they did, the effect upon prices was far from immediate. For these reasons it is difficult to believe that gold could have accomplished the adjustments, at least in the manner described.

Thus, we realize today that neither gold flows nor the shift of trade terms in the direction indicated was a necessary or inevitable means of equilibration, perhaps not even the major influence. Nevertheless, it remains true that almost any appreciable disequilibrium in the balance of payments under the gold standard will cause either gold flows or a diversion of the course of newly mined gold. Though these flows may not be large, especially on balance, usually they do influence bank policy and the volume of money. Whether or not these changes actually influence

[19] See Angell, *The Theory of International Prices*, p. 401; Herbert Feis, "The Mechanism of Adjustment of International Trade Balances," *American Economic Review* (hereinafter *Amer. Econ. Rev.*), XVI (1926), 601.

[20] Even the Bank of England exercised considerable discretion in this regard. When it did raise the Rate, because of an outflow of gold, the purpose was to affect the flow of short-term credits, not prices. Thus, it often strove to keep such a rise in the Bank of England Rate from having deflationary internal effects, or, as an alternative measure, took direct steps to control the gold market and prevent gold flows. Sayers, *Bank of England Operations, 1890–1914*, chaps. vi–vii. Even less was Bank Rate used to raise prices in the face of gold inflow. Walker notes the obvious "asymmetry" of the following explanation of Bank-Rate policy before the American Monetary Commission, in 1910:

"Bank-rate is raised with the object either of preventing gold from leaving the country or of attracting gold to the country, and lowered when it is completely out of touch with the market rate and circumstances do not render it necessary to induce the import of gold," "The Working of the Pre-War Gold Standard," *Rev. Econ. Studies*, I (1934), 199.

In fact, in view of the observation already made that gold flows were more often the result than the cause of interest rate differentials, there is serious question as to whether central banks should have lowered rates when the gold flowed in and raised them when it flowed out. If the rise in interest rates which attracted the gold was the result of the pressure of domestic and foreign investment upon limited reserves, a lowering of rates would have aggravated rather than ameliorated the internal and external situation. See Walker, "The Working of the Pre-War Gold Standard," *Rev. Econ. Studies*, I (1934), 196–209; Whale, "The Working of the Pre-War Gold Standard," *Economica*, n.s., IV (1937), 20–21, 31. On the Bank's policies after the World War see pp. 174–77, 199–203, below.

relative prices, the gold flow does at least make complete and two-sided the shift in buying power and in this way facilitates adjustment on the purchasing power plane. Gold movements should then be regarded merely as a more effective secondary shift of purchasing power; but as such they may be extremely important.

The manner in which a shift in purchasing power operates upon the balance of payments has been discussed in the literature almost exclusively in relation to the "transfer" of large unilateral payments. This is, perhaps, because disequilibria of this type are the neatest and most striking cases, perhaps, also, because of the general inclination of economists to regard capital movements as mainly causal and the trade balance as normally passive. In the following discussion we shall attempt to treat the problem more generally, since the disequilibrium giving rise to the initial net purchasing power flow may result from a change in any item in the balance of payments.

It is almost impossible for heavy unilateral payments even to begin to be transferred in real terms unless the monetary transfer has first been accomplished. It is the money payment by means of an inflow of short-term capital, in the manner described above, which sets in motion the purchasing-power factors which tend to effect an enduring adjustment of the balance of payments. In times of instability it may be impossible to make this beginning. When a currency's strength is in doubt, no exchange or interest-rate inducement may be sufficient to attract the needed short-term funds. Funds may be repelled instead of attracted, and the country may not have enough gold or foreign exchange resources to start the transfer, let alone to meet a capital flight precipitated by its weakness.[21]

[21] In his rather vague realization of this lay one of Keynes's strongest criticisms of Ohlin in their famous controversy over reparations. Keynes assumed fairly consistently that Germany had insufficient gold and foreign exchange to make the initial payment and that lack of faith in the mark prevented foreign countries from accepting deposits in Germany. Hence, he argued, there could occur no increase in foreign purchasing power, available for purchase of German goods, and German exports could increase only as a result of a relative decline in German prices, which Ohlin dismissed as unnecessary. Ohlin really assumed that Germany would be able to make the initial payment by a reverse short-term credit flow, thus setting in motion the purchasing power factors. *Interregional and International Trade*, pp. 432–33; see also Angell, "Reparations and the Cash Transfer Problem," *Political Science Quarterly*, XLI (1926), 337–43. However, if, as Keynes argued, Germany's only means of making the payment and thus transferring the purchasing power was first to increase her exports: "the increased 'buying power,' due to the fact of Germany paying . . . will have been *already* used up in buying the exports, the sale of which has made the Reparation payments possible." "The Reparation

The only way in which the transfer may be effected in such a case will be by continuous deflation in the remitting country, B. If the funds are actually raised internally, e.g., by subscription to new issues or by taxation, and these funds are immobilized awaiting transfer, the deflation of buying power and the consequent reduction of purchases from abroad will provide some needed foreign balances. However, since the exchange thus acquired has already been used by the other countries to buy B's goods, its unilateral transfer merely restores to their previous ratio the levels of buying power in the countries concerned and leaves the provision of more exchange to a continuation of this deflation in B. Such a transfer would in any case be difficult; if the "abnormality" of the times, as a result of which foreigners refused to accept B's currency, consisted in general world deflation, as is probable, the burden of deflation upon B would have to be even greater, and the probabilities of successful transfer even smaller.

Assume that purchasing power has been transferred from B to A. Except to the extent that the change of buying power is offset by a change in saving, in the same direction, A's demand curves for all goods will shift to the right, B's to the left, the shift being equivalent to the total of primary and secondary purchasing-power effects. There will thus be an immediate tendency for the total current balances of A and B to adjust, the degree of adjustment depending upon the marginal propensities to import, and for the bilateral balance between them also to shift, depending upon their reciprocal demand dispositions; for this no change in general price levels is needed.

The shift in purchasing power will tend, in addition, to adjust the respective sales of A and B by causing divergent movements of their prices and costs. These movements need not be absolute, but only relative to each other. Many factors may prevent them—cyclical movements, imperfections of competition, monetary and fiscal policies. They are not inevitable; neither is successful adjustment inevitable. The one, however, tends to facilitate the other.

Prices of imports, set in a world market and based upon foreign costs, will change the least in both A and B. Domestic prices, on the other hand,

---

Problem: a Discussion," *Econ. Jour.*, XXXIX (1929), 181; see also Fanno, *Normal and Abnormal International Capital Transfers*, pp. 38–39. However, Keynes and Fanno both overlook the possibility, discussed in the text below, that purchasing power might have been reduced in Germany before the money transfer was made, thus creating supplies of foreign exchange without need for a shift in terms of trade.

will rise most in A and fall most in B, being unrestrained by competing foreign supplies or demands. Export and import-competing goods' prices will occupy a middle position. Their changes will be retarded by international influences—in A by the competition of foreign products, in B by the existence of foreign markets. However, the relative prosperity of A's domestic industry and the increase of A's demand will tend to raise these prices and costs somewhat; export and import-competing industries may actually suffer a diversion of productive factors to industries supplying the domestic market. Opposite conditions in B will tend to lower such prices and costs in that country. The low prices of A's imports relative to import-competing and domestic goods and the tendency for her export prices to rise must tend to increase her imports and decrease her exports. The high price of B's imports relative to domestic and import-competing goods and the tendency for B's export prices to fall will tend to adjust B's trade balance with the world in the opposite direction. To the extent that A's increased buying power and B's decreased buying power directly affect their reciprocal demands, A's export prices may be kept from rising entirely, and B's from falling. This means merely that if the shift in purchasing power directly affects their bilateral balance there will be neither cause nor occasion for price changes to facilitate the adjustment.

The transfer of purchasing power thus tends to rectify the trade and service balance in two ways: initially, through its primary and secondary effects on total demand for foreign goods in each country, secondly, through differential price and cost effects, the result of changed sectional demand and supply conditions.[22]

[22] This analysis is not so far from the classical gold-flow terms of trade analysis as its leading protagonists seem to assert.

It is true, as is so often said, that relative price changes and gold movements, which are absolutely essential to the classical analysis, are now proved to be unessential. The terms of trade may, indeed, turn either way; at most their role is to facilitate the adjustment. See Ohlin, "The Reparations Problem," *Index*, April, 1928, p. 11, and *passim*. This alteration in the theory represents an important contribution. One scans the writings of Keynes or Taussig absolutely in vain for the slightest recognition that the shift of purchasing power directly influences demand curves, entirely apart from the latters' response to price movements.

Yet the major stress in the "modern" treatment is on the shift of factors of production within the countries as a result of differential movements of sectional domestic demands. See Iversen, *Aspects of the Theory of International Capital Movements*, pp. 461–63, 477–78, and chaps. vii and xii, *passim*; Ohlin, *Interregional and International Trade*, pp. 409 ff., esp. 409–10, 431. Ohlin claims that this shift of productive factors "is partly, but partly only, the consequence of this change in 'sectional price levels.'" "The Reparation

The theoretical tendencies discussed above deserve far more qualification and elucidation than is possible here. The major qualifications center about the inevitable time lags in their operation and the many other factors which operate upon the balance of payments at any moment and may abet, hinder, or entirely thwart their operation. The effects of the initial purchasing power shifts upon the total disposition to spend, upon prices, upon costs, and upon the allocations of productive factors are slow and uncertain.[23] Moreover, a purchasing power flow, once started, may take many and devious routes before it returns to restore equilibrium, if it does return at all. The decrease of B's buying power may be transmitted indirectly and in minor degree to A. A's increased imports may come from E and F, and only after a great lag may some of

---

Problem: a Discussion," *Econ. Jour.*, XXXIX (1929), 175; see pp. 174–76. The mere increase of demand for home market goods in A, and the decline in B is supposed to cause it. *Interregional and International Trade*, pp. 409, 420.

If the factors are actually to be shifted from one line to another, there must be relatively full employment. Under these conditions, how such a shift may be induced other than by changes in sectional prices and hence in relative rates of remuneration is not clear. The only possible line of reasoning under such conditions must be based upon the greater profitability of domestic industry in A, of export and import-competing industry in B, because of the purchasing-power shift—which under full employment can mean *only* differential price changes.

And once the shift of productive factors has occurred, it is difficult to see how it can operate except again through prices. The shift of labor in A from export to domestic industries means a rise in costs, in supply prices in A's export industries. And conversely in B: the shift of productive factors from the depressed domestic goods industries to export industries has not the slightest importance except as it means that costs, supply prices, have fallen in B. The "releasing of more goods for export" in B and "decreasing supply of factors available for production of export goods" in A mean nothing if not that B's export prices tend to fall and A's to rise.

Therefore, the secondary adjustment of balances of payments due to the differential incidence of the purchasing power shift as between various industries, the process which plays so large a role in modern theories, is entirely an adjustment through prices, through terms of trade. It is difficult, therefore, to join the chorus which proclaims that such an important contributing factor as the change in relative prices (trade terms) is negligible and subsidiary. See Haberler, *The Theory of International Trade*, pp. 73–76; Elliott, "Transfer of Means-of-Payment and the Terms of International Trade," *Canadian Journal of Economics and Political Science*, II (1936), 481–92; Pigou, "The Effect of Reparations on the Ratio of International Exchange," *Econ. Jour.*, XLII (1932), 532–43; Iversen, *Aspects of the Theory of International Capital Movements*, pp. 510–12; Viner, *Studies in Theory*, pp. 327 ff., esp. p. 360.

[23] See Angell, *The Theory of International Prices*, p. 416; Iversen, *Aspects of the Theory of International Capital Movements*, p. 486; White, "Haberler's *Der Internationale Handel*; Ohlin's *Interregional and International Trade*," *Quarterly Journal of Economics* (hereinafter Q.J.E.), XLVIII (1934), 734.

the increment reach B. In all countries, decrease or increase of income will probably first affect domestic industry, making international readjustments more devious and more feeble at each turn. It is impossible to say a priori how or along what routes, precisely, the adjustment will work out, or if it will work out at all. History seems to show that the balance works in some such way as we have indicated during more or less normal periods. That impression is, however, due partly to the fact that in this, as in other economic analyses, we tend to designate as "normal" only those periods when the autonomous factors of adjustment in the economic system are successful.

In any case, so long as maladjustment persists, it will beget forces which tend to restore equilibrium. Those forces may not be strong enough: wars, tariffs, cyclical disequilibria, or even heightened secular changes may create maladjustments which the autonomous restorative forces of the balance of payments may be incapable of correcting. Indeed, history is full of instances in which disequilibrating repercussions, growing in strength, put an end to an entire "normal" institutional economic framework and led to the improvisation of other institutions as a matter of sheer self-defense. An enduring equality of inpayments and outpayments may be restored automatically; it may be restored if appropriate policies are pursued, policies which may be more or less feasible, depending upon circumstances. It may be unrestorable short of heroic measures: abandonment of free trade or of the gold standard; it may even be unrestorable short of complete breakdown. The preponderance of forces will be determined only by the particular circumstances in each case.[24]

The previous discussion suggests that any number of concomitant circumstances may affect ease or probability of adjustment: the relative elasticity of demand between the countries involved and between each country and the world (a world demand for B's products which does not respond either to world income changes or to price changes in B, although not likely, might conceivably prevent adjustment); the extent to which the increased or decreased funds are spent or taken from expenditures upon domestic, export, or import goods in the countries initially concerned; the extent to which other countries share indirectly in the income increment or decrement and the way in which their spending

[24] This realistic attitude is a most important asset of Aftalion's *L'Equilibre dans les relations économiques internationales*; see especially p. 169 footnote and pp. 447–55.

changes as a result; the stage of the business cycle at which transfers are made; labor union policies—each is an influential and perhaps an inhibiting factor.

Deliberate decision of policy, above all, may thwart the process of adjustment. Independent credit policies may keep the buying power shifts from taking effect. The difficulties of successful re-equilibration are magnified if the field of international transactions is narrowed or hedged about by increasing restrictions.[25] In a neo-mercantilist world, such as has been evolving, in which sales and employment are preferred to the acquisition of goods and where frequently goods are given away for nothing or for useless gold, in order to keep people employed, the realm of possible autonomous adjustments narrows daily. Nor is this simply a matter of human stupidity; sales and employment are important in the present economic "order," and even free goods may not be worth the difficult problems of adjustment which they entail in an increasingly stratified economic system.

[25] The existence of tariffs may not have any very harmful effect upon the ease of adjustment, as long as a sufficient volume of international trade remains, as long as trade relations have become adjusted to the tariff, and as long as there are still marginal buyers, sellers, and lenders who will be affected by the changes which balance-of-payments disequilibria induce. Progressive rises of tariffs must, however, make adjustments increasingly difficult. Haberler, *The Theory of International Trade*, pp. 79–80.

III. THE NEED FOR AN ORGANIC THEORY

THE ACCEPTED THEORY of international equilibrium tells us little about the real outcome of the process which it purports to explain. Tacitly or explicitly, the "gold standard," for example, has usually been held to have achieved its purpose as long as currency stability was maintained. But currency stability is not an end in itself. Surely the only proper criterion of success is the real counterpart of the equilibrium outcome, the actual level of international economic activity and world income. Yet these are scarcely considered in the theory, a failure which is possibly attributable to the common assumption of a state of full employment.

Currency stability, it is true, sets the stage for a maximization of real income by making possible an optimum amount of international specialization and exchange. But the two are not inevitably associated. Currency instability is usually associated with a decline in international trade and lending, with defaults and unemployment—but not necessarily. Just as the deceptive and inevitable automatic "balance" of debits and credits in the balance of payments tells us nothing about the stability of the situation, so do stable exchange rates and the balancing out of gold and short-term capital flows tell us little about the level of economic activity behind the façade of adjustment.

One may scarcely conclude that a system is "working" if exchange stability is maintained in the face of, perhaps even at the cost of, default, increasing trade and exchange controls, decline in international trade and investment or uneconomic alteration of their settled channels and directions. The gold standard is generally held to have "worked" in the decades before 1914; yet there were long, arid periods in those decades when trade was stagnant, when debtors could not obtain needed funds, whereas creditors had an excess, and resources were unemployed for want of markets. The fact that an equilibrium may be maintained, according to certain inadequate criteria, must not be permitted to hide the fact that the underlying situation may be one of stagnation.

Moreover, the theory does not prove that there will be adjustment to disturbances. It proves only that if equilibrium is disturbed, various factors tending to restore it will be set in motion. The theory cannot promise that these forces will be successful or prophesy what drastic moves will have to be made before success can be attained. It can only assert that if these forces do not succeed, they will continue to operate. The proof, if the argument may be dignified by that name, is entirely negative.

Beyond the truism that in the long run no country can buy, give, or lend on long term more than it sells, receives, or borrows on long term, nothing is certain. This inevitable equation of a country's accounts is maintained by fluctuations in its real buying power, its command over world goods, services, and claims to wealth. Such fluctuations may entail changes in money incomes or in what money will buy. The latter may come about through the terms of international exchange, through fluctuations, either of price levels or of the relative exchange valuations of currencies. The former may come about through changes in income rates (e.g., wage rates), or in total employment. The attainment of equilibrium may therefore involve, or at least need not avoid, currency instability, default, and depression, even though equilibrating factors tend to bring adjustment without these ills. Whether the inevitable equation will involve simple monetary adjustments or severe fluctuations in the levels of economic activity cannot be determined a priori.

New net international lending must, it is asserted, take the form of a flow of goods and services. By transferring the money from B to A, so the argument runs, the nationals of B, who are saving, are transferring some of their current claims over the world's physical output to nationals of A, whose savings are inadequate to meet their investment requirements for goods. As a result, more of the world's goods will inevitably go to A and less to B, on balance, by precisely that amount.[1]

Although this is the essential character of capital flows, the transfer is initially a transfer of money. There is no assurance that in fact the total volume of B's voluntary national money saving is equal to the total of its domestic and foreign money investment, or that A's borrowing added to its voluntary saving equals its total investment. If B's nationals are actually saving, voluntarily, less or more than the total of domestic and foreign money investment, they will automatically be renouncing fewer or more claims to the available excess of goods than they are transferring to other countries. The immediate results of these discrepancies will be either a reduction or an increase of B's net foreign short-term assets. It may, then, be said that B is in the first case not really lending as much as the new foreign loans, because it is "borrowing" on short term in order

[1] See, for example, Hobson, *The Export of Capital*, p. xi.

to maintain consumption, while still lending on long term.[2] Or, in the second case, that B is actually lending more to foreign countries than the new loans, because it is "lending" on short term the additional buying power which it does not choose to exercise. This easy answer does not, however, eliminate the disequilibrium and the inherent instability of the situation. On the contrary, it proves that equilibration of the balance of payments to an isolated purchase of foreign securities is by no means automatic.

But if there is disequilibrium, there are forces at work tending to adjust it—to deflate incomes and raise interest rates in B in the first case and to inflate incomes and lower interest rates in the second case, thus effecting a change in either its net current purchases or its foreign lending or in both. Thus, we revert to the negative indirect proof described above. Capital movements do not directly cause movements of goods; they merely set up disturbances which tend in that direction and persist as long as the maladjustments persist.[3]

Precisely the same argument may be applied to a disequilibrium that appears in an excessively weak or strong trade balance. Any attempt to decrease imports, it is argued, can only to an equivalent extent decrease exports (or other net inpayments).[4] A country may permit its market

[2] "The answer to this is, of course, that in this case no net export of British capital has taken place. That the practice of 'lending long and borrowing short' may entail grave dangers, is another story." Iversen, *Aspects of the Theory of International Capital Movements*, p. 91n.

From the point of view of maintenance of equilibrium it is by no means "another story." Nor is it, indeed, from the viewpoint of Iversen, who is at this point discussing the advisability of a country's stipulating that foreign borrowers spend their loan proceeds for goods of the lender in order to forestall balance-of-payments weakness. Elsewhere Iversen again assumes away the problem of equilibrium in the same way (p. 91). And Marco Fanno's similar generalizations, *Normal and Abnormal International Capital Transfer*, pp. 19–21, 40, are based upon a definition of "normal" transfers which involves equivalent voluntary saving by nationals of B.

[3] Hence the conclusion that there is neither reason nor need for a lending country to stipulate that the borrower expend the proceeds in that country (because [1] capital must be transferred in goods in any case, and [2] if a country's goods cannot compete in world markets it will be unable to export capital in the first place) ignores the difficulties and maladjustments of the transition. It assumes a direct immediate causal relation from loans to goods, or goods to loans. For a flagrant example, see Cassel, "The International Movements of Capital," *Foreign Investments*, p. 39.

[4] The converse proposition, concerning removal of import restrictions in order to eliminate an excessively strong trade balance, is less often heard, because such action is always considered a boon. Ray Hall has, however, applied the argument to the case of the American tariff, the American position of the 1920's being commonly considered excessively strong for so important a creditor: "The feeling is prevalent . . . that Amer-

to be flooded with foreign goods in a period of temporary world stress. Since it cannot buy more than it sells, any such increased purchases must either increase sales as well or cut down the volume of purchases to an equilibrium level.

However, the adjustments are not definite and automatic, but devious, and there may occur in the interim any degree of instability or break-down, and of any duration. Thus, the nature of the transition during which the factors of equilibration operate, with only the assurance that they will continue to operate as long as they are not successful, must be accorded theoretical significance; its pains and pleasures must be weighed in the balance. It cannot merely be assumed that it is of zero duration for theoretical purposes, nor can a negative theory prove its negligibility. Surely the country concerned will be greatly interested in whether the relative deflation of its purchasing power, which is required to equate exports and imports, will involve absolute deflation as well, whether its displaced productive factors will shift easily to other lines, whether, in short, the transition will be easy and brief or troublesome and long. Hence, there may be justification for a policy of attempting to ease whatever pains occur: for a tariff to relieve the balance-of-payments pressure

---

ica's trade balance is a lumpy, insoluble thing which has so tipped the scales of America's international payments as to deprive most of the outside world of gold badly needed there. . . . [But] Fluctuations of gold movements have shown scarcely any relation-ship to America's trade-balance fluctuations, in the post-war years. There is strong evidence that fluctuations of international lending, not of trade balances, have principally determined America's gold movements. America's trade balances—far from being lumpy or insoluble, capable of being balanced only by gold imports—seem also to have been principally determined by fluctuations in international lending." *International Transactions of the United States*, p. 105.

The answer to this highly sophisticated yet excessively simple argument is not difficult. The fact that in the 1920's changes in America's capital flows appear to have been the marginal causal factor influencing gold movements in no sense alters the possibility that a persistently strong trade balance may have continually tended to cause gold inflows. The argument that changes in capital flows seem to have induced changes in trade balances simply ignores the contention that there was a lasting, enduring, more fundamental disequilibrium.

In point of fact, America did gain gold in these years, a process retarded only by highly uncertain and fluctuating foreign lending; her position was too strong from the point view of other countries; her trade balance was not so elastic as to remove this underlying strength.

It is extreme short-sightedness to conclude from the fact that the trade balance has not changed, except in the face of changed capital movements, that therefore it need not change—by arguing, simply, that if it needed to change it would change. Such an argument assumes the existence of equilibrium once before starting and again before closing and attempts thereby to prove that disequilibrium could not exist.

and to prevent unemployment during the transition when productive factors are displaced by imports.

Nor, if the adjusting forces are successful, is there any assurance as to the nature of the outcome. A drastic increase in purchases may finally be adjusted by an increase in the amount of sales. It may, on the contrary, result in a deflation of buying power acute enough to reduce purchases not only to the previous lower level, but even for a time below that level, until the short-term debt position, altered by the temporary buying spurt, is restored to normal. In such an extreme case the trials of transition, on the one hand, and the temporary saving by reduced import prices, on the other, may be the only pains and pleasures to be weighed.

The outcome thus likewise depends upon "outside" factors, that is, factors outside the scope of traditional theory. If the world economy is expanding, adjustment may involve expansion of exports rather than limitation of imports—a slower inflation or expansion rather than absolute deflation and contraction. The adjustment of productive factors may involve simply more rapid growth of some industries than of others, not the absolute decline of any. Adjustment will be difficult and will involve deflation of money and real incomes in proportion to the amount of specialization in the particular lines affected in the country injured by increased foreign competition; the shift will be smooth and the income loss small if the injured country has a great variety of alternatives (because of its adaptability or varied resources). The height of tariff barriers will be another determinant; the stage of the business cycle, still another. It cannot be assumed that the adjustability of long-term capital balances to interest rates, of trade balances to small price changes, the flexibility of money costs is the same in all places and at all times. These factors will help to determine both the ease of adjustment and the type of adjustment. Propitious circumstances will make not only for easy adjustment but also for an equilibrium in which the optimum levels and channels of international activity are least disturbed. The dividing line between transition and the outcome of the process of equilibration, usually sharply distinguished, is fast becoming vague. One additional consideration is enough to eradicate it entirely.

The transition must be accorded theoretical status not only because it may be long enough to deserve weighing in the balance but also because actually the process of transition is perpetual. The world economy is constantly in a state of flux, and balances of payments are constantly being adjusted and being disturbed. How, then, can one distinguish between a temporary "transition" and "normal equilibrium"? It seems impossible to avoid the conclusion that actually they are the same thing. The active and passive factors which produce this perpetual process of change, make it easy or difficult and determine the actual nature of the more or less constant equilibrium become, then, an inherent part of the theory of equilibrium. Yet in the generally accepted theory they are the *ceteris paribus*. That is why this theory offers no explanation whatever of the cyclical ebb and flow of international economic activity which constitutes the major continuous problem of equilibration and within which and in accordance with which the processes of disturbance and adjustment operate.

It may be suggested that such a theory, which subsumes these factors under the head of *cetera*, "other things," is inadequate, not merely as a basis of historical and current analysis but as pure theory as well. One cannot quarrel with a method which explicitly sets aside the consideration of truly extraneous and passive factors or takes for granted a certain type of conditioning institutional framework, while recognizing that changes in that framework may well vitiate the functioning organism under consideration. But a theory which omits the dynamic determinants, factors which do not merely impede or facilitate any extraneous adjustments, but are part of the continuous process of equilibration itself, does not fully explain that process.

Not only does such a theory afford no basis for knowing when the mechanism will operate as expected and when it will not. Even in those concrete situations in which balances of payments have actually seemed to function according to prescription, the theory seems quite inadequate. It almost invariably abstracts single causal sequences when in fact adjustment was the cumulation of a host of dynamic cyclical and secular factors operating interdependently to determine the process and its outcome. In instances in which these forces contributed actively to an easy settlement, the theory is confounded by that ease of adjustment; indeed, the "adjustment" often appears to have preceded the "disturbance," because the outcome did not emerge from a single causal sequence operating in a single direction over a period of time, but grew, rather, out of an organic complex of economic changes.

The division between outside institutional framework and the functioning organism is not clear-cut. The framework is itself part of the organism, and its changes, rapid or slow, are part of the evolutionary process. The functioning international economic mechanism known as the "gold standard," for example, was something more than an abstract set of rules. It was a product of those secular forces which made England the world's leading manufacturing country and the world's undisputed financial center and made for the rise of her competitors and the development of backward areas and conditioned the complementary economic intercourse between these countries. These forces created a certain kind of international order, and the formal redeemability of currencies in gold was but a single symbol and a single instrument of that order. The standard of 1925 to 1931 may have been called by the same name as the earlier standard, but it was actually in many ways fundamentally altered by that same complex of forces which was producing great new international disequilibria and changing the methods of adjustment. Even the passive outside institutional framework has changed and continues to change with great rapidity; these changes have greatly affected the operation of the whole.

Even less can the theory afford to ignore omnipresent and active cyclical influences. These dominate the patterns of demand and supply dispositions, interest rates, national incomes, marginal efficiencies of capital, saving and spending and investing dispositions, which in turn condition the shifting commodity and capital flows, in an endless process of disequilibration and re-equilibration of the world's balances of payments. The balances fluctuate in cyclical patterns, not as a result of random single causes which operate in simple straight-line sequences of change. The changes in balances of payments, like the myriad day-to-day transactions which constitute them, represent an inextricable blend in a moving pattern of independent and interdependent factors as broad and complex, in origin and operation, as the pattern of the world economy itself. This is not obfuscation, but the basis of understanding.

On the basis of these criticisms and because the theoretical scheme is inadequate for any analysis of concrete situations, the need for an "organic" theory of international equilibrium is suggested. The sole fruitful analysis of the balance of payments must be in terms of actual cyclical and secular process, of actual complex patterns of cause and effect in mutual interplay and in continual transition, constantly disrupting and readjusting in a real world. Only thus can we understand the process of equilibration and the kind of equilibrium actually existent. Whether the complex of activity seems to operate so as to vindicate the simple theory, or overrides the influence of the abstracted set of tendencies, in either case the distilled and purified one-way causal explanation is inadequate, for it is the whole pattern of determinants which is operative.

It is the belief of the author that such a theory can be formulated on a priori grounds. But it must be only part of a broader general theory of business cycles and of economic development, a task clearly beyond the scope of the present study. It is hoped that our analysis of the changes in the British international economic position after 1914 will indicate the lines of analysis which are believed to be fruitful. This work is offered, in part, as a sort of case study of an organic theory. It is not, however, a clear case, and the following brief comments on two other very familiar historical examples are offered as a more concrete embodiment of the suggested lines of approach.

CASE STUDIES: CANADA, 1900–1913, AND GERMAN REPARATIONS

A great part of the literature on international equilibrium theory has centered about two cases: the great Canadian borrowings, from 1900 to 1913, and German reparations. The attractiveness of the first, the subject of a classic study by Professor Viner, lies probably in the nicety of the example, the relative absence of disturbing factors, and the ease of transfer. The second was a burning political issue, and economists were turned to as authorities, to control, predict, and advise. The first was an excellent example of the "pure" working of the international balance under the "normal" conditions of the old world gold standard. The second was a muddle; the literature is inconclusive, and conflicting points of view find in it corroboration in one way or another for their own predilections. Times were askew; the old world norm was disintegrating. The following general comments represent an attempt to elucidate the type of "organic" theory of international equilibrium which, it is believed, best explains these diverse experiences.

Professor Viner's explanation of the extremely rapid and easy adjustment of the Canadian balance of payments to the huge inflow of capital in the period 1900–1913 is a familiar one.[5] In general, his study is held to provide inductive verification of the theoretical schema presented in Chapter II, above.

Robert Carr took exception to Viner's interpretation. Viner, he argued, accepts the capital movements as prime and original cause, almost as if they originated outside the economic process. This assumption did not

---

[5] *Canada's Balance;* see also the elaboration by Angell, *The Theory of International Prices,* pp. 505–10.

seem to Carr to square with the fact that the relative rise of Canadian prices preceded both the capital inflow and increased demand deposits. He suggested therefore that the dominating element was not foreign capital inflow, but the enormous "change and industrial growth" within Canada; the great rise of internal demand for labor and materials induced a cost and price rise, which caused Canada to borrow abroad "in order to purchase the greater volume of foreign commodities demanded and to facilitate increased business activity at home at the higher price levels." [6]

There are weak points in Carr's argument. First of all, in most cases Canadians do not seem to have borrowed specifically in order to purchase foreign goods. Nor does there seem to be much validity in his stress upon the time sequence of changes in the variables. The fact that divergence of Canadian from world prices was greatest at the end of the period need not prove, as he alleges, that this divergence could not have caused the adjustment of the trade balance. Nor need the fact that price movements in many cases led those of capital and gold prove that the former were the causes, the latter the effects.[7] Carr's error is basically the same as Viner's—the attempt to draw a single line of causation, overlooking, except initially, the basic conditioning factors behind all the changes and overlooking, too, the complete interdependence and mutual interplay of the various series.

Certainly the fundamental factor, as Carr points out, must have been the high prospective marginal efficiency of capital in Canada after 1900. The increased demand for credit, operating against a slender domestic savings base and limited bank reserves, soon entailed a profit and then some price inflation. Foreign capital must have been attracted almost from the first; Canada normally relied upon foreign savings, and little or no additional formal interest rate differential was required to start British capital flowing. The great increase of investment engendered much business activity, rising prices, and an increasingly adverse trade balance—the latter for two reasons, the growing price differential and the faster rise of domestic income and industrial demands. On the monetary side, increases of velocity of deposit turnover may have accounted for the fact that price rises preceded those of bank deposits. Whether the expansion of the latter preceded or succeeded the capital inflows

[6] "The Role of Price in the International Trade Mechanism," Q.J.E., XLV (1931), 718; see 710–19.
[7] See the criticisms of White, *The French International Accounts, 1880–1913*, pp. 13–15.

and the increase of reserves is a matter of indifference; the two had to go together. Without continuous growth of capital imports, domestic expansion would have stopped much sooner.

Again, whether the adverse trade balance preceded or succeeded the capital imports is also a matter of indifference. The two were inseparable. Although certainly the former could not have persisted without the latter and was undoubtedly increased by it, both were the result in addition of the more basic determinants. This was precisely the reason why the enormous transfer succeeded: the flows of both capital and goods were the product of antecedent circumstances tending to that end. Changing cyclical conditions involved simultaneous and interrelated changes in incomes, prices, interest rates, investment, international lending, and the trade balances. Because the capital flows fitted in as a necessary part of the process of differential rates of world growth and expansion, their "transfer" occasioned little pressure or distress.

And the whole was effected in an international pattern which was propitious for related reasons. The expansion of newer areas and the growth of investment therein called forth simultaneous flows of money and real capital from the world's creditors. Equipment was needed for construction, and consumer goods to satisfy the rising money incomes in regions where investment was outstripping real voluntary saving, and only foreign capital (i.e., a surplus of foreign goods over what these areas could command by current sales) could feed such expansion. This growth thus imparted a leaven to the entire world economy, and all areas, new and old, shared in the expansion. Transfers were easily effected by relatively greater inflation in the receiving countries rather than by absolute deflation of prices and incomes in the lending countries. It is extremely instructive, in this regard, that it was Canada's imports which corresponded most closely to the capital inflow, the capital being transferred by increased sales to Canada rather than by decreased purchases by the lenders. There is no presumption in the accepted theory that this should be the case. The extraordinary ease of international adjustments to the rapid changes of the years 1900–1913 was the result of a complex of interdependent dynamic world-wide cyclical and secular conditions rather than of the simple balance-of-payments adjustment to a capital flow induced by autonomous external factors.

Contrast with this the muddle of reparations! Reparations were a lost atom, buffeted about by forces much more powerful than any which they alone might have set in motion. Their history may be said to illustrate both the possibility and the impossibility of transfer. It shows how elastic is the international transfer mechanism and how futile such adjustability is in the face of greater and more powerful economic forces, to say nothing of political choice and determination.

Reparations differed inherently from the Canadian borrowings. They were an arbitrary political imposition, which happened to conflict completely with the usual economic determinants which move capital and goods from regions where they are plentiful to those where they are scarce. Whereas on the one hand the task was already half done in Canada because the underlying economic situation called for borrowing and prepared the adjustment, in the case of reparations the underlying situation called for just the opposite movement.[8]

In the inflation period reparations were among the factors which broke the mark. But there were so many other contributing factors that here obviously no fair test was provided of German ability to pay. The same was true in the years 1924 to 1928, following stabilization, when the balance of payments was dominated, not by reparations outpayments, but by a far greater influx of long- and short-term capital. By making possible a rapid recovery of the German economy, the foreign capital not only rendered unnecessary any absolute reduction of consumption to finance domestic investment and reparations but actually permitted a great rise in consumption, directly and through government public works and social services.[9] And it provided more than enough foreign exchange for reparations, immediately, without the slightest pressure on the mark or deflationary consequences in Germany.[10] Again, from 1929 to 1932 reparation payments were completely overshadowed by outside factors: abrupt cessation of the capital flow, world depression, and capital flight. While the real burden of reparations was greatly aggravated by world deflation, by far the greatest burdens upon the balance of payments were the shrinking of foreign markets, and capital withdrawals.

The adjustment of German trade to the abrupt reversal of capital flows was striking. From a passive balance of 3½ billion marks in 1927, she developed export surpluses of almost one billion in 1930 and almost

[8] Keynes, A Treatise on Money, I, 338; Robertson, "The Transfer Problem," Economic Essays and Addresses, pp. 178–79.

[9] Joseph A. Schumpeter, Business Cycles, New York, McGraw Hill, 1939, II, 717–23.

[10] See J. W. Angell, The Recovery of Germany, New Haven, Yale University, 1929, pp. 328–33; Haberler, The Theory of International Trade, p. 107; Ohlin, "The Reparations Problem," Index, March, 1928, pp. 3–13, passim.

2½ billions in 1931, exclusive of reparations in kind. Here is an excellent case for the theory of automatic adjustments. Even here, however, other factors were responsible besides the purchasing power effects of slackening capital imports from 1928 on. The gradual reconstruction of German industry and the regaining of foreign markets produced a remarkable continuous recovery of exports from 1924 to 1929 and accounted for a decline in the passive trade balance from 3.5 to 1.9 billion marks between 1927 and 1928, while capital and commodity imports remained roughly constant. This recovery must have contributed to the continued decline of the trade balance after 1928. Other contributory factors were either temporary or more or less extraneous: heavy export dumping, exhaustion of existent stocks of food and raw materials, and a temporary windfall of a greater drop in import than export prices.

Equilibrium was, however, never attained; adjustments were inevitably insufficient. In 1931 Germany lost 1,050 million marks of gold, and German banking assets held abroad were depleted by about 2,100 millions.[11] The huge commodity export surplus could not be maintained in a disintegrating world economy. The depression, currency depreciations, and the spread of foreign trade restrictions reduced German sales, and struck most directly at such active bilateral trade balances as she was attempting to maintain and increase.[12] The active trade balance dwindled after 1931, and Germany defaulted on most of her obligations.[13] Neither the experience of 1929–31 nor that of 1931–33 proves or disproves her ability to pay under any circumstances. They indicate only the remarkable adjustability of the balance of payments, on the one hand, and the impossibility of maintaining equilibrium, as defined, when "outside" circumstances were adverse.

Even if the adjustment of the export trade balance after 1929 had been adequate, as it was not, it is difficult to believe that any people could have continued to believe such adjustments worth the cost. In a period of falling prices, the real burden of reparations became increasingly heavy. Since funds received abroad were held idle or used to repay debts, the German payments failed almost entirely to increase actual buying by the recipient countries. As a result, in contrast with capital flows

---

[11] Statistics from League of Nations, *Balances of Payments*; see also Aftalion, *L'Equilibre dans les relations économiques internationales*, p. 292.

[12] See below, p. 251.

[13] In connection with most of the above see Bank for International Settlements (hereinafter B.I.S.), Special Advisory Committee, *Report* (Gr. Brit., Cmd. 3995, 1932), pp. 4–5; Aftalion, *L'Equilibre dans les relations économiques internationales*, pp. 297–300.

in periods of expansion, the onus of adjustment was now entirely on the payer.[14] Transfer of continued payments could be accomplished only by a greater deflation in Germany than in the rest of the world. The intensity of the resulting German deflation and import controls is mirrored in the cutting of imports by 1932 to 35 percent of their 1929 level. The costs were unemployment, heavy wage cuts, high taxes, reduced industrial activity, and a heavy fall in consumption. Belt tightening, postponed until then by heavy capital inflows, was now intensified by world depression and a gigantic capital outflow. It was early evident that a violent political struggle might be precipitated by a continued attempt to exact payment, under these circumstances.[15] So, by 1932 it was perfectly clear that reparations, as well as other foreign claims upon Germany, were at least temporarily doomed. Their transfer became actually impossible, because normal channels of international banking were clogged by distrust, flights of capital, and currency instability—and because, under these circumstances, no people would have been willing to pay the price of meeting their obligations.

Payment of German reparations was never physically impossible. The abundant energy and capacity for belt-tightening and for vigorous economic reorganization and rehabilitation which Germany has demonstrated since 1933 to make possible an orgy of unproductive investment might easily have made reparations transfer possible if directed to that end instead. In any event, in view of the enormous obstacles to autonomous adjustment, the result would have had to be such a complete reorientation of the German economy as has actually occurred. And the new "equilibrium" would have been as shockingly different from that conceived by the traditional theory as is the "equilibrium" which Germany did actually attain.

Canada's borrowings in the years 1900–1913 were made in a prosperous, expanding world, in an environment of expanding prices, trade, production, and population, with a relatively small burden of international debt, and a relatively unhampered and flexible mechanism of adjustment, external and internal. Reparations were imposed upon a world disrupted by war, going through serious depressions separated by a prosperity of falling prices, in an economic system increasingly in-

---

[14] Kindleberger, *International Short-Term Capital Movements*, pp. 164–66.

[15] See Gideonse, "Comment on Reparation Payments," *Amer. Econ. Rev.*, XX (1930), 694; Robertson, "World Finance," *Economic Essays and Addresses*, p. 204; Keynes, "The German Transfer Problem," *Econ. Jour.*, XXXIX (1929), 7; B.I.S., Special Advisory Committee, *Report*, p. 7.

flexible, hampered and limited by economic nationalism and burdened by heavy fixed international obligations. The theory of international equilibrium, which in itself offers no explanation of these widely divergent experiences, is clearly meaningless without consideration of the world scene and the cyclical and secular forces which in reality condition and determine the forces whose operation it purports to describe.

England also experienced during the period 1919 to 1939 a readjustment to a condition of disequilibrium of her balance of payments. At first she sought consciously to re-establish the old institutional framework and to leave the rest to the operation of more or less autonomous forces. But the world-wide changes had been too great, and her position was too precarious. Her final adjustment, partly under the impact of more or less autonomous forces, partly as the result of conscious policy, differed markedly from the old, although by no means as markedly as the German adjustment. There was no return to the pre-war "norm" either in institutional framework or in the nature of her balance of international payments.

It is this adjustment of the British economy, in its internal as well as external aspects, which is the theme of our study.

Part Two
Great Britain's Position in a Changing World

---◆◆◆---

IV. BRITAIN'S PROBLEMS IN A CHANGING WORLD ECONOMY

THE RADICAL CHANGES in Britain's position in the world economy in the period 1919–39 resulted not merely from factors peculiar to Great Britain alone. They were to at least an equal extent attributable to the radical transformation of the world economy which has been in process since 1914. Before turning our attention specifically to Britain's problems, it is necessary to investigate the broader, worldwide economic developments to which they have been inseparably related.

THE CHANGING INSTITUTIONAL FRAMEWORK AND MECHANISM
OF ADJUSTMENT

The traditional economic system is disappearing—both its framework of a free competitive market and of governmental laissez faire and the flexible mechanism of autonomous price adjustments operating within that framework. Wars and technological, institutional, cyclical, and secular changes have imposed upon this decreasingly flexible system enormous new maladjustments between supply and demand, in the allocation of labor and capital, in prices and costs, and between different industries and countries. The great discrepancies and fluctuations of prices, exchange rates, and interest rates which have resulted in recent years are, paradoxically, an evidence of this inflexibility: they are symptoms of breakdown, of a snapping under cumulative pressure, rather than of adjustment. They would not in fact have been so great or so violent had the processes of continuous adjustment been more successful. The result has been increased governmental and private controls to ease, obviate the need for, or prevent the required adjustments, and these controls have in turn enhanced the rigidities which in large measure evoked them. Thus, re-equilibration, instead of occurring within the old institutional system, has been accomplished by deserting that system.

There is reason to believe that even without World War I nations would have experienced a temporary easing off, if not a considerable cyclical reaction, after the rapid development of the decade preceding 1914. The war left an additional legacy of unsettled problems, with its violent disruption of established internal and international economic relationships, its widespread destruction, and its creation of great new inflexible internal and international burdens of debt. As the solution to these problems, Great Britain sought from the start to restore "normalcy" by reconstructing the unified international order of 1913. True, she did not go all the way back, even in her own policy: various protective duties were imposed or renewed during the 1920's; the Bank of England "played the game" of the gold standard hesitantly; and foreign investment remained subject to sporadic unofficial controls. Nevertheless, in general Britain did more than her share. The interests of the great export trades and of the financial community, and the traditional popular association of free trade with cheap food, successfully resisted protectionist onslaughts and the like. The pound was restored to pre-war parity, the budget balanced, and wartime controls were abandoned.[1] The belief reigned that revival and readjustment would automatically be effected if only other countries would do the same.

For a time it looked as if this effort would succeed. By the close of the first post-war decade there had occurred a remarkable world recovery, and a measure of order and stability appeared to have been attained.[2] But at that very time the end was near. A posteriori we can see why the effort had to fail. Whether less human frailty would have made it a success, it is impossible to say. Great new strains remained not far beneath the surface, and mere nominal reconstitution of the old framework could not easily eliminate them, even with the best of will.

Among the most important disequilibrating factors during the period 1919 to 1939 was a persistent tendency toward overproduction of certain staple primary commodities. The rapid development of the world's primary producing areas in the decade before 1914, the stimulus of war, and the spread of large-scale mechanized farming, were the major factors

---

[1] Francis, *Britain's Economic Strategy*, pp. 15–54.
[2] Salter, *World Trade and Its Future*, pp. 30–35.

on the supply side. Meanwhile, a declining rate of population growth and a distinct tendency toward diminished per capita consumption of many primary foods slowed down the expansion of a demand whose inelasticity in the face of the considerable expansion of productive capacity would in any case have threatened a serious price fall. Various governmental attempts to prevent this price decline by restricting output and by insulating home markets against foreign competition merely intensified the basic maladjustment by preventing the necessary reduction of productive capacity and by imposing even greater strains on free world market prices.[3]

Closely related to this weakness of primary prices was a change in the nature and total of international investment. In major part, international capital before 1914 went into the development of primary producing countries, which repaid their debts relatively easily by feeding the rapidly growing populations and industries of the world out of their expanding output. After the World War, however, a greatly increased proportion went into European reconstruction. It seems likely, in any case, that a long cycle of investment in primary producing countries was coming to an end by the late twenties. Thus, these countries were even before 1929 under increasing pressure to meet their debt service. After 1928 the combination of an abrupt decline of new lending, which greatly increased this pressure, and a cyclical decline in world demand for their products caused a precipitous fall in prices, which, in turn, made the shrinkage of investment even greater. Each decline thus reinforced the other in cumulative fashion. The situation of European debtors was little better, when the flow of new capital ceased. Far more than in the case of the major prewar debtors, their products were directly competitive with those of their creditors, whose markets were thus less open to them. Besides, much of their borrowed funds had gone into "investment" not directly productive of a heightened ability to export, being used in repayment of old obligations (e.g., reparations), to accumulate gold and foreign-exchange reserves or for public works and armaments.[4]

It was largely this unstable situation of primary producers and the related disturbance of debtor-creditor relations which combined to make

[3] See Ohlin, *The Course and Phases of the World Economic Depression* (hereinafter *The World Economic Depression*), pp. 19–23, 38–54; also pp. 54–65, 99–104; Great Britain, Committee on Finance and Industry (hereinafter the MacM. Comm.), *Report*, pp. 60–63; Royal Institute (of International Affairs), *The Problem of International Investment*, pp. 26–31.

[4] Royal Institute, *op. cit.*, pp. 13, 20.

the ensuing cyclical down turn so sharp and devastating in its long-run consequences. The result was monetary and financial collapse, involving a frenzied quest for liquidity, a scramble for gold, a panic of hoarding by debtor and creditor alike, an increase of trade and currency controls to maintain solvency and to avoid unemployment, and ever-deepening deflation—all these steps in a competitive race of mutual frustration and grinding depression which all were forced to join.[5] Not only did international trade and investment shrink as a result; the world economic pattern, reconstructed with such labor, was again completely shattered, apparently forever. This was not merely a severe depression but also the breaking up of an economic system.[6]

Even before 1929 the world had failed to attain the monetary stability of the pre-war gold standard. War and inflation had enduring effects upon people's confidence in their own and foreign currencies and in their willingness to hold claims in other than the most liquid forms. The result was the phenomenon of hot money, a huge volume of fluid capital, quick to move from one center to another at the slightest suspicion of the strength of any given currency. Hot money, the product of currency instability, itself made impossible enduring currency stability under a free economy; only confidence in a currency makes it in fact worthy of confidence. Other factors as well contributed to this greatly increased mobile fund of truly international short-term capital: the increased popularity of international stock exchange speculation and interest and exchange arbitrage, heavy national post-war income taxation, and the spread of the gold exchange standard.[7]

Hot money was dangerous, first, because its quick response to interest rate differentials prevented full adjustments of balances of payment. High interest rates in a country with a weak balance of payments attracted a huge volume of capital, which prevented gold flows and thus obviated temporarily the need for deflation of buying power. The precipitancy of the subsequent withdrawals made the necessary adjustments at that time quite impossible. In the interim price disequilibria were perpetu-

---

[5] See Ohlin, *The World Economic Depression*, pp. 99–104; Morgan-Webb, *The Rise and Fall of the Gold Standard*, p. 119, chap. ix.

[6] Salter, *World Trade and Its Future*, pp. 35–62.

[7] See Jones, "The Gold Standard," *Econ. Jour.*, XLIII (1933), 567–68; Einzig, "Some New Features of Gold Movements," *Econ. Jour.*, XL (1930), 56–60, and *The Tragedy of the Pound*, p. 46; W. A. Brown, *The Int. Gold Stand.*, II, 746–47, 768–70. The foreign exchange holdings of European central banks have been estimated at $250–$400 million before the war, $900 million in 1924, and $2,500 at the end of 1928. *Ibid.*, pp. 747–48, also see chap. xx, *passim.*

ated.[8] The widespread introduction of the gold exchange standard contributed to this substitution of temporary for enduring re-equilibration. Changes in the gold country's balance of payments vis-à-vis the gold exchange countries resulted, not in gold flows, with consequent effects upon its credit policy, but merely in a net rise or fall in its total shortterm foreign liabilities at the expense of, or in favor of, domestic liabilities.[9]

Secondly, the greatly increased "independent" movements of shortterm capital—i.e., those which were not directly or indirectly a response to balance-of-payments disequilibria and hence a substitute for gold flows, but which tended, rather, to bring gold with them, in the same direction —were themselves serious disequilibrating factors. The very speed and size of their movement made adjustments other than by gold flows impossible. And even after the gold flowed there was much less tendency toward enduring adaptation. Primary purchasing power effects were slight, because the capital was held as idle deposits or went chiefly into short-term money markets or security speculation. Moreover, the funds by no means necessarily went to countries which were in particularly great need of foreign goods, let alone those of the "lender." And their secondary purchasing power effects were frequently forestalled by policies of offsetting the gold flows which they induced. Central banks were well aware that these flows were not the result of balance of payments or price disequilibria, but of truly "external" factors, and were therefore subject to reversal at any time. Therefore they felt, justifiably, that it would be dangerous to absorb the gold into the credit system of the receiving country and undesirable to institute the required deflation in the

[8] Mlynarski, *The Functioning of the Gold Standard*, pp. 15–17. True, as we have seen, even before 1914 short-term capital flowed customarily in response to interest rate differentials. But the flows were in such cases apparently not a means of tiding over consistently adverse balances of payments and thus avoiding necessary enduring adjustments. That is why the capital usually brought gold with it, instead of obviating a gold flow in the opposite direction.

[9] Thus the economy of gold, so often proclaimed to be an advantage of this system, amounted in fact to a dangerous credit expansion by both gold and gold exchange standard countries on the basis of the same gold. The secondary purchasing power effects of balance of payments disequilibria upon the gold standard country were effectively forestalled, unless that country looked upon net changes in its total foreign liabilities in the same way as opposite movements in its gold stocks. In the latter event, there would have been no economy of gold. Only in disequilibria between the gold exchange standard countries were complete reciprocal purchasing power effects and the concentration of reserves compatible. See pp. 14–15, above. Also Viner, *Studies in Theory*, p. 411; Keynes, *A Treatise on Money*, I, 350 ff.; Heilperin, *International Monetary Economics*, pp. 211–18; Mlynarski, *The Functioning of the Gold Standard*, pp. 18–21.

remitting country.[10] So strong were the forces giving rise to these movements that cessation or reversal alike were usually difficult or impossible. Thus, gold flows in the post-war period became increasingly erratic, and, because of the inadaptability of balances of payments, larger and more continuous.[11] They had exceedingly unsettling effects; they contributed to and were part of the post-war liquidity mania, which threatened the stability of the gold standard of 1925–29 and greatly intensified the subsequent deflation and financial crises.

The monetary instability of the post-war world was in large measure the result of the growing threat to the financial supremacy of London by New York and Paris (the latter after inflation and stabilization of the franc). This was, of course, not simply or even primarily a monetary phenomenon. The financial strength of a country is fundamentally its *real* wealth and productive power, on which depend, among other things, the size of its savings, its ability to send those savings abroad in the form of goods and services, and its consequent ability to attract gold. To a very marked extent, after the first World War, Great Britain lost this power, and the United States and France gained it, at least temporarily. America's industrial pre-eminence, the undervalued franc and the capital repatriations after its stabilization, the world's tribute in reparations and war debts to both countries—these were the causes of American and French ascendancy.

In the pre-war system Britain's financial predominance had given her enormous power over world credit conditions. She was the "conductor of the international orchestra," [12] and other countries were perforce on a sterling standard; they had to follow England if they wished to share in the long and short credit which she supplied.[13] Because of her immense power to attract and hold gold and foreign deposits (just as a banker has the power to hold the deposits of his clients), and because of her inherently strong balance-of-payments position, Britain could afford to pursue a policy of laissez faire in foreign lending and international trade. In time of stringency she could easily draw in foreign deposits and

[10] See above, p. 20*n*; Kindleberger, *International Short-Term Capital Movements*, pp. 211-12, 221, 228.

[11] Other reasons for this phenomenon are suggested by Einzig, *International Gold Movements*, chap. vi, and W. A. Brown, *The Int. Gold Stand.*, I, 631–35, and *England and the New Gold Standard*, pp. 274–77.

[12] Keynes, *A Treatise on Money*, II, 307.

[13] Williams, "Monetary Stabilization from an International Point of View," *Amer. Econ. Rev.*, Suppl., March 1935, p. 161.

gold and curtail her lending by raising the Bank Rate. But at all times her great free and open market permitted debtors to meet their obligations to her in goods with comparative ease.[14] And credit-worthy borrowers could almost always obtain accommodation, at a price, without stipulation as to the expenditure of the proceeds.[15] Thus, Britain did not drain the world of gold, but, on the contrary, worked traditionally with a very modest gold reserve. Because her income from exports and other income from abroad were so important to her, she was impelled to manage the "sterling standard" in the interest of world stability. This was not altruism, but pure self-interest.[16]

It was no coincidence that British economists provided the theoretical rationale for the international system over which Britain presided. Sterling provided the system with the medium of exchange and trade credit instrument which bound it together. The concentration of world deposits in one center permitted the bulk of world payments to be made and offset by book transfers with a minimum need for gold flows. The location in England of the world's major commodity (including gold) markets, where world supply and demand met to fix a world price, helped create a true international price level. The pre-war world economy operated and grew just as it did and as smoothly as it did largely because of Britain's predominant financial and commercial position and the policies she pursued.[17]

For purely technical reasons the disintegration of this central financial nucleus created obstacles to the stability of the world economy. The benefits of the clearing principle are, of course, maximized when all clearings are effected through one center; otherwise the transacting countries must keep balances in several centers and the economies and greater security of concentrated reserves are reduced. Now each clearing center be-

[14] The British market absorbed an extraordinarily large proportion of the world's total exports of various staple products—no less than 99 percent of the bacon and hams, and 96 percent of the mutton and lamb in 1930. Other percentages for the same year were as follows: butter 63, eggs 62, beef 59, cheese 46, wool 32, and wheat and wheat flour 28. Figures from K. A. H. Murray and Ruth L. Cohen, *The Planning of Britain's Food Imports*, as reproduced in Bidwell, *Our Trade with Britain*, pp. 71–72.
[15] W. A. Brown, *The Int. Gold Stand.*, I, 157–58.
[16] See the excellent discussion by Morgan-Webb, *The Rise and Fall of the Gold Standard*, pp. 55–67; also Sir George Paish, *The Way to Recovery*, New York, Putnam, 1931, pp. 37–39.
[17] See W. A. Brown, *The Int. Gold Stand.*, II, 774–78, and *passim*, this being Brown's major thesis; also Morgan-Webb, *The Rise and Fall of the Gold Standard*, pp. 50–54, and Condliffe, *The Reconstruction of World Trade*, pp. 144–45, 272–73.

came dependent upon the policies and the balance of payments of the other with the rest of the world. Each became subject to gold drain or embarrassing gold influx because of the other's excessively strong or weak position, just as individual banks lose or gain reserves by extending credit more or less generously than other banks. This was true also because to keep working foreign balances in any one center there was little but temporary considerations of safety or profit.[18] In addition, the purchasing-power flows making for re-equilibration are at their maximum effectiveness when all international payments are made with claims upon a single center. Only, then, in the case of payments between the clearing center and the rest of the world will the shift be only one-sided,[19] a situation which is, moreover, easily susceptible to the control of the clearing center if it prudently exercises its financial strength. With the rise of other clearing centers, payments involving only unilateral purchasing-power effects multiply in number. The problems of prudent credit control increase, while responsibility for a consistent co-ordinated policy and power to enforce it are dissipated.

Neither France nor the United States had the tradition or the economic compulsion to behave as Britain had behaved. The French propensity to hoard has always been strong, France's banking habits are relatively undeveloped, and her tendency to accumulate great gold supplies is inveterate. Her foreign lending was further restricted to short-term loans in the post-war years as a result of the heavy wartime losses on continental investments. In fact, this "lending" consisted mainly of huge liquid balances fleeing a depreciating franc; these balances were a constant menace, and their repatriations increased the world's maldistribution of gold. Neither in France nor in the United States were there strong groups and interests dictating a free-trade policy or free foreign lending, and both lacked a broad stable market for foreign securities. Having attracted gold, they failed to expand credit as much as Britain had customarily done. The Bank of France has seldom been willing to vary its credit policy because of external conditions, and the far greater importance of the American internal market inclined the Federal Reserve authorities, however willing to co-operate with other central banks, in the same direction. The violent business cycle in the United States and her lack of a steady foreign-investing class made her international lending very fitful; she could still experience sudden huge inflows of capital, as

[18] W. A. Brown, *The Int. Gold Stand.*, II, 786–89.
[19] See above, pp. 11–12, 45.

in 1928–29, because of the superior attractions of American investment outlets and the prospects for speculative gain. For all these reasons the increased financial power of the United States and France was particularly disruptive of international financial stability.[20]

Great Britain's financial pre-eminence, which had in the past permitted uncontrolled foreign lending and free trade, trusting to the forces of autonomous adjustment to retain equilibrium, was now undermined. When because of a weak balance of payments she was forced to attract and hold foreign short-term capital, to avoid a loss of gold, she had to compete with New York and Paris. The transfer of many of her normal customer balances to these centers, and in addition their strong balances of payments with the rest of the world, put a large portion of the claims on London in the hands of these creditor countries.[21] These balances no longer inevitably stayed in London; they had to be induced to stay.[22] When America reduced her foreign lending, Britain promptly experienced a withdrawal of foreign balances by the debtor countries thus weakened and a drain of gold to the United States, pounds being offered heavily for dollars.[23] Britain's financial position was, manifestly, far more precarious than it had formerly been.

Because of her altered financial position, but even more because of her underlying weaknesses, Britain's place in the new world gold standard was untenable. After an unhappy experience from 1925 on, she was finally forced off gold in 1931. Concomitantly she abandoned the other bulwarks of the traditional policy on which the old world "sterling standard" had been based—free trade [24] and uncontrolled foreign lend-

[20] For fuller discussions of the implications and consequences of the rise of France and the United States, the reader is referred to Einzig, *The Fight for Financial Supremacy;* W. A. Brown, *The Int. Gold Stand.*, I, 330–32, 551–54; Gayer, *Monetary Policy and Economic Stabilization*, pp. 30–31, 77, 154; Morgan-Webb, *The Rise and Fall of the Gold Standard*, pp. 75–76, 80–89, 102–3; Ohlin, *The World Economic Depression*, pp. 35–36; Gold Delegation, Financial Comm., *Interim Report*, League of Nations, Geneva, 1930, p. 110; O. M. W. Sprague, "The Working of the Gold Standard under Present Conditions," *Selected Documents* submitted to the Gold Delegation of the Financial Comm., League of Nations, Geneva, 1930, p. 54.

[21] France's heavy reparation receipts, for example, paid in large measure by British loans to Germany, thus turned up as French claims on London, subject to instantaneous recall. MacM. Comm., *Evidence*, II, 199.

[22] W. A. Brown, *The Int. Gold Stand.*, I, 669–72.

[23] *Ibid.*, I, chap. xvii, pp. 518–23, 725–26; Mlynarski, *The Functioning of the Gold Standard*, pp. 21–23; MacM. Comm., *Evidence*, II, 199.

[24] "In spite of the increasing use of the tariff for political or non-revenue purposes, the tariff up to 1931 could still be regarded as a free trade measure. Every imported article was free of duty unless listed. . . . [By] 1932 our tariff policy had completed its turn-

ing. Trade and lending controls and currency flexibility as the means of adjustment to basic balance-of-payments disequilibria became for the first time the accepted rule of peacetime policy. Credit policy became attuned primarily to the needs of the home market rather than primarily to the requirements of currency stability, and the domestic money supply was shielded from the effects of international gold and capital flows. Free competitive adjustments were further restricted internally by a greatly increased concentration of business control. Thus, in Britain after 1931, as in the world as a whole, the flexibilities of autonomous adjustments via the price mechanism were superseded by the flexibilities (such as they are) of monetary and trade policies, and the rigid rules controlling and limiting governmental actions were made untenable by an increasing rigidity and stratification of the economic organism. The two changes, greatly accelerated in the years 1913–39, occurred together and reinforced each other; together they are molding the world economy of the future.

By falling in with world trends after 1931, Britain greatly reinforced them. The intricate web of international transactions which still customarily cleared through London, the settled financial and trade connections to which English traders and bankers were a party were disrupted by the decline and fluctuations of sterling. Central banks suffered losses on their sterling reserves. Many debtors who had customarily met their obligations largely by sales of goods and securities in England were severely hit by the fall of the pound, by the tariff, empire preference, and lending restrictions. The scramble for liquidity, the vicious cycle of deflation and of trade and currency restrictions and controls was intensified. As a result, in the British system and in the world system, negotiation, discrimination, bilateralism, and government controls increasingly took the place of laissez faire.[25]

In many respects, thus, the years 1931–32 are a real turning point, a revolutionary readaptation of government policy after an attempt to rebuild along traditional lines. However, the major real determinants of the British economic position were independent economic forces largely beyond the power of British policy to alter over any period of time.

---

over from free trade to protection. Every imported article from a non-Empire country is now dutiable unless listed as free." McGuire, *The British Tariff System*, pp. 232–33.

[25] The effect of British policy in this regard must not be exaggerated. The world economy was disintegrating without Britain's assistance. Further, Britain's policy in some respects restored a degree of stability—for example, by the development of a new sterling standard. See Francis, *Britain's Economic Strategy*, pp. 290–93.

Policy changes contributed to the greater or lesser success of her adjustments, but they merely supplemented a process of autonomous adaptation throughout the years 1919–39. In these major respects the period 1919–39 does not break at 1931–32, but represents, rather, a single continuous series embodying striking long-run trends.

The "technical" potential weaknesses of Britain's monetary position after 1925, as we have suggested, cannot be separated from her real weaknesses. The deteriorating competitive position of British industry was what made her balance of payments weak, making it necessary for her to struggle to retain foreign balances. The new monetary situation was important, but it was itself the product of a changing real world situation —for example, the enormous productive power of American industry— and its threat to Britain was great mainly because of her changing real position in that world.

In the impact upon Britain of the transformed world economy, similarly, it was not so much the procedural or structural changes in the latter which were important, as the serious real alterations of long-run trends and levels of economic activity, these alterations being partly the cause, partly the result of the formal changes. Secular trends of growth of certain regions and industries, of total international trade and investment, have been seriously modified. These apparent secular changes may simply be aspects of a long and severe cyclical fluctuation; it is difficult as yet to be certain. In any event, the cyclical fluctuations, if they are such, have been of greatly increased intensity and duration and have entailed what appear to be lasting effects. It is these changes which we propose next to investigate.

BRITAIN'S CHANGING REAL POSITION

During the latter half of the eighteenth century Great Britain appears customarily to have exported more goods than she imported. After a transitional period at the beginning of the nineteenth century, the commodity balance became regularly and heavily passive, but exports of goods and services together were still considerably in excess of imports. After about 1870 these receipts, too, proved inadequate, and thenceforth Britain was able to import as much as she did only because of her income from previous investments. Thus, despite her heavy continuous foreign investment, England had for decades before 1914 provided a decreasing proportion of her own total consumption of goods and services, either directly or by current exchange for foreign goods and services.

These changes clearly mirror an evolving international financial position. In her earlier period as a creditor Britain naturally exported more capital than she received in income from past savings invested abroad. However, new foreign investments cannot indefinitely exceed the growing income from the old. Foreign investment reduces the differential between domestic and foreign marginal productivity of capital which initially induces it. There are dynamic offsets to this tendency, but of these at least one, the world's geographical expansion, is not unlimited. Furthermore, the continued development of younger areas means an expansion of their own capital resources and a diminished relative need for foreign capital. So eventually, as part of an inevitable process of financial maturing, Britain passed from a stage in which she produced more goods and services than she consumed to one where the opposite was true; she became a *rentier* nation.

As an essential counterpart to this financial evolution was the development of Britain's industrial position, in which we are particularly interested. The foreign demand for British savings and Britain's ability to satisfy it were results of her industrial leadership. In turn, the relative decline of the world's demand for those savings and the beginning of net interest and dividend repayments were the counterpart of a rise in the productive power of debtor areas relatively greater than the rise of productive power in Britain herself—an inescapable result of the spread of technology and the tapping of immense resources within those debtor areas.

The impact of these long-run determinants of Britain's financial and industrial position was intensified during the 1870's by the abrupt termination of a period of extremely heavy investment, so that that decade became a fairly clear signpost in this development.[26] The heavy imports of American agricultural products which followed were in part simply a return on past investment. They dramatized, also, the secular emergence of the American producer and the corresponding relative decline of the British producer. Similarly, the slower expansion of British exports was only partly the token and result of a decreased marginal efficiency of capital abroad; it was also the result of the development of competing foreign manufacturing industries. When the expanded output of foreign areas began to pour forth, when increasing foreign tariffs revealed the diminished world need for British goods and when world prices and

[26] See Jenks, *The Migration of British Capital to 1875*, chap. xi, "At the End of the Surplus."

profits sagged under the impact, Englishmen began to be uncomfortably conscious of their dependence upon world markets to keep them employed. Business men complained, and a Royal Commission of Inquiry was appointed to investigate the increasingly successful competition by foreign producers. British agriculture lost out rapidly to cheap American and Russian grain. The following decades were marked by a revival of protectionist sentiment and by agitation for empire preference. The British people, as producers, were beginning to look for security and protection against cheap foreign goods, even though those goods were raising their real incomes enormously.[27]

Whatever the net effect of these changes upon real British incomes and living standards, the fact that as a producer Britain was growing more slowly than the rest of the world had an ominous aspect. Britain's high incomes rested in large measure not simply upon cheap imports but also upon her ability to command those imports by her own superior industrial ability. The development of foreign productive powers, to the extent, however slight, that they were competitive, involved definite losses, as certain British producers found themselves less able than before to compete in the world market. Had Britain's predominance been based on a superior agriculture, a greater portion of the country would have suffered the fate of the British farmer from 1875 to 1900, and the gains from cheap food would have been offset by an even more severe reduction than actually occurred in her ability to command that food. As her dependence upon foreign foods and materials grew, Britain's ability to command them declined.

The fact remains that British real income increased throughout the nineteenth century. For one thing, the progressive alteration of her balance of payments was to some extent the result simply of the secular financial evolution described above. To this extent British productive factors were merely being reallocated, moved from export and import competing lines, without reduction of marginal productivity, to satisfy increased domestic purchasing power. It should be noted, however, that even this potential increment to British current living standards involved some counterbalancing loss of income, for the increased available

[27] Some recognized the signs of secular change: see Bourne, "The Growing Preponderance of Imports over Exports," *Journal of the Royal Statistical Society* (hereinafter J.R.S.S.), XL (1877), 30–34, *Trade, Population, and Food*, p. 284 and *passim*. Also Alfred Marshall, *Industry and Trade*, chap. v, *passim*; Clapham, *An Economic History of Modern Britain*, II, 111–13, III, 35–38, 44–45, 48–49; C. R. Fay, *Great Britain from Adam Smith to the Present Day*, 3d ed., London, Longmans Green, 1932, pp. 222, 243–44.

purchasing power was seldom completely employed. A sudden decrease of foreign lending almost invariably involved considerable unemployment in export trades, since effective domestic spending or investment failed to take up the slack completely.

The other offset to the relative decline in world demand for British goods was for a long time more than sufficient: the absolutely increasing productive and hence consuming power of the world. Expansion of younger economies supplied Britain with growing markets for her manufactures not merely on current account but also in the form of capital attracted by the rich opportunities for investment therein, and this permitted the extension of that international division of labor which contributed so much to the great economic advance of the century. The development of oversea primary producers was mainly complementary to her own industry,[28] and Britain undoubtedly gained more than she lost thereby. The rapid changes of the century before 1914 naturally demanded continual adjustments. But as long as there was no radical break with the past, as long as changes were reasonably consistent and followed continuous trends, as long as the whole move upward, the international economic pattern was not disrupted and England, by and large, felt relatively little strain.

The most important real problems faced by Britain in the years 1919 to 1939 arose out of the continuation and intensification of these long-run factors, with two important differences of degree. First of all, foreign countries developed industries along increasingly competitive lines. And secondly, the vital mitigating factors—expanding world markets and increasing international investments—seem not to have been equally operative. The significance of these various factors may perhaps be best illustrated by a theoretical argument.

Here is a wealthy country, B, formerly the manufacturing center of the world because of the skill of her labor, the size and quality of her equipment, her established connections, and her head start in the development of these assets. Assume that a previously backward area, A, by adopting modern techniques, accumulating domestic capital, and using superior resources, has attained superiority over B, at a given point of

---

[28] "Competitive" and "complementary" foreign production are not absolute concepts. There is an entire range of international trade based upon comparative (not absolute) advantage, between industries far more competitive than British coal and Portuguese wine. The difference is one of degree, but it is none the less actual. British real incomes are clearly less injured by the growth of jute plantations than of textile factories in India.

time, in the production of the latter's export goods. What will be the effect on B's exports? On B's real incomes?

The tendency will be for B's exports to decline. If world demand is absolutely constant, clearly B must sell absolutely less and A absolutely more in world markets.[29] Actually, however, world output must be increasing by the amount of the increased efficiency of A. Assuming hereafter that aside from this expansion of A world output is stationary, the question whether or by how much B's trade will fall absolutely depends upon the nature of the reciprocal demands between B and the outside world.

The additional income of the world—both the income in A and the income in A's markets now released by the greater cheapness of their imports—may turn either toward goods in the production of which B has special advantages or to goods concerning which B is at a disadvantage and in the production of which it will concentrate only if it is under great compulsion to export. In the extreme case, the added demand may go into goods and services which do not enter into international trade— buildings, parks, baseball players, or leisure.

In the former case (if world demand for B's goods has high income elasticity), B's exports may be saved from absolute decrease and may in extreme cases even increase. The latter is possible if A's cheaper products underbid those of other countries as well, thus potentially releasing for the purchase of B's goods more demand than B previously lost through A's competition. Otherwise B can at best merely hold all the demand which it lost. If world demand for B's goods has a low income elasticity (a probable condition of a decline in B's general competitive position in relation to the world), there will be an absolute fall in the total value of her exports. The extent of this decline will depend very largely upon the income elasticity of B's demand for foreign goods and the price elasticity of world demand for B's goods.[30] If B's demand for its accustomed imports does not contract, the volume of exports may well be

[29] The effect might be an initial tendency for B also to buy more, A's producers invading her home market. This is not likely to occur at once, however, in view of the probability (especially if the transportation cost factor be included) that the industries concerned operate, in the long run, under increasing cost conditions. Under these conditions, A's continued encroachments will become increasingly more difficult, and B's resistance progressively easier with falling marginal costs. The probabilities are that B will lose its markets in A first, and its home market last. In any case, a rise in B's imports as well does not alter our reasoning or conclusions.

[30] Price elasticity of B's demand is relatively unimportant, since there is little reason to anticipate a change in the world price of B's imports.

maintained at the cost of greatly deteriorated terms of trade. How far they will have to deteriorate will depend upon the price elasticity of the world's demand for B's goods.

What does this mean in terms of B's national income? B's physical productivity has not diminished. Any change in income must therefore result from a change in the quantum of exports required to obtain a given quantum of imports, i.e., in the barter terms of trade.

In conditions wherein B's exports will decline (if world demand for her goods has low income elasticity), her income derived therefrom must obviously decline as well. The weakness of B's balance of payments resulting from the general deterioration of her competitive position must be equilibrated by a net decline in her real purchasing power over foreign goods. This decline must be permanent, in the absence of external changes, for balance-of-payments equilibrium to be sustained in the face of the permanent net fall in the world's demand for B's goods. Her displaced factors of production may shift from export to domestic lines of production rather than remain unemployed; but, by assumption, the total amount of imports which these factors will be able to command through their new product will be less. In any case, the result must be, in the absence of an independent rise of domestic demand (for consumption or investment), a general decline in their marginal productivity—i.e., in B's real income.

Those factors determining the extent to which B's national income will actually fall as a result will be the same as in the case of exports: the income elasticity of B's demand for imports and the price elasticity of world demand for B's goods. If, in the extreme case, the price and income elasticity of world demand for B's goods is low and B's demand for imports is highly inelastic, then B's income reduction will be great. That reduction may take any or all of the following forms: a severe decline of terms of trade, heavy unemployment, income deflation required to keep the demand for imports within bounds, or a shift of her factors into very unremunerative export lines in order to sustain the imports which B continues to require. And balance-of-payments equilibration will require this heavy decline. If, under similar conditions of world demand, however, B's demand for foreign goods is very elastic, then B's imports will fall as far as exports without any necessarily equivalent reduction in real income, since B's factors will not have to take to these very unremunerative lines, and her terms of trade will change but little. Income received from exports will, it is true, decline heavily, but income from domestic sales will rise almost equivalently. And balance-of-payments equilibration will not require an appreciable income decline.[31] Only, however, if all the demand released by the economic progress of A (assuming that only B's producers have been supplanted) turns to products in which B has sufficient relative advantages will B not suffer some absolute fall in national income.

These considerations by no means exhaust the possibilities, but the following general conclusions seem justified. It is probable that B's national income and foreign trade will decline in absolute terms. The extent of the decline will depend largely upon B's adaptability—her ability to shift to other lines of production to satisfy the released world demand. However, it is quite possible that B's trade may fall much farther than her income: if B's demand for foreign goods is relatively elastic, her productive factors will be released to supply the home market, and will be utilized there to only slightly less advantage, because B's population favors foreign goods only slightly over domestic.[32]

Thus, under the initial assumption of a stationary world economy, except for progress in A, B will be spared a fall in total trade and income only under rather unusual circumstances. Eliminate that assumption, however, introduce an expanding world economy, and this is by no means necessary. B, though supplanted in wheat production, may well become the world's center for the production of cotton manufactures, the demand for which may grow as the world economy expands. The shift of B's factors of production from old lines to new will be far easier, since B's exports are sustained by world demand. B's farming population may simply cease to grow, rather than decline absolutely. In an expanding world economy the relative gains of A need by no means mean absolute losses for B.

Remove, again, the expanding world economy or expanding world trade (with hence a possibility of increase of demand for B's goods). In the worst case B may become a decadent economy, highly specialized,

[31] See p. 13, above. Here we have a concrete substantiation of our contention of Chapter III, above, that the processes of the "transition" and of the "long run" are one and the same. The income or purchasing power shifts of the adjusting balance of payments mechanism and the income changes involved in such "long run" factors as permanent changes in world demand for the goods of any country are precisely the same. And hence, obviously, the same factors (e.g., B's marginal propensity to import, the direction of the world's new demands) will make both—the "transitional" unemployment and the permanent loss to B's income—great or small.

[32] Charles R. Whittlesey has discussed some aspects of these problems in "Foreign Investment and the Terms of Trade," Q.J.E., XLVI (1932), 444–64.

extremely prosperous as long as it was predominant in its specialty, and extremely depressed as soon as others learned to produce those goods more efficiently.

Here are suggested some of the fundamental problems of Britain in a changing world. To what extent has she lost her leadership in world manufacture? To what extent has she been able to compensate for losses in older lines by relatively increasing specialization in new, in satisfying the demands released by rising world incomes? To what extent did world markets continue to expand? How elastic was the British demand for foreign goods? How did the British balance of payments, and the entire economy adjust themselves to the changing world situation? Were the effects of these changes imparted by relative monetary deflation in Britain, by fluctuations in the external value of sterling, or by fluctuations of employment? What was the influence in this regard of conscious government and business and labor controls? Were there other, "external," changes bearing upon Britain's situation?

It is generally recognized that an unprecedented rate of population growth, the extension of the geographical frontiers of the capitalist economy, and rapid technological advance were essential contributory factors to the enormous world-wide economic expansion of the century before 1914. It is also recognized that the diminution of the rate of population growth and the disappearance of geographical frontiers have rendered more and more unlikely a continued advance at anything like the earlier rates and along the old lines. The one remaining field for future advance is the intensive margin, which offers the opportunity of increasing the standards of living of the existing population within existing geographical areas by fuller application of the means already at hand and by further technological advance. While these remaining frontiers offer ample possibility for continued expansion, it would appear probable that world economic growth will be slower in the future than in the past, if only because the productive factors "land" and "labor" will cease growing.[33]

There is a second and more serious threat: that the capitalist world will be less and less able to make full use of its existing potentialities because of a growing discrepancy between savings and investment outlets under the changed conditions. The secular tendency, noted by Keynes, the tendency for an increasing share of a rising national income to go into

[33] Alvin H. Hansen, "Economic Progress and Declining Population Growth," *Amer. Econ. Rev.*, XXIX (1939), 1-15; J. M. Keynes, "Some Economic Consequences of a Declining Population," *Eugenics Review*, XXIX (April, 1937), 13-17; A. R. Sweezy, "Population Growth and Investment Opportunity," *Q.J.E.*, LV (1940), 64-79.

savings is probably intensified if that rising income is spread over a stationary population. This is, however, not essential. A decrease in the size of families may involve less rather than more saving; decreased "investment" in children may lead to increased "investment" in houses or durable consumer goods. In any case, however, the disappearance of two major factors providing outlets for continuous investment in the nineteenth century—the equipment of a growing labor force, and the development of new areas—augurs at least a tendency to underinvestment and hence to underemployment. Other factors may reinforce that tendency. Continued technological progress in the provision of the essentials and slower expansion in the demand for them will release a greater proportion of the labor force for the satisfaction of other desires. Hence there will be an increasingly urgent necessity for new effective demands to provide full employment.[34] Moreover, since the demand for luxuries is far more subject to fluctuation with changing income expectations, full employment may be sustained only precariously.

The geographical incidence of this increased underemployment and that of a slower rate of world economic advance may be very unequal. The weight of adjustment will fall especially heavily upon the advanced economies which have been geared to a steady outflow of capital (and also labor) to expanding younger foreign economies. Even if the world economy continues to expand by learning to cultivate at the intensive margins, these foreign outlets for the output of older countries beyond their own ability or willingness to consume have definitely ceased to grow as rapidly, and it is problematical whether they will ever grow again as before.[35]

Britain has been such an imperialistic economy par excellence. During the nineteenth century she opened her home markets freely and sacrificed her agriculture in order to attain and to maintain her position as the world's leading exporter of manufactured goods.[36] In the process undeveloped areas became customers, and customers became competitors. But a rapidly expanding world population offered a growing market to farmers, who were not therefore impelled, most of them, to go into

[34] Glenday, "The Future of Export Trade," International Affairs, XVIII (1939), 646–51.
[35] See Salter, World Trade and Its Future, pp. 21–23.
[36] The reader is reminded that this exposition of Britain's peculiar specialized international position gives an incomplete and oversimplified picture of the whole British economy. Agriculture, for example, remains an important industry, which supplies an important portion of domestic requirements. See, for example, Political and Economic Planning (hereinafter P.E.P.), Report on International Trade, pp. 204–5; Liberal Industrial Inquiry, Britain's Industrial Future, pp. 318–19.

manufacturing and so to compete with Britain. Even if they did, new markets for British manufactures were constantly being opened up. Moreover, continued British technical advance enabled her to specialize increasingly in higher grades and qualities of manufactures—finer consumer goods, machinery, shipbuilding—and so in part to adapt herself to the industrialization of former agricultural customers.

The burden was by no means thrown entirely upon the latter method of adjustment. Had Britain's only means of maintaining her real income levels been by maintaining her technological leadership, the pressure exerted by others who were catching up would have been felt much earlier. So a slower rate of expansion of international trade and investment outlets, such as seems actually to have characterized the years since 1914, or at least since 1929, is fraught with serious danger. The rise of previous customers to economic maturity has not been adequately compensated by the opening of new markets. The pressure of competition in existing markets has grown, and an enhanced tendency toward underemployment has intensified the bitterness of the competitive struggle.

It became apparent again to the British people, as it did in the 1870's, that the price of their specialization was insecurity and dependence upon the market. Of the food needed to sustain a greatly increased population, domestic farmers produced an inadequate share. Of the raw materials required by her industry, Britain produced only coal in abundance. Her ability to command these vitally essential goods over any period of time depended primarily upon her ability to export. Hence her living standards were subject perpetually to the vagaries of the competitive struggle, and the maximization of her income under that system demanded willingness and ability to make all the necessary adjustments to changed external conditions.

Ever since 1870, and much earlier in some cases, other countries, faced with an inflow of cheap foreign goods, made decisions of policy which represented a choice, conscious or otherwise, of security and stability over the maximum potential income which free trade is supposed to offer. They were led to protect themselves not only against the transitional difficulties of adjustment but also against the ultimate consequences: the economically and politically precarious specialization which would result from complete obedience to the rules of the game.[37]

---

[37] See Allen, *British Industries and Their Organization*, pp. 9–16. Josiah Stamp argued before the MacMillan Committee for abandonment of laissez faire in foreign lending, in the interests of stability. "What is the good of having a higher standard of life

This trend toward economic nationalism has been and probably will continue to be reinforced by a retardation of world economic growth. The problems of adjustment are much greater in a period of relative contraction than in times of rapid expansion, so the clamor for protection and other state intervention grows. Historically, situations in which economic vistas are narrowing have not been conducive to unregulated individualism; they tend rather toward combination in industrial control [38] and protection in national policy, and each of these outcomes reinforces the other.[39] Dwindling agricultural profits led to tariffs on manufactures in order to develop domestic industry. Wars and threats of wars and the deep depression of the thirties also have reinforced the trend, and none of these more recent calamities can be said to be unrelated to the above-mentioned secular phenomena, which have intensified the struggle over existing markets, and increased the economic difficulties of debtor and creditor nations alike. The British position has been made possible largely by international division of labor and mutual trade. As that system breaks down, Britain suffers from her great specialization. If other countries more capable than she by virtue of superior natural resources decide to play a completely different game, refuse to buy her goods, and thus force her people also to live within themselves, the results in the way of declining living standards will be more serious for her than for most others.

These nationalistic restrictions have in turn undoubtedly slowed still further the increase of world output, especially the increase of international trade and investment. But the entire relative lag in trade and investment can scarcely be attributed to them. Our discussion suggests other more basic causes. One such cause has been the virtual halt to the development of new areas and markets, a development which supplied an important stimulus to international investment and trade in the past. Secondly, a more even spread of technology has tended to diminish the differential national advantages which make international specialization most desirable. Certain modern scientific advances, notably the use of hydroelectric power and petroleum, and the synthetic manufacture of raw materials, have had the same effect, by diminishing local advantages

if you are everlastingly falling short of it?" *Evidence*, I, 256; also 255, and Royal Inst., *The Problem of International Investment*, pp. 31, 33.

[38] See Myron W. Watkins, *Industrial Combinations and Public Policy*, New York, Houghton Mifflin, 1927, pp. 9–14.

[39] See Lionel Robbins, *Economic Planning and International Order*, London, Macmillan, 1938.

based on possession of necessary raw materials.[40] These changes have
had the added effect of making less costly policies of national insulation
through protection and hence of encouraging them.[41] Finally, there may
be noted an apparently universal tendency for an increasing proportion
of rising incomes to go into services: distribution, the professions, entertainment, and possibly housing, which for the most part do not enter into
international trade. Similarly, the related decline of international investment has had other basic causes than perverse policy. Among these were
the increased financial self-sufficiency of debtor areas, and the decreased
opportunities for profitable investment in younger primary producing
regions, for reasons already indicated. The disastrous results of the heavy
lending of the 1920's, which choked off international investment in the
following decade, were in large measure attributable to these underlying
factors and to the failure of alternative investments in countries whose
trade was not essentially complementary with that of the creditors.

There have no doubt been forces operating in the opposite direction.
The growth of wealth and new consumer demands and the progress of
technology have tended to increase international tourist traffic and trade
in specialty manufactures and in raw materials such as oil and rubber.[42]
Technological advance may tend to augment international trade by reducing transport costs or by increasing the advantages of concentrating
large-scale output in one area. However, in the modern world technology
is international and "head starts" are difficult to get and follow up. Except where propinquity to raw materials is desirable, economy of size
may not prevent the more or less simultaneous establishment of similar
industries in many countries, each protected against the others by tariffs
or cartel agreements.

International trade has since 1913 failed to keep pace with total production of exportable goods, as Table 1 clearly shows.[43] Compared with

---

[40] The margins of comparative advantage have by no means been obliterated. Nevertheless, a revival of international trade is not so essential as it has been in the past
to many countries. India, for example, has learned enough of modern techniques and
has accumulated enough capital so that its continued progress is truly far less dependent
than it was, say, fifty years ago, upon foreign goods and capital.

[41] Robertson, "The Future of International Trade," *Econ. Jour.*, XLVIII (1938), 9,
and *passim*.

[42] On the other hand, the automobile has also increased the importance of service and
distributive trades—repair shops, filling stations, parking lots. See Whale, *International
Trade*, pp. 236–42.

[43] The trade indexes should be compared with output indexes for industrial and primary
production together. The figures are very rough, but the declining ratio is quite appar-

world income, which includes the expanding output of service trades, the lag has been even greater.[44] As we have argued, this lag would probably have occurred even in the absence of adverse commercial policies. However, the revival of the late twenties, when world trade expanded at least as rapidly as physical output, indicates that a more stable international order, with less restrictive trade policies, would undoubtedly have gone far to prevent such a decline.

TABLE I

QUANTUM INDEXES OF PRODUCTION AND TRADE [a]

	1913	1925	1929	1937
B.I.S. world indexes				
Industrial production	100	...	139.0	152.0
Trade	100	...	130.0	123.0
Ratio trade: production	100	...	94.0	81.0
League of Nations world indexes				
Trade	100	107.0	127.0	123.5
Primary goods output	100	117.0	130.0	143.0
Industrial output				
Hypothetical [b]	100	123.0	146.0	152.0
Including U.S.S.R.	...	...	100.0	120.0
Exports U.K. goods [c]	100	79.4	86.6	71.6

[a] Sources: B.I.S., *Ninth Annual Report*, p. 37; League of Nations, *Memoranda on Production and Trade* and *World Production and Prices*. All indexes are very rough and cannot be used with any precision.

[b] This is offered as compensation for the B.I.S. index, which seems low for the year 1929, in light of League estimates. The 1913–25–29 figures are the League's indexes of raw material production. They are used as a minimum estimate for industrial production, in view of the League statements that the rise of the latter undoubtedly exceeded the rise of the former in these years. The 1929–37 interval is from a League estimate, which excludes the U.S.S.R.

[c] See Table 18, below.

---

ent. The falling ratios from 1913 to 1929 can probably not be attributed entirely to tariff policy. The official Committee on Industry and Trade (hereinafter, Balfour Comm.) reported in 1925 that the ad valorem incidence of tariffs on British goods had not increased appreciably, as compared with 1913, although other informal obstructions had multiplied. *Survey of Overseas Markets*, pp. 14–20. The League study of tariff levels substantiates this conclusion. International Economic Conference, *Tariff Level Indices* (publications II, 1927, No. 34). However, the creation of new countries meant thousands of miles of new customs frontiers. Further, the ad valorem incidence of unchanged specific tariffs was automatically increased by gradually falling prices after 1925. See Per Jacobsson, "Some Foreign Trade Problems of Today," *Index*, V (1930), 187–88.
[44] In addition, the lack of adequate data for the greatly expanded building industry causes it to be almost entirely neglected by the League index.

And, as Table 1 shows, the decline in British exports was great and continuous. Here was Britain's major single problem of the period 1919–39. The world was learning to dispense more and more with her manufactures. And world economic progress, particularly the growth of total world trade, was not sufficient to keep her losses from turning, for the first time in the memory of Englishmen, into a long painful secular decline.

V. THE DETERIORATING POSITION OF BRITISH INDUSTRY

THE SERIOUS QUESTIONS which arose in the period 1919–39 concerning the future of Britain in a changed world economy arose because of the seriously diminished competitive power of her industry. Of course, it had been perfectly evident long before that British pre-eminence could not persist. By 1875 she was seriously challenged; by 1913 she was probably no longer the world's leading or even second industrial nation, and others were not far behind her. But it was not until after the war that the impact of these long-run factors was fully felt and the need for drastic readjustment made perfectly clear. Even from 1873 to 1896, during the so-called "Great Depression," absolute progress was extremely rapid in real terms. In the period 1919–39, on the contrary, there were unprecedented harsh secular declines, radical breaks with the great continuous upward trends of the preceding century.

THE STAPLE INDUSTRIES

Britain's economy rested on a relatively narrow industrial base. A few basic industries, the sources and the products of the "Industrial Revolution," were the foundation of her growth and supremacy. There was the basic source of power—coal—which ran machinery, ships, and trains. There was a basic metal—iron (and steel)—produced with that coal and itself the main component of the machines, ships, and trains which revolutioned production and transport. And, finally, there were the cheap mass-produced finished products, the textiles thus manufactured and transported, which made Britain the world's leading exporter.[1] These basic interconnected trades were almost exclusively the foundation of British industry: coal, iron and steel, textiles, and "engineering," the latter embracing machinery, ships, railway materials, all goods made mainly of iron and steel and using mainly coal for power.

In 1907, the first year in which a comprehensive production census was taken, the net output of the three industrial groups, coal mining, iron and steel (including engineering and shipbuilding), and textiles,

---

[1] Textiles alone made up 60 percent of Britain's exports in 1850 and 46 percent in 1880–84. Clapham, *An Economic History of Modern Britain*, II, 228–29. They were still 38 percent of the total in 1907.

was roughly 46 percent of the total "value added by manufacture" of the United Kingdom industry.[2] Since, in addition, a large part of the clothing industry represents the last stage of textile manufacture, we may conclude that these staple industries produced one half, at least, of the total British net output. Similarly, they accounted in 1921 for perhaps 51 percent of the people in Great Britain gainfully employed in industry (including mining and utilities) according to the decennial census of that year—or approximately to 20–25 percent of the total gainfully employed population.[3]

Even these bare figures do not convey the full importance of the staple industries. It was the expansion of just these which had been almost entirely responsible for the "industrial revolution" of the previous century. The absolute rise of building, food, clothing, printing, the professions, services, and the like was mainly the result of the growth of population and living standards which that "revolution" made possible. This dynamic surge was largely dependent upon the opening up of foreign markets. It was only on the basis of a broad foreign market, reached by British ships, that British industry could produce on a large scale at low costs. It was the growing export trades which were mainly responsible for the large profits and rising national income, out of which the heavy capital accumulation and investment were made and which rendered possible the purchase of the increasing quantities and varieties of foreign foods that rising British living standards demanded. And these same staple trades were the great export trades.

Exports of coal, iron and steel, textiles, engineering products (machinery, other than electrical, new ships, and railway equipment), cutlery, tools, and hardware amounted in 1907 to no less than 70.3 percent

[2] Figure computed from Gr. Brit., Board of Trade, First Census of Production, *Final Report*. The "United Kingdom" includes Great Britain (England, Scotland, and Wales) and all of Ireland before 1924, but excludes the Free State thereafter. Although often in general discussion we use the names "England," "Britain," and the "United Kingdom" more or less interchangeably, in all specific references to statistical data the various titles must be taken in their precise meaning.

[3] Computed from data in Gr. Brit., Ministry of Labour, *Abstracts of Labour Statistics*. The 51 percent includes those classified under coal mining, textiles, and those parts of the large metal-engineering-vehicles category which seem to belong, i.e., eliminating, among other groups, electrical industries and automobiles, which belong rather to the new industrial era. If we take the "basic" industries as a whole, i.e., including the entire engineering-metal-vehicles group, the proportion becomes 56.2 percent. In a sense, these later developments are modern substitutes for steam machinery and locomotives, and should be included to give an accurate picture of the relative importance of the older industries before the war, when comparable data are not available.

and in 1913 to 65.5 percent of the total exports of domestic produce from the United Kingdom. They were already losing ground, relatively, to such rising products as automobiles and electrical equipment. Nevertheless, they remained the firm foundation for the British export trade, as they had been throughout the preceding century.[4] So in 1907, while making up roughly 50 percent of the total net domestic industrial production and giving employment to perhaps 20–25 percent of the total gainfully occupied population, the staple trades constituted 70 percent of Britain's exports.

In 1907 about 30 percent of the output of British industry and a somewhat higher portion of the output of exportable goods alone was exported.[5] For reasons in part already suggested, even this 30 percent does not give a true picture of the real importance of exports. Being in a sense marginal, they meant the difference between prosperity and extreme depression. Most important, much of the internally consumed industrial output was the manifestation of a level of incomes and of population in large part made possible by an economic growth based primarily on exports, and sustained by the imported foods which the exports made possible.

The British staple industries depended upon exports to a far greater extent than the others, as Table 2 clearly shows. The most obvious case is that of cotton, where exports supplied virtually the entire market.[6] The dependence upon foreign markets of the woolen and engineering trades is also far above the national average. The importance of exports to the iron and steel trades is understated even by the 39 percent for the industry as a whole, in 1907, in view of the heavy sales abroad of the many domestically produced goods for which iron and steel are raw materials.[7] The same is true of coal; the foreign demand for many

[4] Their relative importance in the export trade was even greater in earlier years. A roughly comparable group of exports made up 74–77 percent of the British total in the cyclical peak years 1860, 1866, and 1872, 71 percent in 1882, and 69 percent in 1900 and 1907. For an excellent discussion of the central position of the staple industries in the British economy see Allen, *British Industries*, chap. ii.

[5] The British total includes the output of building trades, agriculture, mines, and fisheries. Adapted from Gr. Brit., Bd. of Trade, *Final Report*, First Census of Production, pp. 25–26.

[6] The low percentage of yarn exported indicates merely that most of the yarn is used by British weavers and exported in higher stages of manufacture.

[7] This total dependence in 1929 was estimated at 70 percent, a figure which, however, seems unbelievably high. Gr. Brit., National Committee for the Iron and Steel Industry, *Final Report* to the Import Duties Advisory Committee, Cmd. 4181, Session 1931–32, p. 8.

products, notably iron and steel and their manufactures, is equally a demand for "domestically consumed" British coal. Similarly, the relatively low proportion of steamships exported is no measure at all of the dependence of shipbuilding on Britain's export trade, that trade being a major support of the great "domestic" consumer, the British shipping industry.

TABLE 2

GROSS OUTPUT AND EXPORTS IN SELECTED UNITED KINGDOM INDUSTRIES 1907 AND 1930 [a]

(£ooo, *unless otherwise indicated*)

	GROSS OUTPUT		EXPORTS		EXPORTS AS PERCENTAGE OF OUTPUT	
Industrial Group	*1907*	*1930*	*1907*	*1930*	*1907*	*1930*
Total U.K. output [b] £000,000	1,393	2,457	420	535	30.2	21.8
Staple Trades						
Cotton						
Yarns 000,000 lbs.	1,800	1,047	241	137	13.4	13.1
Piece goods [c]	94,572	81,600	81,049	61,305	85.7	75.1
000,000 yards	7,088	3,399	6,298	2,407	88.9	70.8
Industry as a whole [b]	125,717	118,000	105,043	86,205	83.6	73.1
Wool						
Industry as a whole [b]	60,253	85,000	34,090	39,707	56.6	46.7
Wool and worsted tissues [c]	36,741	...	17,705	...	48.2	...
000,000 sq. yds.	397	316	184	114	46.3	35.9
Iron, steel, engineering and shipbuilding [b]	248,000	...	96,668	...	39.0	...
Iron, steel, and m'f'rs [d]	147,289	225,343	46,563	51,261	31.6	22.7
Steam engines	12,708	...	7,900	...	62.2	...
Machinery	38,583	...	22,848	...	59.2	...
Miscellaneous machinery	...	42,175	...	19,603	...	46.5
Textile machinery	13,099	12,398	8,039	8,628	61.4	69.6
P'v't yard shipb'ld'g, steamships:						
Hulls and fittings	19,388	...	6,586	...	34.0	...
Machinery	8,290	...	2,551	...	30.8	...
Coal	119,554	165,733	40,170	45,661	33.6	27.6
000 tons	266,560	243,882	63,601	54,874	23.9	22.5
Bunker coal 000 tons	...	...	18,619	15,617	...	...
Total 000 tons	266,560	243,882	82,220	70,491	30.8	28.9

[a] Sources: *Final Reports*, of the first and third censuses of production, 1907 and 1930; *Annual Statements of Trade of the United Kingdom*. Great care has been taken to make the export and output figures comparable, but more than approximate comparability is

TABLE 2—*Continued*

GROSS OUTPUT AND EXPORTS IN SELECTED UNITED KINGDOM INDUSTRIES

1907 AND 1930 [a]

(*£ooo, unless otherwise indicated*)

	GROSS OUTPUT		EXPORTS		EXPORTS AS PERCENTAGE OF OUTPUT	
Industrial Group	*1907*	*1930*	*1907*	*1930*	*1907*	*1930*
Other Trades						
Electrical						
Machinery	4,312	21,164	996	6,434	23.1	30.4
Goods and apparatus	2,865	...	668	...	23.3	...
Lamps, wireless valves	...	4,164	...	923	...	22.2
Other wireless apparatus	...	6,870	...	851	...	12.4
Total machinery, goods,						
wire and cable, etc.	12,439	68,298	3,466	15,957	27.9	23.4
Road vehicles						
Complete motor cars no.	9,800	200,574	2,300	22,712	23.5	11.3
Motorcycles, tricars no.	3,800	125,030	800	42,631	21.1	34.1
Cycles (not mechanically						
propelled) no.	623,800	882,105	102,400	247,147	16.4	28.0
Total motor cars, all cycles						
and parts (exc. tires) [b]	11,900	102,500	2,666	14,319	22.4	14.0
Silk and rayon yarns and						
m'f'rs, exc. apparel [d]	...	29,573	...	1,556	...	5.3
Hosiery 000 doz. prs.[e]						
Stockings and hose	...	24,029	...	3,309	...	13.8
Underwear	...	8,509	...	416	...	4.9
Wooden furniture and cabi-						
netware [f]	...	22,723	...	1,129	...	5.0

unattainable. There are two major sources of error: exports are f.o.b. and output figures value at the factory, thereby overstating the importance of the former; secondly, except where very rough estimates free of duplication are made by the census, the relative importance of exports is seriously understated to the extent that the gross output figures involve double counting, the value of goods sold by one firm to another within the industry for further fabrication (e.g., cotton yarns sold to weavers) appearing in the gross sales values of both.

[b] Output figures are free of duplication.

[c] Output of finishing trades is apportioned between the various textile industries and included therein. Cotton piece goods output for 1907 linear, for 1930 square, yards.

[d] Considerable duplication in output figures.

[e] 1924 data show a much higher proportion of exports: of stockings and hose 20.5 percent, of underwear 10.7 percent.

[f] Comparison is very rough, the share of exports being overstated, as a large part of output escaped record due to exclusion of small firms. While exports were £1,129,000, retained imports were £874,000.

The contrast between all the older staples and the expanding British industries of the twentieth century is striking. Producers of electrical goods (other than machinery), automobiles, silk and rayon, hosiery, and furniture concentrate primarily on domestic demand, and in many cases, before the tariff, they were able to meet only a relatively small share of that demand.[8] It goes without saying that this is true of the other leading expanding lines of employment—building and building materials, gas, water and electricity supply, and various service and distributive trades,[9] where in the nature of the case exports are impractical.

Table 2 indicates the sharply declining importance of exports in British industry during the years 1919–39.[10] This decline had two aspects: a shift toward a greater relative importance of those industries in which exports were at all times less important and a decreasing importance of exports in each individual industry. The table shows some exceptions to the latter trend: electrical machinery, textile machinery, motorcycles, and bicycles. Nevertheless, for each larger category of which these are a part—machinery, electrical products, road vehicles—the proportion of exports fell. Even in those instances where it rose, by far the greater absolute expansion was for the home market, except for textile machinery, increased exports of which reflect less the strength of that industry than the relative stagnation of Britain's own textile manufactures.

The nineteenth century, then, produced in England an economy resting upon a few staple industries, themselves peculiarly dependent upon foreign markets. England's superiority in these industries had been disappearing long before 1914, as others learned to produce the old products better and more cheaply and began to sell them abroad more aggressively. After the first World War new products and new methods, the result of changing technology and shifting consumer tastes, further increased the pressure of competition upon the older trades.

[8] Although exports of automobiles were in 1907 almost one-fourth of production, the preponderant importance of the home market is indicated by the fact that in that year imports were almost twice as large as exports. Similarly, a rather high percentage of finished silk manufactures were exported in 1930: over one-third of the silk piece goods (wholly or partly of silk) produced. However, retained imports were twelve times the size of exports, British products thus supplying only about one-seventh of the home market. 1930 Census, I, 127.

[9] This is not to ignore the very important exports of shipping, banking, insurance, and other similar services. However, in all such cases, British greatness was firmly rooted and grew during the nineteenth century. Shipping and banking were in a sense also staple trades of the pre-war British economy.

[10] It must be noted, however, that 1930 was a year of incipient depression, when exports contracted more than output.

To these secular problems the war added its own. War industries expanded far beyond peacetime needs and were left, when peace came, with excessive plants built at high prices, heavy fixed charges, and high unit costs because of their having to run at less than full capacity. From 1911 to 1921, the number of persons (in Great Britain, ten years of age and over) engaged in coal mining and the manufacture of metals, implements, machines, and conveyances increased 30.6 percent, continuing and aggravating a disproportionate growth in the first decade of the century,[11] while the total gainfully employed population increased only 5.5 percent. The price inflation of the post-war boom increased many of these maladjustments. The cotton industry, spurred by a heavy temporary foreign demand, and shipping and shipbuilding, starved of capital during the war, went heavily into debt at high interest rates, in expectation of continued soaring prices and profit margins.[12] There were also great wage disparities between various industries and disparities also between wages and the rapidly fluctuating price level, a situation which led to bitter strikes, notably in coal and railways. For six full years, 1914 to 1920, years which themselves succeeded a boom decade, industry was shielded from the necessity for normal adjustments. Inefficient firms remained in business, money costs soared, and normal stimuli to reduce costs were largely inoperative.[13]

Basically, however, the need for adjustment was greater than ever. For meanwhile foreign markets had been closing. Exporting industries had been cut off from their markets, and competitors in the United States and Japan, and in protected domestic industries, were springing up to fill the gap.[14] The demand for coal was cut by war-induced conservation measures and by the development of substitutes, for iron and steel and machinery by a general post-war scarcity of capital and hence diminished investment demand, for ships by the slow recovery of world trade. In 1928, when the volume of sea-borne trade was about at 1913 levels, the world's merchant fleet was about 50 percent above its 1913 tonnage.[15]

---

[11] From 1901 to 1911, according to the census of population, the total gainfully employed population increased by 12.5 percent, those engaged in coal mining, and the manufacture of metals, machines, and conveyances by 26.7 percent.

[12] New domestic issues in 1920 were £325 million, according to the Midland Bank; this compares with the highest figures thereafter of £219 million in 1928 and £176 in 1927. See especially Henry W. Macrosty, "Inflation and Deflation in the United States and the United Kingdom, 1919–23," J.R.S.S., XC (1927), 71–72; Grant, *A Study of the Capital Market in Post-War Britain*, pp. 136–41.

[13] Clay, *The Post-War Unemployment Problem*, pp. 19–23, 88–92.

[14] See Balfour Comm., *Survey of Overseas Markets*, pp. 9–21.

[15] Liberal Industrial Inquiry, *Britain's Industrial Future*, p. 11.

When the slump came, it was the heavy staple exporting industries which were hardest hit. For a time it was believed that the difficulties were simply a temporary result of the disruption and uncertainty of the world economy after the war, as in large measure they were. Peace and the return to normalcy would, it was felt, bring a return to prosperity. However, though Britain did benefit from the ensuing revival of world trade, these industries by no means recovered fully. General improvement from 1923 on and mild prosperity in the late twenties left the staple industries and special areas still severely depressed, because of the failure of their exports.[16]

UNDERLYING EXPLANATIONS

Although the bulk of discussion about the problems of British industry in the inter-war period stressed British mistakes, faults, and shortcomings, there can be no doubt that the basic causes were secular, impersonal, and inevitable.

From perhaps 1875–1900 a new technology has been emerging to take the place of the "paleotechnology" of coal, steam, and iron and steel. It is a technology of physics and chemistry, of the scientific industrial research laboratory, of electricity and petroleum, the dynamo and internal combustion engine, nonferrous metals, special-purpose alloys, and synthetics. In its emphasis on machine-standardized-mass production, the new technology is merely an intensification of previous development. But change in techniques, sources of power, and materials has been so great and so rapid that it amounts almost to a change in kind.[17]

Britain had excelled in the old. She had had special advantages— ideally situated coal (and, for a time, iron), cheap transportation, giving her easy access to foreign raw materials and markets, a skilled labor supply, and an ample head start.[18] It was inconceivable that she should

[16] British Association, *Britain in Depression*, pp. 6–11.

[17] See Lewis Mumford, *Technics and Civilization*, New York, Harcourt Brace, 1934, chap. v; Thorstein Veblen, *Absentee Ownership*, New York, Huebsch, 1923, pp. 258–59, 264–66, 270–72.

[18] The importance of wars and other noneconomic factors in giving her this head start has often been ignored. Before 1789 or 1763 it would have been difficult to predict that England would surpass France. By 1815 the result was clear. Although England had other advantages, it is interesting to speculate what would have happened had Louis XIV built a navy and preferred overseas to continental expansion, had England not won a colonial empire from France, or had there been no devastating Napoleonic wars on the continent.

have similar advantages, most of them necessarily transitory, in the new.[19] In fact, it would seem almost inevitable that the new technology develop elsewhere, in countries with different natural advantages and aptitudes and less hampered by a business leadership trained and steeped in the traditionally successful methods as well as by a heavy capital investment in the old.

Even without radical changes in world techniques it was inevitable that England should lose her relative advantages. Gradually, and long before 1914, the great staple trades lost their quasi-monopoly. Cotton, one of the first industries to be transformed in the eighteenth century, was one of the easiest for others to copy. Britain's portion of the world's total spindleage declined from 54 percent in 1881–84 to 39 percent in 1913, although in absolute terms her growth was rapid.[20] Her pig iron and steel output were exceeded by America and Germany long before 1913, and her share of the world's total production of both declined rapidly.[21] Superior foreign resources were one factor; real costs of coal in Britain were already rising, and she was increasingly dependent upon foreign iron ores. Technical changes also helped undermine her position: for example, the decline of wrought iron, in which British leadership depended largely on the high degree of skill involved in its production, and the Thomas process, permitting the use of the great continental phosphoric ores. Nevertheless, Britain imported more and more ore and pig iron, specialized increasingly in the higher stages of manufacture, and her industry grew steadily.[22]

In addition, consumer demand has changed radically, especially since the World War, to the direct and indirect detriment of Britain. For one thing, the particularly heavy depression of primary producing countries hurt English producers only less than it hurt the suffering countries themselves. Far more than most other manufacturing countries, she depended especially on these areas for markets.[23] Not only did these markets buy

[19] Jevons predicted in 1865 that Britain's cheap coal and technical leadership would prove but transitory advantages, and he foresaw poverty and unemployment as the ultimate consequences. *The Coal Question*, especially Preface to second edition.

[20] Allen, *British Industries*, pp. 215–16; Edgar Crammond, "The Economic Relations of the British and German Empires," J.R.S.S., LXXVII (1914), 783–85, 817.

[21] Allen, *op. cit.*, pp. 91–92; statistics in M. S. Birkett, "The Iron and Steel Industry since the War," J.R.S.S., XCIII (1930), 372–73.

[22] Allen, *op. cit.*, pp. 88, 92–96.

[23] Taking the first ten of British markets in 1928 which can be fairly accurately described as primary producers and manufacturing countries, respectively (on the one side, India,

less; they also bought goods of poorer quality, supplied to them at very low prices by competitors of England, employing relatively unskilled labor. In addition, the depression and mechanization of agriculture forced labor off the land, and these countries began, aided by protective tariffs, to produce a larger proportion of the manufactures which they previously had imported.[24]

A large portion of the world's income previously expended for primary commodities was released by declining need for them and by their falling prices. But the demand so released, as well as demand created by generally rising incomes, failed to turn appreciably to British manufactures. Instead of demanding fine, durable British cottons and woolens, china, or cutlery, consumers in protected markets, subjected to high-pressure salesmanship, turned to new mass-produced cheap luxuries—silks and rayons, radios, automobiles, household gadgets, movies, phonographs—and to home market goods and services—electric light, newspapers and books, sports, housing, and leisure.[25] Almost none of these new demands offered Britain compensation for her losses in the old lines. In producing the newer goods, where fresh mechanical and marketing techniques were involved, Britain failed to take anything like the pre-eminent position she once enjoyed. It was scarcely conceivable that she should. Consider how much better adapted to the new production was United States industry, with its mechanically ingenious leadership, its younger and bolder "captains of industry," its expansive and less conservative home market. British tastes, like British industrial methods, continued to stress workmanship and quality, although undoubtedly greater adaptability in industry and in marketing would have produced corresponding changes in taste.

Britain was undoubtedly hampered by the lack of a market as broad and as uniform as that of America, a market for which she might produce

---

Australia, Eire, Canada, South Africa, Argentina, New Zealand, Brazil, Straits Settlements, Egypt, on the other, the United States, Germany, France, the Netherlands, Belgium, Japan, Sweden, Switzerland, Poland and Czechoslovakia), we find that the former took 45.6 percent, the latter 26.4 percent of Britain's total exports of home products.

[24] Allen, *British Industries*, pp. 278–80; Robertson, *Economic Essays and Addresses*, pp. 163–69; Pigou and Clark, *The Economic Position of Great Britain*, pp. 26–29. It will be recalled that the British enclosures and the related agricultural advances of the century before 1750 provided a body of landless labor which was one condition of the rise of mass industry.

[25] Siegfried, *England's Crisis*, pp. 114–19. Cf., on a more optimistic note, Plummer, *New British Industries in the Twentieth Century*; also Loveday, *Britain and World Trade*, pp. 86–92; Ohlin, *The World Economic Depression*, pp. 19–25.

standardized products on a large scale. Her markets were diverse, un-regimented, and variegated; and none of them was secure, for competi-tion and tariffs made them all precarious. The resultant production of a great range of products on a small scale in small individual productive units is well illustrated by the engineering industry. British machine makers rely on a high degree of skill and an equipment of general-purpose tools to manufacture a much greater variety of products than are put out by individual American plants organized for mass production. This description may, very broadly, be taken as true of British industry generally, in contrast with the American. British producers had to de-pend on exports for a regular large portion of their sales, unlike many American and German producers, for whom exports were often a "sur-plus" which might be sold merely to cover direct costs. Besides, the un-protected home market would not bear all the overhead; any discrim-inatory price policy would at once bring increased imports.

These various factors were essentially secular and inevitable. Britain's competitive power was deteriorating because of the spread abroad of the old technology and of new products and methods in which she was, if anything, positively handicapped by nature, by the inadequacies of her market, and by indoctrination in the old methods, and finally because of the not unrelated changed nature of world demand. The spread of power machinery for the most intricate operations made her skilled labor supply much less of an advantage and its customary high wages a positive disad-vantage. As a result, British goods were in many cases simply too ex-pensive. Their high prices were often no longer even justified by better quality, as modern standardized mass production in many lines combined quality with cheapness.[26]

If British industry were to regain its position after the World War, a drastic renovation of its methods and plant was necessary. Its very back-wardness in turn made such renovation extremely difficult. Industry came out of the war and post-war boom in poor financial condition, and demand for its products was weak. Excess capacity, overcapitalization, heavy fixed charges made it difficult for iron and steel, cotton, coal, and shipbuilding even to set aside sufficient reserves for depreciation, let alone to finance a comprehensive program of scrapping and rebuilding. The credit of these industries was low. An excess of intensely competitive

[26] Over and over one finds the complaint, especially in the Far Eastern markets, where price was a prime determinant, that British producers were being undersold. For example, *Board of Trade Journal* (hereinafter B. of T.J.), CXXVI (1931), 627–28.

small units, of varying grades of efficiency, increased their difficulties. Attempts at amalgamation often merely perpetuated their overcapitalization, because of the high prices exacted by those selling out. Bankruptcy, slow in any case, was further retarded by the unwillingness of banks to force reorganization upon their failing debtors. Here was a vicious circle of competitive weakness, because of their failure to reorganize, bringing financial weakness, and financial weakness in turn making it impossible to attract the capital necessary to effect reorganization.

On the other hand, the major foreign competitors of Great Britain had special advantages. The collapse of the mark wiped out German business debt, and her industrialists promptly took advantage of their clean slate, their great profits of the inflation (worthless except when immediately reinvested in goods), and the influx of foreign capital, to install the most modern equipment. In France and Belgium to similar benefits of currency depreciation were added heavy government expenditures for reconstruction of war-torn areas. England returned instead to pre-war parity, and the burden of business debt incurred in the days of soaring prices was thereby magnified many times.[27]

The burden of a vastly increased government debt was also intensified in the same way; this, plus the expanded costs of normal government operation, largely because of the "social services," also diminished the capital available to British industry. The cost was born primarily by extremely heavy increases in income and inheritance taxes, which were probably partly responsible for the decline of private and business savings in Britain after the war.[28] Henry Clay attributes the inability of the old traditionally self-financing industries to finance their own rehabilitation in large measure to heavily increased taxes on their profits.[29]

[27] Clay, *The Post-War Unemployment Problem*, pp. 98–102.
[28] See below, pp. 137–38. See, however, Grant, *The Capital Market in Post-War Britain*, p. 181. There were other greatly increased taxes which injured British industry, notably the local rates, which were until 1929 a major means of financing the social services, and which were particularly pernicious in their incidence. See Liberal Industrial Inquiry, *Britain's Industrial Future*, pp. 433–36; Dennison, *The Location of Industry and the Depressed Areas*, pp. 82–86; P.E.P., *Report on the Location of Industry*, p. 71. The payroll tax levied to finance the unemployment insurance scheme was in effect a tax on employment: the levy thus committed the error of contributing to the problem which the scheme sought to alleviate.
[29] *The Post-War Unemployment Problem*, pp. 138–45; also Thomas, *British Banks and the Finance of Industry*, pp. 218–28. E. M. Burns contends in a review of Professor Clay's book that this self-financing was the cause of the excess capacity which plagued these industries after the war, and deserved to be discouraged. *Amer. Econ. Rev.*, XX (1930), 316. There seems little merit in this argument. Wartime and post-war overexpansion would

Largely because of this scarcity of capital from the usual sources, there was mounting complaint in the 1920's of the inadequate facilities offered by the British banking system and new issue markets to home industry. Exporters complained of a lack of credit facilities for the intermediate financing of exports of capital goods, while American and German firms, they asserted, were getting foreign contracts by virtue of such assistance from their banks.[30] Since British industry had previously been accustomed to finance capital extensions in large measure by reinvestment of profits, with outside aid, if any, coming from local banks and investors, and since, on the other hand, the London banks and issue houses had concentrated largely on short-term credits to finance domestic and foreign trade and on long-term foreign issues, the contact between British industries and the London money markets was not very intimate. In consequence, when, in the post-war period, domestic industry lacked sufficient internal capital, complaints about the foreign investment bias of London became persistent. Again the question arose as to whether, in her new and more vulnerable international position, Britain could afford to lend abroad freely, while industries at home had difficulty in obtaining accommodation.[31]

It is not easy to demonstrate that London showed uneconomic bias in favor of foreign issues. The prospective returns from foreign investments, and at least until 1929 the actual returns, really were higher than on domestic investment.[32] With the prosperity of the late twenties there was a veritable new home issue boom, particularly in newer British industries, which needed fresh capital and promised high returns.[33] Complaints against the British credit system were a result of the altered competitive position of the staple industries, and of their consequent need for outside capital. A re-examination of traditional British attitudes toward

have occurred regardless of the type of financing. Furthermore, excess capacity was the result of a subsequent decline in demand, not an initial cause of the difficulties of these industries. In any case, the fact remains that they did suffer a scarcity of capital during the 1920's.

[30] MacM. Comm., *Report*, pp. 170–71, *Evidence*, I, 118; Balfour Comm., *Final Report*, pp. 48–49; Thomas, *British Banks and the Finance of Industry*, chaps. iv–vi, especially, pp. 246–50 ff.

[31] See Allen W. Rather, *Is Britain Decadent?* London, Sampson Low, 1931, p. 52; MacM. Comm., *Report*, pp. 161–67; Clay, *The Post-War Unemployment Problem*, pp. 188–89.

[32] Siegfried, *England's Crisis*, pp. 160–63; for pre-war investments see Cairncross, "Did Foreign Investment Pay?," *Rev. Econ. Studies*, III (1935), 73–75; R. A. Lehfeldt, "The Rate of Interest on British and Foreign Investments," *J.R.S.S.*, LXXVI (1913), 204–5.

[33] Grant, *The Capital Market in Post-War Britain*, pp. 143–46.

the function of banking and toward foreign lending was probably necessary. Such a re-examination, however, would probably have involved the substitution of a new system with "uneconomic" bias, according to the old standards: that is, a refusal to leave foreign lending entirely to considerations of maximum individual prospective gain. If this was required, however, it was because of the new situation, not because of inherent defects in the old system. Thus, after 1931, with the cheap-money policy and abatement of pressure of heavy foreign lending upon limited capital resources, with British business becoming increasingly solvent and decreasingly dependent upon bank credit, these complaints became less frequent.[34]

British Inadaptability

Under the circumstances, it is not surprising that one heard much during the inter-war years about the deterioration of the British spirit, the laziness and unreasonable demands of labor, the indolence and rigidity of business leaders. There is much truth in these accusations. Seen in proper historical perspective, however, these facts seem clearly to result from the changed conditions rather than a change in British character. British goods at one time almost sold themselves. Real wages had risen for a century, and British labor had not become any less skilled. Naturally labor fought any reduction of its standards of living. Naturally British industrialists were reluctant to scrap their plants. And naturally British labor and business, trained in the old technology, could not lead in the new. Even a true deterioration of business leadership, third- and fourth-generation indolence, is in a sense responsive to the laws of economic change and an inevitable concomitant of success.

It is difficult, especially for an outsider, to generalize about the relative efficiency of "British business." Inefficiency and efficiency exist side by side in all countries and industries, and England is no exception. Nevertheless, it would certainly seem, partly because this is precisely what one would expect, that British business men were, as a class and particularly in the older industries, less adaptable, less modern, less efficient than many of their foreign competitors. The hard days of the twenties gradually forced some readjustment in these respects, and the thirties even more. But in general the informed consensus of opinion seems to be that British business leadership was backward and uninspired.[35]

[34] *Ibid.*, pp. 186–88.
[35] Liberal Industrial Inquiry, *Britain's Industrial Future*, p. 42; Heaton, *The British Way*

English business men were slow to scrap obsolete plants and to institute the highly mechanized standardized operations which foreign competitors were employing. They did not sufficiently appreciate the possibilities of scientific industrial research. "Practical" men, accustomed to the rule of thumb and traditional methods, held sway. The most modern research laboratories were those of industrial giants in newer lines: Imperial Chemicals, Metropolitan-Vickers, General Electric. Although the state-aided industrial research associations made considerable progress, a good deal of the work consisted merely of routine testing; and, especially in the staple trades, there prevailed a considerable apathy toward practical utilization of the products of the research.[36]

In the face of increasingly aggressive foreign sales policies, the British displayed an attitude amounting almost to apathy in many cases. This comparative lack of aggressiveness in foreign markets seems long to have been a British characteristic,[37] but it now became especially serious. British merchants seemed loath to leave the relative comforts of foreign coastal cities to develop inland trade; their sales staffs seemed to be less active, less solicitous of local tastes and desires and credit needs.[38] The continued use of traditional merchant houses for the marketing of a great line of exports, while foreign manufacturers (and some of Britain's newer trades) were selling abroad directly with their own organizations, was another instance of this gentlemanly lethargy.[39] Neglect of foreign markets, except within the empire, where a closer cultural link and tariff

---

to Recovery, p. 32. These generalizations are based primarily upon the experience of the older staple trades. The general picture in the new lines in all these respects, from technological progress to quickness to "co-operate" and "stabilize," seems rather strikingly different. This again emphasizes the conviction that the inadequacies of management were primarily a result of more basic long run factors, rather than themselves an independent cause.

[36] Balfour Comm., *Final Report*, pp. 212–18 ff.; Gr. Brit., Economic Advisory Council, Committee on New Industrial Development, *Report*, 1932, especially, pp. 10–16.

[37] See Ross J. S. Hoffman, *Great Britain and the German Trade Rivalry, 1875–1914*, Philadelphia, U. of Penn., 1933, p. 80, chap. i and *passim*; Alfred Marshall, "Memorandum on the Fiscal Policy of International Trade," *Official Papers*, London, Macmillan, 1926, pp. 405–6, and *Industry and Trade*, Bk. I, chap. v, *passim*.

[38] Siegfried, *England's Crisis*, p. 27. It seems almost ludicrous, for example, that a commission inquiring into the failure of Sheffield goods to sell well in South America should have to recommend, among other things, that "Catalogues should always be in the language of the country," or that "Terms of payment should, where necessary, be extended to meet foreign competition." B. of T.J., CXXVI (1931), 259–60.

[39] The merchant houses, with their established connections and wide experience, still have a useful function, particularly for the smaller producers who cannot afford to set up their own organizations. P.E.P., *Report on International Trade*, pp. 131–39.

preference made export easier, was further encouraged by cartel agreements and by the relatively greater recovery of the home market demand after 1931.[40]

To many of the problems of British industry the only answer was co-operative industry-wide reorganization, to eliminate the dead wood and secure the advantages of large-scale organization. Surplus capacity in a welter of small competing firms could be overcome only by full-time operation of the more efficient units and closing down of the technically backward. The financially weak had to be eliminated or absorbed by firms with strong credit, who could borrow to tear down and to rebuild along modern lines. The answer to the marketing problem for a great number of small concerns was co-operative selling. Amalgamation and plant specialization were the only solution for small-scale unstandardized output by firms each making a variety of products. British business men, however, typically displayed a suspicious individualism. Jealousy, vested interests, and lack of concern all stood in the way of reform.

In most industries, however, even in the most intensely individualistic ones, there has been a change in this regard, under the pressure of adversity and government action. British business, indeed, seems to have learned only too well to "co-operate." The government has actually had to impose reorganization by law only in a few cases, notably in coal and cotton textiles. In other cases it gave sufficient inducements to force reorganization upon recalcitrant groups—notably a tariff to iron and steel and a subsidy to tramp shipping, both conditional upon thoroughgoing reorganization. In all cases, its mere protection of the domestic market made business combination much more feasible, for obvious reasons.[41]

The result has been no less than a transformation of the British economy. Few markets remain which are free from some form of virtually unsupervised business co-operation and self-regimentation. There has been an almost unanimous abandonment of price competition, and scarcely less widespread are schemes, in endless variety, for output control, co-operative marketing, and restriction against the entrance of outsiders. Distributive channels are closely guarded by boycott, rebates, price maintenance, tying contracts. The schemes vary in effectiveness as widely as

---

[40] See *ibid.*, pp. 129–42; Liberal Industrial Inquiry, *Britain's Industrial Future*, pp. 133–35; Balfour Comm., *Final Report*, pp. 157 ff.

[41] These and the following general comments upon the concentration movement in British business are based almost exclusively upon the two definitive studies, Ben W. Lewis, *Price and Production Control in British Industry*, and Lucas, *Industrial Reconstruction and the Control of Competition*.

they do in form, but the psychology of controlled competition is widespread and generally accepted.

The basic explanation for the spread of this movement, at least in the staple trades, lies in low profits, surplus capacity, and the consequent rigors of competition. The psychology was defensive. The justification was the undoubted need for technical reorganization. In the newer industries, however, where the movement first made headway, the psychology was more aggressive, resembling, rather, the apparent motivation of the American trust movement. Rayons, chemicals, automobiles, and electrical equipment were unimpeded by individualistic traditions or by small, vigorously competing units; the incentive of monopoly profits was undoubtedly strong. With the general tariff and the recovery that followed, the movement gained rather than lost impetus, and it can no longer be said that in general the attitude was defensive. Hence, there was in Britain growing alarm about the dangerous potentialities of the new system of control in a period of rising prices, and this alarm was little abated by the record of the reorganized industries. True, the "combines" or associations have apparently not pursued unreasonable or extortionate price policies. Nor has output control been particularly restrictive.

The dangers are somewhat different. Instead of solving the problem of industrial stultification and stagnation, the new type of industrial control and the tariff have tended to intensify it. In practice the major focus has been on the suppression of competition rather than on technical reform and rehabilitation. Far from weeding out weak firms, these static defensive measures all aim to preserve existing equities, to permit all firms, efficient and inefficient, to retain their share of the market or be bought off at the best price that can be exacted. Prices are set regularly at levels "intended to be fully remunerative, even to most of the less efficient . . . sufficiently profitable, in fact, fully to satisfy these members and 'keep them in line.' " [42] High-cost firms are preserved by giving them a right to a quota share in a protected market; or they are bought off, as in the "reconstruction levies" upon the shipbuilding, flour milling, and cotton textiles industries, whereby the cost of buying out weak plants is saddled upon the industry as a whole (and upon the consumer) for an indefinite period. This is not to say that there has not been considerable technical progress in British industry. But in most cases such progress can scarcely be attributed to the business combination or to the superstructure of price and output control.

[42] Ben W. Lewis, *Price and Production Control in British Industry*, p. 21.

These new developments are no solution for the export industries. To the extent to which their decline was inevitable (e.g., because of an increase of economic nationalism), moderate price control, programs for scrapping excess equipment, and the like mitigated the harshness of inevitable depression and were perhaps salutary in the short run. To the extent to which the problem was one of relative inefficiency and remediable inability to compete in world markets, as in part it was, price controls, tariffs, and similar methods of preserving the unfit were precisely the wrong answer. Each individual industry has been sheltered from the salutary long-run effects of competition as well as from the distressing short-run effects, and no substitute has been created to protect the welfare of the economy as a whole. Such a shortsighted muddling system of stop-gaps runs the risk of sacrificing the long-run welfare of the British people and of British industry itself.[43]

"If capital was stupid, labor was stubborn." [44] In the face of stern competition and the need for downward cost adjustment, it seems clear that British wages were too high and too inflexible on the downward side, during the 1920's. However, wages in the unsheltered export industries fell heavily after 1920; the really rigid wages were in the sheltered home-market industries. Rigid wages could hence have hampered exports only indirectly, by sustaining such "sheltered" costs as railroad rates, for example.[45] Perhaps more important obstacles in the export industries were the various conservative union rules and restrictions—limitations on the use of labor-saving devices, on machines permitting substitution of semi-skilled for skilled workers, on piece-work payment—and jurisdictional controversies, especially in shipbuilding and other branches of engineering. These were the products of the same defensive conservative psychology which in business led to restriction of competition. They were equally understandable and equally dangerous, in the long run. However, it should be noted, the ability of unions to enforce such restrictions was likewise particularly weak in the depressed staple trades.[46]

---

[43] See "The Real Threat to Our Exports," *Economist*, CXXXIV (1939), 234; Alfred Marshall, "Memorandum on the Fiscal Policy of International Trade," *Official Papers*, pp. 408–9; Findlay, *Britain under Protection*, chap. ix; Ben W. Lewis, *Price and Production Control in British Industry*, pp. 32–33.

[44] Heaton, *The British Way to Recovery*, p. 32.

[45] Balfour Comm., *Final Report*, pp. 70–73, 88; Clay, *The Post-War Unemployment Problem*, pp. 96–97, and "Unemployment and Wage Rates," *Econ. Jour.*, XXXVIII (1928), 6–7, 12.

[46] Liberal Industrial Inquiry, *Britain's Industrial Future*, pp. 146–47; Balfour Comm., *Final Report*, pp. 97, 239–42; Cole, *British Trade and Industry*, pp. 341–42.

However understandable it may have been, the unwillingness of the British people to yield any portion of a high living standard, as evidenced, for example, by the system of unemployment insurance paid by a payroll tax or by the inadequacy of available capital, handicapped British industry in its struggle for existence.[47] A loss of competitive ability may well necessitate a decline in both money and real wages if industry is to continue to find foreign markets. In a regime of international competition, particularly for a country in such a precarious position, suppleness and adaptability are at a premium, and these Britain lacked.[48] But the basic causes for the difficulties of the export industries are not to be found in mistaken policies. "Excessively high" British standards of living did not cause the depression of the staple trades; the depression was what made these standards excessive. At the same time, it must be noted at this point that British industry was not stagnant in these years. The productivity of labor rose substantially, justifying a more than slight rise in real wages.[49] Some industries expanded rapidly. Although the years 1927–29 were scarcely characterized by boom conditions, they were prosperous years, except in a few special areas. And in the thirties British industry in general experienced a revival and boom which rivaled any in pre-war years and was the envy of those who had too quickly forecast its demise.

Nevertheless, these special trades and areas were so crucial and their problems so acute that they must be studied in greater detail. With this examination we shall have told most of the story of decline, or relative decline, and we shall be able to proceed to the story of adjustment and recovery. As a whole the period 1919 to 1939, despite the dreary picture so far painted, was one of rising productivity and improved standards of living. But it was a very different industrial structure on an altered base which survived and came into view.

[47] André Siegfried makes much, indeed too much, of this "moral deterioration" of the British people, their inability to tighten their belts, *England's Crisis*, pp. 27–28, 91–105, 132, 175–77.
[48] See Loveday, *Britain and World Trade*, pp. 147–81.
[49] See pp. 264–65, below.

VI. THE DECLINE AND ADJUSTMENTS
OF THE STAPLE TRADES

IT IS SCARCELY an oversimplification to say that the industrial supremacy of Great Britain was founded on three products—coal, iron and steel, and cotton textiles. It is even less an oversimplification to say that the difficulties encountered by British industry in recent years have been, pre-eminently, the difficulties of those same three trades.

COAL

If coal was the very heart of the old industry, it constituted most of the body of the old foreign trade. Though comprising only 9 percent of the total value of British exports in 1924, it accounted for no less than 82 percent of the total tonnage.[1] Were it not for these heavy exports, ships bringing in bulk food and raw material imports would have had to leave British ports almost entirely in ballast. Coal benefited from low outgoing freight rates which the shipping companies were thus willing to charge, and at the same time it made possible low freight rates, which made for shipping supremacy, cheap food, cheap raw materials, and cheap exports.[2]

The plight of coal since 1914 is both the evidence and the result of change in the old industry. As Table 3 shows, the steady secular expansion of coal production in England which characterized the century before 1914 gave way immediately after the war to an abrupt decline, which has since persisted. In all years except 1923–24 the output was far below the 1909–13 annual average of 270 million tons. Exports and bunkers, while only one-third of total output in 1913, were the exclusive causes of this reduction, accounting for 45.7 of the total output decline of 47 millions in the period 1913 to 1937. Domestic consumption was secularly extremely stable, although it fluctuated cyclically.

The entire world coal-mining industry was subject in these years to two factors which seriously reduced demand: increased use of substitutes (hydroelectric power, oil, and lignite) and much more efficient measures of fuel conservation.[3] As a result, world output expanded at a greatly re-

[1] Balfour Comm., *Survey of Overseas Markets*, p. 4.
[2] Jevons, *The Coal Question*, pp. 253–76.
[3] League of Nations, *The Problem of the Coal Industry* (Publications II, 1929, No. 19), pp. 6–7. The proportion of the world's merchant marine adapted to the use of oil increased

TABLE 3

UNITED KINGDOM PRODUCTION AND EXPORTS OF COAL [a]

| | MILLIONS OF GROSS TONS | | | | £ MILLIONS | |
Year	Output	Exports	Bunkers [b]	Exports and Bunkers	Output	Exports
1860	80.0	...	...	7.3 [c]	20.0	3.3 [c]
1880	147.0	...	...	18.7 [c]	62.5	8.4 [c]
1900	225.2	44.1	11.8	55.8	121.7	36.4
1913	287.4	73.4	21.0	94.4	145.5	50.7
1924	267.1	61.7	17.7	79.3	251.7	72.1
1929	257.9	60.3	16.4	76.7	173.2	48.6
1932	208.7	38.9	14.2	53.1	138.4	31.6
1935	222.3	38.7	12.5	51.2	144.5	31.6
1937	240.4	40.3	11.7	52.0	182.7	37.7
1938	227.0	35.9	10.5	46.3	188.8	37.4

[a] Sources: Board of Trade, *Statistical Abstracts for the United Kingdom*; W. M. Page, *Commerce and Industry*, London, Constable, 1919, Vol. II, for pre-war figures.
[b] Includes small amounts of manufactured fuel.
[c] Includes small amounts of coke and cinders.

tarded rate after the World War. Meanwhile, potential supplies were greatly expanded because of the war and the post-war boom, the increasing mechanization of mines, and the development of new mines in new countries, often with governmental encouragement.[4]

Britain's continued relative decline under these circumstances made the plight of her industry particularly acute. For the entire decade before 1925 British producers had been spared serious trouble successively by the war, the post-war boom, the slow return to production of the destroyed continental mines, the American coal strike of 1922, and the Ruhr invasion of 1923. Their production in 1923 was only about 10 million tons below the 1913 level, and their share in total world output roughly unchanged. Therefore, when the weight of increased foreign competition and decreased domestic demand was at last felt and Britain's share in world

from only about 3.4 percent in 1913 to fully 38 percent and 51 percent in 1929 and 1937, respectively. *Ibid.*, p. 7; P.E.P., *Report on the British Coal Industry*, London, P.E.P., 1936, p. 116; I.L.O., *The World Coal Mining Industry*, Studies and Reports, series B, No. 31, Geneva, 1938, I, 86. The I.L.O. Report argues convincingly, however, that fuel conservation has been much more important than substitution in causing the decline of consumption. I, 32 ff., 75–77, 85–89 ff., 100.
[4] I.L.O., *The World Coal Mining Industry*, I, 101–10.

markets declined rapidly as a result,[5] the effect was much more crushing.

The British coal industry suffered seriously from the depressed state of its chief domestic customers, the iron and steel and shipping industries. The increased use of scrap steel, and the rise of the motor ship had in any case permanently diminished their consumption of coal.[6] In addition, the relative decline of the British exporter was very rapid. In the period 1909–13 Britain's coal exports, including bunkers, accounted for 50 percent of the world's total, in 1925–29 (excluding abnormal 1926), only 39.5 percent, and in 1936 it dropped to 34.4 percent. Britain suffered above all in continental European markets; the chief beneficiaries were subsidized Polish and German mines, German coal being released by increased domestic lignite production (stimulated by war exigencies) and exported in part payment of reparations.[7] In addition, countries with growing industries—among them Russia, Japan, China, India, and South Africa—were tapping previously untouched sources.[8]

It had long been evident in England that penetration to less productive mines and a long period of prosperity unconducive to improved efficiency of organization were raising costs excessively. Per capita output declined steadily from its peak in the period 1884–88. After 1904 profits per ton and real wages of miners tended to diminish.[9] There was indeed a very great increase in productivity and mine efficiency in the later twenties and throughout the thirties, with the return of the eight-hour day in 1926 and the greatly increased use of mining machinery. In 1913 only 8 percent of the coal was mined by machinery; in 1924 it was 19 percent, in 1929, 28 percent, in 1933, 42 percent, and in 1937, 57 percent. Progress in all these respects nevertheless still lagged considerably behind foreign technical advance, partly, no doubt, because of penetration to less productive seams.[10]

[5] See statistics in J. H. Jones, "The Present Position of the British Coal Trade," J.R.S.S., XCIII (1930), 28. This relative decline was much slighter between 1928 and 1937 because of Britain's well-sustained domestic demand. Statistics in Frederick H. Saward, *Saward's Annual*.

[6] Estimates of coal consumption in British Iron and Steel Federation, *Statistics of the Iron and Steel Industry of the United Kingdom*; see also P.E.P., *The British Coal Industry*, chap. iii.

[7] I.L.O., *The World Coal Mining Industry*, I, 142–45, 150–52.

[8] *Ibid.*, I, 65, 155; J. H. Jones, "The Present Position of the British Coal Trade," J.R.S.S., XCIII (1930), 15–18, 26; Allen, *British Industries*, p. 37.

[9] Allen, *op. cit.*, pp. 31–33.

[10] British output per man shift increased only 7 percent between 1913 and 1934 (about 30 percent between 1924 and 1934), while that of the Ruhr rose 77 percent, Polish Upper Silesia 63 percent. P.E.P., *The British Coal Industry*, pp. 153 ff. Also British Assoc.,

There was also the familiar inefficiency due to surplus capacity and a great number of excessively small mines, some extremely inefficient and unprofitable, yet by their existence preventing concentration of production in the more efficient mines. Coal suffered from British individualism at its worst. Both management and labor were unenlightened.[11] Resistance to inevitable wage cuts and lengthened hours led to the great strikes in 1921 and 1926, during which Britain lost markets to competitors eager to take full advantage of such opportunities.[12]

The coal industry was for these reasons constantly on the verge of financial collapse in the decade after 1924. It showed net losses in 1927 and 1928.[13] To maintain wages it had required a subsidy from August, 1925, through April, 1926; the removal of the subsidy precipitated the great strike. Unemployment in the industry was throughout far above the national average. The depression after 1929 accelerated the secular decline in exports, despite continued cost reductions. The effects of empire preference, trade agreements, and the decline of the pound were largely offset by foreign retaliation and intensified competition in other markets. With recovery and rearmament, domestic consumption rose to about its 1913 levels; but exports and bunker sales were in 1937 slightly lower, and in 1938 considerably lower, than in 1932.

The response to these conditions in coal, as it was in most British industry, was the evolution of a comprehensive "plan." Frequent demands for suspension of bitter price competition and for industrial reorganization had been unavailing, because too many owners clung tenaciously to their independence. Accordingly, a Coal Mines Act was passed in 1930, forcing adherence to a systematic scheme of output control by quota allocations and of price control administered by the operators themselves. In addition, a Coal Mines Reorganization Commission was set up to encourage, and having some power to enforce, the adoption of reorganization schemes with the aim of cutting costs.

Though the control planned by the act was far-reaching, the results were feeble. The act could not suppress the real conflicts of interest be-

Britain in Depression, pp. 158–59, _Britain in Recovery_, p. 234; Allen, _British Industries_, pp. 43–44, 60–61; "Coal Mining and Coal Prices," _Economist_, CXXXIV (1939), 567–68.
[11] Lucas, _Industrial Reconstruction_, pp. 33, 36; Liberal Industrial Inquiry, _Britain's Industrial Future_, pp. 343–45.
[12] Of all the greatly increased number of working days lost in strikes from 1919 to 1926, coal accounted for 62 percent. Liberal Industrial Inquiry, _Britain's Industrial Future_, p. 144.
[13] Board of Trade, _Statistical Tables_, II, 10; Lucas, _Industrial Reconstruction_, p. 68.

tween more mechanized and less mechanized mines, between poor and
rich mines, between those who exported and those who supplied the home
market. Even the temporary palliatives of price and output regulation
apparently eliminated only the most extreme forms of competition.[14] The
amalgamation provisions, which were intended to meet the longer-run
needs, proved almost a complete failure, because of governmental unwillingness to sanction coercion and the hostility of many producers, the
strong refusing to assume the burdens of the weak, the weak, entrenched
behind protected output quotas, refusing to perpetuate their current position of inferiority in a permanent agreement.[15] A new Coal Mines Act,
passed in 1938, sought to remedy the faults of the old act by creating a
new commission with increased powers to reduce the number of collieries
and enforce reorganization. Provision for national purchase of mine royalties will undoubtedly facilitate the process. However, it seems doubtful whether these measures can do much to reverse the trends of the
inter-war years. They may, at best, if properly administered, succeed better than did the forces of free competition in minimizing the continued
shrinkage of the British coal industry.[16]

IRON AND STEEL

The most striking aspect of the story of British iron and steel in the
inter-war period, as it is in coal and most other staple industries, was the
heavy decline of exports. But the behavior of exports by no means dominated the fortunes of this industry. The sharp decline in pig output can
be only partly attributed to the disappearance of exportation, because, as
Table 4 indicates, most pig iron goes into domestic steel. Again, all iron
and steel exports other than pig were in 1929 once more at the 1913 peak,
yet the industry was depressed during the 1920's. On the other hand,
severely reduced steel exports during the thirties were associated with a
strong rise in production.

The troubles of the steel industry during the 1920's were largely the
result of plant overexpansion during the war. The peak production of
9,717,000 tons in 1917 was not again attained until 1935; yet capacity was
estimated at 12 million tons in 1927.[17] Surplus capacity and the resulting

[14] Lucas, op.cit., pp. 75–90.

[15] Ibid., pp. 91–102; P.E.P., The British Coal Industry, pp. 5, 77–78, 81–82.

[16] For more optimistic views, see Damade, Le Mouvement de réorganisation industrielle
en Grande Bretagne, pp. 146–52, and Ivor Thomas, Coal in the New Era, London, Putnam, 1934; also P.E.P., The British Coal Industry, pp. 125–30.

[17] U.S. Bureau of Foreign and Domestic Commerce, "Iron and Steel Trade and Industry
of Great Britain," (Trade Information Bull. No. 639, 1929), p. 5.

TABLE 4

IRON AND STEEL PRODUCTION AND TRADE OF THE UNITED KINGDOM [a]

(*In ooo tons*)

| | TRADE IN IRON, STEEL, AND MANUFACTURES [b] | | | | PRODUCTION | | |
| | Exports | | | Imports | Pig | | Finished |
Year	Total	Pig [c]	Other		Iron [c]	Steel	Steel
1913	4,971 [d]	1,124	3,847	2,205 [d]	10,260	7,664	...
1920	3,251	580	2,672	1,083	8,035	9,067	6,769
1923	4,318	893	3,425	1,314	7,441	8,482	6,519
1929	4,380	545	3,834	2,813	7,589	9,636	7,625
1931	1,979	202	1,777	2,838	3,773	5,203	4,681
1932	1,887	128	1,760	1,590	3,574	5,261	4,424
1935	2,312	157	2,156	1,149	6,424	9,859	7,126
1937	2,574	167	2,407	2,026	8,493	12,984	9,681
1938	1,915	101	1,814	1,311	6,761	10,398	...

[a] Sources: Board of Trade, *Statistical Abstracts for the United Kingdom; Annual Statements of Trade of the United Kingdom.* Finished steel output from National Federation of Iron and Steel Manufacturers, bulletins and reports (later, British Iron and Steel Federation, *Statistics*).
[b] Net trade: exports of United Kingdom products; retained imports.
[c] Includes ferro alloys.
[d] Hollow ware of iron, steel, and tinplate added to official figures for comparability.

financial weakness throughout the decade made impossible the technical renovation which was essential if exports were to be expanded and the rise of imports checked.

Britain's portion of world pig iron output continued to decline drastically, as before: from 13.2 percent in 1913 to 8.3 percent in 1937.[18] Persisting causes of this decline were insufficiency of domestic ores, substitution of basic steel for cast iron, wrought iron, and acid steels, in which Britain had specialized, increased use of scrap, and the growth of protected domestic furnaces in former markets, India, Japan, Canada, Australia, and on the European continent.[19] To find a figure in pig iron output before 1913 lower than that for 1937, the peak of the entire 1919–38 period, one must go back to 1901; only before 1895 are the figures regularly lower.

British steel, on the contrary, has held its own, relative to world production, except for temporary heavy relative losses between 1925 and

[18] Statistics in League of Nations, *Statistical Yearbooks.*
[19] Allen, *British Industries,* pp. 97–100; M. S. Birkett, "The Iron and Steel Industry Since the War," J.R.S.S., XCIII (1930), 345–46.

1929, with the rapid recovery of continental industry. The relative strength after 1929 was attributable primarily to such temporary factors as continued American depression and the great British recovery after the comparative stagnation of 1927–29; however, the earlier stagnation may also have been in part abnormal, as well as temporary. Steel was able to avoid the absolute decline of pig iron largely by using foreign pig iron, shifting to basic steel, and concentrating increasingly on the higher stages of manufacture. Of the total imports in 1929, crude iron and steel were 42.5 percent, rolling mill products 42.9 percent, and more highly fabricated products (including rails) 14.6 percent. Of the exports, on the other hand, crude iron and steel were only 13.0 percent, rolling mill products 23.1 percent, and more highly finished products 63.9 percent.[20] The output of finished steel products, it will be noted in Table 4, showed great strength during the 1920's.

This concentration on more finished steel products explains in part the survival in Britain of smaller steel plants than were able to survive in other major producing countries, manufacturing a greater variety of products for a series of smaller markets. However, it also mirrors Britain's sheer inability to compete in the bulk lines. From the point of view of maintaining and increasing exports, this adjustment, in so far as it was an adjustment, was quite inadequate.[21]

The fact is that during the 1920's the British industry, in all its branches, suffered from the familiar evils of financial weakness, stagnation of output relative to foreign competitors,[22] inefficiency, and high costs. Individual plants were small and obsolescent, and their products were too unstandardized to compete with the mass bulk output of America and reconstructed Germany.[23]

The great depression after 1929, superimposed upon the trials of the preceding decade, at last compelled drastic measures. Unfortunately, "drastic measures" amounted to a complete program of protection, controlled competition, and retrenchment.[24] Because a more or less freely

[20] Macrosty, "The Overseas Trade of the United Kingdom, 1924–31," J.R.S.S., XCV (1932), 633.

[21] Allen, *British Industries*, pp. 101–2, 106, 117–21.

[22] See Board of Trade, *Statistical Tables*, II, 77.

[23] Lucas, *Industrial Reconstruction*, pp. 105–10; also Liberal Industrial Inquiry, *Britain's Industrial Future*, pp. 33–35; Balfour Comm., *Final Report*, p. 185; Allen, *British Industries*, pp. 115–16; U.S. Bureau of Foreign and Domestic Commerce, "Iron and Steel Trade and Industry of Great Britain," p. 18.

[24] See Ben W. Lewis, *Price and Production Control in British Industry*, pp. 14–16.

competitive regime had failed to effect much needed reorganization, the government made its grant of a tariff in 1932 conditional upon reconstitution of the industry into a responsible centralized unit. In 1934 all conditions were removed, and the duties were made permanent. Suppression of competition, not technical reorganization, seems to have been the prime motive of the British Iron and Steel Federation. Its whole scheme of market control, output quotas, protection, restriction of entrance into the industry, and its agreement of 1935 with the international steel cartel, effectively reserving the home market at the price of accepting an extremely low export quota, has been a means of preserving vested interests, of drawing within a shell in which could be found security and profit. The Federation's motives, as evidenced by its price policy, may not have been flagrantly predatory or exploitative.[25] But it has been at best conservative, following the narrow short-run interests of the producers rather than constructively and aggressively pursuing long-run national interests. And these dangers of monopoly are great enough.[26] Meanwhile, the government has constantly encouraged, mildly cautioned, shunned active interference, and relied upon the word of the industry's leaders that they would act like gentlemen.[27]

The British Iron and Steel Federation, born out of the defensive psychology of depression, remained in the saddle during prosperity. Exports continued to be almost completely neglected. Necessary capital extensions were delayed or discouraged by quota control of output and by the Federation's policy of passing upon all schemes, in keeping with its avowed purpose of preventing a recurrence of the previous malady of surplus capacity.[28] The impact of this protective conservative policy was

[25] Gr. Brit., Import Duties Advisory Committee, *Report on the Present Position and Future Development of the Iron and Steel Industry* (Cmd. 5507, 1937), pp. 48–49, 51–53. The Committee, however, is notoriously sympathetic with the whole self-government of industry movement. See, on the other side, Davies, *"National" Capitalism*, pp. 52–62, and the *Economist*, CXXXIII (1938), 588 for convincing condemnations of the Federation's price policies.

[26] Lucas, *Industrial Reconstruction*, pp. 110–14, 118–22; Allen, *British Industries*, pp. 132 A–F.

[27] This attitude pervades the report of the Import Duties Advisory Committee, cited above. See, for example, pp. 43–44, 56, 59, and *passim*; also Davies, *"National" Capitalism*, chap. iii.

[28] Import Duties Advisory Comm., *Report on the Present Position and Future Development of the Iron and Steel Industry*, pp. 33–42; *Economist*: "Britain's Steel Industry," CXXII (1936), 116; "Policy in the Steel Industry," CXXV (1936), 510: "It is hard to resist the conclusion that, at the moment, the consumer rather than the producer has the best claim

felt when revival turned into boom in 1936 and 1937. Prices soared, as shortages appeared in scrap, ore, and some grades of steel; and exports languished, if only because of the inability of the trade to meet orders.

It was the revival and the great prosperity of 1936–38, rather than any efforts of the Federation, which at length brought true technical advances. Reviving demand was led by the building boom, followed by the growing automobile industry, by a reviving shipbuilding and engineering, and, finally, by rearmament. Steel output in 1935 set new records, and the output of the entire industry (according to the Board of Trade index) was in 1937 30 percent above even the 1935 level. A far greater increase in output than in employment reflected a notable rise in per capita productivity and in average plant size. New modern plants were erected, and capacity was considerably expanded.[29]

By 1939 the iron and steel industry as a whole was greatly expanded, possessed much more modern equipment, and was more prosperous than it had been ever since the first World War. Britain produced almost as great a share of world steel in 1937 as in 1913. This was no decaying trade. But its prosperity was based on domestic demand alone, much of it perhaps ephemeral. And before it really got down to making these noteworthy adjustments, the industry had saddled itself with tariffs, import and export quotas, and a tight, monopolistic leadership which threatens its own future competitive power and the competitive power of its leading industrial consumers as well.[30]

COTTON TEXTILES

The first British industry to be transformed by the Industrial Revolution was cotton textiles. In the period 1919 to 1939 it was in this industry that the plight of the staple trades was most dramatically manifested.

The cotton industry is dependent to an extraordinary degree upon

---

to 'protection.' " "The British Steel Industry," CXXVII (1937), 325; "Commercial History and Review of 1936," *Economist*, Feb. 13, 1937, p. 51; and, especially, "The Lesson of Jarrow," *Economist*, CXXIV (1936), 105. See also Davies, *"National" Capitalism*, pp. 62–71.

[29] *Economist*, CXXX (1938), 132; "Commercial History and Review of 1938," *Economist*, Feb. 18, 1939, p. 52; "Expanding Steel Capacity," *Economist*, CXXVIII (1937), 169–70; Damade, *Le Mouvement de réorganisation industrielle*, pp. 160–66; B. of T.J., CXL (1938), 7.

[30] The *Economist* reported with some glee that "Lord Nuffield is becoming a confirmed free trader." CXXI (1935), 952. Lord Nuffield, a leading automobile manufacturer, had long advocated heavy protection—for automobiles. He was now complaining bitterly about the high price he had to pay for protected steel.

foreign markets. Its almost unbroken decline from 1913 to 1938 was entirely due to declining exports, for domestic consumption increased considerably.[31] The decline has been devastating, as Table 5 clearly shows. To find a value of total cotton yarn and manufactured exports less than the £49.7 million recorded in 1938, one has to go back to 1863.

TABLE 5

UNITED KINGDOM COTTON TEXTILE INDUSTRY PRODUCTION, EXPORTS, RAW COTTON IMPORTS [a]

Year	Net Imports, Raw Cotton	Exports Yarn	PIECE GOODS		Percentage of Production Exported	TOTAL YARNS, MANUFACTURES [b]	
			Production	Exports		Production	Exports
	(In million lbs.)		(In million sq. yds.)			(In £ millions)	
1907	2,056.5	241.1	7,088 [c]	6,298.0 [c]	88.9	126.0	105.0
1913	1,916.7	210.1	...	7,075.3 [c]	...	...	...
1924	1,435.6	163.1	6,027	4,444.0	73.7	256.0	196.2
1925	1,757.3	189.5	...	4,435.6	...	...	...
1929	1,461.5	166.6	...	3,671.6	...	...	...
1930	1,140.1	137.0	3,320	2,406.8	72.5	118.0	86.2
1931	1,049.9	133.5	...	1,716.3	...	...	...
1932	1,204.5	141.5	...	2,197.5	...	...	...
1933	1,350.4	135.1	3,504	2,031.2	58.0	100.0	57.7
1934	1,198.2	130.4	3,457	1,993.5	57.7	103.0	57.7
1935	1,197.6	141.7	3,385	1,948.4	57.6	106.0	58.6
1936	1,485.0	150.9	...	1,916.6	...	...	...
1937	1,600.5	159.0	...	1,921.3	...	...	...
1938	1,161.0	123.0	...	1,386.2	...	...	...

[a] Sources: *Annual Statements of Trade of the United Kingdom;* Great Britain, Board of Trade, *Final Report,* 5th Census of Production and Import Duties Act Inquiry (1935), Part I, *Final Report,* First Census of Production (1907).
[b] Production figure free of duplication. Both figures exclude lace, net, ribbon, etc., and apparel.
[c] Linear yards; comparability with later figures is only slightly affected.

The rise of silk and rayon and the rather slow increase of consumption of all textiles after the war, in the face of enlarged productive capacities, acted as a depressing influence upon all the world's cotton industries.[32]

[31] Of the decline of £150 million in the output of the industry as a whole, between 1924 and 1935, exports accounted for £137.6 million, the fall in prices of home consumption for the rest, while the quantum of home consumption rose.
[32] I.L.O., *The World Textile Industry,* Studies and Reports, series B, No. 27, Geneva, 1937, I, 156–67.

But these factors simply slowed down the rate of growth. The decline of British cottons was primarily British in origin, not the result of factors operating equally on all countries. Table 6 shows very clearly the enormous relative decline of British capacity and output.[33]

According to this table Britain, although possessing almost 40 percent of the world's spindles in 1913, consumed less than 20 percent of the raw cotton. For this there were two causes. Probably the more important was the fact that Britain concentrated upon production of better grades of goods, mainly with mule spindles, which consume less cotton per spindle. Secondly, even in 1913 British equipment was not as fully employed as was the equipment of many of her competitors, where longer hours and even double shifts were common. Between 1913 and 1929 the discrepancy between Britain's relative positions in respect to spindles and raw-cotton consumption became even greater, the sole explanation being the greatly increased amount of excess capacity worked part time or not at all.[34] Between 1929 and 1937, on the contrary, the discrepancy narrowed, as cotton consumption rose absolutely, while spindles (particularly the less cotton-consuming mules) were scrapped or allowed to depreciate.

The rise of competitors caused a continual shifting in the geographical center of gravity of Britain's exports of cotton goods before 1913 as well as after.[35] During all previous shifts, however, the total continued to rise. After 1913 it fell rapidly. The greatest declines were in sales to Far Eastern markets. The purchases of British piece goods by India, China, Japan, and Hong Kong, which in 1913 took 54 percent of the total, declined by 91 percent between 1913 and 1937. Small consolation could Lancashire find, for a loss of 2,700 million yards of exports to India alone, in a rise of 76 millions to the only absolutely expanding markets, South, East, and West Africa. In fact, sales to all countries outside of those Far Eastern markets fell by no less than 49 percent.[36]

One mitigating factor was that the greatest export losses throughout this period were in markets for low-quality goods, markets with rela-

---

[33] The true volume of output is only very roughly measured by the volume of raw cotton consumed, because it does not take account of the higher average quality of the British product throughout, and the shift to still higher quality during these years.

[34] See League of Nations, *Memorandum on Cotton* (International Econ. Conference, 1927), p. 20; Liberal Industrial Inquiry, *Britain's Industrial Future*, pp. 36–37.

[35] Allen, *British Industries*, pp. 213–15.

[36] Statistics on geographical distribution in B. of T.J., CXXV (1930), 129–30, CXLI (1938), 255–56. Exports to the Irish Free State excluded from all compilations, for comparability with 1913. See also P.E.P., *Report on the British Cotton Industry*, pp. 32–47.

TABLE 6

RELATIVE IMPORTANCE OF THE BRITISH COTTON INDUSTRY [a]

A. *Spindles* (*in millions*) [b]

Country	TOTAL			MULE SPINDLES			RING SPINDLES		
	1913	1929	1937	1913	1929	1937	1913	1929	1937
World	143.4	164.2	149.6	64.3	61.5	38.1	65.6	102.7	109.1
Great Britain	55.7	55.9	38.8	40.5	42.8	26.8	9.3	13.1	10.6
U.S.A.[d]	31.5	34.8	27.0	4.1	1.8	.4	27.4	33.0	26.2
Germany	11.2	11.3	9.8	4.8	4.6	2.8	5.6	6.6	7.5
Russia	7.7	7.5	10.1 [c]	2.9	2.6	1.0 [c]	4.2	4.9	9.1 [c]
France	7.4	9.9	10.2	3.9	3.4	2.3	3.3	6.4	7.5
Japan	2.3	6.5	11.9	.1	.0	.0	2.2	6.5	12.3
India	6.1	8.7	9.9	1.3	.9	.5	3.4	7.8	9.2
Great Britain as percentage of total	38.8	34.1	25.9	63.0	69.5	70.2	14.2	12.8	9.7

B. *Cotton Mill Raw Cotton Consumption*
(*000,000 actual bales, for half years*) [e]

	1913	1929	1937
World	10.14	13.01	15.14
Great Britain	1.91	1.36	1.46
U.S.A.	2.89	3.62	4.09
Russia	.97	1.09 [c]	1.06 [c]
Germany	.79	.65	.54
Japan	.79	1.43	2.06
China	. . .	1.01	1.26 [c]
India	.85	1.02	1.54
Great Britain as percentage of world total	18.9	10.5	9.6

[a] Sources: International Federation of Master Cotton Spinners' and Manufacturers' Associations, *International Cotton Statistics*.

[b] Data for 1913 are for end of August, and the division between mule and ring is of spindles in use only. Totals for 1929 and 1937 are for end of July. Figures for mule and ring spindles in 1937 are said to be "for the half year" ending January 31, 1938, which explains their failure to add up to the totals given.

[c] Estimated.

[d] Division between mule and ring spindles approximate.

[e] Regardless of weight of bales, which varies somewhat as between American, Egyptian, and Indian cotton. 1913 figures are for average half year consumption during year ending August 31, 1913; 1929 and 1937 figures are for the half year ending July 31.

tively low per capita incomes.[37] Yardage figures thus overstate the actual "quantum" decline. As a result, until 1928 the Egyptian branch of the spinning industry, which spins the finer counts of cotton, remained relatively prosperous, whereas the American branch, spinning coarser counts, was in a state of deep depression after 1920.[38] The result of the even more precipitous decline in exports of the cheaper grades after 1929 was perforce an intensification of this trend.[39] Whereas in 1935 Japan accounted for 41.0 percent and Britain only 29.9 percent of the total yardage of the world's cotton piece goods exports, in value terms Britain still led with 37.0 percent as against only 27.3 percent for Japan.[40]

However, this specialization, traditional in Britain, unfitted the industry for competition in the modern world and involved the use of obsolete methods and equipment. In the great American industry, as Table 6 shows, mules were scarcely 5 percent of the total spindles; in Britain they constituted more than 75 percent. Mule spindles require skilled labor, generally produce a higher quality product, and are not adaptable to standardized mass machine output. While British labor thus wove the finest cottons, of manifold types for varied markets, other countries were adapting the ring spindle and using the automatic loom and less skilled labor in much cheaper mass production of standardized goods, usually, but not always, of inferior quality.[41] India, the southern United States, China, and Japan had abundant cheap labor, great domestic markets, and ample near-by sources of raw cotton. Japan had a fresh start, an efficient modern plant that was worked in double shifts, and able technical and business management and organization.[42] She was aided, too, by the

[37] Whereas piece-goods exports in the years 1922–24 were only 50 percent (in yards) of the 1913 level in those markets where the purchase price had averaged below £14 per 1,000 yards in the earlier year, they were actually 14 percent above 1913 levels in markets where the price had averaged £17 and above. G. W. Daniels and J. Jewkes, "The Crisis in the Lancashire Cotton Industry," *Econ. Jour.*, XXXVII (1927), 33–37.

[38] Imports of raw cotton from Egypt were in 1928, 88.3 percent and in 1931, 67.0 percent of the 1909–13 annual average; imports of United States raw cotton were only 50.8 percent and 25.8 percent of that average, in those years. P.E.P., *The British Cotton Industry*, pp. 54–56.

[39] League of Nations, *Review of World Trade*, 1937, p. 64.

[40] I.L.O., *The World Textile Industry*, I, 75, 77.

[41] In January, 1934, only 2.4 percent of the British looms were automatic, as against 12.5 percent in Japan, 22.9 percent in Italy, and 68.4 percent in the United States, *ibid.*, I, 54–55; see also 215–17; League of Nations, *Memorandum on Cotton*, p. 9; P.E.P., *The British Cotton Industry*, pp. 94–95; Allen, *British Industries*, pp. 222–26.

[42] I.L.O., *The World Textile Industry*, I, 211–13; Allen, "Recent Changes in the Organisation of the Japanese Cotton Industry," *The Manchester School*, VIII (1937), 1–22; Barnard and Hugh Ellinger, "Japanese Competition in the Cotton Trade," J.R.S.S., XCIII (1930), 206–7.

extreme depreciation of the yen after 1931. The fall in the price of silver after 1920 and the curtailment of agricultural buying power helped to turn Asiatic consumers to lower quality cheaper products. Under these circumstances Britain's retention of leadership in high-quality goods failed to serve as the basis of bulk exports and mass production or to support prosperity. Her industry, financially weak, with a heavy investment in mules and the older looms and trained in the old methods, suffered under these developments; her skilled labor, its relatively high wages no longer justified, refused to be displaced by modern machinery and semi-skilled labor. Heavy overcapitalization as a result of the post-war boom and reluctance on the part of banks to force liquidation and write down their assets plagued the spinning branch. Short working hours—a widely adopted means of spreading work and cutting output—meant a continuation of high unit costs and financial weakness.[43] In contrast with the great increase of per capita productivity in most cotton industries of the world, British productivity declined or at best remained constant during the twenties.[44]

As a result, cheap foreign cottons, Japanese and Indian in the Orient, Italian in the Balkans and Near East, those of the United States in Latin America, not only displaced British cottons but also in primitive countries tapped new lower levels of demand, which the British product could never reach.[45] India tells almost the entire story, for she alone in 1913 took 43 percent of British piece good exports, and between 1913 and 1937 accounted for well over 50 percent of the decline in the total. Japan supplied 0.1 percent of the volume of India's average annual imports of cotton piece goods in the period 1909–13, as against a British share of 97.4 percent. By 1936 the Japanese percentage had risen to 54.6, and the British had fallen to 43.7. However, far more important than Japan's inroads in eliminating British sales was the displacement of all imports by domestic production. Imports from Japan were, at their 1929 peak, less than ⅕ of those from Britain in 1913. The portion of apparent Indian consumption supplied by domestic mills rose from 26.5 percent in the earlier period to 82.0 percent in 1936; moreover, these figures exclude handloom production, which also expanded appreciably.[46]

[43] Econ. Research Section, U. of Manchester, *Re-adjustment in Lancashire*, Manchester, Manchester University Press, 1936, pp. 16–17; P.E.P., *The British Cotton Industry*, pp. 28, 58–60; MacM. Comm., *Evidence*, II, 266.

[44] I.L.O., *The World Textile Industry*, I, 298–303; Allen, *British Industries*, pp. 238–41, 247–49. See below, p. 265n.

[45] Hubbard, *Eastern Industrialization and Its Effect on the West*, pp. 17, 19.

[46] Computations from *Statistical Abstracts of the British Empire* and *Annual Reviews of*

In other markets as well, in the Low Countries, Brazil, Italy, China, and Japan, it was to rising, protected, domestic industries that Britain suffered her greatest losses.[47] After 1930, indeed, it seemed that relative to total world cotton exports, the British exports had ceased to fall.[48] But the absolute fall in that total was enormous, and no exporting country depended as much as Britain upon foreign trade in cottons.[49]

Chaotic industrial organization contributed to technical inferiority. As in coal, the old and almost fanatic individualism was at its worst in the cotton trades; the industry suffered from an excessive number of small, weak firms, unco-ordinated marketing, and too many middlemen. Weaving mills were too small to produce bulk goods cheaply, and many of the merchant houses in charge of marketing were too small for cheap mass distribution. The division of the industry into four major sections (spinning, weaving, finishing, and selling), almost completely segregated, further reduced the chances of rationalization.[50] On its own initiative the cotton industry, except in the fairly well organized finishing branches, seemed incapable of co-operating to remedy this situation.[51] Large enterprises were attempted during the twenties, but the cost of buying out stubborn independents weakened them from the start. Price agreements were ineffective, piecemeal, short-lived, and certainly never thoroughgoing enough to serve as a basis for greatly needed reorganiza-

---

the Trade of India. Years are fiscal years, beginning April 1. See also Hubbard, *Eastern Industrialization;* Royal Institute, *The Problem of International Investment,* pp. 61–64; A. B. Burnett-Hurst, "Lancashire and the Indian Market," J.R.S.S., XCV (1932), 395–440.

[47] I.L.O., *The World Textile Industry,* I, 104–12.

[48] Whereas the British portion of total cotton piece-goods exports from 13 leading countries had fallen from 54.6 percent in 1924 to 40.0 percent in 1930, statistics for 17 countries show British percentages of 37.9 in 1930, 38.0 in 1935, 38.6 in 1936 and 36.2 percent in 1937. Joint Committee of Cotton Trade Organizations, *Cotton Trade Statistics.* The 1936 and 1937 percentages are slightly high, since the total export figures exclude exports by Spain and Portugal, which must have been very small because of the war.

[49] It was estimated in 1930 that roughly ⅘ of total world output of cotton piece goods by weight was consumed within the producing countries. Ellinger, "Japanese Competition in the Cotton Trade," J.R.S.S., XCIII (1930), 185. The British ratio was even at that late date under 30 percent.

[50] The industry consisted in 1930 of ". . . more than 3,000 unco-ordinated small units . . . without cohesion, without nucleus, loose, higgledy-piggledy, rushing hither and thither, jostling, chasing, fighting, the whole curious phenomenon involving an enormous wastage of money, energy, time and power." *Ibid.,* p. 211; see pp. 207–12; also P.E.P., *The British Cotton Industry,* pp. 69 ff.; J. Wisselink, "The Present Condition of the English Cotton Industry," *Harvard Business Review,* VIII (1930), 156–66; *Britain without Capitalists,* chap. viii; Lucas, *Industrial Reconstruction,* pp. 146, 149–50.

[51] Lucas, *op. cit.,* pp. 160–68; Allen, *British Industries,* pp. 238–41.

tion—partly because of the real divergence of interests between different branches of the trade and partly because of the prime importance of exports, which made price control or output control alone no remedy at all.

Support of the government was therefore enlisted. In 1936 a cotton spindles reconstruction levy was imposed by law; many excess spindles were purchased with the proceeds and scrapped, as Table 6 shows. Although this was a step in the right direction, the remaining branches were saddled with the cost of eliminating the surplus capacity, and the need for technical reorganization remained.[52] Agitation continued, therefore, for a more thoroughgoing industry-wide scheme. A bill, passed in 1939, set up administrative machinery for such a plan, giving the industry itself wide powers to effect reorganization, fix prices, and so forth, with scarcely any government supervision. An interesting commentary upon the British attitude is furnished by the comparison of the wide powers given such an autonomous industrial group with the severely restricted operations of the governmental Coal Mines Reorganization Commission of 1930.[53]

These efforts were accompanied by a fair recovery and brighter prospects for cottons than at any time since 1924. World revival checked the trend to cheaper cottons, which had been to the advantage of foreign competitors: from 1935 to 1937 the quantity of Japanese exports of piece goods failed to gain relative to the British.[54] While total exports failed to recover, there was some consolation in the rise of exports to other parts of the empire, except India, aided by imperial preference in the dominions and quotas against the Japanese in the crown colonies.[55] Domestic demand had grown greatly, apparently for the first time enough to compensate, temporarily, for dwindling exports (see Table 5). Net imports of raw cotton, a rough index of production, were in 1936 and 1937 actually above 1929 levels. The long depression had brought some

---

[52] *Statist:* CXXVI (1935), 8, 10; CXXIX (1937), 722; CXXXII (1938), 823–24; Lucas, *Industrial Reconstruction*, pp. 168, 173.

[53] See "The Cartelization of England," *Economist*, CXXXIV (1939), 551–52.

[54] League of Nations, *Review of World Trade*, 1937, p. 65; "Lancashire's Future, II," *Economist*, CXXV (1936), 402–3; "Cotton Trade Revival," *Statist*, CXXIX (1937), 81–82.

[55] Sales to North America, to West, South, and East Africa, were in 1937 considerably above 1929 levels, and to Australia and New Zealand about constant. In East Africa, Ceylon and Malaya, Japan had made alarming inroads between 1929 and 1933. Severe quota restrictions imposed by Britain in 1934 sharply cut down Japanese sales, and the British recovered strongly as a result. See Hubbard, *Eastern Industrialization*, pp. 18–24; British Assoc., *Britain in Recovery*, p. 445.

plant renovation, cost reduction, and writing down of excessive capitalizations, although vastly more remained to be done.[56]

The huge drop in foreign sales in 1938 and the deep depression of the industry in that year, however, marked once more the precarious position of cotton. Domestic demand and a stable relative share of shrinking world exports were not sufficient. Nor could empire preference provide an enduring solution. In fact, Britain's relative share of world exports fell sharply again after 1936.[57] The export of cotton piece goods in the first half of 1938 was the lowest in 90 years, and domestic demand also declined.[58] Cotton may eventually recover and rise above its 1938 levels, but real recovery is impossible without the return of a freer world trade or thorough reorganization of the British industry. Even in the latter event, British cottons can never recover anything like the leadership or prosperity of 1913.

OTHER STAPLE TRADES

The remaining staple industries, a heterogeneous lot, cannot be studied in detail. Their experiences differed in important respects, just as did those of coal, iron and steel, and cotton. But in all appeared some or all of the same general features: relative stagnation, overexpansion of capacity from 1914 to 1921, inability to compete, loss of foreign markets, competition of younger foreign producers, the absence of a boom in the late twenties, and, in most of these industries, recovery based upon a domestic revival after 1933, although exports continued to lag.

The shipbuilding industry of the entire world was depressed throughout the period 1921 to 1938 by two major factors: vast overexpansion of production and capacity during the war and post-war booms, and relative stagnation of world trade thereafter. Under these circumstances the relative decline of Britain brought her severe depression. The secular rise in total non-British shipbuilding to 119 percent of the 1909–13 level in the years 1926–29, and 130 percent, 183 percent and 203 percent in

[56] British Assoc., *Britain in Recovery*, pp. 450–51.

[57] She accounted for 38.0 percent of the exports of 17 leading countries in 1935, 36.2 percent in 1937, and well below 34 percent in 1938. Joint Committee of Cotton Trade Organizations, *Cotton Trade Statistics*. The 1938 figure of 33.9 percent is too high due to the exclusion from the 17 country total of exports from Spain, Portugal, the U.S.S.R., and also the trade between Germany and Austria and parts of Czechoslovakia, after their annexation.

[58] "Banking and Commercial Review," *Statist*, Aug. 20, 1938, pp. 17–19; also CXXXII (1938), 823; CXXXIII (1939), 298–99.

1936, 1937, and 1938, respectively, was directly at the expense of Britain, whose output fell in 1926–29 to 79 percent of the pre-war level and in 1937 to 61 percent. Thus, her portion of total world shipbuilding fell from no less than 61 percent in the earlier period to 51 percent in 1926–29 and 34 percent in 1937 and 1938.[59]

British labor and management must share some of the blame for these changes, although the main causal factors were largely beyond their control. Shipbuilding is irregular work, employing a great variety of relatively skilled craftsmen and consuming the products of a great number of other industries. These conditions, as in building, make for high hourly wages, a welter of minute union restrictions, jurisdictional strikes, and clumsy, archaic organization. Also, there was an important technological factor: just as the British victory over the American builder in the middle of the nineteenth century had been associated with her development of steam and iron while America was experiencing a final glory of sail and wood, so now her own decline was associated with the Diesel engine and the more rapid adoption of the oil motor ship by her competitors. In 1927 Britain was building about three-fifths of the world's steam tonnage and only about two-fifths of its motor tonnage.[60]

The major customer for British ships is the British shipping industry, and that industry has been generally depressed because of subsidized foreign competition and the absolute drop in world trade. In 1914 Britain owned 39.2 percent of the world's ships, in June, 1929, 29.6 percent, and in June, 1937, 26.5 percent.[61] Thus the entire period 1919–39, except during the sharp recoveries of world trade in the periods 1927–29 and 1936–37, and except for the revival of armament demand after 1937, was one of more or less deep depression for British shipbuilding.[62] Surplus capacity brought financial weakness and so impeded technical reorganization. To combat this situation, a private reconstruction levy scheme was undertaken in 1930, as a result of which slightly more than 30 percent of total capacity was bought up and shut down by the end of 1937. The levy seems to have been worth while, according to purely

[59] "Commercial History and Review of 1938," Economist, Feb. 18, 1939, p. 55.
[60] Liberal Industrial Inquiry, Britain's Industrial Future, p. 32. See E. S. Gregg, "The Decline of British Shipbuilding," Harvard Business Review, IV (1926), 290–96; Balfour Comm., Final Report, pp. 66, 138–41.
[61] Bank of England, Statistical Summary, Aug. 1938, p. 100.
[62] Allen, British Industries, pp. 151 ff.; British Assoc., Britain in Recovery, pp. 331–32, 355–56.

economic standards, the cost of purchase having been more than compensated by reduced unit costs resulting from greater concentration.[63] However, the boom conditions of 1937, with the abrupt recovery of world trade, must have been attributable in part to the earlier scrapping of building capacity.[64] In any event, an equally abrupt decline of world trade after 1937 brought another severe fall of freight rates, a sharp rise of idle tonnage, and the secular problems of British shipbuilding, which had been for a short time submerged, again became evident. Shipping and shipbuilding are staple trades par excellence. There can be no recovery based on the home market.

The story of wool is much like the story of cotton. Its difficulties have, however, been far less intense because of the greater importance of the home market and because woolen manufacture is not so readily copied by less industrialized countries. Nevertheless, the problems have been great. They have centered entirely in a decline of exports, as a result of sharp competition from other exporting countries, notably Japan, and (even more) from protected domestic industries in former markets, notably Australia, Argentina, Canada, and the United States. Although Britain remains by far the world's greatest exporter of woolen manufactures,[65] sales have fallen drastically. Exports of woolen and worsted tissues, 219 million square yards in 1913 and 222 million in 1924, were 171 and 156 millions in 1928 and 1929, respectively, and recovered only to 123 millions in 1937. Since domestic sales were relatively stable during the 1920's, the decline of exports entailed severe depression.

However, the industry recovered strongly after 1932, entirely on the basis of sales to the newly protected home market. By 1935 output of tissues regained almost all the ground lost after 1924, largely because of the reduction of imports. Despite the heavy decline of exports, accordingly, in 1935 the total volume of output of the woolen and worsted industries was 9 percent above 1924 and 43 percent above 1930 levels.[66]

The engineering trades are so inclusive and so diversified that it is

---

[63] Damade, *Le Mouvement de réorganisation industrielle*, pp. 230–31; Lucas, *Industrial Reconstruction*, pp. 127–35. The British government has no doubt had occasion frequently since 1939 to regret that noneconomic considerations of military security were not the determining factors instead. The scrapped capacity has probably been sadly missed.
[64] The *Economist* freight rate index, 1913 taken as 100, was 91.1 in October, 1936 (this being little above 1932–35 levels) and 145.0 in September, 1937.
[65] I.L.O., *The World's Textile Industry*, I, 86, 88.
[66] Data from *Final Reports*, 4th and 5th Censuses of Production. See also I.L.O., *The World Textile Industry*, I, 118–19, 143, 182–85; British Assoc., *Britain in Depression*, pp. 359–60, 364; *Britain in Recovery*, pp. 464, 466, 474.

hard to discuss them except qualitatively. Such branches as the manu-facture of electrical machinery, of automobiles and other vehicles, are relatively new British industries. Largely because of their inclusion, the Board of Trade production index for the industry as a whole, including shipbuilding, shows an increase of 21 percent between 1924 and 1929, and a rise after 1934 to unprecedented levels, roughly to 30 percent above the 1929 peak. However, some old branches as well, like steel, show continued secular expansion. Engineering is still a growing branch of industry.

The major staple branches are the older manufactures of machinery and prime movers employing mainly coal and steam: locomotives and agricultural, basic iron and steel, textile, and shipbuilding machinery. This was at best a stationary group during the twenties, and some branches were declining or depressed, for familiar reasons: excessive expansion of capacity during the war, loss of foreign markets in the older lines to competitors, and the shift of demand and techniques (including sources of power) away from those products in which Britain had excelled. In-directly, engineering has suffered from depression within the staple trades which it equips, especially the production of textiles and ships.

As Table 2 showed, exports accounted in 1907 and even in 1930 for at least 50 percent of the output of most of the traditional engineering trades. The sluggishness of the major portion of the industry during the twenties was the result of loss of these markets to foreign competitors; do-mestic demand was stable or strong. The United States took a marked lead in agricultural machinery, especially motor tractors; Germany sup-planted Britain in many markets for textile machinery,[67] and Japan now manufactures much of her own. American and German mass production methods took over the newer products from the start, Britain importing from Germany most of the complex mass-produced precision tools she required, for example. Thus, British exports of machinery (excluding locomotives) were 689,000 tons in 1913, 562,000 in 1929, the post-war peak, and only 438,000 in 1937.[68] Despite the continued decline of ex-ports, there was substantial revival during the thirties, based preponder-antly on domestic sales,[69] behind strong tariff protection. The building

[67] Britain still retained a clear lead in this product. However, whereas in 1913 her ex-ports were fully 75 percent of the total of the five leading exporting countries (United Kingdom, Germany, France, Switzerland, and the U.S.A.), in 1929 she supplied only 47 percent of the total. I.L.O., *The World Textile Industry*, II, 107.

[68] "Commercial History and Review of 1937," *Economist*, Feb. 12, 1938, p. 52.

[69] In mining machinery, exports retained much of their previous importance, with the

boom, a considerable re-equipment of staple industries (notably coal, iron, and steel), and an armament program created boom conditions. In addition, there was a growing market in equipping such rising industries as food, drink, and tobacco, printing and bookbinding, refrigeration, air-conditioning, and so forth.[70]

The period thus ended prosperously. The great danger, as with other staple trades, lay in the excessively narrow basis for that affluence—a home market inflated by prosperity and by a superimposed armament demand, with exports failing to take their accustomed place. Another war, bringing a continuance of temporary well-being, will merely increase the hardships of inevitable readjustment at its close. Nevertheless, in the short run at least, in the engineering trades, as in wool, iron and steel, coal, and even shipbuilding, the middle thirties witnessed an appreciable change for the better. For many of the staple industries the dismal twenties gave way to the hopeful thirties, and this change represented a substantial adjustment to their altered international competitive position.

---

increase of gold, copper, and other mining throughout the empire. See "Engineering Supplement," *Economist*, Nov. 14, 1936, p. 14.

[70] For discussions of the engineering trades see *ibid.*; British Assoc., *Britain in Depression*, pp. 285 ff., *Britain in Recovery*, pp. 391–93; Allen, *British Industries*, pp. 134–44.

VII. THE EXPANDING INDUSTRIES

FOR BRITISH INDUSTRY as a whole the period 1919–39 was not simply one of stagnation or decline. The staple trades were organizing in response to the new competitive situation. In addition, other groups arose to compensate, in part, for the decline of the old. British industry was slowly adapting itself to its new place in the world.

Most of the expanding industries may be classified within three fairly distinct categories. First, and numerically most important, were those nonmanufacturing services—distribution, transportation, personal service, entertainment, the professions, government—whose more than proportional growth is the usual concomitant of an expanding economy, an increasing division of labor, and rising per capita incomes. The cheapness of foreign food in the years 1919–39 was an important additional factor releasing British income for the satisfaction of such "higher" consumer wants. Second was the building industry, with its satellites. The great growth of housing activity in Britain during these years was in part merely the upswing of a long building cycle; but there seems also to have been a permanent increase, still in process, of individual and social interest in housing, slum clearance, and related forms of social planning. This is a huge economic group, including not only actual construction but also great industries supplying building materials and house furnishings, and, in a broader sense, much of the development during these years of roads, government services (e.g., sewerage and water supply), and electrical supply. Finally, there were the new industries—those products of relatively recent technological change in which British industrial skill and capital resources found new outlets when returns in the old diminished —in which lies our major interest.

THE NEW INDUSTRIES

The growth of "new" industries during the years 1919–39 in the fields of power (electricity), transportation (automobiles, airplanes), engineering (electrical machinery), metal manufacture (aluminum), textiles (rayon), and chemistry (synthetic nitrogen and dyes, coal hydrogenation), permeating the entire industrial structure, belies any facile generalizations about Britain's industrial decline, about her lack of adaptability or ingenuity.[1] Their rapid rise and the extremely important posi-

[1] See Plummer, *New British Industries*, pp. 347–48, 366, and *passim*.

TABLE 7

THE RISE OF NEW INDUSTRIES IN THE UNITED KINGDOM [a]

A. *Employment and Production*

	EMPLOYMENT				INDEXES OF VOLUME OF OUTPUT		
Industrial Group	1907	1924	1930	1935	1924	1930	1935
Electrical goods [b]	62,300	150,884	192,322	247,948	55	67	100
Electricity supply [c]	22,618	49,788	78,754	102,157[d]	45	71	100
Automobiles and cycles	54,043	192,708	241,012	279,748	42	61	100
Aircraft	...	11,735	21,322	35,032	23	65	100
Silk and rayon	32,272	40,328	69,957	82,035	20	47	100
Hosiery	57,016	98,104	107,191	116,294	70	69	100
Chemical and allied trades [e]	127,959	178,094	178,151	194,011	67	69	100
Scientific instruments, etc.	14,389	23,816	25,279	29,241[d]	...	...	...
Total of above trades	370,597	745,457	913,988	1,086,466	...	...	...
All U.K. industry [f]	7,087,123	7,339,215	7,172,134	7,102,996[d]	85	88	100
Percentage of above trades to all U.K. industry	5.2	10.2	12.7	15.3	...	...	...

B. *Net Output (£000)*

	1907	1924	1930	1935
Total of above trades	46,282	204,996	257,385	310,959
Total U.K. industry	712,135	1,642,054	1,576,814	1,638,082[d]
Percentage of above trades to all U.K. industry	6.5	12.5	16.3	19.0

[a] Source: Board of Trade, *Final Reports*, Censuses of Production. The compilation of such composite tables as this and Table 8, below, offers great difficulties, due to the frequent, often inadequately explained, changes in classification of trade and census data. Lack of comparability in individual cases is not great enough to vitiate the general conclusions drawn. This table includes all of Ireland in 1907, only North Ireland in other years. Figures for 1907 are for all firms, subsequent years only for those employing more than 10 people on the average. Employment figures, the averages for the year, include outworkers. Net output figures include excise duty payments (estimated, but excluded from census), since they represent a contribution by the industry to national income.

[b] Includes all electrical machinery, apparatus, and appliances. The 1907 figures are estimated.

[c] Output indexes computed from League of Nations, *Statistical Year Books*.

[d] Provisional figures from *Preliminary Reports*, 5th Census of Production (published as supplements to the B. of T.J., 1937).

[e] Output indexes are for chemicals, dyestuffs, and drugs only. These comprised about 40 percent of total net output of all chemical and allied trades in 1935. For the group as a whole the indexes are 90, 89, and 100, respectively.

[f] Output indexes adapted from Board of Trade index of production for total mining and manufacturing.

tion which they came to occupy in the entire British economy are shown in Table 7.[2] In 1907 these trades were responsible for about one-fifteenth and in 1935 almost one-fifth of the total net output of British industry.

The new industries differ sharply from the old in degree of dependence upon export markets. This has been a source of strength in a period of secularly declining world trade. It has also, however, been in many instances an evidence of weakness: the small exports a sign of inability to compete, and the large home sales the result of protection.

These new industries were thus unable to compensate for the loss of export markets by the old. As Table 8 shows, their relative growth as exporters has been rapid and significant, particularly if the chemical industries be omitted.[3] But this swift rise in position was due mainly to the great fall of staple exports. In sharp contrast to the disproportionately great importance of the staple trades in exports, the importance of new industries in exports was considerably less than their share in total output. That discrepancy would be even greater if we excluded from national output such nonexporting trades as building and public utility services. Another indication of the failure of these industries to take over their proportional share of exports is the heavy concentration of their foreign sales within the empire. In 1928 only 42 percent and in 1929 40 percent of the exports of the staple trades (coal, iron, steel and manufactures, nonelectrical machinery, cotton, woolen, and worsted yarns and manufactures, rail vehicles, and new ships) went to the empire, as against 53 percent and 54.5 percent, respectively, of the new industries (listed in Table 8). On the face of it, there is no cause for this especially great dependence of the latter upon relatively sheltered markets, except competitive weakness.[4]

[2] The choice of industries is somewhat arbitrary. In general, however, these are the trades which were rather small before the war, but expanded enormously thereafter and for the most part owe their rise to technological changes of the last half-century or so. The classification is not clear-cut. Not only are many other new industries not included, but, in addition, many chemical manufactures and silk scarcely belong at all. Silk is included mainly because of its close link with rayon, making them often indistinguishable in census figures. Besides, world silk production has been a rising industry since the war, due to technological advances which have cut its price, and encouraged by great changes in fashion and consumer demand.

[3] A large section of these varied trades was already important before 1913 and does not really belong in our category. Hence the relative rise of the chemical industry as a whole was much smaller than that of the others: from 4.6 percent to 5.9 percent of total British exports (1907–37) and from 3.0 percent to 5.6 percent of total net output (1907–35). See also note e, Table 7, above.

[4] Omitting chemicals, for reasons already discussed, the latter percentages were even higher: 56.5 percent and 58 percent, respectively. There are exceptions: iron and steel on

Moreover, the newer products bulked far larger, relatively, in imports. As Table 8 shows, imports in this category were higher than exports throughout 1929 (this discrepancy increased between 1929 and 1931); excluding petroleum products,[5] exports exceeded imports only after 1913, and then not appreciably. Heavy protection invalidates comparisons after 1929. This record contrasts sharply with the far more important staple products, imports of which were of the same order of magnitude, but exports of which were £299, 344, and 379 million in 1907, 1913, and 1929, respectively.[6] Moreover, "new" imports would have been considerably larger during the twenties but for protection. Automobiles and parts were subject to a 33⅓ percent duty from 1915 until August, 1924, and after July 1, 1925. Commercial vehicles and parts became subject to duty in April, 1926, and tires in April, 1927. Reflecting the lapse and reimposition of the former (McKenna) duties, imports of cars and parts (excluding tires) were in 1925 almost double their 1923 and 1926 levels. Silk yarns and manufactures were subject to duty from July 1, 1925, and in 1929 imports were half their 1924 level. Other new products which enjoyed protection in the twenties were certain chemicals (notably various coal tar derivatives) and photographic films (protected up to August, 1924, and after July, 1925; in 1929 the latter made up about ⅖ of the imports of "scientific instruments, etc.").

Previous discussions suggest the causes of this relatively poor showing of the newer industries in foreign trade: Britain's lack of the increasingly important cheap hydroelectric power, petroleum, and nonferrous metals, her habituation to older methods and products, her lack of a broad uniform domestic market. Still, British manufacture of automobiles, silk and rayon, electricity and electrical goods, synthetic dyes, and many other products expanded rapidly. Nor was protection in all cases necessary, as the unprotected electrical manufactures demonstrate. The newer industries attracted men of talent and imagination, less hampered by the conservatism and excessive individualism of the staple trades. They enjoyed more than did the old industries the technical advantages

the one side, and silk on the other, but the contrast remains clear—even, indeed, if we omit from the staple trades coal, which went almost exclusively to continental Europe.

[5] "Manufactured oils," mainly petroleum products, are really a special class of "manufactures," the heavily rising imports resulting from Britain's deficiency in the raw material. Therefore totals which omit these products are also given.

[6] The constituents of the 1929 figure are listed in the preceding paragraph. The two earlier figures have the same composition, except that they include all textiles (excluding apparel).

TABLE 8

THE NEW INDUSTRIES AS EXPORTERS AND IMPORTERS [a]

(*In £000*)

A. Exports

	1907	1924	1929	1930	1935	1937
New Industries [b]	31,660	82,377	99,155	83,053	72,623	91,889
U.K. exports, total	426,035	800,967	729,349	570,755	425,834	521,391
New industries as percentage of U.K. exports	7.4	10.3	13.6	14.6	17.1	17.6
Net output, new trades, as percentage of total U.K. net output [c]	6.5	12.5	...	16.3	19.0	...
New Industries, excluding chemicals, etc.	12,127	47,978	63,939	53,635	46,134	61,359
New industries as percentage of all U.K. exports	2.8	6.0	8.8	9.4	10.8	11.8
Net output, new trades, excluding chemicals, as percentage of total U.K. net output [c]	3.5	8.3	...	11.4	13.4	...

B. Imports

	1907	1913	1924	1929	1935	1937
New products [b]	43,666	58,926	107,692	107,803	61,808	82,151
U.K. imports, total	645,808	768,735	1,277,439	1,220,765	756,041	1,027,824
New products as percentage of U.K. imports	6.8	7.7	8.4	8.8	8.2	8.0
Excluding manufactured oils, etc.:						
New imports	34,427	45,128	68,522	64,376	29,190	35,627
New exports	29,501	42,917	73,456	90,556	67,463	86,012
Total U.K. imports	636,569	754,937	1,238,269	1,177,338	723,423	981,300
New imports as percentage of all U.K. imports	5.4	6.0	5.5	5.5	4.0	3.6
Imports, staple goods [d]	43,509	60,457	75,336	87,030	36,678	64,108
Staple goods imports as percentage of total U.K. imports	6.7	7.9	5.9	7.1	4.8	6.2

[a] Source: *Annual Statements of Trade of the U.K.* See also note a, Table 7, above. Exports are of U.K. products only; imports are gross.

[b] The industries are, in so far as possible, the same as in Table 7, above: electrical machinery, electrical goods and apparatus, all road vehicles and parts (including chassis and tires), silk and rayon yarns and manufactures (excluding apparel), hosiery, chemicals and allied products (chemicals, drugs, dyes, colors, manufactured oils, fats, resins, excluding explosives), and scientific instruments and apparatus (excluding electrical appliances). Imports of new products differ only in excluding cycles and motorcycles, a small group.

[c] From Table 7, above.

[d] Coal, iron, steel and manufactures, cutlery, hardware, etc., machinery (except electrical), new ships, rail vehicles, textile yarns and manufactures (except silk and rayon).

of modern research and of size (and the dangers of monopoly). The heritage of the old economy inevitably carried over into the new, but many of its obstructive traits were much less apparent there.

AUTOMOBILES

In the late 1930's no fewer than 1,300,000 people in Great Britain derived their livelihood from the manufacture, sale, operation, or servicing of motor vehicles. If to this total were added those engaged in producing the huge amounts of raw materials consumed by that industry, the automobile would appear by far the leading employer of British labor.[7]

The motor industry of no country can compare with that of the United States. America's high per capita incomes and great distances gave her the marked and enduring advantage of a huge uniform market for such a standardized and convenient means of cheap transportation. Her industry, young and alert, discovered this market and adapted its general methods to it before 1914, while Europeans were still making a specialized, limited, luxury product.[8] On any other ground than comparison with the American industry the growth of the British industry has been great and noteworthy, as Table 9 shows. A promising development [9] was cut short by the first World War, when plants were converted to war purposes and foreign markets were lost. But recovery was rapid, and the great continuous post-war expansion was only temporarily halted even by the 1929–32 depression. Prices fell steadily throughout (see Table 9), as British producers learned to make low-cost cars in great quantities.

In foreign markets, too, the industry made progress, as Tables 9 and 10 show. Exports bore a remarkably stable relation to total production throughout and constituted a definitely rising proportion of the world's total. They grew steadily, while American cars flooded world markets in the late twenties; when sales of the powerful, heavy gasoline-consuming American car declined sharply during the depression, in the face of tariffs, diminished world buying power and onerous gasoline taxes, the lighter, lower gasoline-consuming British car, better suited to the shorter distances and gentler gradients of England, made the greatest gains by

[7] See "British Motor Industry," *Economist*, Special Section, CXXI (1935), 1129; Society of Motor Manufacturers and Traders, *The Motor Industry of Great Britain*, 1938, p. 51; "The Colossus of Roads," *Economist*, CXXXII (1938), 57; British Assoc., *Britain in Recovery*, p. 311.

[8] Plummer, *New British Industries*, pp. 72–73, 89.

[9] Allen, *British Industries*, pp. 175–76.

TABLE 9

AUTOMOBILE PRICES, PRODUCTION, AND TRADE IN THE UNITED KINGDOM [a]

(*000 cars*)

Year	Output	Price Index [b]	"Real" Price Index [c]	Imports	Exports	Exports as Percentage of Output
1907	12.0	...	...	8.2 [d]	2.5 [d]	20.8
1913	34.0	76.0 [e]	132.8 [e]	13.0	11.0	32.5
1922	73.0	...	...	22.4	3.0	4.2
1924	146.6	100.0	100.0	23.7	15.7	10.1
1925	167.0	97.1	96.6	47.7	29.1	17.4
1929 [f]	238.8	75.0	80.0	37.8	42.0	17.6
1930	236.5	68.1	75.5	11.3	29.8	12.6
1931	226.3	60.8	72.1	3.6	24.3	10.7
1932	232.7	59.6	72.4	3.1	40.2	17.3
1933	286.3	61.4	76.8	4.0	51.7	18.1
1934	342.5	51.8	64.3	12.5	57.6	16.8
1935	403.7	49.8	60.9	15.4	68.2	16.9
1936	461.4	49.0	58.3	14.8	81.7	17.7
1937	507.7	50.5	57.2	23.2	98.5	19.4
1938	447.6	...	...	12.2	82.5	18.4

[a] Sources: Society of Motor Manufacturers and Traders, *The Motor Industry of Great Britain* (annual); 1938 figures from Board of Trade, *Annual Statements of Trade,* and "Commercial History and Review of 1938," *Economist,* Feb. 18, 1939, p. 56. Table includes private cars, taxis, commercial vehicles, and omnibuses.
[b] Private cars only.
[c] Price index adjusted for changes in cost of living.
[d] From trade figures; chassis figures for 1908 used in 1907 totals.
[e] 1914.
[f] Output figures for 1929 and after are for years ending Sept. 30.

far. Depreciation of the pound and empire preference also helped to spur British sales after 1931; but the gain was by no means merely temporary. In 1937 Britain's share in world markets was still far above its 1929 level, sustained by the general failure to remove gasoline taxes in time of recovery, by the spread of good roads, and by the steadily declining price of the British product. As a result, Britain was in 1937 second only to the United States in exports and in total production as well.[10]

Nevertheless, the record of the British motor industry was not one to inspire great optimism concerning its future. What headway was made in international competition was effected primarily by benefit of protec-

[10] *Economist,* CXXXIV (1939), 274, and CXXI (1935), 1194–96.

TABLE 10

EXPORTS OF PRIVATE AND COMMERCIAL AUTOMOBILES BY LEADING COUNTRIES [a]

Years	U.K.	U.S.A.	Canada	France	Italy	Germany	Total
			(000 automobiles)				
1924	15.7	178.7	56.7	48.7	19.0	2.3	321.1
1925	29.1	302.9	74.2	63.8	29.1	1.8	500.7
1929	42.0	537.2	101.7	49.0	23.7	7.8	761.4
1933	51.7	107.0	20.4	25.5	7.5	13.4	225.4
1937	98.5	395.2	65.9	25.1	33.0	64.9	682.6
			(Percentage of total)				
1924	4.9	55.7	17.7	15.2	5.9	0.7	100.0
1925	5.8	60.5	14.8	12.7	5.8	0.4	100.0
1929	5.5	70.6	13.4	6.4	3.1	1.0	100.0
1933	22.9	47.5	9.1	11.3	3.3	5.9	100.0
1937	14.4	57.9	9.6	3.7	4.8	9.5	100.0

[a] Sources: adapted from *Economist*, CXXI (1935), 1195–96; Society of Motor Manufacturers and Traders, *The Motor Industry of Great Britain*, 1938, p. 142.

tion and preference. Exports, which never exceeded 20 percent of domestic production in the inter-war years, were concentrated almost entirely in empire markets, where they benefited throughout by tariff preference.[11] Secondly, its home market had to be heavily protected, as we have seen.

The major cause of this weakness was the predominance of the American producer, who offered more and more power, in standardized models, at less and less cost.[12] However, while it was, perhaps, inevitable that the British should make fewer cars than the Americans, there was little excuse for their production of more varieties, something fatal to maximum efficiency and to minimum prices. It was a common practice of British manufacturers to offer a large number of models, in the hope that one would catch the public fancy and pay for losses on the others. In 1937 the six leading British producers, making roughly 350,000 private cars, turned out more than forty different engine types and an even greater

[11] The empire took 86.7 percent of them (by number) in 1925, 86.4 percent in 1929, 67.4 percent in 1932 (British cars benefiting in non-empire regions during the depression from the partly temporary factors already mentioned, while empire buying power was especially severely deflated), and 84.6 percent in 1937.

[12] Large-scale British production of high-powered cars, such as would be suitable to more rugged foreign terrains, was impeded by a system of taxing domestic cars on the basis of their horsepower.

number of chassis and body models, which was considerably more than the number offered by the three leading producers in the United States, making perhaps 3,500,000 cars.[13]

As with other protected industries, this one, for all its great growth, tended to sit back and enjoy the profitable protected home market. Non-empire markets were neglected, in sharp contrast to America's active world-wide network of sales and service organizations. Joint action to reduce the number of models, to permit greater plant specialization and standard mass production methods, and to provide the necessary but expensive foreign sales and service organizations, which many of the manufacturers could not afford individually, was not forthcoming.

Perhaps in the future the British motor industry will need above all a gradual reduction of the tariff behind which it has thus far found prosperity and excessive comfort. For such comfort cannot endure. The fact that in 1938, for the first time, depression brought a serious fall in total output would appear to indicate that the protected home demand was confined in increasing degree to more readily postponable replacement requirements. For a heretofore expanding industry, whose home market appears to be approaching saturation at existing prices, the only remedies, if expansion is to continue, are a more aggressive sales policy and lower prices. Only thus can lower income levels be tapped and exports expanded. The secular increase of production of a new product for a people with high per capita incomes, in a protected market, by methods copied, without much improvement, from the United States, offers no excuse for smugness. The acid test and *sine qua non* of the British automobile industry will be, in the long run, its efficiency, its growing ability to compete in international markets without protection or special favors.[14] But these fears belong mainly to the future. The period 1919–39 was one of great and continuous growth.

THE ELECTRICAL INDUSTRIES

By their great and satisfying expansion in the years 1919–39, the industries producing electricity, electrical machinery, and other electrical

---

[13] And this 40 was a reduced figure, compared with depression years. *Economist:* "The British Motor Industry, I," CXVII (1933), 756; CXI (1930), 698–99; Allen, *British Industries*, p. 187. It was estimated that in 1937, for fully 26 out of 40 models, sales were less than 5,000 cars apiece. *Economist*, CXXXI (1938), 132.

[14] It was primarily on the basis of the experience of the automobile industry that a minority of the Balfour Committee recommended immediate abolition of the McKenna duties, in 1929. *Final Report*, pp. 281–88. See also *Economist:* CXXXI (1938), 708; CXXX (1938), 169–70; CXI (1930), 698; CX (1930), 62; *Statist*, CXVI (1930), 411–12.

goods and appliances have won a place among the basic industries of Great Britain. They gave employment in 1937 to about 480,000 workers. Even this figure conveys inadequately their true significance. Electricity supplies Britain's main source of industrial power; electrification has been a focal aspect of national economic development and the modernization of industry. Moreover, it promises to expand with national growth, and continuously decreasing unit costs promise to tap ever lower strata of demand.[15]

Expansion of electrical output in Great Britain was long retarded by the same general factors that retarded the modernization of her industrial plant—the real and psychological dead weight of the past. In 1924, according to the Census of Production, only 49.7 percent of total British power in use in industry was electrical, in contrast with 1925 figures of 73 percent for the United States and 67 percent for Germany. In 1930 the percentage (60.6%) was probably still as far behind, proportionately, as was that of 1924. And, as might be expected, this relative deficiency of industrial electrification was most pronounced in the staple trades.[16] Lack of enterprise and vision has also been manifest in the electricity-supply industry itself. Power was long generated by a great multitude of local plants all over the country, varying widely in efficiency, each employing its own frequency and supplying different voltages, all obtaining few of the benefits of co-ordinated large-scale production and transmission and of a broad varied market.[17] As a result, the amount of electric power generated in Great Britain during the 1920's lagged far behind that of the United States and Germany, not only *in toto* but also per capita.

Nevertheless, growth was continuous, in absolute terms, during these years. The output of the authorized public supply companies rose from 4.7 and 4.2 billion units (k.w.h.) in 1920 and 1921, respectively, to 10.3 in 1929. Of the world's six leading producing countries, only Britain and Japan actually expanded their output between 1929 and 1932, and

[15] See British Assoc., *Britain in Recovery*, p. 256; British Electrical and Allied Manufacturers' Association (B.E.A.M.A.), *The Electrical Industry of Great Britain*, pp. 116–17, 181.

[16] On the basis of B.E.A.M.A. estimates of the amount of electrification needed by all British industries *a*) to reach German standards and *b*) to reach a theoretical optimum within existing capacity, coal, iron and steel, and cotton textiles together accounted for *a*) 62 percent and *b*) 74 percent of the respective totals, *ibid.*, pp. 128–30; see pp. 125, 132–34.

[17] "The British Electrical Industries," *Statist*, Suppl., Dec. 17, 1938, pp. 1–2; Plummer, *New British Industries*, pp. 13–14, 20–23.

Britain has since retained a notably higher proportion of world output than in the former year. Her total output rose steadily from 15.8 billion k.w.h. in 1929 to 17.0 in 1932 and 28.8 in 1937.[18]

Britain was catching up. This progress was in large measure the result of a thorough reorganization of the supply industry by the Central Electricity Board under the act of 1926. The board has been responsible for planning and operating a national production system, setting an end to the chaos of numerous small-scale local producers. It established the "Grid," a national network of main transmission lines interconnecting all public supply stations, enabling it to supply electricity in great quantities to authorized distributors and to concentrate the required production in the most efficient plants. Bulk sales, concentration of output, and the general program of reducing the excessive number of generating plants, all entailed steadily falling costs.[19]

As a result partly of the falling costs, partly of the normal expansion of the market for any new source of power as new uses are discovered, the demands for electricity have increased greatly in amount and variety, in the home and in industry. This expansion has been largely coterminous with the adjustments of the entire British economy, with the recovery and re-equipment (and electrification) of the staple trades, the growth of newer industries, such as chemicals, paper, hosiery, rayon, and motor vehicles, most of which used electricity from the start, and with the housing boom, involving a growing demand for electricity in new homes and new regions.

The rapid concomitant growth of electrical manufacturing industries is clearly shown in Table 11. It is difficult to evaluate this growth of the industry taken as a whole. The weakness of exports relative to output shown in Table 11 was apparently moderate before 1930. However, during the late 1920's the rapid recovery of German producers and continued

[18] Years beginning April 1. Output of authorized public supply stations rose even more rapidly, from 10.3 billion units in 1929 to 22.9 in 1937 and 24.4 in 1938. Gr. Brit., Central Electricity Board, *Annual Reports*. Many businesses which had previously been producing their own electricity found it more profitable, as rates fell, to buy it, and closed down their own generating plants. British Assoc., *Britain in Recovery*, pp. 253–54.

[19] Much reorganization, however, remains necessary. The Grid is only a system of production. In distribution there remain much of the duplication, disorganization, inefficiency, and excessively small units, which formerly characterized the production end. The multiplicity of local political and business interests prevents a much needed reorganization. See "The British Electrical Industries," *Statist*, Dec. 17, 1938, pp. 2–3; Plummer, *New British Industries*, pp. 23–29, 31–36; T. E. Elias (ed.), *British Commerce and Industry*, London, Russell-Square, 1934, I, 187 ff.

secular rise of the Americans left British exports far behind.[20] Imports at the same time supplied a rising share of British consumption and far exceeded the imports of her major competitors.[21] While this was in large measure the result of British free trade, it was also the result of her comparative backwardness in particular lines.[22] Thus, it would appear, output for both domestic consumption and export was retarded by some competitive weakness.

On the other hand, after 1930, when exports lagged far behind production, British exporters seem actually to have gained ground in comparison with their rivals,[23] thus indicating that the decline in total world trade, rather than any particular British disability, was the major factor. However, this relative strength was the result in part of trade policy, of the British tariff and of preferential tariff treatment in empire markets,[24] the need for which may indicate a lingering competitive weakness.

The electrical manufacturing industry is in reality a large group of industries which produce a great variety of products and in many respects have had sharply divergent experiences. There is a "heavy" section, producing electrical machinery, which is in general the older branch.

[20] The rise in Britain's share in the exports of these three leading exporting countries from 26.1 to 34.5 percent between 1913 and 1924 was the result of the disorganization of German industry, whose share declined from 54.2 to 30.3 percent in the same period. And even then Britain could not penetrate such German-dominated markets as the continent of Europe (Balfour Comm., *Survey of Metal Industries*, p. 340). Between 1926 and 1929 British exports increased but slightly, and their share among the three leaders declined rapidly: from 32.7 percent in 1927 to 26.3 percent in 1929. Computed from B.E.A.M.A., *The Electrical Industry of Great Britain*, p. 85, and the respective official trade statistics.

[21] See Table 11. Britain in 1925 took about 9.2 percent of total world imports, as against 1.9 percent for Germany and 0.9 percent for the United States. League of Nations, *The Electrical Industry*, pp. 21, 26, International Economic Conference, Publications II, 1927, No. 7.

[22] See below, pp. 118–19, where her imports are shown to have been greatest in those lines in which her industry's efficiency apparently lagged most, and whose exports were in turn the least, relative to production.

[23] "The Electrical Equipment Industry," *Economist*, CXXVII (1937), 665. Using official export figures converted on the basis of average annual exchange rates, the British share of the three-country total ranged from 27.5 to 28.6 percent in the years 1935–37, compared with 26.3 percent in 1929. Such a computation, employing the nominal official German exchange rates, if anything understates the true comparative value of British sales. In 1937 British exports were closer to their 1929 peak of £19.5 million than either the German or the American. Moreover, they spurted from £18.5 million in 1937 to an all-time record of £21.8 million in 1938, while the American declined.

[24] The empire took about 61 percent of total sales, excluding machinery, in the years 1924–28, and, in the years 1934–37, a portion steadily rising from 63 to 71 percent. These contrast with an empire portion of all British exports around 45 percent in the late twenties, and 48 percent in 1935 and 1937.

TABLE 11

GROSS OUTPUT AND TRADE IN ELECTRICAL GOODS IN THE UNITED KINGDOM [a]

(£000)

	1907[b]	1924	1930[c]	1935[c]
Gross output				
Machinery	4,312	19,242	24,273	28,169
Insulated wire and cable	5,262	24,097	24,624	20,906[d]
Other goods and apparatus	4,524	25,622	38,777	57,778
Total	14,098	68,961	87,674	106,853
Exports of U.K. goods				
Machinery	996	5,353	6,313	4,089
Insulated wire and cable	1,802	4,477	4,546	2,685
Other goods and apparatus	668	6,204	7,414	7,014
Total	3,466	16,034	18,274	13,787
Retained imports				
Machinery	570	985	973	330
Insulated wire and cable	365	570	958	239
Other goods and apparatus	716	2,641	6,289	3,009
Total	1,650	4,196	8,220	3,578
Exports as percentage of output				
Machinery	23.1	27.8	26.0	14.5
Insulated wire and cable	34.2	18.6	18.5	12.9
Other goods and apparatus	14.8	24.2	19.1	12.1
Total	24.6	23.3	20.8	12.9
Imports as percentage of consumption				
Machinery	14.7	6.6	5.1	1.4
Insulated wire and cable	9.5	2.8	4.6	1.3
Other goods and apparatus	15.7	12.0	16.7	5.6
Total	13.4	7.3	10.6	3.7

[a] Compiled in detail from *Final Reports*, Census of Production; *Annual Statements of Trade*. Exports are f.o.b, imports c.i.f., gross output figures value at factory, so comparability is only rough. 1907 figures include all of Ireland and firms employing 10 or less; later figures do not.

[b] 1907 trade and output figures for wire and cable exclude telephone and telegraph wire.

[c] All 1930 and 1935 figures include vacuum cleaners with "other goods and apparatus"; in 1907 and 1924, when separate figures are not available, they are left with machinery. Figures for the earlier years must have been small.

[d] Apparently not exactly comparable with earlier figures, the comparable 1930 figure given by 1935 census being £21,586 instead of £24,624.

What may be rather arbitrarily designated the "light" section produces miscellaneous electrical goods and apparatus: telephone, telegraph, radio, lighting appliances, batteries, meters, insulating materials, and other equipment, goods generally not far removed from the ultimate consumer. From this second group we have singled out production of electric insulated wire and cable for separate consideration, because its story differs radically from the rest. The second group is in general the younger; the great expansion of output of the lighter goods is more largely a post-war phenomenon. Thus, as Table 11 shows, the gross output of "other goods and apparatus" expanded almost thirteenfold between 1907 and 1935, while electrical machinery and wire and cable were in 1935 only six and one-half times and less than four times their 1907 values, respectively.

As elsewhere, Britain fared better in the older lines. The new "American" methods, mass production with machines and semi-skilled labor of standardized products for a broad consumer market, has revolutionized particularly the "light" section, where the price factor is dominant. Such methods and considerations are far less applicable to the installation of electrical equipment, involving heavy capital expenditures, where quality and skill remain most important.[25] To this lag in newer lines, the relative backwardness of the British home market for electrical products contributed. In 1925, when British, American, and German exports were all about equal, total British output of these goods was only half the German and less than one-fourth the American.[26] Moreover, the chaos within the electrical supply industry, with its variety of voltages and frequencies, helped to perpetuate a profusion of small-scale firms, producing a large variety of products, thus retarding standardization of output, which would have lowered costs and enhanced competitive ability, particularly in the newer lines. The machinery and wire and cable branches, which were best able to compete, were in fact much more closely knit, better organized, with fewer and larger producers, who could afford to push exports.[27]

Thus, the enormous expansion of British output in the lighter branches, far more than in the heavy groups, was essentially for the home market alone, as Table 11 clearly shows. Similarly, of the exports of electrical goods by the six leading countries in 1927, Britain supplied 32 percent

[25] B.E.A.M.A., *The Electrical Industry of Great Britain*, pp. 3–13, 22–23.
[26] League of Nations, *The Electrical Industry*, p. 21.
[27] "The British Electrical Industries," *Statist*, Suppl., Dec. 17, 1938, pp. 4, 7; Balfour Comm., *Survey of Metal Industries*, pp. 286–87, 302.

of the machinery and fully 54 percent of the less important wire and cable group, but only 22 percent of the already most important group of "other goods and apparatus." [28] The same factors which made free-trade Britain a relatively weak exporter of these miscellaneous lighter goods, while demand rose very rapidly, made her also a heavy importer. Imports of these goods supplied a greater portion of domestic consumption than did imports in the other categories, and as foreign (mainly American) radios, vacuum cleaners, batteries, etc., poured into the British market from 1924 to 1930, the ratio rose from 12.0 to 16.7 percent. These products thus offer unique instances in which before 1932 British exports of manufactures were much smaller than her imports. Thereafter, the tariff cut imports sharply, but they remained far more important than in other branches throughout, both relative to total output and in absolute amounts (see Table 11).

However, there is evidence that the balance was being redressed. Exports in the lighter branch of the industry expanded more rapidly than in the other branches throughout this period, both proportionately and absolutely. Shipments of wire and cable reached their peak in 1926. Those of machinery fell after 1927, although in 1938 the 1927 figure was exceeded. Exports of other electrical goods continued their strong rise throughout 1929, and in 1937 they alone of the three groups had surpassed 1929 levels.

Increased domestic sales, rationalization and expansion of electricity supply, industrial combination, increased research activities, co-operative extensions of sales and export organizations have steadily lowered costs and enhanced the competitive ability of the manufacturing industries.[29] The enlarged demand created by the growing electricity supply system, by the re-equipment of old and the upsurge of new industries, by railway electrification, the housing boom, and a rising effective consumer desire for all the electrical amenities of modern living, have made this a period of great prosperity. Since exports of the lighter branches were above 1929 levels in 1937 and 1938, and of machinery in 1938, their decline relative to output was not a depressing influence. It was probably in larger measure the consequence of the increase in foreign trade barriers and of a resultant preoccupation with the domestic market rather than of inadequate

[28] Adapted from figures in B.E.A.M.A., *The Electrical Industry of Great Britain*, Appendix B, Table I; see also pp. 74–75, 223–29; League of Nations, *The Electrical Industry*, pp. 76–78 ff.

[29] B.E.A.M.A., *op. cit.*, pp. 45–56, 61–63, 180; Balfour Comm., *Survey of Metal Industries*, pp. 289–91, 303, 306–8; Plummer, *New British Industries*, pp. 47–52.

competitive strength compared with other exporting countries.[30] The home market promises to continue to grow, with increased electrification of the railroads and of the virtually untouched rural areas, with slum clearance and post-war reconstruction. The need for exports, which the British economy as a whole will soon feel again, will not effect the electrical industries for some time.

RAYON

The British rayon industry has also expanded considerably. The output of rayon yarn, so small that it was not recorded separately in the 1907 Census of Production, rose rapidly with technical development, improved quality, increased attractiveness, and falling prices, to about 6.6 million pounds in 1913, 24 million in 1924, 57 million in 1929, and 120 million in 1937. A mass market for cheap clothing luxuries is being tapped as prices continue to fall.[31]

In its international aspects, however, the British rayon industry has not shown great strength. In 1924, before the 1925 tariff drastically reduced them, yarn imports exceeded exports by 60 percent, supplying almost 40 percent of British consumption. Although exports of piece goods were fully 36.8 percent of output in 1930, imports were not much smaller, amounting to 32.2 percent of consumption. Exports of all rayon manufactures declined rapidly after 1928; imports, on the contrary, expanded greatly both in value and quantity throughout 1931, despite duties imposed from July 1, 1925. Since in 1937 exports could not have exceeded their 1928 quanta (they were far below in value), it was exclusively for a secularly expanding home market that output increased so enormously (rayon piece-goods production was 178 million square yards in 1930 and 464 million in 1935).

In 1925 Britain appears to have been the world's leading exporter of rayon manufactures.[32] Rather incomplete data show that in 1935, on the contrary, Japan led all other exporters by a vast amount, with exports probably twice as great as those of France, Italy, Germany, and the United Kingdom combined. The predominant part of British exports has

[30] British Assoc., *Britain in Recovery*, pp. 271–74; "The British Electrical Industry," *Statist*, Suppl., Dec. 17, 1938, pp. 7–8.

[31] Balfour Comm., *Survey of Textile Industries*, pp. 281 ff.; "The Rayon Industry," *Statist*, CXXVII (1936), 941–42. All statistics of British and foreign output of yarn are from League of Nations, *Statistical Year Books*, and annual "Commercial Histories and Reviews" of the *Economist*. Figures on British piece goods production from Censuses of Production.

[32] "The Artificial Silk Industry," *Economist*, Monthly Suppl., Dec. 26, 1925, p. 47.

gone to the empire, favored by preferential duties, and, since 1934, by severe quotas against Japan in the crown colonies.[33]

Despite the remarkable growth in her output of filament rayon, Britain has been steadily losing ground in comparison with other nations. In 1913, according to an estimate of the League of Nations, she led all others, accounting for some 32 percent of world output.[34] Her share declined steadily after the war, to 16.5 percent in 1924, 12.9 percent in 1929, and 10.7 percent in 1938, until it was far behind those of Japan, the United States, and Germany.[35]

The dangers of excessive attention to a protected home market and of weak exports (except to empire markets) will undoubtedly become more apparent in the future, when rapid expansion of home demand ceases. Nevertheless, as in other new industries, the dangers still lie in the future.

THE BUILDING INDUSTRIES

The second large group of expanding occupations is building and its ancillary trades. These industries have virtually no direct international significance. Yet precisely because of that fact, their growth was an essential aspect of the evolving international position of the British economy.

The building industry is extremely important and has expanded greatly, as Table 12 shows. Together with the few trades most directly linked with it, it accounted in 1938 for more than one-fifth of the total (insured) employment in manufacturing in the United Kingdom. In fact, its domain spreads even wider, encompassing a large part of the expansion, during these years, of such industries as the quarrying or fabrication of natural and artificial stone, slate, gravel, and concrete; the manufacture of iron and steel for manifold building uses; the production of glass, paints, carpets, oilcloth, and linoleum; of stoves, grates, pipes, and all manner of heating and ventilating apparatus; the supply of electricity, electrical wiring and contracting, and so forth.

Building activity expanded almost uninterruptedly in the years 1924 to 1939. This long-lived boom was a boom in housing. While the amount

[33] I.L.O., *The World Textile Industry*, I, 96; "Banking and Commercial Review," *Statist*, Feb. 19, 1938, p. 20; Plummer, *New British Industries*, pp. 223–24.
[34] Only 27 percent, according to the Balfour Comm., *Survey of Textile Industries*, p. 305.
[35] If the figures for output of staple fiber were included, the relative British decline would be far greater. This product owes its phenomenal rise in recent years to its uses as a substitute for raw cotton and wool, which has led to a rapid subsidized development by totalitarian countries. *Statist*, CXXVII (1936), 941.

TABLE 12

NUMBERS OF INSURED WORKERS IN THE BUILDING INDUSTRIES [a]
(*ooo workers*)

Industry	July, 1923 Aged 16 and Older	July, 1938 Aged 16 to 64 [b]
All United Kingdom		
(1) Total (insured) workers	11,485.8	13,904.8
(2) Total in mfg. industries [c]	6,711.4	7,923.4
All "new" industries [d]	868.5	1,431.4
Building and related industries:		
(3) Building and contracting	844.0	1,378.2
Brick, tile, pipe, etc.	61.2	107.8
Constructional eng'ring	23.2	46.7
Furniture and upholstery	94.1	150.4
(4) Total	1,022.5	1,683.1
(3) as percentage of (1)	7.3	9.9
(4) as percentage of (1)	8.9	12.1
(3) as percentage of (2)	12.6	17.4
(4) as percentage of (2)	15.2	21.2

[a] Compiled in detail from Gr. Brit., Ministry of Labour, *Gazette*, XLVI (Nov., 1938), 446–47.
[b] Excludes throughout various classes of domestic workers brought under the act in that year.
[c] Building and contracting included; gas, water, and electricity supply not included.
[d] Covering, as nearly as possible, the same range of industries as in Tables 7 and 8, above. However, the inclusion here of the entire chemical, and gas, water, and electricity trades definitely exaggerates the total of truly "new" industries.

of other building increased more rapidly in both periods 1924–29 and 1932–37, it also declined far more in the years between. House building, on the contrary, was almost impervious to the usual cyclical influences.[36] The huge industrial rebuilding after 1933, which came with renovation of the staple trades, continued expansion of new trades, and the armament boom, was also very important, but this building can scarcely be classed with the expanding industries of the entire period 1919–39.

Housing was stimulated by special conditions, which had little influence on other forms of building activity. During most of the twenties, as

[36] See *Economist* index of building activity and data in *Abstracts of Labour Statistics, Statistical Abstracts for the United Kingdom*, and the *Annual Reports* of the Ministry of Health.

indicated by the predominance of and the considerable fluctuation in government and government-subsidized building, a major factor was government subsidy.[37] By the late twenties, however, these essentially temporary post-war subsidies were withdrawn, and the government confined itself to granting assistance to local authorities for slum clearance.

The true boom occurred in private unsubsidized construction of houses, mainly for sale. This activity was remarkably stable throughout the depression, began to rise late in 1932, and reached boom proportions late in 1933 and 1934. A steady decline in building costs until early in 1935 undoubtedly stimulated and sustained the boom, just as their rather sharp subsequent rise must have contributed to the leveling off of activity after the 1935 peak. The great decline in interest rates after 1931 stimulated an industry in which interest burdens are very important. However, the cost factor must not be exaggerated. Housing activity was remarkably well maintained from 1929 to 1932, when building costs, according to the *Economist* index, fell much less than did wholesale prices. The effective interest rate made available by building societies, which financed the greater part of the boom, actually fell very slowly. Nor is it conceivable that the less than 10 percent fall in costs from 1929 to 1932 could have been responsible for the subsequent 100 percent increase of output.

The major cause seems clearly to have been increased demand.[38] The migration of labor, with changing locations of industry, the spread of factories and residences to the outskirts of towns, facilitated by the automobile, created an unusual demand for homes. So did a considerable rise in real incomes of the employed in the years 1929–31. Behind all this was a driving force which translated all these possibilities into reality: "an almost revolutionary conception of what are tolerable housing standards among a vast section of the population . . . public appetite has over large areas become omniverous."[39]

In the first half of 1935 private unassisted housing development leveled off. Building activity was sustained by increased subsidized local gov-

---

[37] British Assoc., *Britain in Depression*, pp. 326–28; Kaethe K. Liepmann, "English Housing Policy since the War," *Amer. Econ. Rev.*, XXVII (1937), 503–18.

[38] See the excellent discussions, British Assoc., *Britain in Recovery*, pp. 399 ff., and especially pp. 418, 425–29; "The Housing Boom, I," *Economist*, CXXI (1935), 795–96; Stolper, "British Monetary Policy and the Housing Boom," Q.J.E., Nov. 1941, Part II (Suppl.); also p. 262, below.

[39] British Assoc., *Britain in Recovery*, pp. 432–33; see also Marian Bowley, "Fluctuations in House-Building and the Trade Cycle," *Rev. Econ. Studies*, IV (1937), 174.

ernment expenditures on slum control, by a large increase of industrial capital extensions and replacements, and by rearmament. But with increasing building costs, and a rising cost of living, private housing activity was reaching the saturation point, although it remained at a high level as late as 1938.

This does not mean that the real need for adequate housing had been satisfied. This upsurge of private building was undertaken to meet a great middle-class and lower-middle-class demand. Most of the houses were built for sale, not for rent. The cost was undoubtedly beyond the reach of the bulk of the self-supporting laboring population. Slum clearance programs, on the other hand, the only building which continued to receive government subsidy, touched only the very bottom strata.[40] In the absence of some revolutionary technical advance in building, there seems little doubt that the future satisfaction of this still largely unsatisfied demand, a demand turned into an active need by the destruction of a long war, must increasingly be undertaken by the government.

All Great Britain's rising industries of the years 1919–39 were of one pattern, typified by housing. The greatly increased sales of owner-driven automobiles, of new houses, the increased domestic and industrial consumption of electricity and electrical goods, and the accompanying technological progress and falling unit costs and prices reflect a rising standard of living for the bulk of the population (at least for those who were employed), a growing enjoyment of the amenities of modern existence, with real wages mounting and (after 1932) unemployment diminishing. The total pattern represents, in large measure, a successful adjustment by the British economy to the altered international position of British industry.

[40] Liepmann, "English Housing Policy Since the War," *Amer. Econ. Rev.*, XXVII (1937), 515–18; "The Housing Boom, I," *Economist*, CXXI (1935), 795; Stolper, "British Monetary Policy and the Housing Boom," Q.J.E., Nov. 1941, Part II, pp. 9–20, 147. The political aspects of this problem seem to have been significant. Under Labor government subsidies, considerable numbers of houses were built by local authorities for rent to poorer classes. Conservative governments abolished these subsidies, largely at the complaint of private builders, and buildings thenceforth were constructed mainly for sale. See Ernest Davies, *"National" Capitalism*, chap. iv, *passim*; Norman McKellen, "Housing the People," *Transactions of the Manchester Statistical Society*, Feb. 13, 1935, pp. 9–11.

Part Three
The British Balance of International Payments

VIII. BASIC TRENDS IN THE BRITISH BALANCE OF PAYMENTS

THE MAJOR real determinants of Great Britain's changing position in the world economy, we have stated, were autonomous economic forces largely independent of and beyond the control of British policy. It is the purpose of this chapter to analyze the evolution of the British balance of payments under the impact of these forces.

BEFORE 1914

Throughout the century before the first World War, Great Britain was by far the leading international creditor. Her balances on current account for 1907, 1910, and 1913, presented in Table 14, show how her people were able to add something to their capital abroad in virtually every year from 1850 on,[1] and as much as 100, 150, and even 200 millions annually in these years. For one thing, the British bought almost all their imports of goods and services by equivalent exports; in 1913 Britain was still the world's leading shipper, banker, and exporter of manufactured goods.[2] While in the aggregate the British were thus enabled by their heavy income on past investments to consume more foreign goods and services than they gave in exchange, most of this income was saved and reinvested.

[1] Only during the bad harvests of the late seventies does Britain seem actually to have consumed some very small amounts of her foreign capital, on balance. All references to pre-war balances of payments, unless otherwise noted, are to the estimates of Hobson, *The Export of Capital*, pp. 170, 197.
[2] Even in 1899, a year of war and of practically no capital export, British merchandise exports (£320 million) and service income (£105 million, net) were together almost sufficient to buy her imports (£485 million). Even if British foreign lending and income from past investments had ceased, her people would thus have been able to support by far the major part of their commodity imports by sale of goods and services.

Table 13

Balance of International Payments of the United Kingdom, 1924–38 [a]

(In millions of pounds sterling)

	1924	1925	1926	1927	1928	1929	1930	1931	1932	1933	1934	1935	1936	1937	1938 [b]
Current Balance															
Merchandise trade															
Imports (−)	1,291	1,331	1,253	1,226	1,206	1,229	1,053	870	710	685	754	797	865	1,048	939
Exports	953	940	790	839	853	848	666	461	422	422	460	536	519	606	562
Balance	−338	−392	−463	−386	−353	−381	−387	−408	−287	−263	−294	−261	−345	−442	−377
Net shipping receipts	140	124	120	140	130	130	105	80	70	65	70	70	85	130	100
Net income, overseas investment	220	250	250	250	250	250	220	170	150	160	170	185	200	210	200
Short interest, commissions, etc.	60	60	60	63	65	65	55	30	25	30	30	30	35	40	35
Other receipts	15	15	15	15	15	15	15	10	15	10	10	10	10	10	0
Govt. transactions	−25	−11	4	1	15	24	19	14	−24	−2	7	−2	−3	−4	−3 [c]
Balance on Current Account	72	46	−14	83	122	103	27	−104	−51	0	−7	32	−18	−56	−45
Net Gold Movements	−1	11 [b]	−7	−1	−1	7	−2	31	−15 [c]	−195	107	−115	−166	−190	204
Capital Account															
New Issues, London	−134	−88	−112	−139	−143	−96	−98	−41	−37	−83	−63	−51	−61	−60	−29
Repayments			27	34	35	49	39	27	48	67	42	81	107	61	39
Other long-term movements [a]							40	15	10	10	−15	−70	−20	10	30
Short-term capital															
Bank & Treasury advances									−123	133	15				
London bank liabilities					84	−52	−16	74	67						
Sterling area liabilities								−200				−40	20	13	−72
London bill holdings, foreign account					−61	25	15	35	15						
Residual	63	31	106	23	−36	−36	−5	163	101	68	−79	163	138	222	−127

[a] Sources indicated in Appendix, pp. 293–99, below. The reader is referred to that Appendix for all explanations of the figures in this Table.

[b] 1938 current balance tentative.

[c] See Appendix for explanation of these specific figures.

TABLE 14

UNITED KINGDOM BALANCE ON CURRENT ACCOUNT [a]

(£000,000)

Items	1907	1910	1913
Net outgo on mdse. account (including gold)	142	159	158
Net income from			
Shipping	85	90	94
Interest and dividends	160	187	210
Short interest, commissions, etc.	25	25	25
Other sources	10	10	10
Total	280	312	339
Current balance (+)	138	153	181

[a] Source: *Board of Trade Journal*, CX (1923), 386. These are the only pre-war years for which official estimates are available.

The years 1907, 1910, and 1913 were, however, peak years of a peak decade, and comparisons of the years 1919–39 with them alone are deceptive. Never before had Britain exported so much capital, in absolute quantities, and only in a few periods (1871–74 and 1886–90) as much in proportion to her foreign interest income. The estimates of Table 15 supply a better perspective.

Certain characteristics of the pre-war balances remained unchanged. The trade balance had been passive since 1825 at least, and probably decades before that year.[3] Invisible incomes mounted fairly steadily throughout, in real terms, with the regular accumulation of foreign investments, and expansion of the volume of world trade. They grew faster or more slowly—but they grew.

The most striking fluctuations were the corresponding inverse changes in the balance of trade and in capital exports.[4] These fluctuations were

[3] It is impossible to assign definite dates to these changes because of the arbitrary official valuations of exports and imports before 1854. Stephen Bourne places the change around 1825, in "The Growing Preponderance of Imports over Exports," J.R.S.S., XL (1877), 21–23; see also his *Trade, Population and Food*, pp. 15–20, 31–33. A recent more elaborate investigation shows that the balance was fairly regularly passive at least from 1801 on, and definitely, regularly, and appreciably so (by over £10 million) only after 1824. Schlote, *Entwicklung und Strukturwandlungen des englischen Aussenhandels von 1700 bis zur Gegenwart*, pp. 37, 124–25.

[4] They correspond statistically, because the latter is taken as the converse of the current balance, of which merchandise trade (for which alone accurate figures are available) is

TABLE 15

ANNUAL AVERAGES OF UNITED KINGDOM BALANCES OF PAYMENT, CURRENT
ACCOUNT [a]

(£000,000)

| Period [b] | MERCHANDISE TRADE [c] | | | Net Service Income | Net Investment Income | Balance (Net capital outflow) |
	Imports (−)	Exports (+)	Balance (−)			
1870–74	378.3	317.1	61.2	74.0	48.0	60.8
1875–80	411.1	290.4	120.7	76.6	47.9	3.8
1881–85	419.6	316.1	103.5	77.4	56.0	29.9
1886–90	414.0	320.7	93.3	82.1	82.1	70.9
1891–99	480.3	331.5	148.8	87.2	92.6	31.0
1900–1904	571.0	384.0	186.9	103.5	104.7	21.3
1905–9	669.5	514.0	155.5	126.8	138.2	109.5
1910	. . .	. . .	159.0	125.0	187.0	153.0
1913	. . .	. . .	158.0	129.0	210.0	181.0

[a] Sources: 1910 and 1913 from Table 14, above; all other years from Hobson, *The Export of Capital*, pp. 170, 197. These estimates are extremely rough and contain considerable error. However, they are the only complete series available.
[b] These periods are chosen, although they are of uneven lengths, in order best to demonstrate the fluctuations of the current balance.
[c] Includes coin and bullion.

conditioned by two major factors. First, there were long- and short-run changes in British and world demand and supply functions. Secondly, there were shifting relative marginal efficiencies of capital in different regions of the world. During the nineteenth century the development of the world's debtor countries, by means of international and domestic capital, probably fluctuated between greater extremes than did domestic investment in an older country like Great Britain. This was partly because the more exotic foreign ventures were naturally subject to greater vagaries of public psychology, within both debtor and creditor countries. Exuberant optimism and overexpansion and bankruptcy and excessive pessimism followed each other with monotonous regularity. Moreover, the real profitableness of investment in "younger" countries varied greatly as new geographical areas were opened and settled, new natural resources discovered and exploited, new means of transportation invented

the largest and most variable part. Actually, however, whenever more accurate evidence is available, it appears to be true that capital movements and commodity trade balances show the closest (inverse) correspondence.

and applied, and as, after each initial spurt, short-run diminishing returns inevitably set in. Such fluctuating investment brought wide, continually recurring fluctuations in relative levels of buying power in different regions of the world. This meant, in turn, continual changes in reciprocal trade balances along lines determined by world conditions of supply and demand, which themselves were unstable.

In periods culminating in the years 1870–73, 1888–90, and 1911–13, under the influence of this configuration of factors, the incomes of the world's debtor countries increased rapidly, Britain lent heavily abroad, and her exports rose correspondingly. The period from about 1850 to 1873 was one of rapid development of continental Europe and the United States; it witnessed also the beginning of heavy investment in the empire and other outlying regions, mainly in a sustained world-wide railway construction boom. In these years, moreover, the British producer enjoyed a pre-eminence never again matched.[5] Heavy world investment required specifically British ships, rails, locomotives and other capital goods; [6] and rising world incomes inevitably meant a demand for British textiles and clothing. Only Britain was wealthy enough to help younger countries finance their development; she exported capital to them in the form of contractors and managers, capital and consumption goods, and services. In such cyclical upswings British exports expanded far more rapidly than imports, with a definite tendency for the adverse trade balance to diminish (a tendency more or less offset by rising prices), as buying power of the developing foreign countries expanded more violently than her own.[7] The absolute decline or slow ascent of the trade balance (see Table 15), in conjunction with rapidly rising invisible incomes,[8] constituted her huge foreign lending.

The converse was true in the downswing. With the rapid decline of investment in debtor countries by their own nationals and by Englishmen, a situation usually accompanied by severe contraction of over-

---

[5] Clapham, *An Economic History of Modern Britain*, II, 7–8, 13–21.

[6] See Jenks, *The Migration of British Capital to 1875*, pp. 173–75, 420.

[7] Kindleberger, *International Short-Term Capital Movements*, pp. 141–43; see statistics in Bourne, *Trade Population and Food*, pp. 53–54, 57, 174; and Table 16, below.

[8] The growth of income from past investment was not so much the result of world prosperity as of the enormous increase of new investments. The increase of £1,000,000,000 of Britain's foreign security holdings in the years 1907–8 to 1913, estimated by Sir George Paish ("Great Britain's Capital Investments in Other Lands," J.R.S.S., LXXII, 1909, 475; "The Export of Capital and the Cost of Living," *Statist*, Suppl., Feb. 14, 1914, pp. v–vi), at 5–6 percent (a modest return in such prosperous times) would account for a rise in annual income of £50 to £60 million in just those six years.

inflated money and credit structures, these countries suffered especially great income deflation. Previous overinvestment left the world with greatly expanded and not entirely assimilated productive powers, while the great effective demand for goods for investment and consumption suddenly fell off. There ensued a decline in demand for British goods which was not merely cyclical. As we argued in Chapter 5, above, this growth of foreign productive power contributed to a secular deterioration of Britain's competitive position as well. So, in each subsequent cyclical phase, she encountered increasing difficulties due to the trade barriers and intensified competition of countries increasingly capable of meeting their own and others' needs on current and capital account. And in the downswing, with this conjuncture of cyclical and secular changes, British exports lagged considerably behind imports in both value and volume, as foreign lending declined correspondingly.[9]

These fluctuations in Britain's international trading and financial position were accomplished primarily by alterations in the rate of growth of her merchandise exports. It is apparent from Table 16 that imports grew secularly at a much steadier rate than did exports, with the rise of British population, industry, and real incomes and a decline in that proportion of needed food and raw materials which her own productive factors could supply.[10] In times of diminished lending (e.g., 1890–99), this relieved debtor countries of deflationary pressure and hence diminished their need absolutely to cut their purchases from Britain. Thus, Britain suffered no absolute declines in the volume of her exports over any appreciable length of time (i.e., between ten-year cyclical peaks). With the continuous secular expansion of trade, adjustments to these changing capital flows were relatively easy for the British creditor, as well as for the foreign debtor.

The years 1905 to 1913 represented in a sense the last and greatest effort, when a broad new expansion of younger regions far more than offset a secularly diminished British competitive strength. And just as previous investment booms had ended in long periods of relative stagnation and a weaker British balance of payments, so, it was to be ex-

[9] As Table 15 shows, exports rose but 5 percent in value from 1870–74 to 1891–99, while imports increased 27 percent. Correction for the price fall would show an even greater relative rise of imports, prices of which fell faster than prices of exports. See also Table 16.
[10] See also C. K. Hobson, "Export of Capital in Relation to Unemployment," in *Is Unemployment Inevitable?* London, Macmillan, 1924, p. 168. Table 15 shows only one slight decline in the value of imports, in the period 1886–90, and this greatly facilitated a heavy transfer of capital.

TABLE 16

VOLUME OF UNITED KINGDOM TRADE: AVERAGE ANNUAL RATE OF GROWTH IN
PERCENT [a]

Period	Gross Imports	Exports U.K. Goods	Re-exports
1700–1770	1.2	1.2	. . .
1780–1800	5.5	6.1	. . .
1800–1825	1.3	1.2	2.1
1825–1840	3.3	4.0	4.6
1840–1860	4.5	5.3	5.5
1860–1870	4.4	4.4	3.9
1870–1890	2.9	2.1	2.0
1890–1900	2.6	0.7	0.8
1900–1913	1.5	3.3	3.7
1913–1929	1.1	−0.5	−0.4

[a] Source: Schlote, *Entwicklung und Strukturwandlungen des englischen Aussenhandels*, p. 46. Imports, being gross, should properly be compared with exports and re-exports together.

pected, would this one. Nevertheless, earlier peaks were as important as this one, in proportion to the smaller total of international transactions and in view of the higher prices of the later years. And even apart from these peaks Britain had always been adding to her foreign investments and selling a steadily increasing volume of exports. The years 1905–13 differed from preceding decades only in degree, not in kind.

POST-WAR YEARS; THE TRADE ASPECT

If we are to compare the years after 1919 with peak pre-war years in a study of long-run changes, it is necessary also to take the best years of the later period, as we do in Table 17.[11] This comparison and the data of Table 13, above,[12] show in unmistakable terms the most striking and significant general change in the British balance of payments during the inter-war years—the decline and disappearance of the available surplus for investment abroad, the balance on current account. The reduction of this balance by 40 percent in value and perhaps 60 percent in real

[11] The balance of payments mirrors only one aspect of an economy. A "strong" balance of payments is not necessarily the strongest or most desirable total economic position. British living standards increased many times more in the years 1875–1900, when the balance of payments was generally weak, than in the years 1900–1913, when it was strong. See chapter XIV, below.

[12] Allowance should be made for abnormal 1926, the year of the coal strike.

TABLE 17

U.K. CURRENT BALANCES OF INTERNATIONAL PAYMENTS, 1907–38 ANNUAL
AVERAGES, PEAK YEARS [a]

(£000,000)

	1907, 1910, 1913	1927–29	1933–35
Merchandise, including silver			
Imports	712.5	1,220.3	745.3
Exports	577.9	847.7	472.7
	134.6 [b]	373.0	273.0
Shipping	89.7	133.3	68.3
Interest and dividends	185.7	250.0	171.7
Short interest, commissions, etc.	25.0	64.3	30.0
Other receipts	10.0	15.0	10.0
Government transactions	. . .	13.3	1.0
	310.3	476.0	281.0
Balance (+)	176.0	103.0	8.0

[a] Source, *Board of Trade Journal* (annual issues). Gold is excluded.
[b] Merchandise figures given by the official Board of Trade estimates include gold and differ therefore from these, which are from the *Statistical Abstracts for the United Kingdom*.

TABLE 18

UNITED KINGDOM AND WORLD EXPORTS AND IMPORTS [a]

	U.K. VOLUME INDEXES [b]		U.K. AS PERCENTAGE OF WORLD [c]	
Year	Net Exports	Net Imports	Exports	Imports
1913	100.0	100.0	13.11	15.24
1924	80.0	106.4	12.94	17.62
1927	81.8	118.3	11.10	15.92
1929 [c]	86.6	121.3	10.86	15.40
1929			10.75	15.19
1932	54.5	106.9	9.92	16.30
1936	65.4	124.6	10.30	17.60
1937	71.6	132.5	9.87	17.03

[a] Sources: indexes from *Board of Trade Journal*, and Balfour Committee, *Survey of Overseas Markets*, pp. 4, 638. Percentages of world trade from Board of Trade, *Statistical Tables* (1924–30), I, 164–65, and League of Nations, *Reviews of World Trade*.
[b] Official figures for 1924–37 have been linked to 1913 by the Balfour Commission estimates, which make allowance for exclusion of Irish Free State after 1923 and for improved quality of exports, 1913–24.
[c] First series, through 1929 (first figure), from Board of Trade, second, from 1929 (second figure), from League of Nations. No allowance made for exclusion of Irish Free State after 1913. The effect is to conceal part of the decline of Britain as an exporter (its sales to Ireland exceeding Irish exports to the rest of the world) and to exaggerate its rise as an importer (its purchases from the Free State exceeding the latter's purchases from the world outside Britain).

terms [13] between 1907, 1910, 1913, and 1927–29, and to a level barely, if at all, positive after 1930, was the result of a far greater strength of merchandise imports than of exports, while invisible incomes lagged. Such regular passive balances as occurred after 1930 were apparently without precedent in the century before 1913.

The severe absolute decline in volume of British exports (see Table 18) in the period 1919–39 is attributable primarily to the deteriorating competitive position of her industry in a world where the volume of trade was expanding much less rapidly than real income. In the 1920's it was the relative decline of Britain which was the more important. She was the world's leading exporting country in 1913; in 1929 her share in world exports was only 10.86 percent, in contrast with 15.77 percent for the United States. After 1929, on the other hand, the major factor was the great absolute weakness of all world trade, in the face of which Britain's relatively stable share provided but poor consolation. In both cases, as might be expected, the staple trades bore the brunt of the constriction. This is shown in Table 19. The rising exports come for the most part from the newer industries. Only machinery was an inter-

TABLE 19

INDEXES OF EXPORT VOLUME, UNITED KINGDOM PRODUCTS, 1924–37 [a]

Commodity Group	1924	1929	1937
Rising			
Vehicles [b]	100.0	206.1	214.2
"Other" textile manufactures [c]	100.0	129.7	143.0
Chemicals, drugs, dyes, etc.	100.0	129.7	136.4
Electrical goods and apparatus	100.0	130.8	126.7
Nonferrous metals and manufactures	100.0	124.6	119.7
Food, drink and tobacco	100.0	119.5	115.4
Machinery	100.0	123.7	100.5
Declining			
Iron, steel and manufactures	100.0	115.7	77.3
Coal	100.0	96.3	64.3
Wool, worsted yarns and manufactures	100.0	77.0	62.9
Apparel	100.0	93.9	61.0
Cotton yarns and manufactures	100.0	88.4	58.0
All U.K. products	100.0	108.3	90.1

[a] Computed from indexes (annual) in *Board of Trade Journal*. In these indexes are linked together three separate series. The results are therefore only roughly comparable. The products included amounted in 1937 to over 75 percent of total exports.
[b] Road vehicles predominantly.
[c] Excluding cottons, woolens, and silks. Mainly rayon yarns and manufactures.

[13] The mean of the 1927–29 Board of Trade indexes of wholesale prices was 139.5, 1913 base. Prices in 1913 were already above 1907 and 1910 levels.

mediate case, partly because this group includes the growing electrical group, but primarily because the manufacture of machinery to equip the growing industries of the world is, like steel manufacture, still a secularly expanding trade. Exports of machinery, like those of steel, were thus not so weak as were exports of other staples, particularly during the recovery of world investment during the 1920's. However, this recovery of many staple exports, like the rise of the British total, in most cases failed to bring the volume back to 1913 levels, leaving unbroken the long-run decline from 1913 to 1937.

Cottons constitute the clearest and most important case. Between 1913 and 1937, when total British exports were £525 and £521 million, respectively, exports of cotton piece goods declined from £98 to £45 million. This loss of 53 millions constituted in itself a large portion of the postwar balance-of-payments problem.[14]

The rising exports were far from sufficient to compensate for the falling segment. Their rise did keep the total value of British exports in 1937 at the 1913 level, but they could not check a decline of almost 30 percent in the total quantum in this period.

While the volume of British exports and Britain's share of the world total fell steadily, her imports rose almost as steadily in both respects (see Table 18). There were several prominent causes of this phenomenon. One was the great fall in price of foreign foods, in the face of which British demand showed a surprising elasticity. While Britain's population increased roughly by 11 percent between 1913 and 1937, the volume of food purchased from abroad increased by 38.6 percent, despite the introduction of agricultural protection. The British people were eating better in the years 1919–39. Cheaper food and a marked decline of savings after the war released additional income for purchases of other foreign consumption goods as well, before the imposition of the tariff.

The backwardness of British industry was another factor contributing to a rise in imports. We have already seen how imports of both the staples and the newer products increased before the 1931 tariff, despite important instances of tariff protection. The volume of British imports of manufactured goods was in 1929 roughly 142 percent and of exports

[14] See Royal Institute, *The Problem of International Investment*, pp. 61–64. Some of this particular decline was the result of equilibrating tendencies of the British balance of payments, and even more of debtor primary-producing countries' balances, aided by protectionist policy. Hence, had cottons not fallen, no doubt other goods would have felt greater pressure.

only 90 percent of their respective 1913 levels.[15] The tariff, which in large measure merely compensated for the many tariffs faced by British exports, partly restored this balance, but could not check so sharp a recovery of imports of manufactures from 1935 to 1937 as to surpass 1929 quanta in the latter year, while exports continued their secular decline. It should be noted that this was the result primarily of the limitations of Britain's natural resources. By far the greatest share in the rise of "manufactured" imports consisted of raw materials only partially fabricated—especially the newer petroleum and nonferrous metal products, which Great Britain could not possibly produce—some of them for the use of British industry in higher grade industrial operations.[16] Nevertheless, whatever the cause, a decline in competitive ability was indicated.[17]

The weakness of Britain's consumption of the traditionally central raw materials must be blamed for the decline of her imports from 1924 to 1929, and their failure appreciably to rise from 1913 to 1929, both relative to the imports of the whole world. While purchases of foreign food, drink, and tobacco in 1929 were 31.2 percent above the 1913 level and of "manufactures" 42.1 percent above that level, those of raw materials (according to the rather faulty official classification) were but 1.6 percent higher. This was the result of stagnation in the staple industries, whose raw material imports recovered only moderately from 1924 to 1929, offsetting a notable rise of other, "newer" imports. The great rise of British imports before 1932 was thus in goods for consumption, as Table 20 shows. After 1932, on the contrary, the great expansion took place in imports for use of industry, as a result of protection, rising food prices, and a great industrial revival.[18] There occurred a marked expansion of imports of nonferrous metals, petroleum products, rubber, paper-making materials for the greatly expanding printing and publishing trades, and,

---

[15] All volume indexes, series of Board of Trade (B. of T.J.) and the Balfour Comm., *Survey of Overseas Markets*, pp. 4, 638–40, linked. Exports roughly corrected for inclusion of sales to the Irish Free State and for higher average quality between 1913 and 1924.

[16] Clark, "Statistical Studies Relating to the Present Economic Position of Great Britain," *Econ. Jour.*, XLI (1931), 350–52; "Ten Years of Trade," *Economist*, CXIX (1934), 768.

[17] See Snow, "The Balance of Trade," J.R.S.S., XCV (1932), 79–81; Vicose, *Le Commerce extérieur de la Grande Bretagne*, pp. 133, 194, 199–200; H. V. Hodson, in *British Commerce and Industry* (T. E. Elias, ed.), I, 12–14; Macrosty, "The Overseas Trade of the United Kingdom, 1924–31," J.R.S.S., XCV (1932), 611–12.

[18] See Schlie, *Die britische Handelspolitik seit Ottawa*, pp. 36–39.

in the boom years 1936–37, iron and steel and machinery, while electrical goods, textiles, and other manufactured consumption goods remained at their 1929 levels or below them.

TABLE 20

INDEXES OF VOLUME OF UNITED KINGDOM RETAINED IMPORTS [a]

Year	Total	For Use in Industry and Agriculture	Ready for Consumption
1924	100	100	100
1930	113	107	120
1935	108	109	107
1936	116	117	112

[a] Source, Butterworth and Campion, "Changes in British Import Trade, 1924–36," *Manchester School*, VIII (1937), 52.

This heavy rise of imports was to some extent equilibrative. Increased purchases of foreign consumption goods in the 1920's were in part the result of the decrease in British savings, which contributed at the same time to a corresponding decline in foreign lending. Increased imports for the use of industry in the 1930's involved a more subtle type of equilibration. The building boom and the expansion of the printing industry, with correspondingly rising imports of wood and paper materials, are outstanding examples of what happened to British purchasing power released from both foreign lending and the purchase of foreign consumption goods, the former by the disappearance of profitable investment opportunities abroad, the latter by the tariff and cheaper foreign food. It led, not directly to increased compensatory imports, but instead to the increased purchase of domestic products. The rapid recovery of an industry expanding to satisfy the protected home market in turn required greatly increased quantities of foreign raw materials, with the result that in the years 1936–38 any strength imparted to the balance of payments by the tariff or by decreased foreign lending was gone.

However, these imports were not an equilibrating offset to persistently strong balances of payment. They were, on the contrary, themselves an independent and enduring source of British weakness, as we shall see.

Just as the secular expansion of Britain's new foreign investments had been mainly responsible for the secular rise of income from them before 1914, so the loss of investments during the war and the failure to reinvest thereafter at anything like the old rate accounted in large measure for the weakness of this credit item after 1918. The *Economist* estimates that the British lost £850 to £1,000 million, one-fifth to one-fourth of their 1913 foreign investments, as a result of the war, because of sales to raise badly needed foreign exchange and belligerents' defaults.[19] An additional cause of the long-run decline of this income was the weak position of Britain's debtors. For a time they met their fixed obligations out of incomes sustained by new borrowing. After 1928, with the disappearance of new lending and the long depression of world trade, came defaults, transfer moratoria, and rapidly declining returns of equity investments. The resultant failure of Britain to add to her foreign investments and, in the recovery period, heavy repayments of past debts and conversions in London at lower interest rates reinforced this tendency, indicating that there has been a secular decline, attributable to the world's decreasing (effective) demand for British capital as for British goods.

The income earned by Britain's shippers, bankers, underwriters, acceptance houses and insurance companies are also in major part dependent upon the volume of international commercial and financial activity. They, too, suffered during these years from the lag of this activity and from the deteriorating relative position of the British supplier.

POST-WAR YEARS; THE CAPITAL ASPECT

In the years following 1913 real British savings were considerably smaller than in the immediate pre-war years.[20] Inequality in the distribution of British income seems to have reached a peak around 1913, partly as the result of high profits in industry and large income from oversea investments in that year, and to have diminished considerably afterward.[21] The effect of heavy taxes on business profits, incomes, and

---

[19] "British Capital Abroad," CXXIX (1937), 359; CXI (1930), 895–96; see also Kindersley, "A New Study of British Foreign Investments," *Economic Journal*, XXXIX (1929), 9. All subsequent references to Kindersley are to his studies of Britain's foreign investments appearing annually in the *Economic Journal*, from 1929 to 1939.

[20] Clark, *The Conditions of Economic Progress*, p. 397, and *National Income and Outlay*, pp. 249–50; Gr. Brit., Comm. on National Debt and Taxation (hereinafter referred to as Colwyn Comm.), *Report* (Cmd. 2800, 1927), pp. 16–17; Bowley, *Some Economic Consequences of the Great War*, p. 136; Kindersley, in *Econ. Jour.*, XXXIX (1929), 22–23.

[21] Clark, *ibid.*, p. 430. E. A. Radice, on the basis of British experience, casts some doubt upon the usually assumed positive correlation between inequality of income and personal

inheritances and of government social service expenditures after the war has already been mentioned. In addition, real wages rose in the post-war years, due largely to the rigidity of money wages. The greatest gainers were unskilled workers, whose earnings and savings were smallest; hardest hit were business profits, which accounted for perhaps two-fifths of total national saving in 1924.[22] The staple trades, traditionally accustomed to reinvest a large part of their earnings, were especially depressed. Finally, the poor showing of income from oversea investments most adversely affected the investing *rentier* classes. The middle and upper classes, their incomes reduced by these many factors and by depression after 1929, kept up consumption at the expense of savings.[23]

Britain's ability to supply all domestic and foreign demands for her capital was thus diminished. The brunt of this decline was borne by foreign investments, which for perhaps a decade before the war had taken 50 percent or more of national savings. Clark's data show that they accounted for 56 percent of total British (net) capital accumulation in 1907, 22 percent and 33 percent in 1924 and 1929, respectively, and (less than) zero in 1937.[24] As Table 21 shows, 45 percent of all new issues floated in London in 1910–13 were foreign, and only 2 percent in 1934–38.[25]

For only a small part of this decline of foreign lending can discriminatory government policy be held responsible. The sporadic government controls of the 1920's could scarcely have been sufficient to explain it, and the continuous effective official controls of the 1930's, although a restraining influence, were hardly necessary. The major causes in the latter years were the collapse of international credit and the diminished opportunities for international investment. As a result of this diminution of investment outlets and of the continued economic growth

---

savings. However, if business savings, the medium through which the wealthy do most of their own saving, are taken into account, the familiar relation seems to hold. *Savings in Great Britain, 1922–1935,* London, Humphrey Milford, 1939, pp. 20–22, 67, 72.

[22] Colwyn Comm., *Report*, pp. 17–19; Clark, *National Income and Outlay*, p. 96.

[23] Clark, *National Income and Outlay*, pp. 250–54; Radice, *Savings in Great Britain*, p. 22. See also Bowley, *Some Economic Consequences of the Great War*, chap. vi, and pp. 80–82, 114; Liberal Industrial Inquiry, *Britain's Industrial Future*, pp. 245–46, 253–54.

[24] *The Conditions of Economic Progress*, p. 397; Herbert Feis, *Europe, the World's Banker*, p. 5.

[25] See Kindersley, in *Econ. Jour.*, XXXIX (1929), 23; Gregory, "Great Britain and Foreign Investments," in *Foreign Investments*, pp. 120 ff., especially 131, 136; Liberal Industrial Inquiry, *Britain's Industrial Future*, pp. 19–20.

TABLE 21

ANNUAL AVERAGES OF NEW ISSUES IN LONDON [a]

In £000	1910–13	1926–30	1934–38
For the U.K.	43,966	164,560	138,199
Empire	76,864	70,064	25,601
Non-empire	100,570	49,457	4,047
Total	221,400	284,082	167,848
As percentage of total			
For the U.K.	19.9	57.9	82.3
Empire	34.7	24.7	15.3
Non-empire	45.4	17.4	2.4
Total	100.0	100.0	100.0

[a] Compiled from annual year-end estimates of the *Statist* (1910–13), and *Midland Bank Monthly Review* (1926–38). Excludes conversions and shares issued to vendors. The Midland Bank figures explicitly exclude refundings; those of the *Statist* are believed to exclude them also. The two are fairly comparable.

of debtor countries, those countries became increasingly self-sufficient, and were thus enabled to repay large portions of their external debt.

In the 1920's, however, high interest rates reflected considerable demand for capital. The losses resulting from war and the inadequately restored international stability of the first post-war decade both doubtless helped to dampen the ardor of investors. But perhaps most important in Britain's case was her decreased ability to lend. First of all, growing new domestic industries, incapable of financing their own development and promising high returns, pressed against her diminished supply of savings. Secondly, her balance of payments was weak.[26]

The result of strong foreign demands, pressing against a limited supply, was a stiffening of British interest rates during the 1920's, both automatically and through conscious policy of the Bank of England. Consequently non-empire debtors could as a general rule borrow more cheaply in New York than in London.[27] Only empire countries (with the ex-

[26] This weakness may be said to have resulted from an attempt to transfer abroad more capital than voluntary savings (minus domestic investment) would permit and hence may not be considered an independent or additional factor.

[27] See table in Royal Institute, *The Problem of International Investment*, p. 135. The American rates shown there are probably understated for comparison with the British figures for non-empire borrowing, by the inclusion in the former of the cost of Canadian and Australian issues in New York. Empire borrowers probably obtained better rates in New York as well as in London.

ception of Canada)[28] continued to borrow predominantly in London; they obtained more favorable rates because of the psychological preferences of British investors, and the statutory grant to most of their issues, if duly registered and meeting certain requirements, of trustee status, which increased their marketability.[29] Because of this and also because the 1920's witnessed a considerable investment boom in large sections of the empire, these countries took a rising share of the diminished total of Britain's foreign lending (see Table 21).

A decline of Britain's foreign lending, from causes partly external to the current balance—such as actually occurred—might have made for a strong balance of payments. The current balance would then have been induced to adjust thereto via higher British purchasing power and prices. Export costs would have risen relative to those of other countries, as the relative prosperity of domestic industry attracted factors of production from export industries. This is not what happened. During the 1920's it was foreign lending which had to be squeezed down by high interest rates and spasmodic government embargoes to fit an excessively weak current position. There occurred a relative deflation of British prices and purchasing power; wages in export industries were forced down considerably compared with competing exporting countries, and factors of production in these industries were unemployed. Domestic industries, it is true, were more prosperous than export, partly because of factors such as the decline in savings, which contributed also to the reduction of foreign lending. Furthermore, British export costs were thus somewhat enhanced. But the major problem in Britain was not the difficulty of attracting workers actually engaged in export production to domestic industries by higher wages. Instead it was hoped that lower wages in sheltered trades would help absorb workers already unemployed by the fall of exports. Therefore, despite the fact that capital exports were at a lower level than before the war, they were excessive in relation to the current balance. At least until 1931, the preponderant causal influences proceeded from trade, not from the capital side of the balance of payments.

[28] Whereas in the years 1927–30 Canadian new issues sold in the United States exceeded repayments of issues originally sold there by almost $800 million, vis-à-vis England repayments exceeded new issues by $70 million. Tables in *The Canadian Balance of International Payments*, pp. 193–95; also pp. 112, 116–17, 121, 124; Hans Schlie, *Die britische Handelspolitik*, p. 30.
[29] "British Capital Abroad," *Economist*, CXXIX (1937), 364–65; Gregory, in *Foreign Investments*, pp. 105–8.

After 1931 net foreign investment and the positive current balance virtually disappeared. Weakness of the current balance in this period can scarcely be considered the major cause of weakness of foreign investment, despite the fact that the dubious responsiveness of trade to any attempt to transfer large investments precluded any substantial revival of lending. The decline of capital exports was not so much the result of diminished ability to lend as of prohibitively low prospective gain. The interrelationships between the two balances were complex and devious. The maintenance of consumption out of savings during the depression and the release of buying power as a result of cheaper food created a quickened demand in Britain for new goods, houses, newspapers, the cinema and for domestic investment to produce them. Whereas in the twenties much of this demand leaked abroad, for foreign goods and securities, and interest rates were maintained at a high level by the superior attractions of foreign investment, now the collapse of foreign lending, the existence of the tariff, and the fall of the pound all brought easy money and a limitation of the increased demand to home goods. The balance-of-payments situation was eased. Production for the home market and domestic investment recovered rapidly. In time, however, the relative ease of the balance of payments vanished, as domestic revival eventually entailed heavy imports of raw materials and manufactures required by booming home industry. The current balance again became negative, as a result, after 1935. This was in a sense a delayed adjustment to decreased lending.[30]

As in the 1920's, however, the continued change in Britain's current balance must have been the result of factors operating initially upon trade rather than upon capital. The reappearance of heavy adverse balances after 1935 was, if an adjustment to anything, as much an adjustment to the tariff and the depreciated pound, which had helped to ease the years 1932–35, as an adjustment to lending, which had been small ever since 1932. Had it not been for the tariff, the current balance would have fallen much sooner and more rapidly, a fall which would scarcely have been attributable to, or in adjustment of, decreased foreign lending. Britain's weakened competitive position, the great decline in the lending of other countries as well, the relatively long-run difficulties of primary

---

[30] This is even more clearly true of the failure of income from oversea investments to recover to 1929 levels, because new issues no longer offset repayments, and because cheap money in Britain, largely attributable to decreased foreign lending, led debtors to undertake extensive conversion operations.

producers, the spread of economic nationalism, all these factors affecting both her ability to sell and the ability of others to make payments to her, would have, even more than in the 1920's, caused a deterioration of her current balance beyond that dictated by capital factors, regardless of the trend of her foreign loans. It cannot be doubted that the decline of the current balance after 1935 was largely a reflection of the continued operation of these factors—from Britain's point of view, factors from the trade side.

Although thus the disappearance of foreign lending was to a large extent in the 1920's, and primarily in the 1930's, the result of "factors from the capital side"—i.e., decline of savings and of the effective foreign demand for British capital—and although British exports were undoubtedly lower as a result, the evidence indicates that the long-run decline of the current balance was not in major part an adjustment thereto. The reasons are clear. For one thing, even the decline in voluntary savings, by entailing an increased consumption of foreign goods, diminished the current balance far more directly and quickly than it curtailed the attempt to lend abroad. For another, even when Britain did lend in the 1920's, her commodity exports were much less likely to be stimulated than in earlier decades. Just as it was increasingly true in pre-war years, so in the post-war years, a far greater portion of the loans were made to countries who needed British goods less than they needed foreign foods and raw materials, gold, or exchange with which to pay such obligations as reparations. Similarly, more of Britain's capital helped to rebuild industries which within a very short time began to take foreign markets away from her.[31] Finally, not only British but also total international lending was considerably less in the post-war years.[32] And, as we have seen, this was only one of the causes for the diminished buying power of Britain's debtor markets. All these factors, involving a change in world supply-and-demand dispositions which made British industry less able to meet world demands, were more important causes for the decline of British exports than her own decreased lending. For her this decline in sales was thus an initial disequilibrating factor.

The "competitive position" of a country's industry, it appears, is no simple concept. Two separate complements of factors may be distin-

[31] See Royal Inst., *The Problem of International Investment*, pp. 20–22; B.E.A.M.A., *The Electrical Industry of Great Britain*, pp. 182–84; Loftus, *A Main Cause of Unemployment*, p. 55.
[32] Cassel, "The International Movements of Capital," in *Foreign Investments*, pp. 53–60; Ohlin, *Interregional and International Trade*, p. 456.

guished, even though in reality their effects may be utterly indistinguishable. The first, and the more obvious, consists of the supply functions of that country in relation to the supply-and-demand dispositions of the rest of the world, at given levels of purchasing power. The second we may term the "purchasing power factors," changing levels of buying power which result from net changes in balances of payments and levels of investment activity, both of which shift total demand (and to a lesser extent cost) curves of different countries relative to each other and thus favor or hamper various competing suppliers.

Because of certain changes in the world's demand for and supply of primary goods, and because a cycle of heavy investment in the development of these productive facilities was coming to an end, the countries specializing in their production suffered a depression of incomes in comparison with the rest of the world in the years 1919–39. Because Britain's sales were particularly heavily concentrated in those markets, this shift in world demand made for a deterioration of her competitive ability. Supply curves were also thereby altered to her detriment. On the one hand, the factors causing a decline in her own lending also helped to sustain British export costs. This was the minor factor, we have concluded. On the other hand, the primary producing countries were in this way impelled the more rapidly to speed the secular rise of their own manufactures, by government policy and by automatic adjustment, the latter resulting from a release to import-competing lines of labor previously engaged in their export trades.[33] To the primary producing countries the cut in their purchases of British goods was an equilibrative adjustment. For Britain it was in major part an external disequilibrating factor.

Although both complements of causes from the trade side meant the same thing to Britain—a poorer competitive position and a tendency to lower incomes—it is important to note the difference between them, in order to stress the fact that it was a concurrence of many changes which conspired drastically to alter her position in the years 1919 to 1939. Britain's ills sprang only partly from simple technological and managerial backwardness. They were in very large measure the result also of fluctua-

---

[33] That this was not simply an adjustment to decreased imports of capital (let alone British capital only) is indicated by the fact that debtors went into import-competing lines not so much because of a depression of home market industries, caused by a decline of borrowing, but because of the depression of their exports, for other reasons. And their prices and costs fell not so much because of declining domestic purchasing power as because of a decline in foreign demand for their goods.

tions in world levels of buying power, arising outside her balance of payments, factors over which she had not the remotest possibility of control.

THE TERMS OF TRADE

The changing terms at which a country's exports exchange against foreign goods and services are determined in the same processes and by the same factors as determine its competitive position, and the structure and the fluctuations of its balance of payments.[34]

TABLE 22

INDEXES OF THE UNITED KINGDOM BARTER TERMS OF TRADE [a]

(*1913 = 100*)

Period	Import Prices	Export Prices	Terms of Trade
	(1)	(2)	(2) ÷ (1)
1694	68.0	197.0	290.0
1801–15	203.3	288.0	141.7
1816–28	144.7	178.8	123.6
1829–42	117.4	117.6	100.2
1843–50	100.8	93.1	92.4
1851–59	110.0	90.7	82.6
1860–69	129.2	111.1	86.0
1870–76	118.6	108.9	92.0
1877–85	103.5	85.3	82.4
1886–93	87.1	77.4	88.8
1894–03	79.6	77.7	97.6
1904–10	90.8	88.7	97.7
1911–13	98.3	96.7	98.5
1914–18	160.2	150.0	93.6
1919–23	202.8	264.0	130.1
1924–32	127.7	158.5	124.1
1933–37	89.6	123.4	138.0

[a] Source: Clark, *The Conditions of Economic Progress*, p. 453.

[34] The reader is reminded of the classification of these factors adopted above: reciprocal demand and supply dispositions, the product of an enormous variety of technological, institutional, cyclical, and other determinants, and changes in levels of purchasing power, resulting from net changes in balances of payments and levels of investment activity. See pp. 7, 128, 142–43. For an interesting indirect corroboration of the validity of this distinction between two sets of causative factors, in a different connection, see Machlup, *International Trade and the National Income Multiplier*, pp. 115–16.

The most striking technological changes of the century from 1760 to 1860 were those which increased the productivity of Britain's manufacturing industry, and effected equivalent reductions of the unit costs of her exports.[35] Consequently, from perhaps 1700, and more certainly from 1800 to 1860, Britain's terms of international trade deteriorated continuously and markedly (see Table 22).[36] A very large share of the benefits of her industrialization was going to the foreign consumer.[37]

After 1860 the opening of new areas producing food and raw materials, aided by exports of British men and capital, by the railroad, the steam (and refrigerated) ship, and the mechanization of agriculture, bore fruit. Britain relied increasingly upon foreign food supplies and benefited more and more from their falling costs. In more recent years this relative weakness of primary prices was aggravated by the combination of factors already discussed and by a greater downward rigidity of industrial prices than of primary prices, for institutional reasons. As a result, this long-drawn decline of Britain's trade terms at last ceased around 1860 and gave way to an almost equally great and continuous improvement up to the present, although with important reactions or plateaus from 1873 to 1880, 1900 to 1913, and 1924 to 1929.

The fluctuations and the long-run development of these supply and demand factors were intimately related to the operation of a "purchasing power cycle," following much the same tendencies whether it covered a century, ten years, or forty months.[38] Some of the aspects of this

[35] The efficiency of British agriculture too had long been increasing. This had the same effect as cheaper manufactures, for until 1760 Britain was on balance also a heavy exporter of foods.

[36] We refer always hereafter to the barter terms of trade, as measured by the ratio of export to import price indexes; a deterioration or change to Britain's disadvantage is a decline in this ratio, a fall of Britain's export relative to import prices.

[37] Most of the following factual material concerning the terms of trade and volume of exports and imports before 1914 is from Clark's *The Conditions of Economic Progress*, pp. 450–54, and Schlote, *Entwicklung und Strukturwandlungen des englischen Aussenhandels*, pp. 51–52. Another indication of the long-run deterioration of the terms of trade is the effect of the use until 1854 of official valuations, fixed in 1694, for British imports and exports. Whereas these official figures still show a very large active trade balance in 1854, declared values, mirroring the rapid relative fall of export prices, show instead a heavy passive balance.

[38] Tendencies toward three-year cycles of the type about to be outlined in terms of trade and capital movements are demonstrated by Folke Hilgerdt, "Foreign Trade and the Short Business Cycle," *Economic Essays in Honour of Gustav Cassel*, London, Allen and Unwin, 1933, pp. 273–91; see also I.L.O., *Employment, Wages and International Trade*, pp. 29–43.

cycle as manifested in the nineteenth-century British balance of payments have already been briefly explored.[39]

What we may arbitrarily designate the "first phase," it will be recalled, usually experienced a great surge of purchasing power and need for goods in the younger, primary producing countries, both internal credit expansion and import of capital financing a considerable excess of domestic investment over limited voluntary domestic savings. Meanwhile, the opening of these new areas, by construction of railroads and similar investment activities, created a diversion of their productive factors from the provision for their needs or from the production of goods which might be exported in exchange for those required. The pressure of a greatly expanded domestic demand against supply capacities reduced by the pull of factors of production into investment industries usually caused home-market and export costs and prices to rise rapidly. Meanwhile, the more mature creditor economies came to be geared to export of capital and goods, the relative (but seldom absolute) diminution of their domestic investment and consumption demands usually making it possible to satisfy the increased foreign demand for their goods with a relatively small advance in their export prices. Thus, their terms of trade tended to become less favorable.

Just as a creditor country must eventually reach, in its secular development, the stage at which it begins to receive more goods from abroad in income from past investments than it lends abroad in new,[40] so eventually debtor countries must attain the corresponding stage of maturity. In the shorter cycles, these turning points were reached periodically, as we have seen, because of the spasmodic character of such investment activity. They introduced the second phase of the cycle. As voluntary saving capacity in the younger countries increased, investment required perhaps proportionately less credit expansion and certainly proportionately less foreign borrowing. Extreme upward fluctuations in domestic purchasing power tended as a result to be damped down; in the shorter cycles a sharp fall usually occurred. On the supply side, the long time-consuming construction needed to open up new areas, diverting resources for an extended period from the production of needed goods, became relatively less important. In addition, the increased burden of debt put pressure upon producers to expand sales. Increased supply capacities in the face of relatively declining domestic demand resulted in a tendency for export costs and prices in the debtor countries to fall, especially because of the in-

[39] See above, pp. 127-30.   [40] See above, p. 52.

elasticity of the demand for their primary products.[41] Meanwhile, in the creditor countries the relative decrease of foreign demands for goods and capital, the release of capital for domestic investment, and the further augmentation of domestic buying power by the inflow of income from past loans, all tended to attract productive factors from export industries, with consequent reduction of supply of export goods, and to maintain domestic costs and prices.[42] Terms of trade therefore tended, in the second phase, to become more favorable to the lending countries.

These tendencies were more or less offset by the effects of the purchasing-power cycle upon the reciprocal demand curves of the countries involved. True, the relatively declining purchasing power of creditor countries in the upswing could not have seriously depressed primary prices, in view of the low income elasticity of their demand for these goods. However, there are frequent instances, in the shorter cycles before 1914, when the rapidly increasing demands of debtor countries for the coal, iron and steel, and machinery of the creditors actually turned the terms of trade in favor of the latter. Similarly, in the mature stage the more important offset, again particularly effective in the shorter cycles, was the decline in the demand for industrial products with the diminution of investment activity in younger countries. The extreme character of these fluctuations in investment and income of debtor areas in large measure set the pace of world cyclical history in the nineteenth century. As a result, in the upswings the prices of creditor countries seldom fell in absolute terms, and in the downswings their relative rise seldom prevented an absolute decline.

This purchasing-power cycle is inseparable from a cycle of reciprocal demand and supply functions. Historically, the prelude to the "first" phase (the upswing) was usually heavy investment in the manufacturing creditor countries. The increased productive capacities of these countries and the eventual slackening of home investment, depressing prices and interest rates, forced investors, contractors, and manufacturers to seek

[41] It must be remembered, however, that the price inelasticity of demand for food and raw materials (the latter determined primarily by the state of industrial activity) is an elasticity of total demand, and not for the output of any single area. The relative price fluctuations of goods produced by debtor countries will therefore not be as extreme in these two phases as might be expected. In the first phase there is bound to be a tendency toward increased consumption of domestic products in the creditor countries, e.g., a revival of domestic agriculture. And in the second, falling prices of imported goods is likely to lead to a considerable increase in their consumption, as domestic producers in creditor countries are displaced.

[42] See Clark, *The Conditions of Economic Progress*, pp. 466–67.

foreign outlets for their respective funds, talents, and goods, outlets which they found in the first phase. In the second phase, the greatly increased output of the debtor primary producers, their productive power usually expanded beyond the world's immediate ability to absorb the product, in turn forced down their export prices. Shorter cycles continued in this fashion. Thus, in the second phase creditor countries turned again to domestic investment, finding added incentives in the new abundance of capital. The stage was thus eventually set for another spurt of development of debtor areas, with the discovery of new regions, or because increasing world population and industry had again more than caught up with previously overexpanded primary productive abilities.

The two major sweeps of Britain's trade terms, downward until 1860 and definitely upward after 1880, seem clearly to represent one such enormous cycle. Whether or not the idea of so long a cycle, covering perhaps 150 years, seems excessively metaphysical, such factors as we have described were without doubt responsible for the indisputable secular movements. It will be remembered that a crucial turning point in the British balance of payments also occurred around 1875, partly as a result of these price changes, partly as a result of the longer-run industrial (supply-demand) and financial (purchasing power) factors underlying them.[43]

An interesting break in the secular movement occurred between 1900 and 1913, when the previously rapidly improving terms of trade leveled off; indeed, during most of the intervening years they were slightly less favorable to Britain than in the period immediately preceding.[44] These years witnessed the upswing of a shorter cycle of the type outlined. Purchasing-power factors alone tended to alter the terms of trade in favor of debtor countries and against Britain.[45] Factors of supply and

[43] See above, pp. 51–53.

[44] It is difficult to make of the period anything worse than a plateau in the long-run development, for by 1911–13 the trade terms were almost back at their extremely (and abnormally) high 1899–1900 level. See the indexes of Taussig, "The Change in Great Britain's Foreign Trade Terms after 1900," *Econ. Jour.*, XXXV (1925), 4, and Silverman, "Monthly Index Numbers of British Export and Import Prices, 1880–1913," *Review of Economic Statistics* (hereinafter *Rev. Econ. Stat.*), XII (1930), 147. Nevertheless, this leveling off of a marked earlier improvement was an important phenomenon, with important effects. It is difficult to agree with Sir William Beveridge that there was no break with pre-1900 trends. "Mr. Keynes' Evidence for Overpopulation," *Economica*, IV (1924), 5–9.

[45] Since British capital exports were far from being the sole causal factor or even neces-

demand had the same effect. The previous decade had witnessed a substantially reduced investment in the development of the world's capacity for producing food and raw materials. Supplies were further limited by the attainment of extensive agricultural frontiers and by an incipient drift of population from countryside to town. As a result, the steadily increasing demands of the world's growing population and industries caused primary prices to recover well in advance of appreciable international flows of capital.[46] On the other hand, the industrialization of Western countries, which had been proceeding rapidly in the nineties, greatly increased the competition of manufactures in world markets, and hence held down the prices of British exports.[47] By 1912 and 1913 the situation was being redressed. The terms of trade turned rather rapidly again in favor of Britain when supplies of primary products began to show the effect of the heavy investment, and rapidly rising interest and dividend receipts largely offset the effects of the greatly heightened outflow of capital. The second phase of the cycle was approaching.

These shifting price levels lubricated the long-run flows of capital and of income therefrom. Schlote demonstrates clearly the regular converse fluctuations of Britain's terms of trade and the ratio of export to import volume, the correspondence being particularly close for the longer sweeps.[48] The relative price movements helped to attract or to repel capital and goods together, and the capital flows helped in turn to main-

---

sarily the initial factor, there is not the slightest theoretical necessity for the price movements to correspond with any exactitude to the fluctuations in these capital exports. In fact, the short-run correspondence is very poor.

[46] Sir George Paish, "The Export of Capital and the Cost of Living," *Statist*, Suppl., Feb. 14, 1914, p. iii. Rising farm prices encouraged the renewal of investment; the resultant increase of agricultural output had by 1913 only begun to have its effect on farm prices, which might therefore have been expected to decline in the future on this account alone. *Ibid.*, pp. iv–vii.

[47] Keynes attributed the terms of trade experience from 1900 to 1911 "to the operation of the law of diminishing return for raw products," *Econ. Jour.*, XXII (1912), 631. See also Angell, *If Britain Is to Live*, pp. 56–57. He doubtless erred in mistaking what was in large part a cyclical for a secular phenomenon. Beveridge objected to Keynes's interpretation: "The change observed is just as good evidence of increasing returns in industry." "Mr. Keynes' Evidence for Overpopulation," *Economica*, IV (1924), 15. However, Beveridge did not seem to realize that even the second case need by no means entail a continued rise of real British incomes, which was Keynes's primary concern. ("A Reply to Sir William Beveridge," *Econ. Jour.*, XXXIII [1923], 481–83.) The change *was* partly the result of increasing returns in industry, but it was probably American, German, and Belgian more than British industry. Britain could therefore only lose by her poorer terms of trade.

[48] *Entwicklung und Strukturwandlungen des englischen Aussenhandels*, pp. 51–52. Compare Tables 16 and 22 above.

tain the price and purchasing-power differentials which bound capital and goods in equilibrium.

Nevertheless, any inductive attempt to correlate British capital exports (a function of the ratio of export to import values), year by year, with converse movements of the terms of trade, is bound to fail. The export of capital is very largely a short cyclical phenomenon. Therefore one cannot ignore the abrupt shorter cycles, with peaks in 1871–73, 1886–90, 1904–7, 1909–13, and 1922–28, which do not fit the simple theoretical scheme nearly so well as do the longer sweeps.

The major factor disrupting the neat pattern was the competitive predominance of Great Britain in precisely those goods for which short cyclical demand fluctuated most widely.[49] As a result of the huge international investment activity of the years 1860–73, for example, foreign demand for Britain's goods outgrew her ability to supply them, her terms of trade improved markedly [50] (contrary to "theoretical" expectation), and finally export volume grew despite this fully as rapidly as did import volume. For the same reasons, in the downswing of 1873–80 the collapse of this investment demand and the rise of new industrial competitors of Britain outweighed other influences, causing both a deterioration of her terms of trade and a more rapid decline of export than of import volume. A. G. Silverman has shown that such behavior of terms of trade and capital flows was in fact characteristic of the short cycles in the period 1890–1913. He discovered that an annual increase of capital exports was associated with an improvement of terms of trade, and a decrease with a worsening, more often than the reverse, for the reasons already indicated.[51]

The evidence of rapidly improving British terms of trade accompanying increasing capital exports is no doubt discomfiting to a theory which

[49] See p. 147, above.

[50] Coal export prices, for example, which had averaged 9 to 10.4 s. in the years 1860–71, soared to 15.8 s. in 1872 and 20.9 s. in 1873. See Bourne, *Trade Population and Food*, pp. 242–43.

[51] "Monthly Index Numbers," *Rev. Econ. Stat.*, XII (1930), 145–46; "Some International Trade Factors," *Rev. Econ. Stat.*, XIII (1931), 122, 124. One can easily verify this cyclical relationship by comparing the price indexes with Hobson's capital export figures. In the period 1883–90, when capital export increased greatly, reaching its peak in 1888–90, the terms of trade continued slightly to improve, and improved very rapidly in just the peak years 1888–90. Again from 1904–7, years of very rapid increase of capital export, terms of trade remained approximately constant, and from 1910–13 they actually improved considerably, despite another great rise of lending. See also Ohlin, *Interregional and International Trade*, pp. 470–72; Iversen, *Aspects of the Theory of International Capital Movements*, pp. 368–69.

starts with the capital flow as the initial outside cause to which trade must adjust, via price fluctuations. Nevertheless, such a theory as we have suggested, which makes the change of trade terms part of the pattern, not of one-sided adjustment to capital movements, but of mutual adjustment in which prices and lending are but two interacting components, is by no means disproved thereby. In such a theory neither the exact chronology nor the exact simple behavior of trade and prices demanded by the earlier single line of causation explanations is necessary. There is ample long-run evidence for the place of terms of trade fluctuations in the mechanism of adjustment, as we have already seen. In fact, there is also ample short-run evidence of the same thing, in the very period surveyed by Silverman. But to find such evidence, relative prices must be regarded as one participant, indeed, a whole series of participants, in a complex, ever-changing organic pattern, comprising also changing world demand and supply functions, marginal efficiencies of capital, price and income levels, as well as international lending operations.[52] The failure of orthodox theory to include these various determinants would seem to be explained by the fact that it virtually ignores the business cycle, in accordance with which their greatest fluctuations occur.[53]

It was the concurrent operation of these many interacting factors which sustained the balance of payments so effectively in equilibrium before 1914. The adjustment of trade and capital movements was too

---

[52] Thus the substantial improvement of Britain's terms of trade in the years 1888–90 and 1910–13, years of very heaviest foreign lending, can be explained by factors in our theoretical pattern. The transition to the downswing of the purchasing-power cycle was already taking place, in fruition of the heavy foreign investments of the years immediately preceding. As a result and as a further indication of this, the volume of British imports increased far more in these periods relative to exports than in the preceding years. In addition there was the concurrent heavy cyclical foreign investment demand for British coal, iron and steel.

The considerable deterioration of Britain's terms of trade from 1900–1901 to 1905, despite continued low capital exports, suggests a relative recovery of the price of primary goods, due partly, perhaps, to a revival of domestic investment in those producing countries, partly to their failure to expand productive capacity in the preceding decade. This rise of primary prices in time helped to induce a flow of British capital. But before this occurred the volume of British exports expanded far more than did imports, facilitated by the changed terms of trade, and resulting from the increased foreign need for British goods, for construction, and to satisfy rising consumption demands.

For the considerable improvement of British terms of trade, 1905–7, despite expanding capital exports, and their deterioration 1907–9, one must look again to the great cyclical increase and decrease in investment demand for British goods. British capital exports were often the least rapidly responding part of the pattern, rather than the independent outside initial cause.

[53] See pp. 7–8, above.

efficient to be accomplished in the single causal sequence, depending upon the shift in trade terms outlined by Taussig and others. But it was also too smooth and quick to be induced by the simple mechanism of purchasing power flows described by the more modern theorists, Ohlin and Iversen.[54] It is only when treated as we have indicated, as both determined by many other factors and facilitating their adjustments, that the terms of trade can again take their proper theoretical place, their role and behavior not overemphasized, or underemphasized, or oversimplified.

THE PROBLEMS OF ADJUSTMENT, 1919–39

The basic explanation for the strong rise of British terms of trade in the years 1919–39 is to be found in the superimposition upon the long-run factors operative since around 1880 of the mature phase of a shorter cycle, the earlier period of which culminated in 1913, but was prolonged and intensified in many ways by the war and by the investment boom of the 1920's. During the 1920's a revival of international lending, recovering industrial demand for raw materials, and the spread of valorization schemes all sustained primary prices and kept Britain's terms of trade roughly stable from 1924 to 1929, below the extremely high point of 1921.[55] The great improvement from 1929 to 1933 was, like that of 1920–21, in large measure temporary, but the 1937–38 terms were far above the 1929, and for most of the 1930's they were even farther above the stable 1924–29 level (see Table 23).

The only factors tending to deteriorate Britain's terms of trade were those changes of world supply and demand which made for a deteriorating competitive position of British industry.[56] The decline of world de-

---

[54] Taussig was frankly diffident in his explanation and puzzled at its inadequacy to explain the British experience: "The goods . . . seem to move . . . almost as if there were an automatic connection between these financial operations and the commodity exports or imports." "I find it impossible to see how there can be a complete skipping of the intermediate stage—anything in the nature of an automatic connection." "It must be confessed that here we have phenomena not fully understood." *International Trade*, pp. 239, 261; see also pp. 241–43. By permission of the Macmillan Company, publishers.

The difficulty was not in his inability to find an automatic connection, but rather that he viewed the capital movements as an outside determinant, to which, by some direct or devious single route of causation, trade had to adjust. And into this error the later purchasing-power theorists, claiming therein to have found the sought-for automatic connection, have also fallen.

[55] See John Inman, "The Terms of Trade," *The Manchester School*, VI (1935), 46–48. The use of the very favorable 1913 index as a base minimizes the real improvement thereafter. See also note *b*, Table 23.

[56] See pp. 55–57, above.

TABLE 23

INDEXES OF UNITED KINGDOM TERMS OF TRADE, 1913–38 [a]

(*1913 = 100*)

Year	Trade Terms	Year	Trade Terms
1913	100.0	1930	121.6
		1931	134.2
		1932	134.5
1924	112.8	1933	139.7
1925	116.1	1934	136.4
1926	114.4	1935	134.0
1927	112.7	1936	130.1
1928	112.4	1937	123.6
1929	114.5 [b]	1938	133.3

[a] Source: Balfour Committee, *Survey of Overseas Markets*, 1913–24 series. *Statistical Abstracts for the United Kingdom*, 1924–38. The series is only roughly consistent, being composed of four different series of indexes. The indexes represent the price index for exports of United Kingdom goods divided by the price index for retained imports.

[b] Balfour Committee (p. 4) implies an index of 120 for 1924, which would make all succeeding indexes correspondingly higher, by giving an export price index of 180, an import of 150. Its own data seem to show, on the contrary, an import price rise of 57.2 percent, when corrected for exclusion of Irish Free State. See pp. 636, 638, 655–56. The improvement of trade terms shown in the table for all years compared with 1913 may therefore be taken as a minimum.

mand for British goods, for whatever cause, must have entailed a tendency to a relative fall in her export prices. The failure of this tendency to prevail was the result primarily of the far more serious plight of the countries producing her imports. Another reason, however, was the inflexibility of British prices and costs. The average values of British manufactured exports increased after 1913 more than not only the average prices of food and raw material but of manufactured imports as well. Although this doubtless reflected among other things an increased British concentration in goods of higher quality and an equilibrating price adjustment to decreased foreign lending, it also indicated excessively high British export prices, a result of relative inefficiency.[57]

A simple price adjustment to a deteriorated competitive position, by a decline in terms of trade, was not inevitable in any case. For one thing, the disappearance of foreign lending and the tariff to some extent removed the necessity for the price change. Besides, the relative decline of effective British buying power called for by and inevitably resulting from decreased foreign purchases of her goods might (and did) occur

[57] Daniels, "Overseas Trade of the United Kingdom," *The Manchester School*, **II** (1931), 8.

just as much through deflation of money incomes and unemployment; these changes, too, reduced the discrepancy between reciprocal British and foreign demands and hence obviated the need for a decline in barter terms of trade.

A decline in a country's competitive ability may take the form of poorer terms of trade and be equilibrated in that way. But if its prices do not decline, or if extraneous factors cause other prices to decline more, and if its balance of payments is not sufficiently equilibrated in other ways (e.g., by a rapid expansion of world income, by a decline of its lending, or by a curtailment of its imports), a serious decline in the volume of its sales must ensue instead. The improvement in Britain's terms of trade was thus an additional factor tending to reduce the volume of her exports, relative to that of imports. The elasticity of demand for the products of any one country's manufactures being usually great, and British demand for foreign products showing surprising elasticity, as we have seen, the price factor was responsible for a drastic decline of the ratio of British export volume to import volume—this apart from the nonprice factors tending to have the same effect.

Of itself, an improvement in terms of trade provides an opportunity for windfall addition to national income. A given unit of British labor in 1929 was able to purchase at least 13 percent and in 1937 at least 24 percent more imports than it could have purchased in 1913, on this account alone. In an expanding world economy, from 1880 to 1900, such a change did not prevent the volume of British exports from increasing steadily, thus making possible an even more rapidly increasing volume of imports. In the years 1913–39 it merely intensified the tendencies toward absolute reduction in foreign demand for British goods. Clearly, the extent to which British real income could benefit from the greater cheapness of foreign goods depended upon the ability of those factors of production displaced from her export and import-competing industries to be absorbed into other lines. Whether they went into production of other exports (in order to permit the British people to consume more foreign goods with the same amount of labor) or into production for the home market (imports being unchanged, but procured with less labor) depended upon the British propensity to import. In either case, maximization of British benefits required maximum adaptability.

Before the general tariff British demand for foreign goods was great and growing, and her demand for foreign securities remained strong. Yet she failed to develop old or new export lines sufficiently to pay for them.

The higher sale prices of her exports than of her imports were of little benefit if she was unable to sell enough at such prices to pay for what she required.[58] To some extent, accordingly, the better trade terms were untenable and had to be sacrificed, that is to say, dissipated, in unemployment, by income deflation, and later by a falling pound in order to maintain balance-of-payments equilibrium. Nevertheless, in major part the improved terms were tenable, and the decline of Britain's foreign lending and the operation of the tariff increased that part by further reducing the amount of labor needed in export lines to make possible the purchase of foreign goods and securities.

Therefore there was required, primarily, a transfer to the supply of the home market of British labor that had been displaced from export industries. To the extent that resources were not absorbed, but were simply unemployed, these potential gains from improved terms of trade were wasted.[59]

A necessity for precisely the same kind of adjustment was placed upon the British economy by her changing international financial position. The great decrease in new foreign lending relative to receipts of interest, dividends, or repayments from old loans meant of itself greater use of the fruits of past savings, growing net enjoyment of the output of foreign factors of production, in the form of broader domestic consumption and investment. Like the improved terms of trade, this made possible for Englishmen a life better than their own factors of production had previously been providing.[60]

[58] This is Keynes's thesis, "A Reply to Sir William Beveridge," *Econ. Jour.*, XXXIII (1923), 481–83. However, Keynes seems to treat all, or a major part of, the change of trade terms as the result of British competitive weakness, i.e., as an indication of export prices that were too high. He seems to ignore the fact that the major portion was, rather, windfall gain, so that now less exports were required relative to imports. See Robertson, *Economic Essays and Addresses*, pp. 134–35; also pp. 163–69.

The extent to which this change was favorable depended upon how much of imports of foreign goods and securities the British continued to require, and how much productive equipment could therefore really in the long run be dispensed with in export trades— how much, that is, was simply being dispensed with because it had become less efficient in supplying world demands. A decline of exports because less are needed to procure the same amount of imports is sheer gain. A decline because of decreased foreign demand entails a loss.

[59] Robertson, *Economic Essays and Addresses*, p. 135, and in MacM. Comm., *Evidence*, I, 326; Inman, "The Terms of Trade," *The Manchester School*, VI (1935), 49–50.

[60] This changing creditor position was, of course, closely related to the changing terms of trade. The decrease of lending helped to bring an additional windfall to British living standards in the more favorable trade terms which it in part caused. In turn, the secular demand-supply factors depressing debtors' prices, themselves also partly the result of heavy

Before 1932 Britain was disposed to use a large portion of these increments to her purchasing power, accruing from her changing creditor position, to purchase foreign goods, and to that extent the transfers were
effected without deflationary effect upon debtor countries. However, the
rapidity of the change after 1913 and 1929, the fact that other countries
as well had reduced their lending and were less willing than Britain to
take their net income in goods, and the other secular weaknesses of debtor
countries also made for considerable deflation among the latter, with
resultant absolute decrease of British exports.

British factors of production were therefore displaced from export-
and import-competing lines by this net increase of payments from foreign
countries and decrease of unilateral payments to them.[61] The diminished ability of the outside world to purchase the products of British
factors of production served to offset the potential benefits and the improved terms of trade which the changed flows of payments in part
brought. Only by absorbing the displaced factors into enlarged production for the home market could the benefits be maximized, the losses
minimized. As a matter of fact, this transition was arduous. But there was
compensation for these trials in the benefits which Great Britain won
from higher levels of consumption, from cheaper food, and from the re-
equipment of old industries and the building of new ones, designed to
enhance her competitive ability in world markets and to supply her own
consumers cheaply with the pleasures of modern existence.

There were three highly important and quite interdependent aspects
of the long-run evolution of Britain's balance of payments in the years
1919–39: the decreased competitive ability of her industry, the changing international financial position, and the improved terms of trade.
In each and in all will be recognized the concurrence of purchasing power
and supply-and-demand factors tending to reduce British exports and to
weaken her ability to go on accumulating foreign investments. All thereby
forced upon the British economy the need for important readjustments,
a need aggravated in the years 1919–39 by the changed nature of the
world economy and of Britain's place therein and by the suddenness and
greatness of the changes. But, whereas the first aspect, the deteriorated

previous lending and investment, discouraged further lending. Here was the downward
phase of the purchasing-power cycle described above.

[61] See Loftus, *A Main Cause of Unemployment*, pp. 28–29, 46–48. Like Keynes, however,
Loftus ignores completely the benefits of getting something for nothing—benefits by no
means wholly lost in unemployment.

competitive position, necessitated the best possible adjustment to a bad situation, the second and third aspects had very much more agreeable consequences. Adjustment to them involved taking best advantage of a basically favorable situation, and made for a real advance in the living standards of the British people.

IX. PROBLEMS OF EQUILIBRIUM AND ADJUSTMENTS OF POLICY, 1924–31

THE SECULAR DETERMINANTS of the international economic position of Great Britain in the years after the first World War were continuously operative during the period 1919–39. But in respect to government policy and the shorter-run problems of equilibrium, the years from 1924, when most of the world had returned to at least superficial normality, divide sharply into two shorter periods. In the first, Britain especially and the world in general sought to restore the traditional world economy. After September, 1931, Britain gave up that attempt and cut herself off from the disintegrating international "order." [1]

THE CURRENT BALANCE

The great increase, in real terms, of Britain's adverse balance of trade, as compared with 1913, occurred at the outset of the period 1924–31: from £210.4 million in 1923 to £338 in 1924 and £392 in 1925. The great decline of British exports as a percentage of the world's total likewise occurred in the mid-twenties (see Table 18). The particular difficulties of the export trades became apparent only when they failed to share appreciably in the recovery of world trade in the second half of that decade, while reconstructed continental European industries and coal mines began at last to regain (partly from the British) their former position in world markets.[2]

Coal and the closely related iron and steel manufactures were most sensitive to these variations. The fall of coal exports between 1923 and

[1] See above, pp. 42, 49–51.
[2] By 1929 the value of world exports had risen to 7.6 percent and that of the United States to 7.0 percent above their respective 1925 levels, while British exports had declined by 9.8 percent. Between 1927 and 1929 world and United States exports increased by 5.6 and 8.4 percent, respectively, and British by only 1.1 percent. Between 1913 and 1925 the total value of British exports increased by 46 percent, Europe's (excluding U.S.S.R. and the Netherlands, but including Britain) only by 41 percent. By 1927, however, the British were only 35 percent above 1913, Europe's 45 percent. And from 1927 to 1929 the gap widened, British export values rising by 3 percent, Europe's (excluding only U.S.S.R.) by 7 percent. Statistics in League of Nations, *Memoranda on Trade and Balances of Payments* and *Reviews of World Trade*. See also B. of T.J., CXXV (1930), 659; Loveday, *Britain and World Trade*, p. 154.

1925 was no less than £50 million. The return of the Ruhr to production after the French invasion in the former year and German reparations deliveries into European markets,[3] added to the impact of longer-run factors, were behind the depression which culminated in the great coal strike of 1926. The strike was entirely responsible for the great increase of Britain's passive trade balance in that year.[4]

An additional factor, after 1923, was the return of sterling to pre-war parity. In view of the considerable elasticity of world demand for the goods of any one country, and the relative inelasticity of British costs, the overvalued pound must have depressed British exports considerably, at least initially, and perhaps for many years after 1925. Capping the already inevitable difficulties of the coal industry (as of the other staple trades), this helped put pressure upon coal prices and wages which in turn caused the strike. Throughout 1924 and 1925 British exporters found they could not meet foreign competition largely because of the rising exchange.[5]

The merchandise balance showed some improvement from 1927 until the last third of 1929. Industry recovered from the coal strike; there was some adjustment of prices and costs to the new value of sterling; international trade increased, and British exports shared therein. According to the official (Board of Trade) index, the volume of exports increased by 5.9 percent between 1927 and 1929, as against but 2.5 percent for imports. The passive merchandise trade balance declined steadily from its peak of £490 million, for the year ending March, 1927, to £349 million during the twelve months ending July, 1929.[6]

With the onset of depression, improvement ceased, and the unfavor-

---

[3] These were, of course, not of coal alone. B.E.A.M.A., *The Electrical Industry of Great Britain*, pp. 99–106.

[4] See Macrosty, "The Overseas Trade of the United Kingdom, 1924–31," J.R.S.S., XCV (1932), 609–11. The decline in exports and the increase in imports of coal and iron and steel between 1925 and 1926, directly attributable to the strike, amounted to £94 million. The fact that the total trade balance increased only by £71 million may indicate that it would otherwise have improved. However, it undoubtedly also mirrors some automatic adjustment of other trade, e.g., as a result of the severe decline in the income of the workers participating and otherwise affected by the strike.

[5] The question of whether or not sterling was "overvalued" is discussed below. See also Keynes, *The Economic Consequences of Mr. Churchill*, pp. 20–22; Brown, *England and the New Gold Standard*, p. 219; Gregory, *The First Year of the Gold Standard*, pp. 53, 61–62; Clay, *The Post-War Unemployment Problem*, pp. 74–77; MacM. Comm., *Evidence*, II, 184–85; "Commercial History and Review of 1925," *Economist*, Feb. 13, 1926, pp. 3–4.

[6] Monthly trade data in Board of Trade, *Accounts Relating to the Trade and Navigation of the United Kingdom*.

able trade balance grew again, reaching £407 million in 1931,[7] despite
the prodigious fall of prices. While export volume fell between 1929 and
1931 by 37.6 percent, the volume of imports actually rose slightly, a
strength only in minor part explained by the inrush of goods toward the
close of 1931 in anticipation of the tariff. Extreme foreign deflation and
the spread of protectionism were the major causes of this sharp fall in
sales; the inability of British producers to supply the goods as cheaply
as competitors was probably a minor factor. Imports, on the other hand,
were sustained because the distress selling of foreign producers, among
other factors, made them cheap, because the British market was unprotected and because British buying power was maintained by rigid
money wages,[8] unemployment compensation, and curtailment of savings and foreign lending. The volume of food imports (1924 base) increased from 104.7 in 1929 to no less than 114.3 in 1931, of "manufactured" imports from 135.3 to 139.1.[9] Despite the improved terms of
trade, this meant in value terms an export decline of 46 percent, an import decline of only 28 percent, a poor showing virtually unduplicated
by any other major country.[10] The rise of the passive trade balance was,
of course, far greater in real than in money terms. With other income
declining cyclically, the resultant pressure upon the balance of payments
was enormous.

Even during the world prosperity of 1925–29 Britain's invisible incomes were weak, although the stability of their estimated value is due
largely to inadequacy of data. Shipping income declined after 1927, with
falling freight rates, under the pressure of competition by expanded foreign merchant marines. Only government transactions showed a notable
rise, mainly because of growing reparations receipts; and these were in
large measure made possible only by British capital exports to Germany.
Finally, income from such important groups of foreign investments as
rubber, tea, and nitrates, which enjoyed great earnings in the earlier

[7] The peak was 416 millions, in the 12 months ending November, 1931. However, most
of this rise over 1930 came in October–November, with heavy dumping in anticipation of
the tariff. The balance for the year ending September, 1931, was 392 millions.

[8] It is possible that, by their adverse effect upon employment, rigid money wages had the
net result of reducing the income of the working class. It is not possible to reach a final
determination of this issue here. The fact is that the incomes of British workers were remarkably well sustained.

[9] Imports of the many manufactures consumed by industry declined considerably, thus
hiding an even greater rise in the imports of manufactures for consumption. Vicose, *Le
Commerce extérieur de la Grande Bretagne*, pp. 363–73.

[10] *Ibid.*, pp. 334–46; Snow, "The Balance of Trade," J.R.S.S., XCV (1932), 77–79.

1920's, was now depressed by the persistent tendencies toward overproduction of these goods.

In 1930 and 1931 the deep depression of Britain's debtors and the rapid contraction of international trade and investment brought a great decline of invisible incomes, due to both reduced earnings and transfer difficulties. Their fall of 37 percent from 1929 to 1931 contrasts with the slight increase of the adverse trade balance, and with a decline of 23 percent in wholesale prices (Board of Trade index). Income from overseas investments, according to Kindersley, fell only by 27 percent in these years. The relative strength of this particular source of income was attributable in part to the maintenance of distributions at the expense of reserves and in part to the fixed contractual nature of some of these obligations. The former is indicated by the greater decline (32%) in the Board of Trade figure, which included the reinvested undistributed earnings of the years of prosperity (see Appendix). As for the latter, it will be noted in Table 25 (page 187) that income from government loans actually increased slightly in this period, the returns from new issues of 1929 and 1930 being as yet offset by few serious defaults.

Long-Term Lending

Before 1914 the British government pursued a fairly strict laissez-faire policy toward foreign lending. From 1914 onward, first because of the war, later in a conscious effort to sustain the pound, the authorities and the Bank of England periodically exercised a more or less stringent extralegal control over foreign issues in the London market. It became customary for issuers to obtain the Bank's permission. The Stock Exchange forbade dealings in shares when such permission had not been granted. For the period of about a year preceding and following the return to gold (November, 1924, to November, 1925), the Bank of England, in co-operation with leading financial houses, maintained an unofficial embargo, with some exceptions (certain empire, reconstruction, and refunding loans), in support of the pound. The last period of relative freedom, which followed, was terminated late in 1929 under stress of depression and heavy withdrawals of short-term capital.[11]

Along with these temporary limited prohibitions went an even more sporadic policy of encouraging investments which would directly foster exports and would therefore avoid the danger of weakening the cur-

[11] "Foreign Loans," *The Banker*, July, 1930, p. 11; Royal Institute, *The Problem of International Investment*, p. 77; Richardson, *British Economic Foreign Policy*, pp. 62–63.

rency. This was one purpose of the Trade Facilities Act of 1921, which empowered the Treasury to guarantee foreign and domestic loans where the effect would be to provide employment in England, and of the Export Credits Guarantee Department, established in 1926, to extend guarantees, where necessary, on short and medium credits to importers of United Kingdom goods. Foreign loans were encouraged for other reasons as well. The League and reparations loans enjoyed at least tacit government approval and one, to Austria in 1923, received official guarantee. Empire issues were likewise stimulated by the preferential trustee status conferred upon them by the Colonial Stock Act of 1900.[12]

With the possible exception of the encouragement of League loans, which were part of an attempt to restore the old international order, these were indisputable breaches in the traditional national economic policy.[13] Nevertheless, the breaches were still relatively unimportant in the 1920's. Embargoes were temporary, and heavy, relatively free lending continued. In fact, had there not been a great number of governmentally encouraged issues, the total would probably have been lower rather than higher, even if all restraints had been removed.

Of the eleven years, 1921–31, in only three—1925, 1929, and 1931 —were new overseas issues (Midland Bank figures) smaller than £100 million, and in only the last were they very much smaller. The year 1925 was a year of government embargo; relaxation of the embargo in November and December released so many commercial issues that their total for the year as a whole surpassed that of 1924.[14] The low figure in 1929 was entirely the result of an almost complete cessation of activity in the latter half of the year, the first half witnessing a continuation and extension of the 1926–28 recovery. This decline was the result of higher money rates—attributable mainly to the pull of funds to the United States, France, and Germany—disappointment in the results of previous speculation, and the world-wide collapse of security values. The annual average of new issues for the years 1921–30, inclusive, was £125 million. Adjustment of this average for net repayments and foreign participation therein, on the basis of the estimates which Kindersley has made for the years after 1927, would appear to leave a net outpayment of perhaps

[12] "British Capital Abroad," *Economist*, CXXIX (1937), 365; see p. 140, above.
[13] See Iversen, *Aspects of the Theory of International Capital Movements*, pp. 82–85, 121–22.
[14] Most of the information on year-to-year new issues is from the annual articles and estimates in the *Midland Bank Monthly Review*, the *Economist* annual "Commercial Histories and Reviews," and its review of new issues in the last issue of each year, and Kindersley's articles.

80 to 90 millions. This was hardly stagnation. Not until 1931 were the full effects of the depression felt. Foreign lending fell to insignificance by the end of the year; to this decline the official embargo, higher interest rates, and departure from gold also contributed.

Very little information is available concerning other long-term capital transactions. Of the extensive dealings in existing securities,[15] purchases by Englishmen of foreign dollar securities seem to have been most important. The exuberance of New York underwriters in the 1920's seems regularly to have exceeded the willingness of Americans to absorb foreign bonds, with the result that large quantities flowed to London, through the direct efforts of American salesmen and automatically because of an apparently regular spread between quotations of the same securities in the two markets.[16] In the late twenties the chief offset to this outflow of capital was the apparently steady repurchase by foreign nationals and sinking funds of their sterling debt, especially governmental debt.[17] Another offset was the repayment to the Bank of England by the Bank of France of its obligations incurred in franc stabilization. It was Keynes's opinion, in 1927, that these various flows were roughly offsetting, on balance.[18]

In 1930 and 1931, on the other hand, our own very rough estimates of the net effects of some of these transactions show an appreciable capital inflow into Britain. In both years there must have been considerable net sales of British holdings to foreigners, particularly in repatriations of government obligations and in securities of foreign companies. We have estimated British receipts on these accounts at fully £40 million in 1930.[19]

[15] The *Economist* said in 1929 that their gross total probably exceeded new issues. "The Export of New Capital," CIX (1929), 753.

[16] Keynes, "The British Balance of Trade, 1925-27," *Econ. Jour.*, XXXVII (1927), 554; (Kindersley) MacM. Comm., *Evidence*, I, 80; Einzig, *The Fight for Financial Supremacy*, pp. 53-54, 74-76.

[17] Kindersley, in *Econ. Jour.*, XL (1930), 181-82, XLI (1931), 372-73. Kindersley's figures show an almost continuous decline in the total of British investments in non-empire government issues from 1928 to 1932.

[18] See his estimates, "The British Balance of Trade, 1925-27," *Econ. Jour.*, XXXVII (1927), 551, 555.

[19] See Table 13 (p. 126) and Appendix. New issues of oversea government loans, less repayments, amounted to £58 million; yet nominal British holdings of these public issues rose only £25 million. Since there were no defaults, any reduction in nominal values must have been due to repurchases by foreign nationals (Kindersley, in *Econ. Jour.*, XLII [1932], 180-81). Nominal investment in foreign companies fell by £56 million. Much of this change represented a revision by Kindersley of the earlier estimate, but mining shares, U.S. rails, and other securities were sold in large amounts. Declines in market value cut down actual receipts. See *ibid.*, pp. 194-95.

The lower estimate of £15 million in 1931 is the product of a probable decline in the volume of sales and a growing discrepancy between actual receipts and the nominal values of the securities sold.[20]

The evidence seems to indicate that on balance Britain exported capital at the rate of £75 to £100 million annually from 1924 to 1928. However, in 1929 smaller new issues may have resulted in some reduction of this net total. In 1930 and 1931 heavy repayments and repatriations of outstanding securities, in addition to a heavy decline of new issues in the latter year, apparently brought net long-term capital flows down almost to zero, presaging the experience of later years.

GOLD, SHORT-TERM CAPITAL, BANK POLICY, AND THE PROBLEMS OF EQUILIBRIUM

Gold and short-term capital flows are the barometers of equilibrium in the balance of payments. They may be substitutes for each other, or they may flow together, the one becoming almost a measure of the other. In either case, it is convenient to discuss them together, along with the closely interrelated problems of Bank of England policy and balance of payments equilibrium.[21]

The years 1924 to mid-1928 were characterized in general by an influx of short-term capital into Britain. Net gold movements for these years were virtually nil, however, except for considerable losses in 1925 and gains in the first half of 1928. In contrast to England's ability regularly to retain an appreciable portion of the newly mined gold passing through the London market in pre-war years, this experience suggests than on the whole the capital flows were equilibrative, tending to offset a weak balance of payments rather than independently to make for a strong one. This conclusion is reinforced by a consideration of the constant vigilance required of the Bank of England to hold the balances and prevent gold losses.

[20] Repayments of non-empire government securities amounted to £10.7 million, new issues to only £0.2 million, but the total of such holdings fell by £20 instead of £10.5 million. The difference, Kindersley says, was the result of repatriations. *Econ. Jour.*, XLIII (1933), 189. See also Royal Institute, *The Problem of International Investment*, pp. 318–19. There seem also to have been small continued sales of foreign company investments, at lower market prices, and also of unquoted investments, partly to take advantage of the fall of the pound.

[21] The financial history of these years is familiar. Much of the following factual survey is merely a sketchy summary of discussions in the financial journals, in works cited in the following footnotes; also British Association, *Britain in Depression*, pp. 25–51; MacM. Comm., *Evidence*, I, 192–97, and its *Report*.

It is true that some of the inflows of short-term capital were apparently autonomous, offering independent support to sterling. There were heavy speculative purchases of pounds, and repatriations of capital which had fled in 1923, related to the recovery and stabilization of the pound in late 1924 and early 1925. Also, up to 1928 foreign central banks were on balance acquiring sterling preparatory to establishment of a gold exchange or gold standard. Last of all, there were the intense flights of French capital to Britain before final franc stabilization. However, even these inflows had in large measure to be induced by a British policy, seeking first to raise sterling to $4.86 and striving continuously thereafter to keep it at that level without loss of gold. While America pursued a cheap-money policy from late in 1923 through 1924, British money rates were maintained by informal agreement among the London clearing banks, apparently under Bank of England pressure. The mere official decision to return to gold further attracted foreign funds. When, early in 1925, the New York rediscount rate was raised from 3 to 3½ percent, the Bank of England Rate was promptly raised to 5 percent. The considerable losses of gold late in 1925, which resulted from a reduced Bank of England Rate, a weak current balance of payments, and the renewal of foreign lending with removal of the embargo, necessitated a return to 5 percent in December, at which high level Bank Rate remained until April, 1927.

For most of 1927, as well, British market rates were above the American, as a result of co-operation between the two monetary authorities. The result was a diversion of trade bills from London to New York and some borrowing by London banks in the latter market. In addition, the Bank of France and the Reichsbank were prevailed upon to agree to mitigate their gold demands upon London. The commitment by the Bank of France was in keeping with its determination to prevent a rise of the franc; it acquired great amounts of sterling in the period of *de facto* franc stabilization (December, 1926, to June, 1928) to offset the exchange effects of the heavy repatriations of French capital and of a favorable French balance of payments.[22]

Keynes's rough estimate of the British balance of payments for the years 1925–27, inclusive, shows an inflow of short-term capital of some 150 millions—primarily, it appears, of an equilibrative nature: [23]

[22] W. A. Brown, *The Int. Gold Stand.*, I, 446–58.
[23] "The British Balance of Trade," *Econ. Jour.*, XXXVII (1927), 562; see pp. 555–62.

Debit	£ mill.	Credit	£ mill.
New foreign issues in London	300	Surplus, current account	100
		Bank of France, repayment	50
Other long-term capital, net	0	Net decrease, liquid international assets	150
	300		300

Much of the "inflow" was an automatic or semi-automatic adjustment to the low current balance, in 1926, and to heavy foreign lending. Undoubtedly British banks drew heavily upon their foreign balances, foreign exporters extended commercial credits to English importers to pay for the greatly increased purchases, and borrowers retained in London a large portion of the proceeds of their loans, some of which were for the express purpose of acquiring sterling reserves. These operations doubtless form the major part of the large residual item in 1926 and the smaller ones in 1925 and 1927 in our balance-of-payments estimates.[24]

This aspect of the British balance of payments shifted rather abruptly in mid-1928,[25] and from then until September, 1931, the flow of short-term capital was in general outward. This persistent flow was far from being mainly equilibrative, however; it contributed an independent additional pressure upon an already weak sterling and consequently caused considerable loss of gold. The superior attractions of Wall Street cut off America's foreign lending, and early in 1928 yields on short-term money in New York rose above similar returns in London and remained there. Debtors, unable to borrow in the United States, drew upon sterling balances to meet gaps in their balances of payments; funds were withdrawn from and borrowed in London in order to lend in New York. Sterling was accordingly weak and remained so until the Wall Street crash.[26] Even thereafter the strain was prolonged by the difficulties of primary producing debtor countries on the gold exchange standard, for they defended their currencies by heavy liquidations of sterling balances.[27]

[24] See "Britain's Balance of Payments," *Midland Bk. Mo. Rev.*, Jan.–Feb. 1927, pp. 6–8; "The Export of New Capital," *Economist*, CIX (1929), 753–55.

[25] Indeed, in the first half of 1928 the Bank of England for the first time gained considerable amounts of gold, and the pound was unusually strong in terms of the dollar. The balance of payments position was improved in 1928, as we have seen, and was in addition seasonally strong in this part of the year.

[26] See the interesting study of "The Dollar Exchange, Commodity Prices and Money Rates," *Midland Bk. Mo. Rev.*, Dec., 1929–Jan., 1930, pp. 1–4.

[27] B.I.S., *Ninth Annual Report*, p. 81.

Even more important were the heavy gold drains consequent on French and German liquidations of sterling balances, especially in mid-1928, 1929, and 1930. These countries were passing from the half-way house of the gold exchange standard to the pure gold standard. Their central banks could, or would, no longer extend credit on the basis of sterling holdings, and sold what they had for gold. Their strong balances of payments—the result of franc undervaluation, continued French repatriations, seasonal influx of tourists, and heavy German borrowing —created a heavy continuous offer of sterling for marks and francs. Marks and francs were also in great demand domestically, and interest rates were high, because of domestic recovery, rising prices and wages, heavy hoarding after 1929, and for other reasons. Since the central banks were unwilling or unable to meet these requirements by domestic credit expansion, the commercial banks were forced to sell their accumulated and accruing pounds for gold and to turn the gold into liquid domestic assets.[28] In these ways the financial strength of France, Germany, and the United States and their inability or disinclination to "play the game" subjected Britain to serious strains.

The average value of sterling in terms of the dollar was below par in no less than 60 of the 76 months from May, 1925, to September, 1931. The London price of gold tended persistently to remain at or near the Bank of England selling price, and the Bank could therefore acquire it, as a rule, only by exceeding its statutory buying price.[29] It is clear that, with few exceptions, in all the years Britain was on gold her balance of payments showed a persistent weakness indicative of basic disequilibrium. This was particularly clear in the years 1924 to 1927, when the balance was adjusted only by a fairly continual inflow of short-term capital. A comparison of the current balances and the Midland Bank figures for new issues during these years shows a continuous excess of the latter over the former, although errors and omissions in the available data render any such simple statistical verifications nugatory. The accumulation of French and other balances in London and the necessity for relatively

[28] MacM. Comm., *Report*, pp. 73–75; Einzig, *The Fight for Financial Supremacy*, pp. 94–97; *Economist*: "France and the Gold Influx," CXI (1930), 269; "France and Gold," CXI (1930), 1157–59; see also pp. 46–49, above.

[29] See Watrous Henry Irons, *A Study of the Causes Underlying the International Gold Crisis*, Philadelphia, Univ. of Penn., 1938, p. 157; Brown, *The Int. Gold Stand.*, I, 709, also pp. 706–30. The Bank was saved from more serious gold loss in 1930 by the exhaustion of its fine gold stocks; standard gold being unacceptable to the Bank of France, the franc rate went beyond the British gold export point. Einzig, *The Fight for Financial Supremacy*, pp. 110–17.

higher London money rates in 1925 and 1927 and for the temporary loan embargo in 1925 all indicate that this situation was something more than the temporary effect of the 1926 coal strike.[30]

This balancing of the accounts in the period 1924–27 by increasing the net foreign liabilities of London merely increased the precariousness of her financial position. A higher Bank of England Rate did not reduce new lending so much as it increased liquid foreign liabilities, thus weakening the short position of sterling without effecting any lasting solution of the balance of payments problem. The fact that London was the center for the reserves of the gold-exchange countries aggravated this vulnerability, subjecting her to drains when and if these countries decided to adopt a pure gold standard or if their balances of payments with some other country became weak. Whereas before the war Britain's foreign short-term assets and liabilities were probably fairly well balanced, in 1931 the latter may have been twice as large as the former. And whereas, on the one hand, London's relative ability to hold the increased foreign balances had greatly decreased, on the other, the liquidity of her "short-term" assets was greatly diminished.[31]

A frequently heard diagnosis of the British situation of 1925–31 is that she was "borrowing short and lending long." The disequilibrium of her balance of payments, necessitating these inflows of short-term credits (which occurred in general only before mid-1928), is thus attributed to an attempt to transfer more capital on long-term than the current balance permitted.[32] This interpretation is supported by the existence of factors indisputably tending to sustain foreign lending and to make such lending less responsive to the current balance and to available voluntary savings: notably the traditional connection of the new-issue market with foreign borrowers, the relative lack of bias in favor of domestic investment,[33] and the definite encouragement of the League of Nations loans and empire issues mentioned above.

[30] Royal Institute, *The Problem of International Investment*, pp. 138–41; see, on the other hand, Gregory, in *Foreign Investments*, pp. 120 ff., especially pp. 129–31, and H. V. Hodson, *Slump and Recovery 1929–1937*, London, Oxford Univ. Press, 1938, pp. 83–84. Nevertheless, Hodson does admit (p. 85) that London's short-term liabilities to foreigners would have been less but for her high interest rates, dictated by the pressure upon gold reserves of a weak balance of payments.

[31] Albert Aftalion, *L'Or et sa distribution mondiale*, Paris, Dalloz, 1932, pp. 100–8; MacM. Comm., *Report*, pp. 149–50; Hall, *The Exchange Equalisation Account*, pp. 17–21; Kindleberger, *International Short-Term Capital Movements*, pp. 40–41; Grant, *The Capital Market in Post-War Britain*, pp. 106–7, 112.

[32] Gregory, in *Foreign Investments*, pp. 112–15; Sir Josiah Stamp, "The Monetary Question in Great Britain," *Economic Essays in Honour of Gustav Cassel*, pp. 602–3.

[33] Lord Stamp maintained that increased taxation of business profits in order to meet

However, Britain was not "borrowing short" in order to "lend long" any more than she was "borrowing short" in order to buy more than she could earn on current account or, indeed, in order to "lend short." She was no more "overlending" than "underselling" or "overbuying." Unresilient elements and biases on both trade and capital sides made for lack of mutual adjustment. The automatic forces tending to bring the two balances together were not effective enough. Tiding over disequilibria by the inflow of short-term capital mitigated the deflation of British purchasing power. And the strength of Britain's demand for foreign goods vitiated such deflation as did occur. The causes leading to the flow of capital less readily led to corresponding increased purchases of British goods; as we have seen, this was especially true of the lending to continental Europe. Tariffs and subsidies also blocked the relatively easy adjustment of trade and services. On the other hand, the dwindling British current balance did not readily induce the required curtailment of foreign lending. For one thing, there was a connection in the reverse direction, the low profits of a large segment of British industry increasing the relative attractiveness of foreign as compared with domestic investment and therefore encouraging lending in the face of a decline in the current balance.[34] For another, the anticipated adjustment of interest rates was inadequate; short-term rates were, naturally, far more responsive than the pertinent long-term rates; and even to the extent to which a rise in the latter did occur, its effectiveness was probably limited by the fact that foreign demand for British capital was less elastic than the domestic demand.[35] Certainly the Australian government and capital-starved Germany, offering high returns to investors (regardless of their ultimate ability to pay), were less likely to be discouraged by relatively high long-term rates than were Britain's staple trades.

The causes for the inadequate equilibration of the British balance of payments derived from both the trade and the capital side, and from the outside as well, and the characterization of "overlending" or "lend-

---

national debt service took funds from those more likely to reinvest at home and gave them to investors who were just as willing to subscribe to foreign loans. MacM. Comm., *Evidence*, I, 255-57.

[34] (O. M. W. Sprague), MacM. Comm., *Evidence*, II, 302; Haberler, *The Theory of International Trade*, p. 270.

[35] See Hobson, *Export of Capital*, pp. 40-41. Interest rates sufficiently high to reduce foreign lending to the extent necessary therefore would probably have had serious effects on domestic investment and employment.

ing long and borrowing short" is simply an inadequate explanation.[36]

The disequilibrium of the balance of payments in these years has very often been attributed also to the overvaluation of the pound in its 1925 stabilization at $4.86. According to this interpretation, British costs proved so high and unyielding, in the face of an overvalued currency, that the current balance decreased, and lending which might otherwise have been easily transferred now became excessive.[37]

Currency valuation is customarily judged in terms of purchasing power parities. This criterion has many familiar shortcomings, practical and theoretical, but it is generally agreed that the great recovery of sterling in the latter part of 1924, which occurred counter to, rather than in accordance with, price parities did necessitate some relative decline of British costs.[38] The determining factor in raising the value of the pound was the inflow of capital; British prices in fact rose relative to American prices. Partly as a result of the divergent movements of the exchange and of prices, the trade balance deteriorated considerably roughly in step with the relative rises of market rates over parity exchange rates.[39]

[36] See Gregory, "The Causes of Gold Movements into and out of Great Britain," *Selected Documents on the Distribution of Gold*, pp. 23–24.

[37] For example, Keynes, *A Treatise on Money*, I, 348n.

[38] Gregory, *The First Year of the Gold Standard*, pp. 50–53; Keynes, *The Economic Consequences of Mr. Churchill*, p. 32.

[39] Purchasing power parity rates, based upon the U.S.A. Bureau of Labor Statistics and the British Board of Trade wholesale price indexes, show an almost unbroken fall from a peak of $4.58 in February, 1923, to $4.03 in October, 1924, and a rapid rise thereafter to $4.39 in April, 1925, when the market rate was back at par. The actual rate fell with the parity rate throughout 1923 (largely due to a flight of capital), remaining thus roughly around 103.6 percent of parity, the average for the year. But from 101.4 percent in January, 1924, the market rate rose rapidly to 113.2 percent of parity in November, and 113.9 percent in January, 1925. The more rapid adaptation of prices thenceforth (doubtless largely enforced by the rising market value of sterling) reduced this overvaluation, but it was still 9.2 percent in April, 1925.

A 12-month moving total of the adverse trade balances follows these fluctuations quite closely. From January and April to September, 1922, the market exchange rate declined from 108.7 and 108.8 to a low of 98.7 percent of parity, and the trade balance declined steadily from £268 million in (12 months ending) January to £237 in April and a low of £161 million in September. From September, 1922, to April, 1923, the market rate rose from 98.7 to 104.0 percent of parity, remaining thereafter around the 103.6 percent average for the year. The trade balances in the same period rose from £161 to £216 million and then also stayed around £195–220 for the entire year 1923. Then, corresponding to the increasing overvaluation of sterling from January to November, 1924, and January, 1925, the trade balance totals rose from the low in (12 months ending) February of 212 millions to 329 in November and 368 in January, 1925. Thereafter, however, while the overvaluation declined to but 1.5 percent in November, the trade balance continued to

There is evidence that from January, 1925, prices were adjusting, largely under the influence of the higher pound, and by the end of the year wholesale prices were almost at their 1913 ratio to the American.[40] However, costs could scarcely have been corrected as rapidly as the more or less automatically adjusting prices of international staples, which predominate in the wholesale index.[41] After 1925 it becomes impossible therefore to evaluate the restrictive effect of the original overvaluation of sterling, in terms of the relative price changes since 1913. The coal strike introduced a new overvaluation in terms of British and American wholesale prices, which was only gradually adjusted through 1927 and apparently did not disappear completely until late in 1928.[42]

Overvaluation or undervaluation of a currency can have meaning only with reference to a balance of payments equilibrium which would presumably be attained by a correct valuation. Following our own definition, the correct valuation of a national currency is one at which, given existing supply and demand curves, prices, marginal efficiencies of capital, etc., nationals buy and lend abroad as much as they sell and borrow (on long term) without need for government controls. But since these given conditioning factors are constantly changing and fluctuating, the "correct"

---

rise somewhat, reaching £405 million in April, £416 in June; they stayed throughout the year at an average of about £396 million. Computations by the author. See also Brown, *England and the New Gold Standard*, pp. 214–19; Henry Clay, *The Post-War Unemployment Problem*, pp. 69–73.

[40] The parity rate rose from $4.20 in January to $4.77 in November and $4.87 in March–April, 1926.

[41] See Keynes, "The Committee on the Currency," *Econ. Jour.*, XXXV (1925), 301, and *The Economic Consequences of Mr. Churchill*, pp. 10–11.

[42] The parity rate fell from $4.87 in April, 1926, to a low of $4.51 in November, leaving the market rate 7.6 percent above parity. And the trade balance became increasingly adverse. That both were the result of the strike is clear; the slight rise in the Board of Trade general price index was attributable solely to a very great rise in the price of coal—from 146 to 185 (1913 base). The parity rate recovered only gradually, reaching $4.79 by December, 1927, and $4.89 in August, 1928, and the trade balance recovered, although by no means in close month-by-month correlation with the market-parity ratio.

Comparison of price indexes over as long a period as from 1913 to 1928 is a procedure of doubtful validity. Nevertheless, the return of the price ratios almost precisely to the 1913 level in the years of relative stability, 1927–29, in accordance with theoretical expectation —the actual rate averaged 101.2 percent of parity in 1928, and 99.7 percent in 1929— indicates that this procedure is even more than roughly accurate.

On the other hand, the use of wholesale price indexes affords inadequate indication of what we are seeking because of the inevitable correspondence between price ratios of international staple products and exchange ratios. Nevertheless, the ability of the price ratios, i.e., the parity rate, to diverge so considerably from market exchange ratios in the short run proves that wholesale prices are not useless on this account.

valuation of the currency may itself be constantly shifting, without equivalent domestic price fluctuations.[43] Or there may occur compensating fluctuations in the price variables, which would indicate a shift in the parity rate, yet which might be an instrument or essential condition of continuing equilibrium at the existing market rate. Domestic prices are only one series of shifting variables in the interrelated pattern of causes and effects which condition balance of payments equilibrium and disequilibrium.[44]

Thus, we can no longer be certain about even the initial overvaluation of sterling, from the evidence of price parities alone. Many of the basic determinants of the British balance of payments had changed. Of the factors which diminished the current balance, not all entailed or resulted from relatively high British export prices. Lacking the necessary price adjustments, the pound may therefore have appeared to be at an equilibrium level when in fact it was overvalued; and if the price adjustments were made, purchasing power parities alone would fallaciously indicate an undervaluation. Operating in the opposite direction were the fall in British lending and (considering the dollar rate) the rise in American. Since many of the more important causes from the trade side were price factors, it is impossible to say which of these tendencies caused the greater bias in price parities. Similarly, there were various non-price considerations behind the decision to return to $4.86: the expectation of enhanced financial prestige and higher financial earnings as a result, and the fact that the major part of foreign obligations to Britain were fixed in terms of sterling and would buy less foreign goods if Britain consciously chose poorer barter terms of trade, in a lower pound.[45] As a matter of fact these expectations of a stronger balance of payments as a result of higher sterling value were, it is generally conceded, not fulfilled.

In view of these many non-price factors and considerations the entire balance of payments must be the only satisfactory criterion of the correct valuation of a currency. The evidence of flows of gold and short-term capital, the necessity for embargoes on new issues and high interest rates, may be taken clearly to indicate British currency overvaluation from 1925 onward.[46] While such a condition could probably have been elim-

[43] This Hawtrey calls a "virtual" price change, in itself a "virtual" admission of the inadequacy of price parities as a guide to equilibrium valuation of currencies. *Currency and Credit*, pp. 71, 74, 85–86.

[44] See Ohlin, "International Price Relations," *Index*, V (1930), 158–59; see pp. 156–63.

[45] Argued by Gordon, *Capital in Sterling*, pp. 33–37.

[46] Milton Gilbert, *Currency Depreciation and Monetary Policy*, pp. 37–40.

inated by relative shifts in the external or internal purchasing power of the pound, it might equally well have been eliminated by relative income deflation, or alteration in the level of employment, or a rise in long-term interest rates. The concept of currency overvaluation or undervaluation thus either becomes synonymous with that of disequilibrium, for any reason, or it is misleading, because it stresses only one of the possible causes of disequilibrium or methods of adjustment. In the case of Britain in the 1920's, there can be no doubt that the price (or exchange rate) factor was not the only factor, and perhaps not even the most important one.

There is evidence that the initial overvaluation of sterling in 1924–25 was a significant factor contributing to disequilibrium. However, had the competitive position of British industry not declined for other reasons, such disequilibrium might have been slight and easily eliminated by such price and cost adjustments as did in fact occur. If foreign lending had fallen more readily, sterling would have ceased to be "overvalued." [47] The increase of the adverse trade balance, almost *pari passu* with the increasing overvaluation of sterling relative to purchasing power parity, must be attributed in very large measure to outside factors, notably the return of the Ruhr coal mines and industries to active operation after the French invasion of 1923. It will be remembered that this heavy adverse balance continued after January, 1925, despite an apparent gradual price adjustment. It was the combination of the many factors already discussed, including the choice of a $4.86 pound, which created the difficulties of the period 1925–31.[48] To subsume them all under the statement "sterling was overvalued" is either misleading or leaves that concept with very little meaning.

In 1929 and 1930 the flows of short-term credit were outward, as we have seen. Inflows, it would appear, were no longer essential to continuous balance.[49] The balance of payments was indeed in some respects stronger than in the earlier years—in 1929 because of a somewhat larger current balance, and in both years because of considerably reduced net long-term foreign lending. However, foreign balances flowed out, not so much because London could dispense with them as because she could

---

[47] See Harris, in *Explorations in Economics*, pp. 35–45.

[48] This by no means denies the importance of the high stabilization in 1925, which these other factors made more onerous than it would otherwise have been, but which in turn also made their incidence more severe. See Loveday, *Britain and World Trade*, pp. 147–81, and S. J. Catiforis's sensible refutation of Loveday's minimization of the return to gold, *Le Crise de la monnaie Anglaise*, Paris, Recueil Sirey, 1933, p. 81.

[49] MacM. Comm., *Report*, p. 113.

not possibly hold them. The inadequacy of any adjustments to their outflow is indicated by the heavy losses of gold whenever this occurred.
London's financial position remained technically weak. The damage had
already been done, and one cannot read the contemporary financial
chronicles without perceiving the constant feeling of constraint in view
of the always imminent danger of serious gold loss.

There were only two possible solutions within the framework of
liberal laissez-faire policy to this inherently weak position. One was a
deflation of British prices and incomes, sufficiently severe not only to
restore current equilibrium but also to create a strong enough balance
of payments to dissipate gradually the precarious accumulated short-
term credit position. The other alternative was to free the pound and to
start over again.

The Bank of England, as ever, conceived its first duty to be the maintenance of the external value of sterling. To this end it kept its Rate at a
level which was extremely high for a long period of time, both by pre-
war standards and in comparison with contemporaneous rates in the
United States.[50] In the few instances when short-term market rates did
not press closely upon Bank of England Rate, the bank employed informal measures and open market operations to keep them up, i.e., to
make its Rate effective.[51] And it sought to keep the volume of credit
stable. The inflationary effects upon bank reserves of a steady decrease
of notes in circulation from 1925 through 1930 were slightly more than
offset by a similar long-run decline of the bank's security holdings.
Shorter-run fluctuations in bankers' balances at the Bank of England,
due to gold flows, were likewise offset by open market-operations. There
was no attempt to force money into the banking system despite the relatively heavy unemployment, no inclination to risk any sort of easy-
money policy.[52]

There is sufficient evidence that this policy was to some extent deflationary. The very gradual and relatively slight rise of clearing bank

[50] R. G. Hawtrey, *The Gold Standard in Theory and Practice*, 4th ed., London, Longmans
Green, 1939, p. 125; Keynes, *The Economic Consequences of Mr. Churchill*, pp. 14–19.
[51] Hérisson, *Le Contrôle du crédit à court terme par la Banque d'Angleterre*, pp. 238–39;
Brown, *The Int. Gold Stand.*, II, 1018–19.
[52] See Hérisson, *op. cit.*, p. 250. This fear of declining short money rates was increased
by the perverse habit of the clearing banks of keeping a fixed proportion of secondary
reserve, i.e., liquid bills and similar assets. Any increase of domestic advances thus led also
to an increased demand for bills, depressing the latter rates, and hence endangering sterling
more than would a mere reduction of rates on industrial loans. MacM. Comm., *Evidence*, I,
60–62, II, 174–79.

deposits through 1930, in the face of a stable and even slightly declining credit base, entailed declining reserve ratios. Even this rise is deceptive, for over the whole period 1923–24 to 1929–30, current accounts (demand deposits) were quite stable, the absolute increase being confined to deposit (time) accounts. Since in this period industrial output was expanding and the population was growing, all this added up to some deflationary influence, though the strength of that influence is unmeasurable.[53]

One reason offered in explanation of the Bank's conservative policy was Britain's outmoded fixed fiduciary issue currency system. This system froze the greater part of the Bank's gold as a reserve against an internal drain no longer possible under the gold bullion standard instituted in 1925. At a time when the gold reserve was £150 million, the Bank could not actually stand an increase of domestic note circulation and exports of gold together totaling more than about £35 million, without its Proportion falling to zero, except by emergency permission of the Treasury to increase its fiduciary circulation.[54] The fact that the conservative Bank and Treasury officials were not anxious to change this system does not, of course, necessarily vitiate this argument.[55] Nevertheless, there was merit in their contention that any formal changes would be unavailing. Greater freedom to insulate the domestic economy from temporary gold losses would not remove the danger and threat of continued gold losses or solve the problems of persistent balance of payments disequilibrium, which gave ultimate justification to the conservative policy.

If the Bank kept a steady downward pressure upon bank reserves and resisted any inflation of the volume of credit, nevertheless, it did not institute a drastic deflationary policy to effect more enduring adjustments. It sought always to maintain a stable volume of credit; gold outflows were equally offset. Within the limits of keeping the pound stable by encouraging short-term capital inflows, there was considerable solicitude for the needs of the domestic economy and for the political pressures which prevented real deflation. The main purpose of the high Bank Rate was to attract foreign funds, not to deflate domestic prices,[56] and the

---

[53] See MacM. Comm., *Report*, pp. 101–2; W. A. Brown, *The Int. Gold Stand.*, I, 698–704, II, 1016–17; W. H. Irons, *The International Gold Crisis*, p. 78. See, however, Grant, *The Capital Market in Post-War Britain*, pp. 108, 115, 141–46.

[54] MacM. Comm., *Evidence*, I, 167–69, 182–83 (J. R. Bellerby), 325 (D. H. Robertson), II, 6–8 (Keynes).

[55] Their extreme, often unreasoning conservatism is exemplified by some of their testimony before the MacMillan Committee; see, e.g., II, 6–7.

[56] (Montague Norman), MacM. Comm., *Evidence*, I, 215–17.

Bank used its Rate much more sparingly than before the war, in order to prevent serious disturbance of the domestic economy.[57]

In this fashion the Bank sought from 1924 on "to avoid the Scylla of domestic deflation and the Charybdis of external depreciation." [58] Here was a pragmatic middle-of-the-road policy which satisfied very few. On the one hand, it effected no basic price readjustments, and, on the other hand, it kept a tight rein on the volume of credit. Nevertheless, that policy kept sterling on gold, however precariously, until international confidence completely broke down. It helped make the balance of payments basically more strong by tending to maintain long-term rates and thus to hold down long-term lending.[59] It protected domestic industry from severe deflation. And it gradually evolved the practice of using open market operations regularly to shelter the domestic economy from the effects of erratic independent flows of short-term capital and gold, to which the balance of payments could not and should not have been expected to adjust.[60]

The Bank has been criticized for not deflating in earnest to eliminate overvaluation of sterling as, it was claimed, it would have done before 1914.[61] It may be replied that the costs and difficulties of such a policy may well have outweighed the advantages, that unemployment would as a result have been even greater and domestic industry even further handicapped by scarcity of funds much needed for re-equipment and

---

[57] Despite heavy gold losses in the second half of 1928, the raising of Bank Rate was postponed as long as possible, and in 1931 England left gold at a 4½ percent Bank Rate. See *ibid.*, II, 180. Figures computed by Charles Walker, from the Bank of England returns, show strikingly the changed practices in post-war years, in contrast with pre-war years: the disinclination to use Bank Rate; the more frequent offsetting open market operations; and the resultant greater fluctuations in the Bank's own reserves, as a result of gold flows and changing internal circulation. "The Working of the Pre-War Gold Standard," *Rev. Econ. Studies*, I, 204–6; see also Brown, *The Int. Gold Stand.*, I, 684–90, and Hérisson, *Le Contrôle du crédit*, pp. 240–46.

[58] Royal Institute, *The Problem of International Investment*, p. 137.

[59] Long-term interest rates did tend to fluctuate in close correspondence with the short, although within a much narrower range. It cannot be doubted that the heavy decline of new lending toward the close of 1929 and the resumption early in 1930 were in large measure the result of the sharp rise and then decline of interest costs, and even the heavy decline in 1931 was in part due to rising rates, all largely attributable in turn to a Bank policy reacting to flows of short-term capital and gold. See Bank of England, *Statistical Summary*, July, 1932, p. 4.

[60] See Mlynarski, *Gold and Central Banks*, New York, Macmillan, 1929, p. 59; "Money in 1928," *Economist*, CVIII (1929), 506; Hérisson, *Le Contrôle du crédit*, p. 397.

[61] Hérisson, *ibid.*, pp. 401–2, 410; Benham, *British Monetary Policy*, pp. 1–45, especially p. 45.

renovation. Even before 1914, as we have seen, Bank Rate policy was devised not so much to operate upon prices as to induce compensatory short-term credit flows; and seldom before the 1920's had the Bank been faced with such an enduring basic disequilibrium. To the many, on the other hand, who criticize the Bank's conservatism and dear-money policy [62] it may be answered that if sterling was to be protected—and few advocated a departure from gold at a time when the world economy was in process of reconstruction—such a policy was probably necessary.[63] If the Bank was conservative, it was also changing and evolving new attitudes and instruments. The disinclination to use Bank Rate and the evolution of a regular offsetting policy—involving recourse to open-market operations, not simply to make Bank Rate effective, but to offset gold flows—were a real change from pre-war practice.

Still, the years 1925–31 were years of constraint and pressure and of unresolved disequilibrium.

The position was a difficult one. The pound was always faced with potential dangers, but nothing could be done to reduce them without increasing unemployment at home and possibly producing a crisis in some . . . weaker countries abroad. . . . For practical purposes there was only one remedy: that of going off the gold standard and starting all over again. The force of events was such that this remedy had unwillingly to be applied in September 1931.[64]

The early part of 1931 witnessed another lull, as in the previous year. Net short-term capital movements were small, and probably, on balance, toward England. The Bank of France lowered its rediscount rates, while the Bank of England, by vigorous open-market operations, forced money rates upward; exchange rates as a result moved in favor of London, and the Bank gained gold. Then came the crisis, and the system was too weak to weather it. The Continental banking crash, panic, and bank failures in the United States, brought an international hoarding panic. Britain's budgetary weakness, her heavy involvement in the Continent, her extremely illiquid position, and the "Naval Mutiny," turned the panic into a run on England. From the end of June to the end of September, London lost about £200 million of short-term foreign funds. Gold credits negotiated in New York and Paris, £50 million to the Bank of England, £80 million for the Treasury, were soon exhausted, some £30 million of

---

[62] MacM. Comm., *Evidence*, I, 145–56, 278–80 (Hawtrey).

[63] See the balanced evaluation by Hérisson, *Le Contrôle du crédit*, pp. 395–404.

[64] Grant, *The Capital Market in Post-War Britain*, p. 113. By permission of the Macmillan Company, publishers.

gold were lost, and foreign exchange holdings reduced, before Britain left gold. The unprecedented adverse current balance of £100 million added to these difficulties. What with these drains and the partial repayment of the New York and Paris credits before the end of the year, there must have been substantial drawing down, perhaps virtual exhaustion of Britain's short-term foreign assets, as is indicated by the residual balance of payments credit of fully £163 million for the year.[65]

Bank of England policy in the crisis was much the same as before. The heavy gold withdrawals of July were in part offset, but the Rate was raised quickly from 2½ to 4½ percent, and the offsetting was not complete. There was certainly neither intention nor desire to leave gold. Nevertheless the Bank cannot be accused of ruthless determination to hold to gold by whatever means necessary. Its Rate never passed 4½ percent. For years the Bank had pursued as deflationary a policy as was politically possible, without fundamental success, and now Britain was in deep depression. When the Rate was raised to 4½ percent, 22 percent of the insured population was unemployed; it is difficult now, and it was even more difficult then, to believe that further struggle to stay "under the harrow" [66] was worth the price. There was in addition serious question whether any measures would serve to stop the capital flight. A 10 percent Bank Rate and a larger New York credit might either have restored confidence in Britain's determination to hold to gold, or intensified the fears which caused the flight. But the current balance could not be made to adjust by any such policy, and the disequilibrium would have remained. In any event, under the circumstances and after the 1925–31 experience, a 10 percent Bank Rate was impossible.[67] So, in September, 1931, Britain, without entirely realizing it, abandoned the goal she had pursued in the preceding decade, and set out on a new path.

[65] See Table 13 (page 126), and "Banking Supplement," *Economist*, May 14, 1932, p. 6; also Gregory, *The Gold Standard and Its Future*, pp. 56–59; Gordon, *Capital in Sterling*, Part I, *passim*; Benham, *British Monetary Policy*, pp. 5–8.
[66] These were Governor Norman's words before the MacMillan Committee in 1931: "We have been continuously under the harrow." *Evidence*, I, 212; see also 23–25.
[67] See W. A. Brown, *The Int. Gold Stand.*, II, 1019–24; Einzig, *The Tragedy of the Pound*, pp. 97–103; Fanno, *Normal and Abnormal International Capital Transfers*, pp. 64–65n; Hérisson, *Le Contrôle du crédit*, pp. 407–8; Gregory, *The Gold Standard and Its Future*, p. 59.

X. PROBLEMS OF EQUILIBRIUM AND ADJUSTMENTS OF POLICY, 1932–39

WITH THE FALL of sterling, with the advent of a government possessing virtual *carte blanche* to meet the crisis, most inhibitions were gone. The attempt to restore free trade and the gold standard had failed to prevent or to remedy unemployment and stagnation and had ended in collapse. Free foreign lending had brought only a harvest of default. English policy was ready now to look first to the domestic needs for capital and employment, to insulate the home economy from foreign and domestic competition and from the erratic international gold and capital flows which had so harassed monetary authorities.[1] Each desertion from the old system begot others. Once the tariff was accepted, for example, the door was open for a further stifling of domestic competition, and for the discrimination and bilateral bargaining of imperial preference and the trade treaties. Particularly was this true under a Conservative government, which could not be said to have resisted with adamantine will the pleas of vested interest for special protection and favor.[2]

These changes in British policy were important, but not crucial in the long-run evolution of the balance of payments. The control of foreign lending was not the major determinant of levels and channels of investment. The effects of trade treaties and empire preference, as other studies have shown, lay rather in diverting and re-canalizing Britain's international transactions than in changing the total.[3] The game of currency depreciation, protection, and trade bargaining is one that all countries can play, and differential net advantages tend to be zero.

THE CURRENT BALANCE

The decline of sterling and the tariff brought a radical change in British trade. The precipitate drop of export volume was abruptly

[1] See Francis, *Britain's Economic Strategy*, chap. vii; Benham, *Great Britain under Protection*, pp. 10–11, 20–24.

[2] An economist is likely to forget the "political" aspects of economics. Davies's *"National" Capitalism* is a well-informed and in many ways convincing criticism of the National Government's economic policies on these grounds.

[3] These interesting changes are analyzed in Chapters XI and XIII, below.

halted and gave way in 1932 to a slight rise. The stubborn stability of import volume was at last halted. The import surplus was thus cut in the years 1932–35 to the lowest levels of the whole period 1924–38.

The divergence between British experience (as shown in Table 24) and that of the rest of the world is striking. In the years 1929–31, while the volume of British imports was stable, the world's declined by 14.6 percent. In value terms the discrepancy was smaller, because of the greater decline of British import prices, but it was still considerable: the British fell 29.2 percent, the world's (dollar value) 41.5 percent, and the American 52.5 percent. Between 1931 and 1932, on the contrary, the British volume was reduced by 12.0 percent, or almost as sharply as the world's 13.3 percent. A partial offset to this in the value figures was the relatively small decline in British import prices (see Table 24), due to the depreciation of sterling, while the index of world (export and import) prices declined by 22 percent in these years.[4]

TABLE 24

INDEXES OF AVERAGE VALUE AND VOLUME, UNITED KINGDOM TRADE [a]

(*1930 = 100*)

| | AVERAGE VALUE | | AVERAGE VOLUME | |
Year	Retained Imports	Exports U.K.Goods	Retained Imports	Exports U.K. Goods
1929	113.4	104.7	102.4	122.1
1930	100.0	100.0	100.0	100.0
1931	81.0	89.4	102.8	76.5
1932	75.3	83.3	90.3	76.8
1933	71.3	81.9	91.7	78.7
1934	73.3	82.2	96.9	84.4
1935	74.5	82.1	98.3	90.8
1936	78.2	83.7	105.2	92.2
1937	89.0	90.5	111.9	100.9
1938	84.0	92.0	106.8	89.5

[a] Source: *Statistical Abstracts for the United Kingdom.* This table is the product of joining three separate official series; comparability is therefore only rough.

[4] Comparison of British (sterling) import values with world (gold) values shows no lessening of the discrepancy in rates of fall after 1931, but only because the world figure for 1932 is greatly reduced by conversion into gold values of the imports of all those countries who left gold in 1931–32. World and U.S.A. data from League of Nations, *Reviews of World Trade.*

British export volume fell 37.4 percent between 1929 and 1931, the world's only by 14.3 percent, but this discrepancy was largely compensated in value terms by the relative stability of British export prices.[5] From 1931 to 1932, however, the depreciation of the pound was strikingly effective in sustaining British exports relative to world exports. While in volume British exports increased slightly, the world's declined further by 12.1 percent; and in value the comparable British and American percentage declines were 8.5 and 33.5 percent.[6]

It cannot be doubted that Britain gained a greater share of world markets, in value as well as volume terms, as a result of the fall of the pound.[7] Although her competitive strength was weakened by the relatively increased cost of imported raw materials, the lag of export costs and prices (both for Britain and for her gold country competitors) was sufficient to leave a considerable advantage.[8] Inflation of sterling prices and costs was precluded by a balanced budget, and because many other countries also went off gold or adopted trade and exchange controls, thus negating tendencies toward absolutely increased demand for British goods. Sterling import prices were likewise restrained, because of the considerable price concessions forced upon suppliers of Britain's imports (in many cases in the form of a depreciation of their own currencies), since the British market was so important to them. With this stability of sterling prices and costs while the pound was falling, Britain's gold export prices declined far more than American and French in competing lines.[9]

However, when it comes to weighing the net effects of the depreciation of sterling upon British foreign trade in absolute terms, one must

[5] World (export and import) prices fell 32.4 percent between 1929 and 1931, British export prices only 14.7 percent.

[6] World exports declined by 31.8 percent, but this far heavier fall than the British is in large measure the result of converting 1932 world trade figures into gold values, the British remaining in sterling.

[7] Harris, *Exchange Depreciation*, pp. xxiv–xxv note, 95–96, 444–45n.

[8] See Vaneetvelde, *La Dépréciation de la livre sterling*, pp. 177–83, 256–64.

[9] P.E.P., *Report on International Trade*, p. 44; Harris, *Exchange Depreciation*, pp. 5–6, 26, 70, 458–64. Of course, gold countries could buy their imports still more cheaply. See Gregory, *The Gold Standard and Its Future*, pp. 70–73; Gordon, *Capital in Sterling*, pp. 60–80. However, in so far as the failure of import prices to rise was the result of Britain's specially favored bargaining position in these particular goods, and because also the costs of imports are but one part of export prices, the other components of which did not rise, Britain did obtain a competitive advantage. See Marchal, "L'Abandon de l'étalon-or en Grande Bretagne et ses conséquences," *Revue éco. internationale*, 1937, Part 3, pp. 249–62; Harris, *Exchange Depreciation*, pp. 438–46.

compare what happened with what would have been had Britain not left gold, and any conclusions savor of predisposition. If the decline of the pound gave Britain a rising share of total world trade, the value of both that share and the total were declining in absolute terms. Sterling depreciation was in considerable measure to blame for this. The intensified competition of British exporters and the discouragement to British imports put extreme pressure upon world balances of payments, forced many suppliers off gold, and thrust extreme price reductions upon others. It was hence directly responsible for much of the ensuing gold-bloc deflation, for the spread of trade and exchange controls (many directed specifically at her), and for currency instability, all of which choked off world trade in general and British sales (and invisible receipts) in particular.[10]

However, it is difficult to see how anyone, observing the course of the world depression from 1929 to September, 1931, can attribute all the deflation and shrinking world trade thereafter to a mistake of British policy on that date.[11] Only if one believes this can one avoid the conclusion that by permitting her currency to decline Britain at least made the best of a deteriorating position.[12] The hoarding panic and spread of economic nationalism had been going on before that and promised to continue. There is little basis for the belief that world recovery would soon have come had sterling not fallen. The only alternative to leaving gold, for Britain, was deflation, protracted and intensified by stern government policies to preserve the pound, and this too would have helped force gold prices farther down. The world's experience since 1929 has shown that measures necessary to preserve stable currencies and to per-

[10] See Marchal, op. cit., pp. 277–82; Benham, British Monetary Policy, pp. 49–65. Some of the criticisms offered by these writers, among others, deserve but brief mention. One cannot, as do many, blame the fall of sterling both for foreign deflation and for the decline in the real value of that part of British income from foreign investments which was fixed in terms of sterling. To the extent that the latter occurred, it would have been because a shilling could now buy less foreign goods than before; i.e., to that extent the decline of the pound could not have forced down gold (British import) prices. In fact, the real value of the fixed income from abroad did not decline notably as a net result, because its transfer was facilitated, and because import prices did fall. It was also frequently predicted that "a default in time of peace" would wreck the financial prestige of London. Surely the experience of 1925–31 demonstrated that clinging precariously to an overvalued currency by maintaining continually high interest rates is not particularly conducive to such prestige either. The willingness of foreign funds to take refuge in London did not hinge simply upon the $4.86 value.

[11] It must be conceded, however, that such a view is possible if one also happens to believe, as does Benham, that ". . . a wider knowledge of certain economic truths would unquestionably have prevented the great depression." British Monetary Policy, p. 71.

[12] See Milton Gilbert, Currency Depreciation, p. 56.

petuate maladjustments between internal and world prices have often disrupted world trade more than devaluations could possibly have done.[13]

While Britain's abandoning gold forced such adjustments upon other countries—adjustments prevented by their own stubborn adherence to gold—nevertheless, the elimination of her own maladjustments was a definite stimulus to recovery. For the end of sterling overvaluation offered a positive contribution by making possible British and hence world reflation. The importance of this income effect of currency depreciation is indicated by the fact that after 1931 the portion of British exports going to paper countries increased, while the share taken by gold countries declined. Although tariffs and preference were very important in this regard, it cannot be doubted also that the earlier recovery of buying power in sterling-bloc countries, while gold countries were forced more deeply into deflation, helped to more than offset the greater competitive advantage of British exports in gold than in paper markets.[14]

Britain's trade policies of the 1930's were almost uniformly illiberal. The Ottawa agreements, wherein general empire tariff preference was instituted, made British protection permanent, and effected more increases in British tariffs than reductions in the already greatly augmented dominion crisis duties. Preference was granted more by raising non-preferential duties than by lowering preferential rates. The imposition of colonial quotas was brazen discrimination against the increasingly successful Japanese competitor; colonial consumers footed the bill. The trade treaties succeeded in cutting some tariffs, but they forced discriminatory concessions in favor of British goods and investors, and discriminated against foreign exporters by forcing upon them smaller quota shares in the British market.[15] Both preference and the treaties thus were a serious break in the most-favored-nation clause, the extension of which had once been the basis for spreading free trade throughout the world.[16] And they played a role consonant with Great Britain's importance in the world economy in reinforcing the drift toward autarchy, trade control, and bilateralism.

[13] See Gayer, *Monetary Policy and Economic Stabilization*, p. 159; Whittlesey, *International Monetary Issues*, New York, McGraw Hill, 1937, pp. 233–36.

[14] See Harris, *Exchange Depreciation*, pp. xxiii–xxiv, 11–12, 130–33, 449–50, 467.

[15] Invisibles were also embraced in provisions specifically allocating to the repayment and service of British debts some of the sterling exchange gained by bilateral excess of sales to Britain.

[16] On the other hand, by insisting upon most-favored-nation treatment in other cases, Britain blocked serious attempts of the smaller countries of Europe to free trade by mutual tariff concessions.

The total results of these policies, whereby Britain sought to expand her exports by negotiation and discrimination, were not great, on balance. Discriminatory advantages in some markets were offset by retaliation and intensified competition in others. Even the relative advantages turned out often to be absolute handicaps on balance; in many cases, for example, Britain succeeded in obtaining reductions of foreign tariffs against her goods amounting to less than previous rises imposed in retaliation for her own tariff and empire agreements.[17]

The period 1932–35 showed remarkable stability at these greatly reduced levels of international activity. The balance of trade averaged only about £275 million and ranged only from 261 to 294. Both import and export prices remained almost stable at their depression lows in these four years, and the volume of imports recovered appreciably only in 1934, with continued domestic recovery (see Table 24, p. 180). The much greater increase of export volume must be attributed, in large measure, to the comparatively rapid recovery of empire and other sterling area countries and to the trade and monetary policies which favored British sales to these areas.

In contrast, 1936–38 were years of great and rapid fluctuations, mirroring world boom and slump. Imports and exports both rose faster in 1936 and 1937 than in any year since 1924, but now the former expanded much more rapidly than the latter, with the result that the passive trade balance soared.[18] The increase through 1937 was attributable primarily to the great rise in raw-material prices at the peak of the boom;[19] export volume rose almost as rapidly as import, high primary prices being associated with a high level of foreign income available for purchase of British goods. Thus, while the collapse of raw material

---

[17] On the foregoing summary conclusions, see pp. 253–56, below.

See also the *Economist:* "Ottawa Supplement," Oct. 22, 1932, "Ottawa Section," CXXVII (1937), 262–71, and "The Empire and the World," CXXVII (1937), 249–50; see the cited works, *passim*, of Schlie, Francis, Findlay; also Jacques Villeneuve, *La Préférence impériale;* P.E.P., *Report on International Trade*, pp. 90–91, 280–95; Tasca, *World Trading Systems, passim.*

[18] The 1935, 1936, 1937, and 1938 figures were £261, £345, £442, and £377 million, respectively. Even the 1938 balance, it will be noted, still exceeded 1932–35 levels by some £100 million. Erratic flows of silver exaggerated these fluctuations. Excluding silver, the balance rose only from £275 million in 1935 to 431 in 1937, and declined only to 388 in 1938. Similarly, of the £33 million improvement of the trade balance between 1934 and 1935, fully 24 million was due to silver. These flows are entirely entrepôt trade: silver exports for the entire period 1933–38 inclusive amounted to £130 million, and imports to 128.5.

[19] See "The Balance of Payments," B. of T.J., CXL (1938), 230.

prices accounted for some improvement of the trade balance in 1938, it resulted also in a far greater decline of export than import volume, imports being further sustained by the rearmament program. British exports could recover appreciably, it appears, only as a result of such a rise of foreign incomes and (primary) prices as would entail on balance an even more rapid expansion in the value of imports! [20]

The sharp cut in the rate of decline of Britain's invisible incomes in 1932 was doubtless attributable in part to the fall of sterling. Transfer to her was facilitated for those countries which remained on gold, and the earlier recovery of those which followed the pound tended likewise to support Britain's receipts from them. The latter factor—the recovery of the sterling area—seems to have been the more important; as with commodity exports, so with this class of income, British earnings from sterling countries were better maintained than from gold countries.[21]

Between 1933 and 1937, while Britain's total income from oversea

---

[20] The British trade statistics show an interesting lagging relation between imports of raw materials and exports of manufactures. This is a natural phenomenon, augmented by the tendency for inventories to be accumulated in fits and starts, in anticipation of price changes.

Another probable reason for this connection is that suggested in the text: increased British raw material imports, largely to satisfy home market industries, helped increase the buying power of raw material producers, who in turn bought more British goods, these offsetting flows of buying power being canalized by empire preference and the trade agreements. See Jean Gommès, *La Baisse de la livre et les exportations Anglaises*, pp. 65–82, *passim*. The quantum indexes for imports of raw materials and exports of manufactures show this relationship especially clearly. There would certainly seem to be some connection between the year-by-year changes in imports and those one year later in exports.

$(1930 = 100)$

Year	Retained Imports Raw Materials	Exports of U.K. M'f'rs.
1931	93.7	. . .
1932	95.7	76.6
1933	104.7	79.1
1934	112.6	85.3
1935	113.1	92.3
1936	125.5	94.2
1937	. . .	103.7

Source: Annual articles in B. of T.J.
The relationship is, of course, rough. It is obscured by other factors, and, in any case, inadequately revealed by yearly figures.

[21] Kindersley, in *Econ. Jour.*, XLII (1932), 193, XLIII (1933), 199, XLV (1935), 441, XLVI (1936), 657. This is indicated in an approximate fashion by Table 25, which shows that dividends distributed by British companies operating abroad, which have a relatively greater concentration in sterling regions, reached their low point in 1932, whereas those of foreign companies continued to fall in 1933.

investments increased by 32 percent, income from government loans fell by 11 percent.[22] The almost unbroken decline from 1929 to 1938 in the debt service by non-empire governments was almost entirely the result of defaults, a product of excessive borrowing, transfer difficulties, and declining local income, due largely to a shrunken foreign trade. In addition, repatriations steadily reduced the total of British holdings of foreign government bonds before 1933. However, the main repatriations were of greatly depreciated, defaulted issues, income from which would in any event have been slight or nil.

In the case of empire government loans, defaults were scant, in no small measure because British commercial policy made transfer easy. Income from these loans rose steadily from 1928 to 1934, as new issues increased the total nominal value of such British investments. However, the rate of return on this rising total fell persistently after 1932 (see Table 25), as a result of heavy refundings and conversions undertaken in the cheap London money market, especially by Australia.[23] After 1934 new lending was not forthcoming to offset this falling rate of return, and the total income dropped rapidly. In addition, empire government repayments during the 1933–38 period were extremely heavy.[24] After 1934 they exceeded new issues, and Britain's total nominal holdings of these loans declined by £74 million (6 percent) between that year and 1937 as a result. So default by foreign governments, conversions and repayments, mainly of empire governments, and repatriations of both explain the 17 percent fall of interest on overseas government loans between its 1931 peak and 1937.

The larger income from commercial investments followed the business cycle much more closely, and with particular sensitivity because of its heavy dependence upon the more widely fluctuating primary prices. But here, too, conversions, repayments, defaults, repatriations and the lack of new lending made for a long-run decline. Between 1933 and 1937, with the rapid recovery of primary prices, profits and dividends recovered considerably. Leading this great advance were gold mines, which enjoyed great prosperity as a result of the rise in the world price of

[22] See Table 25 and Kindersley's articles for most of the following. Unless otherwise noted, the statistical references to nominal investments in various categories are all Kindersley's estimates.

[23] See Royal Institute, *The Problem of International Investment*, pp. 313–14. Of the 53 Dominion government issues outstanding in December, 1930, which were paying over 4½ percent, only 23 were left at the end of 1937. The number paying 4½ percent or less declined only from 98 to 92. Kindersley, in *Econ. Jour.*, XLVIII (1938), 614.

[24] See Table 26 (p. 191), below.

TABLE 25

INCOME FROM UNITED KINGDOM OVERSEAS INVESTMENTS [a]

(£000,000)

	1929	1930	1931	1932	1933	1934	1935	1936	1937	1938
I. Government loans										
A. Empire										
Income	46.4	46.9	48.4	48.9	49.1	49.1	48.2	46.4	42.9	42.7
Rate %	4.4	4.3	4.4	4.4	4.3	4.2	4.2	4.2	3.9	3.9
B. Non-empire										
Income	18.2	17.8	17.5	13.5	12.0	12.0	12.3	12.5	11.7	9.6
Rate %	5.2	5.0	5.2	4.2	3.6	3.6	3.6	3.7	3.5	3.0
C. Total										
Income	64.6	64.7	65.9	62.4	61.1	61.1	60.5	58.9	54.6	52.3
Rate %	4.6	4.5	4.6	4.4	4.1	4.1	4.0	4.1	3.8	3.7
II. British companies										
A. Interest	18.3	17.5	15.5	13.5	12.5	13.1	14.0	13.6	13.5	12.1
Rate %	4.7	4.5	3.9	3.5	3.2	3.4	3.6	3.6	3.7	3.4
B. Dividends	67.7	59.0	33.3	29.0	29.5	32.4	37.8	43.4	57.9	57.5
Rate %	8.4	7.1	4.1	3.6	3.6	3.9	4.5	5.2	6.8	6.7
III. Foreign companies										
A. Interest	19.7	19.3	18.2	17.1	14.7	13.8	13.7	13.4	12.8	11.4
Rate %	4.9	4.9	4.7	4.6	4.2	4.1	4.2	4.1	3.9	3.7
B. Dividends	42.0	31.7	22.7	22.1	20.5	26.0	29.7	35.1	37.8	31.6
Rate %	9.6	8.1	6.0	6.4	5.9	7.4	8.0	9.3	9.7	8.4
Unquoted investment										
Income	18.5	16.8	13.2	12.3	11.4	12.8	15.9	19.6	21.1	20.0
Total income	230.9	209.0	168.7	156.4	149.7	159.2	171.6	184.0	197.7	184.9

[a] Source: Kindersley, annual articles in the *Economic Journal*.

gold. They alone accounted for more than 50 percent of the increase between 1933 and 1936 in British income from all quoted commercial investments (Group II and III, Table 25).[25] British investments in and income from copper, lead, oil, rubber, and tin also expanded greatly. Improved exchange positions of South American countries released arrears of preferred stock dividends, and transfer problems dwindled. In 1938 exchange difficulties again occurred, and, along with the Spanish and Chinese wars and the Mexican oil expropriations, again reduced these earnings. Interest income from commercial investments, meanwhile, remained stable. Its failure to recover is explained by defaults, exchange

[25] Kindersley, in *Econ. Jour.*, XLVII (1937), 649, 655; XLVI (1936), 656.

restrictions, conversion operations, and by particularly heavy repayments and repatriations of foreign company bonds.

Even cyclical recovery could not restore Britain's income from overseas investments to 1929 levels. Here we see the result, in part, of a long-run decline in the world's effective need for British capital, and a parallel decline in Britain's ability to maintain, let alone add to, her foreign investments.

Long-Term Lending

Under stress of depression and the necessity for defending sterling before and after the departure from gold, the government re-established its control over new foreign issues—a control which soon became a consistent part of the newly evolving pattern of British economic policy. The first aim was support of sterling; hence relaxation of the embargo was used as an inducement to foreign countries to tie their currencies to the pound. A second aim was to foster British exports and to reward countries which offered special concessions to British goods. An added consideration was that domestic producers should have a prior claim on available capital, with empire producers next. Political-diplomatic factors, it was openly admitted, would also be considered in granting or withholding permission.

The first major step was a request by the Chancellor of the Exchequer, in June, 1932, for a complete cessation of new issues, pending the great government debt conversion. Two months later this embargo was relaxed in favor of domestic and empire conversions, and after October it applied only to non-empire new issues. In July, 1934, the chancellor announced that sterling area country loans would henceforth be exempt, if their purpose was to acquire sterling reserves or if they would increase British exports. With the appointment, in April, 1936, of the Foreign Transactions Advisory Committee to co-operate with the Treasury and the Bank of England in controlling new issues along these lines, the basis for a settled policy seemed to have been laid down. In recent years, moreover, attempts have been made to plug up other possible outlets for long-term capital. However, the purchase abroad of new issues, or of existing securities, by individuals, and the right of anyone to turn sterling into foreign currency, for whatever purpose, remained uncontrolled.[26]

[26] Stewart, "Great Britain's Foreign Loan Policy," *Economica*, n.s., V (1938), 45–60, and "Instruments of British Policy in the Sterling Area," *Pol. Sc. Q.*, LII (1937), 184–90; B.I.S., *Eighth Annual Report* (1938), p. 69; Royal Institute, *The Problem of International Investment*, pp. 77–81, 134; "British Capital Abroad," *Economist*, CXXIX (1937), 365.

With world recovery, the embargo must have had an appreciable effect. Just as temporary trade measures adopted under stress of depression came at that time under increasing fire, with the end of the emergency and the increasingly evident need for longer range planning, so it was urged that the London new issue market be freed in order to make its contribution to a revival of international trade.[27] Needy debtors might thus have obtained more capital, and a reawakening Wall Street less. But there was no such basic reconsideration, and war brought the need for more, rather than less, control.

The expanded operations of the Export Credits Guarantee Department were in keeping with these trends. The legal ceiling on the amount of guarantees which it might have outstanding at any time was raised twice from the original £25,000,000, reaching £75,000,000 in 1938, and intermediate and even long-term guarantees were offered. The year-to-year increases in the total of these outstanding loans, amounting to 8–10 millions on the average in the period 1933–38,[28] were a poor substitute for the free long-term lending of an earlier era. In 1939 the department was used widely as a political warfare fund, guarantees being undertaken in loans to potential allies, Poland and Greece.[29] Thus, as elsewhere "peace-time" policies of the thirties were adapted gracefully to the needs of war.

The period 1931–38 was one of uninterruptedly low new capital issues. The annual average of £33 million (conversion and refunding issues excluded) compares with 117 in the period 1924–30 (Midland Bank), and the figures are uniformly low throughout. Non-empire issues declined by no less than 91.8 percent (annual averages) between 1924–29 and 1932–38, and empire issues by 61.0 percent. The low British interest rates were meaningless for most of her potential borrowers.[30]

Of the few non-empire issues permitted, the majority had some special justification. In 1933 there was a British government-guaranteed 4.5 million "loan" to Austria, funding the "short-term" credit granted that country by the Bank of England in the summer of 1931 and a £1 million loan to the Danish government for construction of a bridge by a British company. In 1937 a £5 million issue was permitted the Belgian government to bolster the belga. Private non-empire issues were very small

---

[27] For example, P.E.P., *Report on International Trade*, pp. 182–85; Stewart, "Great Britain's Foreign Loan Policy," *Economica*, n.s., V (1938), 59–60.

[28] Figures in B.I.S., *Ninth Annual Report* (1939), p. 86.

[29] Tasca, *World Trading Systems*, pp. 133–35; B. of T.J., CXLIII (1939), 94, 224.

[30] See *Economist*: "New Capital in 1935," CXXI (1935), 1305–6; "Borrowers in the Boom," CXXV (1936), 625–26.

throughout—one to three millions annually in the recovery years.

Empire issues held up considerably better, not only because of British policy, but also because of the default-free record of their governments, their earlier recovery, and their rich gold mines. Empire government borrowing fell off considerably after 1933–34, as gold exports and recovery brought them increased financial self-sufficiency. But private issues recovered substantially in 1934 and were relatively large thereafter; their average of £21 million in the years 1934–37 compares with £33 million in 1928. Of these, gold-mining securities predominated, especially at the start, but copper and tin mines also took a growing share, and other industries as well, particularly with the spread of prosperity in South Africa, Rhodesia, and Australia.[31]

Meanwhile, with rising raw material prices, gold exports, and a strengthening of their balance-of-payments positions, British debtor countries (particularly the dominion governments) began to use accumulating London balances to redeem large amounts of their sterling debt. Many of these repayments were apparent only, being made out of the proceeds of refunding issues in London, induced by cheap money there. A comparison of the Midland Bank's new issue figures with those of Kindersley, which include refundings (see Table 26), indicates how large such issues were after 1932, i.e., after the coming of cheap long-term money rates.[32] But the volume of real net repayments alone was very large. Thus, as Table 26 shows, in 1932, 1935, 1936, 1937, and 1938, total repayments exceeded the total of refundings and new issues, a phenomenon almost without precedent.

Empire governments participated to a particularly great extent in all these operations. In the years 1932, 1933, and 1934 they floated numerous conversion and refunding issues, to take advantage of the extremely low London rates of interest.[33] In the following years, however, these governments made extremely heavy real redemptions, their gross repayments reaching the unprecedented peak of £77 million in 1936. Heaviest repayments were made by Australia, the Union of South

[31] See p. 162n., above.

[32] Even this understates the actual amount, since Kindersley's figures also deduct estimated foreign subscriptions to the issues. See Royal Institute, *The Problem of International Investment*, p. 314.

[33] Kindersley, in *Econ. Jour.*, XLII (1932), 181. Taking 1932 and 1933 together, empire government "repayments" of £65.4 million (Table 26) were associated with a rise of £43 million in total nominal British investment in these loans (Kindersley). Since new issues, excluding refundings, were £50.6 million (Midland Bank), the remaining discrepancy suggests refunding issues of no less than £58 million in these two years.

TABLE 26

New Capital Issues in the United Kingdom and Offsetting Repayments,
1929–38 [a]

(£000,000)

| | NEW ISSUES | | REPAYMENTS | | | | |
| | | | GOVERNMENT | | COMMERCIAL | | *Total* |
Year	*Midland Bank* [b]	*Kinders-ley* [c]	Empire	Non-empire	*British Companies*	*Foreign Companies*	*Repay-ments*
1929	94.3	96.0	20.3	10.1	8.5	9.6	48.5
1930	108.8	98.0	9.8	9.8	9.6	9.7	38.9
1931	46.1	41.0	5.5	10.7	4.9	5.6	26.8
1932	29.2	37.0	26.8	12.9	4.8	3.6	48.0
1933	37.8	83.0	38.6	10.8	7.8	9.6	66.8
1934	43.4	63.0	15.0	8.1	13.3	5.5	42.0
1935	20.9	51.0	45.7	10.5	12.4	12.5	81.1
1936	26.4	61.0	77.1	10.4	12.5	6.5	106.5
1937	32.1	60.0	20.9	6.8	24.5	9.3	61.5
1938	25.4	29.0	15.5	5.9	10.9	6.9	39.2

[a] Sources: *Midland Bk. Mo. Rev.*, and Kindersley, annual articles in *Economic Journal*.
[b] Excluding refundings and conversion issues.
[c] Includes refundings, excludes conversions and estimated foreign subscriptions.

Africa, and India.[34] In these years, therefore, total British holdings of empire government securities fell precipitately.

The same things happened to a lesser extent in the case of non-empire government and various commercial bonds, although these debtors were less able to refund or to convert in London. In the years 1933–35, inclusive, however, the nominal total of British investments in such loans increased, despite the fact that repayments went on undiminished. The explanation for this discrepancy is to be found in heavy "new issues," which were actually fundings of unpaid accruals of interest and sinking-fund credits due Britain, "funded" because the British had no alternative. With these "loans" excluded, it becomes clear that the total value of British investments of this category declined approximately by the amount of these regular repayments.[35]

There remain the very important dealings in existing securities, Brit-

[34] Kindersley, in *Econ. Jour.*, XLVII (1937), 645–46, 661.
[35] The total of such fundings from 1930 on was estimated by Kindersley in 1938 at £32.5 million. XLVIII (1938), 611, 618; see also XLV (1935), 443; XLVII (1937), 646.

ish participation in foreign issues, and direct investments, our estimates
of which, it may be repeated, are offered only as being faintly illuminating, nothing more.[36] In 1932 and 1933 the British appear to have
gone on selling securities, on balance, although receipts were low (our
estimates are £10 million annually) because of diminished sales and
shrunken market values.[37] The major sales seem to have been of foreign
company securities and unquoted American investments—the latter stimulated in 1932 by the depreciated pound, in 1933 by the uncertainties concerning the dollar. The year 1933 seems also to have witnessed some
repatriation of greatly depreciated foreign government bonds.[38]

Although government control and distrust of new foreign securities
kept down Britain's foreign lending through the London new issue
market, they did not prevent very substantial purchases of outstanding
foreign securities in a recovering world. In addition, direct investments
were made abroad, behind foreign tariff barriers. Particularly important
was the capital flow to the United States, after the dollar was stabilized
and Wall Street began to revive, a flow beginning in 1934 and reaching

[36] See Appendix, especially Table 31, below.

[37] The direct investments made in Britain behind her tariff provided an additional capital
inflow. The annual Board of Trade *Surveys of Industrial Development* show that from
1932 through 1938, inclusive, 284 new foreign (or foreign-assisted) factories opened in
Britain. The 224 set up in the period 1932 through 1935 employed a total of 14,200
people at the end of their respective years of opening. Since the board, in its annual balance-
of-payments articles, estimates that outpayments on income from foreign investments within
Britain rose only from £10 million in 1933 to 15 in 1937, the year-to-year increases in
these investments could not have been very great in relation to other forms of capital movement.

[38] In 1932: (*a*) British holdings of foreign company securities declined by £41 million,
and although the greater part was the result of drastic writing down of capital values,
some small part must have been the result of liquidation. Repayments were only £3.6
million. (*b*) Kindersley estimates a fall of £5 million in unquoted investments. See also
B.I.S., *Third Annual Report* (1933), p. 12; *The Canadian Balance of International Payments*, p. 23.

In 1933: (*a*) An unexplained fall of £15 million in holdings of foreign company bonds
was due partly to conversions of bonds into stocks, but partly also to repatriations.
(*b*) Kindersley estimates a fall of £5 million of unquoted investments, mainly due to
British withdrawals from America during the banking crisis and the period of uncertainty over the dollar. (*c*) An offset to these receipts was a repurchase of £6.5 million of
American-held shares in the British Boots Pure Drug Co. Deducting the effects of new
issues and repayments from the changing total of Britain's foreign investments gives a
balance of payments debit of £10 million in 1933 instead of the credit which we have
estimated. (See Table 31.) However, this net rise of the investment total (i.e., a debit)
includes £15–20 million of issues refunding unpaid interest and sinking fund payments on
foreign government bonds, and involving no actual cash transfer. In subsequent years also
these "loans" continue to cause the original estimates of capital outflow to be overstated.

large proportions in 1935 and 1936. There were offsets to this flow, particularly in 1936; foreign nationals continued to repatriate their commercial securities, and empire governments used accumulating internal taxes and sterling balances to buy up external debt, besides making the heavy formal repayments noted elsewhere. Thus, despite increased absolute capital outflow in 1936, the net outflow was greatly reduced. On balance, it is estimated that, on these accounts, Britain exported capital to the extent of £15, £70, and £20 million in 1934, 1935, and 1936, respectively.[39]

In 1937 and to a greater extent in 1938 the net movement seems again to have turned inward, with the collapse of world prosperity. The evidence is scanty, but what little there is tends to corroborate the showing of Table 31 (p. 298) that there were net sales, slight in 1937, heavier in

---

[39] In 1934: (a) Again a slight credit should be recorded as a result of continued sales to foreigners of their governments' sterling debts, and (b) another of uncertain amount from foreign purchases of British-held South African gold mine shares. (c) On the other hand, there occurred both increased purchases of American and other listed foreign securities, and a rise of £20 million in the total of unquoted investments. Our net estimate is, if anything, probably too low.

In 1935: (a) The residual increase of £104 million in total foreign investment (see Table 31) is overstated by continued fictional non-empire government issues (funding arrears and defaults). Nominal investments in all other quoted securities rose 33 millions, approximately, net of new issues and repayments. Since appreciation of nominal capital values was probably fairly small, most of this must have represented actual capital outflow. (b) In addition, unquoted investments show a rise of 50 millions, a capital flow mostly to America, where the inflow of British capital in these forms was officially estimated at 218 million dollars, or about 44 millions, sterling. U.S. Treasury Dept., *Bulletin*, Feb., 1942, p. 63. (c) An additional £5 million were involved in repurchase of British shares in General Electric and other companies.

In 1936: (a) The U.S. Treasury Department (*ibid.*) records an inflow of British capital, on account of transactions in securities, of $266 million, or about 53 millions sterling. This corresponds to Kindersley's rise of 50 millions, for unquoted investments. However, the nominal value of total British foreign investments in 1936 *fell* by £24 million. Since repayments exceeded new issues by £46 million, dealings in existing securities and capital write-ups could account on balance for an increase of only £22, and perhaps even less, since a small part of that increase seems to have been the effect, as in previous years, of non-empire government issues refunding unpaid arrears. Thus there must have been heavy sales of holdings elsewhere (capital depreciation being an unlikely explanation) amounting almost to £30 million. (b) There probably were considerable sales of commercial investments, particularly of British companies, as is indicated by the fall of nominal investment therein despite an excess of new commercial issues over repayments. Reviving debtor countries were perhaps buying out British interests operating within their borders. (c) Even larger were the repatriations of empire government securities. Kindersley's figures show a regular fall after 1934 in the percentage of outstanding empire government and municipality sterling issues held by Englishmen. The dominions were replacing sterling loans with domestic issues.

1938, of government and commercial securities; our balance of payments estimates are £10 and 30 million, respectively.[40]

The foregoing data permit the following very rough summary of Britain's long-term capital account since 1929. From 1930 through 1933 net long-term capital movements, taking into account repayments, new issues, and dealings in existing securities, were approximately zero on the average, varying from an outflow of perhaps 20 millions in 1930 (on account of the relatively high level of new issues) to an approximately equal inflow in 1932, under the influence of repayments, depression, government embargo, and net sales of existing securities. What new issues there were in this period were almost entirely for empire governments. The major sales of existing securities were repatriations of non-empire government debt by their respective nationals and sales of foreign company securities and unquoted investments, largely American. Real repayments of debt, i.e., excluding the many repayments made through refunding issues, were comparatively small.

In the period 1934–36 and probably in the early part of 1937, a reviving world brought considerable outflows of British capital in the form of direct investments behind foreign tariffs and heavy purchases of American securities. At the same time, however, new issues, held down by government control (and despite a considerable rise of empire mining issues), failed, except in 1934, to keep anywhere near the vastly increased volume of real repayments, the latter mainly by empire governments. In 1934 and 1935 the net flow was outward, but only, perhaps, by £30 to £40 million annually, and in 1936 unprecedented repayments and, apparently, considerable repatriations of foreign debt caused a net capital inflow for the year. This net inflow continued in 1937 and 1938. Smaller repayments still exceeded new issues; in addition, world recession brought a return of British capital by sales of existing investments, while the heavy outflow to the United States ceased.

The period 1930–38 as a whole offers a marked contrast to what the

---

[40] (a) The British-owned portion of empire governments' sterling debt (Kindersley) declined from 90.1 in 1936 to 88.7 and 88.0 percent in 1937 and 1938, respectively. (b) In 1937 holdings of non-empire government bonds fell by £5 million, although new issues and repayments almost balance out. There would seem to have been even larger repatriations in 1938, when nominal investment declined by £19 million, while repayments were only £6 million. The estimated portion of these outstanding securities in British hands declined from 60.2 percent in 1936 to 58.2 in 1937 and 57.5 in 1938. (c) In 1938, there was also an extremely large fall, over and above repayments, in holdings of foreign company securities. Since nominal changes in capital value could scarcely have occurred so rapidly, it is believed that most of this change represents actual sales due to world depression.

British had for decades come to accept as normal. Net capital outflows, even in the best years, were small. For the period as a whole it would seem that Great Britain failed entirely to increase her foreign investments. If anything, they seem to have been decreased.[41]

GOLD, SHORT-TERM CAPITAL MOVEMENTS, MONETARY POLICY, AND THE PROBLEMS OF EQUILIBRIUM

The British balance of payments after 1931 is dominated by huge net movements of gold and roughly equivalent flows of short-term capital.[42] The monetary authorities were preoccupied throughout with controlling the fluctuations in sterling which these flows induced and managing their great potential effects upon the internal economy.[43]

Late 1931 and 1932 witnessed the beginning of a concomitant inflow of gold and short-term capital which became extremely great in subsequent years. First there was the return of funds which had just departed so precipitately. Conservative fiscal and monetary policies immediately following the departure from gold allayed fears of inflation and brought a return of confidence. As Britain cut herself off from the world's deepening depression, this confidence grew, and the inflow continued. Second, and continuing longer, was the accumulation of London balances by sterling area countries. This was made possible by the improvement of their balances of payments, initially by greatly increased gold sales (especially in the earlier stages, by India).[44] Thus the pound recovered sub-

---

[41] And, it would seem, not only in quantity but in quality as well did the investments decline. Apart from repatriations of defaulted non-empire government debt, the heaviest repayments were by the most solvent and credit-worthy debtors. Kindersley, in *Econ. Jour.*, XLVII (1937), 661–62.

[42] The latter doubtless constitute the major part of the balance-of-payments residual, the fluctuations of which, taken with the available specific data of short-term movements, correspond very closely with those of gold.

[43] Most of the following description of gold and short-term capital movements is derived from the following sources: the *Annual Reports* of the B.I.S.; Paish's cited articles in *Economica*, n.s., II (1935), 61–74, III (1936), 78–83, IV (1937), 343–49, and his "Twenty Years of the Floating Debt," *Economica*, n.s., VI (1939), 243–69; Brown, *The Int. Gold Stand.*, II; the *Economist*; and other sources cited below. The reader should also follow the movements in Table 13 (p. 126), above.

[44] Indian gold was usually sold against gold currencies, and the proceeds turned into sterling. See "The Indian Gold Exports," *Midland Bk. Mo. Rev.*, Jan.–Feb., 1932, pp. 4–6. South Africa, however, kept only a limited part of the proceeds of its sales in sterling. B.I.S., *Third Annual Report*, pp. 7–8; *Eighth Annual Report*, pp. 23, 42. See also A. S. J. Baster, "A Note on the Sterling Area," *Econ. Jour.*, XLVII (1937), 568–74; Stewart, "Instruments of British Policy in the Sterling Area," *Pol. Sc. Q.*, LII (1937), 194–200.

stantially in the first months of 1932. Moreover, the Bank of England was able, in May and June, to acquire £15 million of gold (old valuation), and in addition sufficient foreign exchange for the Bank itself and the Treasury to repay easily their foreign debts incurred in 1931.[45]

The inflow of funds in 1932, however, far exceeded any net gains of gold,[46] and the value of sterling fell heavily from April to December. One reason was that the current balance was negative by £51 million, largely because of the lump sum of £29 million in gold paid to the United States in war debts at the end of the year. There were also the repayments, during the first half of the year, of the 1931 American and French credits extended in support of sterling. The first installment of this repayment, late in 1931, was likewise made by the sale of £15 million (nominal value) of gold.

As the sterling areas recovered, while gold countries suffered further deflation, it became more and more apparent that the currencies of the former were far stronger than those of the latter. Increasingly, therefore, after 1932, funds fleeing gold countries in quest of security were added to the inflow of sterling area reserves. In 1933 the flood descended, with the American banking crisis, the flight from the dollar, and a series of flights from the franc, the first following the failure of the London conference. Thus, by the close of 1933 the total of foreign short-term funds in London had probably recovered to 1930 levels,[47] and in this one year the British authorities gained perhaps £200 million of gold on balance.

The year 1934 was exceptional, for it seems to have been characterized by heavy short-term capital withdrawals and gold losses. The pound was weak almost from beginning to end. Dollar stabilization and recovery in the United States and renewed confidence in the determination of gold bloc countries to adhere to gold, caused funds to flow steadily back to

[45] *Economist,* CXIV (1932), 229, 507; testimony of O. M. W. Sprague, U.S. House Comm. on Banking and Currency, on bill "To establish the Federal Monetary Authority," 1934, p. 320.

[46] England was no longer on a gold standard. An increased demand for pounds no longer necessitated equivalent gold inflows unless, and until, sterling appreciated to the old gold parity, where the Bank of England's continued legal obligation to buy gold at the old rate would become effective. Below that point, the tie of gold to short-term credit inflows consisted in the desire of the British authorities to stabilize sterling. To prevent a rise they might offer the desired pounds for gold currencies (which they fairly regularly converted into gold), or purchase gold in the gold market. Similarly, gold would be lost only if the authorities chose to prevent a decline of sterling, by offering gold currencies or selling gold in the gold market. See pp. 199–203, below.

[47] B.I.S., *Fourth Annual Report,* pp. 28–29.

these countries. South Africa, never fully on a sterling standard, decided to retain her gold and used up her sterling to meet balance-of-payments deficiencies. Other empire countries seem in general to have suffered a weakening of their balances of payments in competition with an under-valued dollar, and in the face of progressive shrinkage of their non-empire markets by trade and exchange controls.[48] Official British hold-ings of gold as a result were considerably reduced in 1934, to support a pound weakened by these various outflows of short-term credits. For the most part this gold, bought with sterling, was never exported. On the contrary, whereas official holdings appear to have declined by more than £100 million, physically England imported no less than £134 million, on balance. The difference of almost £250 million represents enormously increased foreign gold holdings in London.[49]

The heavy inflows of short-term capital and the equivalent increase in official gold holdings resumed in 1935, soon offset the 1934 losses and continued in 1936 and 1937. Improving sterling area balances of pay-ments, extreme distrust of gold bloc currencies, with exchange crises, de-valuations, and flights of capital, created almost continuous necessity for sales of sterling for francs and gold in order to lessen the rise of the pound. Gold accumulations became particularly great in the first part of 1937, because of the "gold scare." This resulted from rumors that to prevent inflation the United States was going to reduce its gold buy-ing price, and led to heavy sales of foreign-owned gold for sterling and dollars.[50] The gold scare was transformed by the American depression of the latter part of the year into a "dollar scare," the fear of further dol-lar devaluation to combat the slump. Despite the great flight from the dollar which resulted, British gold gains were small, the great return of funds into gold hoards (in expectation of its appreciation) forcing the Exchange Account to supply large quantities of the metal to the market. For the year as a whole official holdings rose by £190 million, as estimated

[48] B.I.S., *Fifth Annual Report*, pp. 20–21, 33; League of Nations, *World Economic Sur-vey*, 1934–35, pp. 29, 194–96. De Vegh's compilations show some deterioration of empire balances of payments, but not of the whole sterling area. *The Pound Sterling*, Appendices.
[49] See Appendix, below; also Paish, "The British Exchange Equalisation Fund," *Eco-nomica*, n.s., II (1935), 68; B.I.S., *Fifth Annual Report*, p. 25.
[50] A lower gold price meant a higher dollar, hence the very great demand for dollars, and the flow of gold to America in unprecedented quantities. The panic wave of gold dis-hoarding probably cut foreign holdings of gold in London by more than half. See B.I.S., *Eighth Annual Report*, pp. 45–46; Paish, "The Exchange Equalisation Fund," *Economica*, n.s., IV (1937), 345; Waight, *The History and Mechanism of the Exchange Equalisation Account*, pp. 109–11.

in Table 13, yet export-import statistics show a net flow of gold into England of only £79.5 million, the reversal of the 1934 discrepancy. The explanation lies, of course, in the heavy net foreign dishoardings during the gold scare.[51]

Most of 1938 and all of 1939 represent a definite departure from the trends of 1932–33 and 1935–37. The new picture shows extreme weakness of the pound, periodic capital flights, a great withdrawal of short-term funds by British people as well as foreigners, and great consequent losses of gold by the Bank of England and the Exchange Account.[52] The first strain came with the final franc stabilization in May, 1938, which was followed by heavy French repatriations. The second was the autumn Munich crisis and the increasingly clear inevitability of war in 1939. The future of Great Britain itself was in doubt; only the United States and the dollar seemed secure. Added to these strains were the increasing balance-of-payments hardships of the sterling countries, hit by the decline of raw material prices after mid-1937. From mid-1937 to the end of 1938 their London balances were reduced by fully £120 million,[53] partly for these reasons, partly also because these countries, too, were deserting sterling for gold.[54] As a result of these irresistible forces and despite strong official support, shown in gold losses of no less than £275 million in the year April 1, 1938, to March 31, 1939, the pound was driven down from $5.02 in February to $4.67 in December, 1938, remaining roughly stable at that level until the outbreak of war.

Thus, at the close of the period 1932–39 Britain lost much of the gold and short-term balances which she had attracted during the earlier years. The gold in the Exchange Account and Bank of England, as officially reported (and valued at £7 per fine oz.), declined from its peak of £836 million in March 31, 1938, to £560 million one year later. Nevertheless, the great inflows of the earlier years were far from undone. The Bank of England had started the period with gold worth only about £200 million (121 at the old official value). The balance of payments indicates that foreign funds in London must similarly have remained higher by many hundreds of millions of pounds than they were at the close of 1931 or even before the capital flights of that year.

[51] B.I.S., *Eighth Annual Report*, pp. 19–20, 46, 55.

[52] In 1938 gold losses of roughly 200 millions compare with net physical gold exports of only 63 millions, indicating again a considerable increase of foreign hoarding in London. See B.I.S., *Ninth Annual Report*, p. 63; also pp. 83–84.

[53] See B.I.S., *Ninth Annual Report*, pp. 25–26, 32–33 ff., 82.

[54] De Vegh, *The Pound Sterling*, pp. 45–46, 86.

Britain had regained and far surpassed her net short-term debtor position of 1931, with all its attendant uncertainties, risks of capital flight, and inherent weaknesses. Her short-term liabilities were greater, her short-term assets (excluding gold) much decreased, with the decline of her international banking business.[55] Her enormous gold gains were attributable solely to greatly increased short-term borrowing and were therefore no indication of greater basic strength.[56] In the summer of 1931 declining confidence in the pound, political uncertainty, and an extremely adverse current balance brought a flight of capital, a loss of gold, and abandonment of the gold standard. So in 1938 and 1939 war and rumors of war and an adverse current balance again brought capital flight, great gold losses, and finally strict wartime exchange control.

There, however, the resemblance ends. In 1938 Britain possessed a mechanism and a policy evolved in the years after 1931 which permitted her to view almost with equanimity these great pressures and gold losses occurring as a result of factors beyond her control.

In leaving the gold standard, Britain definitely renounced any system which would set currency stability above the freedom of domestic credit policy. Only under a thoroughgoing exchange control could these two be reconciled, and Britain was not ready for the complete economic regimentation which that would have entailed. However, she could not leave the pound free to fluctuate with the vagaries of enormous capital flows or the caprices of the uncontrolled speculation to which such a situation would give rise. Nor did she wish to permit the domestic money supply to run alternately hot and cold under these influences. Some sort of exchange control was called for, but if the above goals were to be attained it would have to be a flexible and unremitting discretionary management. In each case a decision would have to be made as to which exchange fluctuations were undesirable and ought to be resisted, which represented underlying tendencies that could be resisted only at the cost of more drastic adjustments of the internal economy. In either event, a method of internal credit control had to be devised to offset the influence of these extraneous factors. The mechanism of the Exchange Equalisation Account (the EEA), organized in June, 1932, was such a system.[57]

In general terms the function of the EEA was to prevent short-term nonequilibrative fluctuations of sterling, due to speculative flows of cap-

[55] See B.I.S., *Eighth Annual Report*, pp. 70–71.
[56] See "Britain's Gold Holdings," *Economist*, CXXX (1938), 71–72.
[57] See the cited works of Waight, Hall, and F. W. Paish.

ital, by buying and selling foreign exchange in the open market. Sterling was to be kept at the value consistent with long-run balance-of-payments equilibrium. By the same token the EEA was not to resist long-run equilibrative movements of the exchange—i.e., in response to relative price levels, to the demand and supply of exchange for trade, services, or long-term capital transfers.[58] In addition the domestic money system was to be shielded from the consequences of these external factors. These unstable foreign credits were not to be absorbed into the money structure on coming in or to cause internal contraction on their departure.

The system evolved accomplished both internal and external offsetting simultaneously. The Account's resources consisted initially of Treasury bills. In case of an inflow of foreign capital it sold its bills for sterling, with which it bought the foreign currencies offered, turning them into gold. In case of outflow it sold its gold for foreign currencies, offered the latter for sterling, which it converted again into Treasury bills. The exchange effect was thus offset by its supplying the deficiency of pounds or foreign exchange to the open market. The internal effect was offset, essentially, by providing the influx of foreign lenders with bills in which to invest, and taking the bills back from them when they withdrew. The alternate sales and purchases of Treasury bills had the effect of open-market operations, taking off the market the net increase of deposits (provided by it to foreigners), or putting back in the market the funds withdrawn when the (foreign-owned) deposits were resold to it. The gold neither entered the money system nor came out of it, being merely hoarded by the Account, except in so far as it was sold to the Bank of England with conscious intent to increase the credit base.[59]

In practice the problems and methods were far less simple. The day-to-day decisions as to which exchange fluctuations ought and which ought

[58] Noel F. Hall's statement of the criteria by which the EEA could be guided (*The Exchange Equalisation Account*, pp. 4–5) intimates that an equilibrating inflow of short-term credits, tiding over balance-of-payments disequilibrium (sterling overvaluation in this case) should not be offset, i.e., should be permitted to maintain the exchange value of sterling. This, it is submitted, is an error. It would be as much a mistake for the Account to permit sterling to be maintained at an overvalued level by attraction of short-term capital, as to permit it to be raised to an overvalued level by an inflow of independent short-term credits.

[59] After the fall of the franc, in 1936, direct purchases and sales on the London gold market took the place of dealings in foreign exchange as the instrument of exchange stabilization. The way in which this operated is described by F. Lutz, "A Note on Gold Movements in the Present International Monetary System," *Rev. Econ. Studies*, V (1937), 66–69; see also Robertson, "British Monetary Policy," *Lloyd's Bk. Ltd. Mo. Rev.*, n.s., X (1939), 155–56.

not to be resisted required the exercise of discretion. The problems of internal offsetting were even more complex. When the EEA's Treasury bill transactions were with banks, the above-described offsetting operations were not technically accurate.[60] In the case of a capital inflow, for example, the sale of bills by the EEA, to obtain the needed sterling, equalized the effect of capital inflow on bank reserves, but effected no equivalent offsetting extinction of deposits. The net result was hence an increase of (foreign-owned) deposits, unchanged reserves, a decline of the cash ratio, and hence deflationary pressure. So in the case of a capital outflow, there was often a tendency to an inflationary rise in cash ratios, when the purchase of bills from the banks restored their reserves, but failed to create a deposit equivalent to the decrease created by foreign withdrawals. Simple offsetting thus tended in each case to go too far. In so far as foreign funds were hoarded in British bank notes these effects of simple offsetting were far more serious. In the case of a capital inflow, regular offsetting produced an absolute decline in bank reserves, there being no initial increase of (foreign-owned) deposits, or reserves, with a deflationary effect therefore ten times that of a mere fall of cash ratios. And in the case of capital outflow, offsetting thus produced an inflationary effect ten times as great.[61]

No cut and dried procedures could be followed. For these deficiencies of offsetting additional instruments had to be devised to fit the circumstances. To prevent the inflationary consequences of full primary offsetting, for example, the EEA might simply permit its sterling receipts to accumulate in Public Deposits at the Bank of England, rather than turn them all into bills. The extent of offsetting varied with the circumstances. The actual decisions were not made in a vacuum, but were influ-

---

[60] "Technically accurate" offsetting is taken to consist in keeping the volume of bank deposits and reserves stable. Such variables as differential rates of turnover of foreign and domestically owned deposits, not to mention changing cyclical influences all, of course, complicated *real* offsetting.

[61] See the *Economist:* "The Mechanism of Exchange Funds," CXXV (1936), 68–69, 216, "The Exchange Equalisation Account," CXXVIII (1937), 22–23; Waight, *The Exchange Equalisation Account*, pp. 46–47, 53–62, 70–71, 125; W. A. Brown, *The Int. Gold Stand.*, II, 1119–26.

It seems nowhere to be stated precisely why this effect of offsetting *is* inflationary or deflationary, if it merely induces banks to restore their cash ratios by increasing or reducing deposits to their previous total. (This is apart from the much clearer case of hoarding of bank notes.) The explanation would seem to be the more limited and perhaps slower circulation of foreign-owned deposits; an increase of these at the expense of domestic (with capital inflow) is therefore deflationary, a relative decrease inflationary. The volume of credit extended at home is definitely altered in each case.

enced by all other relevant considerations, such as the nature of the capital flows and the tenor of domestic business conditions. Thus, an off-setting purchase of Treasury bills by the Account might, by reducing the supply of bills available to the banks for secondary reserve, have serious deflationary effects. This dilemma arose in acute form with the heavy and rapid French repatriations in 1938 and called for still other expedients.[62] This increased flexibility characterized the operations of the Bank of England as well. Gold purchases from the EEA were used to reduce the fiduciary issue, leaving a possibility of future increase in case of emergency, and permitting expansion of note circulation with domestic revival and increased foreign hoarding. Statutory authority was more readily asked for and given to raise the limit; a large rise was granted in January, 1939, to permit gold transfers to the EEA for defense of sterling.[63]

Perhaps the most important underlying consideration behind the operations of the EEA was the cheap money policy and the prevention of a rise in sterling which would threaten that policy. The Account was created at a time when the government and the Bank of England were embarking upon a regime of cheap money. The appreciation of the pound from its low point at the close of 1931 had caused the earlier feeling of relief that inflation was to be avoided to change to one of alarm lest cheap money and the chances of internal recovery be endangered. A new over-valuation, it was reasoned, could only be followed by another flight of capital and another resultant enforced return of high domestic money rates.[64] The Bank of England thus bought foreign exchange heavily to offset this rise. The EEA was supposed to continue this type of operation. Since its main assets at the outset were in sterling, it was equipped only to prevent a rise of the pound, scarcely a decline. When the pound began to fall after April, 1932, the Account was evidently able to do little to prevent it.[65] Throughout 1933 and 1934, while the Fund com-

---

[62] For example, the EEA purchased the required bills directly from the Bank of England, the latter in turn accomplishing the actual offsetting by purchase of government bonds in the open market. See Waight, *op. cit.*, pp. 64–73, 77, 119–27; "Financial Policy and Business Confidence," *Midland Bk. Mo. Rev.*, Feb.–March, 1939, pp. 1–3.

[63] The Bank converted the bills it received in return for the gold into gilt-edged securities, thus helping to relieve the great market shortage of bills. See "Sterling and Gold," *Economist*, CXXXIV (1939), 76–77.

[64] N. F. Hall, *The Exchange Equalisation Account*, pp. 34–39; W. A. Brown, *The Int. Gold Stand.*, II, 1106–9, 1117–18.

[65] Hall, *op. cit.*, pp. 39, 45–47, 51–52; Paish, "The Exchange Equalisation Fund,"

batted erratic flows of short-term capital in both directions, it seems clear again that it tried harder to keep the pound from rising than from falling. This was the safer course. It involved accumulating a huge gold reserve, by vigorously buying up all foreign exchange offered, thus increasing the strength and liquidity of Britain's position. As a result, by March–April, 1933, and again later on, its supplies of sterling were exhausted and had to be replenished by heavy gold sales to the Bank of England, and a statutory increase in the size of the Fund. As the dollar depreciated during 1933, the Fund seems to have purchased dollars, thus restraining the rise of the pound in terms of dollars sufficiently to hold the franc rate constant.[66]

Nevertheless, the Exchange Account was an effective influence in the direction of exchange stability. The continuance of gold flows as short-term funds flitted in and out was the measure of its activity. It sold gold freely when there was a flight from the pound, the most notable case being in the huge outflows of 1938–39, which made necessary the return of £200 million of gold (£353 at market price) from the Bank to the Fund, in January, 1939. However, the pound was not defended blindly. The Account sold gold in 1938–39 only at a gradually rising price, partly because it recognized that the heavy recession of American prices had caused sterling to be overvalued. And, because of the business recession, the inflationary domestic effects of primary offsetting were permitted to remain.[67]

The great test of Britain's new instrument of monetary policy came with the enormous capital flights of 1938–39. The ease with which they were met, the comparatively minor effect upon the internal economy of the £275 million gold loss, were a token of its efficiency. By the manipulations of the EEA, sterling had become an example of something fairly close to the optimum combination of stability and flexibility in a wisely managed currency.[68]

Economica, n.s., II (1935), 65–66, "Twenty Years of the Floating Debt," *Economica*, n.s., VI (1939), 254–55.

[66] Thus, despite the strength of sterling in 1933, it was worth 86.1 francs in January and only 83.6 in December (yearly average 84.6). See Brown, *The Int. Gold Stand.*, II, 1269–79, 1289–94, 1299; Hall, *The Exchange Equalisation Account*, pp. 60, 78–83.

[67] See "Great Britain's Gold," *Economist*, CXXXII (1938), 73–75; Waight, *The Exchange Equalisation Account*, pp. 76, 111–12.

[68] See Waight, *op. cit.*, pp. 66–67, 127, 148; Kindleberger, *International Short-Term Capital Movements*, pp. 227–28; Marchal, "L'Abandon de l'étalon-or," *Rev. écon. int.*, 1937, Part 3, pp. 237–48.

These highly important changes in Britain's economic policy after 1931 were in a sense attempted adjustments to the disequilibria of the 1920's. The confused and rapidly changing conditions of the 1930's unfortunately make it impossible to determine with any exactitude whether in fact they succeeded in eliminating that weakness. All the customary criteria are faulty. The enormously increased independent flows of short-term capital, occurring for causes other than balance-of-payments disequilibria, make the net changes in short-term credit position and the resultant fluctuations in gold movements and exchange rates untrustworthy guides. Relative money-market rates are likewise no longer useful in view of the government's adherence to cheap money regardless of the state of the balance of payments.

All that remain are purchasing-power parities [69] and a comparison of long-term capital and current balances, and these too are inadequate except for rough indications of the direction of year-to-year changes. Price parities are especially deceptive because of the greatly altered concomitant circumstances. Furthermore, the theory of overvaluation and undervaluation measured by purchasing power parities is based on a fundamental assumption of freedom of commodities to flow in international trade according to the dictates of price differentials. The rapid spread after 1929 of tariffs, and particularly of quantitative trade restrictions, destroyed the validity of this assumption. Such discriminations against British goods would cause the evidence of price parities to create an erroneous appearance of undervaluation or to hide an actual overvaluation of sterling; [70] the preferential reductions of empire and sterling area duties in Britain's favor would have the opposite effect.

The evidence of much more rigid British than American wages and export prices, in the period 1929-31, taken in conjunction with the enormous decline of Britain's invisible incomes, suggests that sterling was considerably overvalued in September, 1931, apart from the weak short-

---

This was not as true in fact as it was potentially. Lowell M. Pumphrey has demonstrated that, largely because of political factors beyond its control, the EEA was not a free agent, but was perforce committed to a stable dollar-pound rate. Thus, in 1933 and the first half of 1939, it was forced to sustain the pound—in the latter period at a rate definitely excessive—for fear of the consequences of American retaliation. "The Exchange Equalization Account of Great Britain, 1932-1939," *Amer. Econ. Rev.*, XXXII (1942), 803-16.
[69] See Hall, *The Exchange Equalisation Account*, pp. 70-78; Harris, *Exchange Depreciation*, pp. 157-59, 435-36; "The Pound and the Dollar," *Midland Bk. Mo. Rev.*, Dec., 1938-Jan., 1939, pp. 1-3—from which studies much of the following factual data on parities is taken.
[70] "The Decline in Sterling," *Midland Bk. Mo. Rev.*, Nov.-Dec., 1932, p. 2.

term position carried over from the past. Thereafter, however, the tariff and the much slower internal than external depreciation of the currency brought an abrupt change in the opposite direction, tending to rectify the previous overvaluation, if not to bring about "absolute" undervaluation. The balance of payments remained weak in 1932, but from 1933 through 1936 the rough correspondence of current and long-term capital balances seems to indicate an approximation to equilibrium conditions. Short-term capital movements seem as a result to have brought fairly closely corresponding movements of gold, not to have been a means of tiding over a weak balance of payments.

It was an equilibrium at a greatly diminished level of international activity and of heavy unemployment. For some of this, British monetary policy may be blamed. The decline of the dollar may have kept that currency and sterling roughly in line, but relative to the gold bloc the undervaluation of the pound became even greater. The deflationary pressure upon those countries increased, and to this in part may be attributed the intensification of trade and exchange controls from which Britain in turn suffered. Noel Hall argues that rising American costs would have justified a $5.50 pound; had the British authorities permitted this level to be reached, he continues, sterling would have remained stable in gold, and hence the intensification of gold bloc distress could have been avoided.[71] The EEA can, nevertheless, scarcely be blamed for the continued depression in a large portion of the world after the decline of the dollar. The dollar-franc rate was the one most seriously out of line, and this was a gold-fixed rate. Sterling did rise considerably in terms of the dollar, from $3.43 in March, 1933, to an average of $5.04 for 1934. Considering the difficulties before 1932, it was not surprising that the authorities refused to permit the rate to rise more. What was needed now was a fall of the gold bloc currencies.[72]

In the years 1936–38 the balance of payments showed increasing evidence of weakness. The current account became negative in correspondence with net inflows of capital. This was certainly in part an evidence of equilibrating forces. The soaring raw-material prices which caused the deterioration of Britain's trade balance in 1936–37 were at the same time making possible heavy repayments by her debtors. Again, in 1937–38, the American depression led both to British sales of American securities and to the relative fall of American export prices and imports, which con-

---

[71] *The Exchange Equalisation Account*, pp. 60, 63, 80–83.
[72] Brown, *The Int. Gold Stand.*, II, 1307–11, 1326–27, 1334–35.

tributed substantially to the weakness of Britain's current balance. But there were signs of disequilibrium. On the one hand, the heavy capital repayments of 1936 were to some extent simply a result of the coincidence of a great number of maturities, and could not continue at that rate. On the other hand, the great domestic recovery and rearmament boom, in the face of falling American prices and incomes during 1937–38 and of gold bloc devaluations, seem to have brought the return of an overvalued pound, which persisted until the heavy capital flights of 1938–39 forced it down. And even though it may be argued that equilibrium was retained, Britain was drawing down her foreign assets, on balance, instead of living on current account. Her income was too low for her outgo, and consumption of capital threatened to make it lower in the future.

The new British policies seem to have had little lasting effect in this regard. The same long- and short-run problems remained.[73] Even with her greatly increased gold stock, Britain's short-term position was certainly not stronger in 1938 than in 1931. If anything, the balance of payments seems to show a considerably greater net increase of short-term liabilities than of gold holdings in the interim.[74]

The only difference from 1931, and it was a very significant one, was that British policy had learned to make the best of a situation which it could not correct except by steps too drastic to be worth while. Britain had a huge gold reserve which she was free to let go in case of capital flight, with minimum damage to the internal economy. And if gold sales were insufficient, Britain was now willing to have adjustment come via a fall of the pound rather than by internal deflation. Although this change in policy was but an adaptation, not a correction, it was a profoundly successful one, considering the circumstances.

Britain was injured by the disruption of the settled world economy which these changed policies involved and accepted. Such actions as the Tripartite Agreement of 1936 and the Anglo-American trade agreement represented incipient efforts to remedy these evils by reconstituting some measure of world order. Had not war come, such pragmatic international co-operative policies might have been the essential counterpart to the equally pragmatic adjustments of independent national policies. But these faltering steps were inadequate, and Britain was in part to blame. She permitted emergency measures and vested interests to block real progress in these efforts. She allowed a "temporary" shelter-

---

[73] See Francis, *Britain's Economic Strategy*, chap. xiii, pp. 366–68.
[74] See Gayer, *Monetary Policy and Economic Stabilization*, pp. 198–99.

ing of industry to become a permanent bar to drastic renovation at home. Nevertheless, the disintegration of the world order was going on without Britain's help, as was the long-run alteration of her balance of payments. Since she could not expect alone to withstand the flood, she fell in with the ways of the world. If in some respects she suffered from her lack of courage, in others she evolved, pragmatically and experimentally, a system of admirable wisdom and flexibility, which may well be a model for the world economy of the future.

Part Four

The Shifting Geographical Patterns of Great Britain's International Economic Transactions

———◆———

XI. SHIFTING GEOGRAPHICAL PATTERNS OF BRITISH EXPORTS AND IMPORTS, 1815–1939

THE CHANGING international economic position of the British people has entailed a constantly shifting geographical pattern of their international transactions. In part these changes were imposed from the outside. In part they represented a form of adjustment. In the period 1919–39, as earlier, the British economy adapted itself to the vicissitudes of the international competitive struggle by geographical reorientation of its economic relationships. In the following analysis of these changes we are not interested in the geographic or political patterns *per se;* we wish simply to use them as a means of analyzing the general problems, policies, and adjustments of the British economy and the balance of payments in a closer approximation to reality, i.e., to the network of specific international transactions of which they were constituted.

MERCHANDISE EXPORTS

In the growing world economy from 1815 to 1914, British exports to areas developing local competition did not necessarily suffer a net loss. Encroachments of competitors were tempered by the growing incomes and consumption and investment demand in those areas. In addition, British exporters turned to new markets. The exploration of both these outlets helped make possible the unceasing expansion of exports during this century. Perhaps the most interesting feature of the nineteenth-century free trade system was the extent to which Britain's trade expanded in the former fashion, i.e., merely through unbroken progress in old areas and by extension of international specialization in accordance with the dictates of comparative advantage. British exports to all major areas except the highly protectionist United States show a steady upward secular movement, a rise considerably more stable in volume than in value terms.

Nevertheless, the geographical center of gravity of British markets did shift. This shift was in large part the result simply of the more rapid increase in the purchasing power of new as compared with older areas. It resulted also from changes in the relative competitive position of British producers. In the 1820's when the South American revolutionists required guns and ships, and in the forties when France and Belgium needed railway iron, naturally they turned to England, who alone was in a position to supply the goods as well as much of the means of payment. The same was true during the great investment boom of 1850–73, although to a decreasing extent in certain growing industrial areas toward its close. On the other hand, neither the enormous growth of the United States after 1873 nor the great industrial development of Germany from 1880 on or of Canada after 1900 resulted in a commensurate rise in purchases of British goods. Britain fared better in outlying markets of Africa and Asia than within the United States and Germany or in markets (such as Canada, Latin America, continental Europe) geographically close to those major competitors. She fared best of all in empire markets because of the dominance there of the British company under British management, the colonial and Indian government purchases through crown agents resident in London, the natural preference for British goods among populations largely of British descent, and the extension of preferential tariff treatment to British goods by the major countries of the empire from 1897 on.[1] In 1857 Western Europe and the United States took 38.0 percent of British exports and 43.8 percent in 1872; in 1907 and 1913 their portions were only 28.8 and 25.1 percent. On the other hand, the share taken by Australia, India, New Zealand, South Africa, and Canada in the two earlier years was 23.7 percent (this total was abnormally high because of the Australian gold

---

[1] See Hobson, *Export of Capital*, chap. i, p. 31; F. L. McDougall, *Sheltered Markets*, London, Murray, 1925, pp. 20–36, chaps. iv, v; Haberler, *The Theory of International Trade*, pp. 369–70; Feis, *Europe, the World's Banker*, pp. 94–95.

boom) and 17.9 percent, and in the two later years 27.2 and 30.8 percent, respectively.

Except in so far as Britain was able to develop new products to supply the older markets, each succeeding wave of investment abroad could be expected to bring a relatively smaller increase in demand for British goods. Any enhancement of the ability of foreign producers to compete anywhere with British producers inevitably tended *per se* to reduce Britain's exports or her terms of trade. The ability of Britons to exploit new markets in the century from 1815 to 1913 provided an important offset to this tendency.

The most striking change in the distribution of British exports in the period 1913–38 was the continued relative rise of the empire. Omitting India and the Irish Free State, the only two individual exceptions, the empire's share rose in the years 1913–29–37 from 23.8 percent to 29.7 percent to 38.3 percent, respectively.[2] The rise was by no means uniform: for Canada and Australia it was only moderate, whereas the relative importance of the younger New Zealand, South Africa, and the colonies fully doubled.

The greatest relative losses were in the Far East, where industrialization, behind tariff protection, made its greatest inroads. The portion of British exports going to Asia as a whole (empire and non-empire) fell from 25.2 percent in 1913 to 17.1 percent in 1937, in distinct reversal of pre-war trends. India, Britain's leading market until 1936, alone took 13.4 percent in 1913, and only 7.8 percent in 1937. The other heavily declining area was Latin America, whose purchases were sustained until 1929 by heavy British and American loans, and then fell sharply with the turn of another cycle of Latin American boom and default.

On the other hand, sales to Europe as a whole maintained their relative position. Their respective 1913 and 1937 shares were 34.6 percent and 32.7 percent. This total, however, conceals some rather sharply divergent component long-run trends. The shares of Norway, Sweden, and Denmark expanded greatly, while those of Germany, Italy, Russia, and France all declined. Within Europe, as in the entire world, and after 1914 as before, Britain was finding her export markets more and more in the younger, mainly primary producing countries of the world.

But now geographical adjustments were powerless to prevent a steady

---

[2] Whenever comparisons are made with 1913, whether for exports or imports, trade with the Irish Free State, classed as external trade only after April, 1923 by the official statistics, is excluded throughout. Data on geographical distribution of British exports and imports based on annual tables in B. of T.J.

decline in the total volume. Changes in geographical distribution were less often adjustments than simply the result of differential rates of decline. Thus, despite their relative rise, the quantum of exports to the empire as a whole (adjusting the value figures for the index of average value of British exports, from Table 23, p. 153) probably declined slightly between 1913 and 1929, and fell heavily thereafter; the volume of exports only to South Africa, Scandinavia, New Zealand, and the West Indies apparently increased to any substantial degree, between 1913 and 1937.

The relative strength of Britain's exports to the empire was in large measure the result simply of the more rapid rise in the absorptive powers of these younger countries. Indeed, the British share in their total imports has declined secularly. She supplied 44.3 percent of their total imports in 1913, 38.6 percent in 1924, and 31.3 percent in 1929.[3] And although empire tariff preference did for a time thereafter substantially increase her share, over the whole period it was powerless to reverse the long-run tendency for British producers to lose ground relative to competitors. However, preference did arrest that decline almost entirely in the years 1929–38, and that in itself was an important contribution.[4]

[3] Data on trade of empire countries from *Statistical Abstracts for the British Empire*. Data for individual countries from Gr. Brit., Bd. of Trade, *Statistical Tables*, I, 64. Trade of the Irish Free State excluded throughout.

Percentage of Total Imports Coming from the U.K.

	1913	1924	1929		1913	1924	1929
Total empire	44.3	38.6	31.3	India	64.2	54.4	44.0
Four dominions	39.1	36.3	29.1	Australia	51.8	45.2	39.8
Rest of empire				Canada	21.3	19.0	15.2
(excluding India)	32.1	27.7	26.5	New Zealand	59.7	51.1	46.2
				U. of S. Africa	56.8	51.5	43.8

[4] Percentage Share of Total Imports Supplied by Great Britain.

Importing Country	1929	1931	1933	1935	1937	1938
Total empire	34.1	34.1	37.0	36.0	31.3	32.3
British India (by sea)	43.8	36.7	41.8	39.3	29.3	29.8
Empire excluding India	32.0	33.6	36.0	35.3	31.7	32.8
Canada	15.2	18.4	24.3	21.0	18.1	17.6
New Zealand	46.2	49.0	51.3	50.3	49.6	47.9
Australia	39.8	39.2	42.3	43.4	43.1	42.2
Union of South Africa	43.8	45.5	50.3	48.7	42.6	43.3

The reader will note the contrast between the continued rapid British decline in India—in the face of increased protection, agricultural depression, political boycott, and Japanese competition—and its happier experience elsewhere. Trade with the Irish Free State is now included throughout.

Between 1931 and 1933 British exports to the empire, omitting the Irish Free State (which was not a party to the imperial preference system) increased from 35.9 percent to 39.3 percent of the total. The Ottawa Agreements of 1932 were accountable not only for this increase but also in major part for the continued rise to 45.6 percent in 1938. For one thing, they had the negative virtue of putting ceilings over empire tariff levels and freezing margins of preference, while trade restrictions in the rest of the world continued to multiply. More positively, they included pledges by the Dominions to reconsider their tariffs, and some reductions were made later as a result. Finally, at the outset they merely gave Britain an increased share in a greatly decreased total. Total empire imports were extremely low in 1932, because of the particularly severe depression of these predominantly debtor primary-producing areas. When at last the empire's incomes and total imports recovered, preference enabled Britain to share in the rise more than she would otherwise have done.

Nevertheless, the concessions which Britain obtained from empire preference, in the way of an absolute reduction of tariffs against her goods, were extremely disappointing. This was particularly true in the case of the most highly industrialized and hence most highly protectionist dominions, Canada and Australia. Eventually most of their crisis duties were removed, but even then the basic rates remained very high.[5] Preference was meaningless if even preferential rates were prohibitive. The Australian market did not regain its peak 1929 share of total British sales until 1938, and Canada did not reach its 1931 high until 1936, for all the relative advantages which British producers enjoyed in the interim.[6] Liberal British economists argued with considerable justification that Britain would be better off without preference, if only the dominions would make substantial nondiscriminating reductions in their general tariffs.[7]

Other factors besides preference contributed to the continued relative rise of empire markets after 1933. Economic recovery of the empire and

---

[5] Richardson, *Britain's Economic Foreign Policy*, pp. 147–51; Villeneuve, *La Préférence impériale*, pp. 30–32; Findlay, *Britain under Protection*, chaps. xii, xiii; *Economist*, CXV (1932), 833–34; Benham, *Great Britain under Protection*, pp. 94, 98.

[6] This was not entirely due to tariffs. The more widely fluctuating incomes of these countries tended to have the same effect.

[7] Benham, *Great Britain under Protection*, p. 80. From 1935 on, it should be noted, liberal elements gained political power in the dominions, especially in Canada, and tariffs were lowered considerably on British and foreign goods. *Economist:* "Ottawa Section," CXXVII (1937), 264, 268, "Canadian Tariff Concessions," CXXVI (1937), 513–14.

of the sterling bloc in general, which had cut itself off from the vicious deflation of gold prices, preceded that of the rest of the world. Although British exports secured no advantages in these markets by virtue of a depreciated pound, her sales to them were increased by the more rapid recovery of their incomes, as well as by substantial currency stability and a certain revival of international lending within the bloc. Another important factor was the reversal around 1933 of the differential price trends, which had since 1929 sorely oppressed the largely primary producing empire countries.

It is not surprising, therefore, that contrary to a priori expectations one factor alone, the depreciation of sterling, failed to increase British sales to the gold areas more rapidly than to those markets whose currencies depreciated equally. Sales to France, Belgium, and the Netherlands declined continuously in relative importance from 1931 through 1935, and only began to recover slightly in 1936 and 1937, when at last they, too, cut themselves from gold. The share of the United States fell from 4.7 percent in 1931 to 4.1 percent in 1932, recovering only in 1933, when the dollar also was forced down and American reflation began. The same was true in the case of Canada, whose dollar failed to follow sterling. The reason for this apparent failure of the fall of sterling was that it led inevitably to increased trade restrictions, as an alternative to devaluation, by the many countries which were subjected thereby to greater currency pressure.[8] If foreign countries were to maintain their currencies, they had to restrict their purchases by trade controls or deflation, in either case offsetting any competitive advantage of a depreciated sterling. Thus the share of British exports to Europe, excluding the Scandinavian and Baltic states (and Ireland), fell from 28.7 percent in 1931 to 21.6 percent in 1936, under the stress of multiplying tariffs, quotas, exchange controls, and deflation.

Meanwhile, within the sterling bloc, closer economic relations were being built, on the firm basis of economic recovery. The share of British exports taken by the Scandinavian countries rose from 4.3 percent to 7.5 percent and of Russia and the Baltic States from 1.3 percent to 3.6 percent between 1929 and 1938. With all these countries, after 1932, Britain negotiated trade agreements, obtaining tariff and other trade concessions. In addition all of them, except the U.S.S.R. and Lithuania, became at one time or another members of the sterling bloc, British exports to them being thus further aided by currency stability and the

[8] See Findlay, *Britain under Protection*, chap. iv.

British loan policy. A notable instance of the latter was a £10 million loan extended to the U.S.S.R., guaranteed by the Export Credits Guarantee Department, for the purchase of British goods.[9]

Here was apparent the new emergent pattern of Britain's international transactions: a withdrawal into a more closed and regulated regional system, with Britain at the center, attempting to maintain ever closer economic ties with the younger, largely primary producing countries of the empire and the sterling area. Despite the predominant influence of conscious policy this was, it will be noted, but an intensification of secular trends apparent well before 1929, or even 1914.

Merchandise Imports

As long as Britain was a free and open market and her people bought where they pleased, as long as the problem of making payment for imports of goods or securities was never so serious as to force Britain either to suspend convertibility of her currency or to control her trade—so long were the sources of her imports and the size of her bilateral trade balances a matter of comparative indifference. Bilateral balances were in general transferred multilaterally without serious friction, and they and imports were left to take care of themselves. With the disruption of the more or less smoothly adjusting world economy, however, and the failure of free economic forces automatically to bring adjustment, these things have become of increasing significance.

Long before 1914 there was a natural tendency for Britain to obtain an increasing share of her growing food and raw material requirements from the untapped resources of the younger outlying regions of the world, just as British manufactures came increasingly to rely upon these regions for markets. In 1900 Argentina supplied less than 1 percent of total British beef imports, and the United States about 70 percent; in 1913 Argentina's share was more than 70 percent and the United States' now below 1 percent. The shift in maize was scarcely less striking. So, Argentina's share of Britain's total imports rose from 2½ percent to 5½ percent, and that of the empire, for similar reasons, from 21 percent to 25 percent, in these thirteen years.[10] It was to be expected that such

[9] The 1934 trade agreement with the U.S.S.R. had virtually no effect on sales of British goods, Russia simply increasing her purchases of Colonial produce re-exported from Britain.

[10] These shifts from rising industrial countries to younger primary producing suppliers must, however, not be oversimplified, even less in the case of British imports, which were subject to no tariff, than in the case of British exports. In both, the older areas showed

secular shifts would continue after the war, although undoubtedly at a slower rate as the world reached its extensive frontiers. The relative rises between 1913 and 1929 of New Zealand, Denmark, Argentina, non-British Asia and the decline of the United States may thus be attributed mainly to the operation of the same longer-run factors influencing the supply of primary products as were operative throughout the nineteenth century.[11]

In imports as in exports, the most striking change of the period 1913–39 was the creation of closer ties to the empire. The relative rise of the empire supplier was very modest before the great depression, but enormous thereafter, its 1937 share in total British imports of 38.2 percent comparing with 24.9 percent in 1913 and 26.0 percent in 1929. It was also very uneven as between different countries. While the shares of Indian and South African suppliers were about constant, those of Canada, Australia, and New Zealand together rose from 11.6 percent in 1913 to no less than 20.9 percent in 1937. This rise was largely at the expense of the countries of Europe, whose share declined from 40.5 percent in 1913 to 32.0 percent in 1937. The Scandinavian and Baltic countries increased their portions somewhat, but the shares of Germany and France combined fell from 16.5 percent in 1913 to 6.1 percent in 1937. The other heavy decline was in imports from the United States, Britain's greatest single supplier, whose share fell from 18.4 percent in 1913 to 11.3 percent in 1937.

The causes for the slow rise in the relative importance of the empire supplier between 1913 and 1929 are of interest because they help us to evaluate the role of commercial policy in the rapid ascent thereafter. Some causes were temporary; 1929 seems to have been an abnormally poor year, partly because of bad harvests.[12] However, empire producers were also encountering increasing opposition from such growing competitors as Argentina and Denmark, who expanded their share of the

---

surprising strength. Increased imports of German manufactures, for example, helped to raise that country to the rank of Britain's second leading supplier in 1913 with 10½ percent of Britain's total imports, in contrast with 6 percent in 1900.

[11] For example: Argentina's share of the world's meat exports, and New Zealand's portion of the world's exports of butter and cheese both continued to rise rapidly after the war. Bank of England, *Statistical Summary*, April, 1932, p. 10. The more than proportionate rise of Britain's imports from China, Japan, and the Dutch East Indies likewise consisted mainly of primary products.

[12] See tables, *ibid.*; also table from K. A. H. Murray and Ruth L. Cohen, "The Planning of Britain's Food Imports," Oxford U. Agricultural Economics Inst., reproduced in P.E.P., *Report on International Trade*, Appendix I, Table 9.

British market at the expense not only of the once-predominant United States, but to some extent of Canada and Australia as well.[13] Little wonder, then, that the latter countries clamored for preferential treatment by Britain. The relative weakness of their export prices also doubtless retarded their rise compared, for example, with the countries of Europe.

While it might appear that the enormous relative rise of empire suppliers after 1931 was merely a reinforced secular trend, it is thus difficult to attribute much less than the entire responsibility to the British tariff and imperial preference, in view of the 1913 to 1929 experience—the greater strength of Denmark and Argentina and the increasing British consumer and industrial demand for foreign manufactured goods, of which the empire supplied but little. The tariff, directed primarily at manufactured goods, cut down empire sales far less than it did others. Preference, on the other hand, simply diverted orders from foreign to empire producers.[14]

The severest relative losses in sales to Britain between 1931 and 1933 were borne by the manufacturing countries. The combined shares of Germany, Belgium, and France were reduced by the tariff from 16.1 percent to 9.2 percent in these years. Correspondingly, empire participation (excluding the Irish Free State) rose from 24.7 percent to 34.3 percent, because of Britain's decreased total purchases of manufactures and because of the drastic diversion of her food imports from foreign to empire sources.[15] The most important diversions were from Danish

---

[13] Thus there was a marked drop between 1925 and 1929 in the empire's share in meat, butter, tea, and fruits and nuts, as well as grain and flour. Bacon and butter provide clear examples of this displacement, mainly by Denmark.

[14] These generalizations, of course, require some qualification. The tariff doubtless caused some diversion of consumer demands from protected to unprotected products, and tended therefore to increase empire sales in absolute terms. Preference undoubtedly reduced the absolute total of British trade, first by creating new tariffs and increasing and freezing old ones, in order to establish a margin of preference, and second by artificially diverting purchases from cheaper to dearer suppliers. The differential incidence of the new duties of early 1932 and of those added as a result of the Ottawa agreements is illustrated by a table compiled by the *Economist*, "Ottawa Supplement," Oct. 22, 1932, p. 6. The producers of manufactures, it is clear, were especially affected by the original duties, and of these Germany, France, Switzerland, and Belgium were subjected to but slight additional burdens by the Ottawa agreements, as they competed scarcely at all with empire products. On the other hand, predominantly agricultural countries—notably Argentina, Denmark, the U.S.S.R.—which were hit much less than the average by the original duties, suffered from a considerable absolute rise in the later tariffs, because their products competed with those of the empire, and suffered further, of course, because of the preference granted their empire competitors.

[15] According to quantum indexes computed by K. A. H. Murray and Ruth L. Cohen,

pork products and butter, and Argentina's beef and grain; the United States and the Netherlands were also hit.[16] Although this diversion was almost instantaneous, the shares of Denmark and Argentina in Britain's total imports did not begin to decline until after 1933, when cyclical recovery reduced the relative importance of food imports,[17] and increased pressure was put on these producers in favor of their empire competitors and the British farmer, by tariffs and by trade agreements, both measures forcing them to accept smaller shares in the British market.[18]

Meanwhile the empire benefited also by the recovery of British industry and its raw material requirements. Whereas the greatest net (relative) gains in the British market between 1929 and 1933 were made by the predominantly food producing Dominions (excluding the Irish Free State), in the recovery after 1933, with soaring raw material prices, almost all of the further empire increase was in the shares of raw material producers, Canada, the colonies, and India. However, these gains, too, must be very largely attributed to preference, which enabled the empire to participate much more fully than it otherwise would have in the greatly expanded demand for raw materials.

The weight of the other factors influencing the distribution of British

---

reproduced in P.E.P., *Report on International Trade*, Appendix I, Table 9, United Kingdom imports of empire food were in 1933 20.5 percent and in 1936 30 percent above their 1931 level, while purchases of non-empire food declined by 25 percent and 35.3 percent in these same intervals. Their table reveals also how the combination of preference, agricultural protection, the decline of sterling, and rising prices of foods reversed a 17 percent increase in the volume of Britain's total food imports between the 1927–29 average and 1931, and the progressing standards of consumption which they entailed; by 1936 the index was only 5 percent above the 1927–29 level.

[16] P.E.P., *op. cit.*, p. 293. The main American losses because of preference were in timber, nonferrous metals, pig products, apples, and wheat. The main beneficiary in these directions was Canada. American crop restriction and droughts were important contributory factors. See Bidwell, *Our Trade with Britain*, chap. v, and pp. 114–17.

[17] Food, drink and tobacco declined from 52.4 to 43.9 percent of Britain's total retained imports between 1933 and 1937.

[18] This is illustrated most clearly in the case of bacon and hams. Largely because of agricultural protection, Britain's imports of these products declined from 12,200,000 cwts. in 1932 to 7,500,000 in 1938. Imports from the empire rose, however, from 500,000 to 2,100,000, those from foreign countries thus declining all the more, from 11,700,000 to 5,500,000 cwts. Danish producers did not fare as badly as declining volume sales would indicate. Since they controlled the distribution of export licenses, were well organized, and did not undercut one another, they managed to benefit to the maximum from the higher prices which British consumers were forced to pay. While the volume of Denmark's sales declined by more than half in these years, actual money receipts were only 4 to 6 percent lower in 1938 than in 1932. Findlay, *Britain under Protection*, pp. 162–63; Benham, *Great Britain under Protection*, pp. 64, 141, 145–46.

imports is difficult to assess. Changes in currency valuations must have tended to restrict her purchases from gold relative to sterling countries, who were indeed induced to follow the pound largely because of their great dependence upon the British market. British trade agreements helped sustain Britain's imports from non-empire sterling area countries, notably by tariff reductions on Scandinavian and Baltic timber, paper, and other wood products. However, their influence was not great. Britain's concessions were restricted by her empire commitments, which she enforced in the trade agreements. Moreover, it was her definite purpose to use her strong bargaining position, arising from the heavily adverse trade balances with these countries, to redress these balances by obtaining many and giving few concessions. Here, as in exports, the chief determinant in the emergent geographic pattern of Britain's international transactions was conscious policy, whether or not the implications and results of that policy were actually comprehended at the time.

XII. THE PATTERN IN EQUILIBRIUM, 1929

UNDER LAISSEZ FAIRE three categories of variables determine the geographical configuration of merchandise and service trade between the peoples of the world: the total demand dispositions of the various populations, vis-à-vis all the suppliers in the world; the supply functions of each, in conjunction with those of all other producers, vis-à-vis all the markets of the world; and the disposable purchasing power in each area.[1] Strictly speaking, the last is redundant, since it can operate upon the balance only through effective demand or supply curves. However, in the analysis of the balance of payments, where relative shifts of purchasing power play so large a role in shaping and maintaining the equilibrium situation, it is useful to think of supply and demand curves as potential dispositions, at given equilibrium levels of purchasing power, altered and made more or less effective by fluctuations in those levels. Under conditions of equilibrium in the balance of payments, such fluctuations, operating upon given bilateral balances, arise from two sources: unilateral transfers between the two areas concerned and the net balance of payments of each with all the rest of the world except the other.[2] For the total balance of payments, these flows tend constantly to cancel out. But for bilateral balances, where debits and credits need not be equated, they may be continuous in one direction. They are in a sense only intermediate determinants, their size and direction being themselves the products, among other things, of the basic reciprocal supply and demand dispositions. But in their continuous unidirectional flow they mold all bilateral balances and tend to keep the total in equilibrium.

These variables seem to operate so as to cause a great proportion of the payments between any two countries to be balanced bilaterally. International trade has been in large measure a fairly simple bilateral barter

---

[1] See pp. 7, 127–29, 142–44, above.

[2] The real determinant is actual rather than merely potential expenditure (or disposable purchasing power), and this is subject, of course, to internal as well as external influences. However, in postulating conditions of equilibrium, we assume that if one country turns over its money more or less rapidly, or increases or contracts its money supply at a different rate than the rest of the world, the total balance and each bilateral balance are successfully adjusted to that situation.

of primary for manufactured goods, any surpluses being largely offset, bilaterally, by net capital and interest and dividend flows. This has been true largely because the wealthier countries have been producers of a disposable surplus of those goods and services which the more primitive have required. Personal and political ties, the fact that established trading connections, including shipping services, are two-way affairs, increase the presumption of bilateral balance. This presumption is a reasonable one. If there are strong influences at work causing A's balance of payments with the world as a whole to be equilibrated, there must be influences tending toward such an equilibration between A and B and between A and C as well. And only bilateral balances between the countries initially concerned in given transactions are subject to the full reciprocal equilibrating influences at either end. The great bulk of Great Britain's transfers in international transactions seem therefore to have been made on a bilateral basis, even under relatively free trade.[3] According to the few estimates which are available—of which one must be extremely wary—this seems to have been true also of world trade as a whole.[4]

There is nevertheless no ground for presumption that individual bilateral balances can come anywhere near complete equality except by chance or by conscious policy. Before the great depression the amount of multilateral settlement was considerable, and its true importance was incalculable. It was at once the symbol of the organic unity of the old world economy and one of its essential instruments. Its disappearance both made inevitable and was made inevitable by the disruption of that functioning whole and the substitution for it of a regime of economic

[3] Britain's trade with the United States, for example, was for long an extreme example of the importance of multilateral transfer, the bilateral balance of net trade (i.e., excluding heavy British re-exports to the United States) amounting in 1913 to no less than 5/8 of the total trade between the two. However, if account be taken of the various invisible transactions between the two countries (based partly on estimates described on p. 221*n*, below), the net bilateral balance of payments between the two appears to have been on the order of £50 million in that year, out of total transactions of at least £250 million. No less than 80 percent of the transfers were effected without the intermediation of third countries.

[4] See estimates for 1929 by League of Nations, *World Economic Survey*, 1935–36, pp. 181–83; Condliffe, *The Reconstruction of World Trade*, pp. 282–83. Most estimates seem to ignore invisibles entirely and are hence quite unreliable. The one cited by the League, for example, takes as a rough measure of a country's triangular trade the total of individual bilateral trade balances which cancel out against each other. In fact, however, none of these transfers need actually be triangular. Each net trade balance may be offset bilaterally by an exactly equivalent bilateral balance of invisibles.

regionalism and bilateral negotiation. In this process Britain played a major role.

THE MAJOR TRIANGLE: THE GREAT BRITAIN–EMPIRE SIDE

In the following study of Britain's bilateral balances of payments, 1929 is chosen for detailed analysis as a year in which we may find the closest approximation (except, perhaps, for 1928) to conditions of equilibrium under free trade in all the years 1919–39.[5]

In 1929 Great Britain appears to have received from the empire a sum on the order of £150 million from her investments there, and an additional £40 million for the use of her shipping.[6] There were other receipts on balance for her banking, insurance, and other services, and inpayments of a political nature—notably the Indian home charges and Irish land annuities. The former alone amounted, net, to about £24 million in 1929.[7] We have here a sum of perhaps £240 million, which was transferred from the empire to the mother country without serious disequilibrium.[8]

Britain received her invisible incomes from abroad in the form of a heavy passive trade balance, amounting in 1929 to £380 million. The empire as a whole contributed perhaps ⅗ of the income from investments, and ⅓ of the shipping income. Yet, instead of contributing a proportional

---

[5] The latter part of 1929 witnessed the beginnings of serious disequilibria, account of which is taken wherever it appears necessary in the subsequent discussion.

[6] The author has compiled detailed estimates of major components of Britain's bilateral balances of payments in 1913, 1929, and 1937, to which reference is made in this chapter and the one which follows. These estimates, which are too lengthy to reproduce here, are composed of merchandise trade, new issues in the London market, receipts of interest and dividends, and shipping income. The new issue figures for 1913 are those of Paish, *Statist*, Suppl., Feb. 14, 1914, p. v; the post-war figures are taken from the *Midland Bank Monthly Review*. The invisible income figures are computed by applying to the respective Board of Trade balance of payments estimates Paish's geographical breakdown of Britain's overseas investments in 1913 (as amended by Feis, *Europe, the World's Banker*, p. 23), those of Kindersley for 1930 and 1936, and only very roughly applicable statistics of the origins and destinations, by net tonnage, of British ships clearing and entering British ports with cargo. This method involves serious errors and inaccuracies, and the resultant estimates afford no more than a very general indication of the probable order of magnitude of these items.

[7] This excludes interest on Indian government debt, and subtracts payments to the Indian government from England. *Finance and Revenue Accounts of the Government of India.*

[8] True, some empire countries were beginning to feel the coming world crisis; but the peculiar transfer mechanism here described could scarcely be considered the cause of this incipient disequilibrium, for the facts were substantially the same in 1927–28, when transfers were effected without difficulty.

share of the net imports, the empire actually bought from Britain £25.5 million more of goods than it sold to her. Merchandise trade thus added a transfer load of its own, bringing the total to £265 million.

To these burdens there was only one important bilateral offset—the willingness of Britons to accept claims on the future income of these countries. In 1929 some £55 million of new empire issues were floated in London, most of them taken up by British investors. Empire repayments seem, however, to have been on the order of £30 million,[9] leaving a net inflow on long-term capital account (by these inadequate measures alone) of perhaps £25 million. This was considerably less than the issues of previous years, but the 1929 picture is still not unrepresentative in general of the late twenties. There was left, then, a substantial surplus of perhaps £240 million, or £190 million when empire gold sales are deducted,[10] which empire countries obtained on balance elsewhere to transmit to England.[11] The total of merchandise trade between England and the empire was £625 million (net trade). A failure to balance by £190 million out of total payments (both ways) of perhaps £900 to £1,000 million is a sizable discrepancy.

In explanation, we revert to the determinants of bilateral balances listed above. The relative demand and supply situation was, with important exceptions to be discussed below, as follows: (1) empire producers were able to satisfy only a small portion of Britain's import needs, while British producers on the contrary held a strong position in empire markets; (2) Britain imported heavily from non-empire countries, while her place in those markets was relatively weak; (3) empire producers sold heavily to foreign markets, but bought lightly from them. The purchasing-power factor bound these dispositions together and converted them into equal and offsetting bilateral balances between the United Kingdom and the rest of the empire, between the rest of the empire and

[9] A rough estimate based upon partial figures of Sir Robert Kindersley.

[10] See pp. 228, 230, below. There must be deducted from the £60 million of total empire gold exports the £7 million which went directly to other empire countries, and most of the £2.7 million of Britain's gold (re-) exports to empire countries. The reader will note that the figure of £60 million is not for the calendar year and that in the fiscal year after June, 1929, Australia lost heavily of her gold reserves, a result of severe disequilibrium in her balance of payments. The Australian exports are, accordingly, for the year July, 1928, to June, 1929.

[11] These were by no means entirely fixed and unyielding obligations to which other balance of payments items had to adjust. Their size and direction were closely related as effect as well as cause to all these other transactions.

the non-empire world, and between the non-empire world and the United Kingdom, in each case in favor of the area named first. Under equilibrium no single one was possible without the others. Together with the configuration of invisibles, they created continuous flows of buying power from foreign countries to the empire, from the empire to Britain, and from Britain to non-empire areas. Had these flows not been equivalent and balancing, they would have created net uncompensated purchasing power, exchange and interest rate, and price level effects, and hence a persistent tendency to re-equilibration. Each proposition offset, caused, and resulted from the others, via the equilibrating tendencies of the balance of payments.

Britain had a constant net inflow of buying power from her empire and from the world as a whole, in invisible income therefrom, and hence a heavy debit trade balance. Yet she sold to the empire more than she bought of it, and took no larger share of empire exports in 1928 and 1929 than she supplied of empire imports. In 1929 she sold to these countries 44½ percent of her exports and bought from them only 27 percent of her retained imports. The empire was clearly a better customer by far for British goods than Britain was for empire goods.[12]

The effect of these supply-demand dispositions alone may be isolated by use of the data in Table 27. With the first four empire countries listed, Great Britain had an active, with the latter four a passive, balance of merchandise trade. The final ratios are arranged so that a high ratio justifies a presumption that these dispositions favored the British exporter and discouraged the empire exporter. However, the ratios still contain the influence of relative levels of purchasing power, the portion which Britain and the empire countries took of each other's exports being a function in part of the buying power of each relative to that of other markets. For this reason the equality of the two ratios, (1) of empire exports to Britain, to total empire exports and (2) of empire imports from Britain to total empire imports (Table 27 A), by no means indicates an equal reciprocal balance of supply-demand dispositions. It results partly from the fact that because of increments to British purchasing power from invisibles her imports normally are absolutely greater than her exports.

The world as a whole sold to Great Britain 15.40 percent of its total

[12] McDougall, *Sheltered Markets*, chaps. i–iii, *passim;* Beveridge, *Tariffs: the Case Examined*, pp. 135–37.

exports in 1929; it purchased from Great Britain only 10.86 percent of its total imports in that year. The ratio between these two was 0.705.[13] The mere fact that the ratios in Table 27 A for South Africa and the Irish Free State were less than 1.00 (i.e., Britain supplied a smaller share of their imports than she took of their exports) does not mean that reciprocal supply and demand dispositions favored them against Britain. The fact that the discrepancy between the two percentages was smaller than the discrepancy between similar percentages for the trade between Britain and the world as a whole indicates quite the opposite: that in these cases, too, Britain was favored by these dispositions. The relative level of Britain's buying power, taking merchandise trade as the effect entirely of the flow of invisibles, was sufficiently high so that she sold to the world only 70.5 percent of the goods she took from it. The smaller discrepancy in the case of South Africa and the Irish Free State (ratios of 0.88 and 0.84 in 1929) can be attributed only to relative demand and supply dispositions, all other factors being now eliminated.[14]

We may therefore conclude that were it not for the purchasing power factors Britain's trade balance with the Irish Free State would have

---

[13] These percentages (from Table 18, p. 132) represent actually the British share as a market of total world imports and her share as an exporter of total world exports, and the resultant ratio is therefore really:

(1)
$$\frac{\text{U.K. exports}}{\text{World exports}} \div \frac{\text{U.K. imports}}{\text{World imports}}$$

If all trade were uniformly valued, so that total world imports equaled total world exports, this would be precisely what we have said in the text:

(2)
$$\frac{\text{U.K. exports}}{\text{World imports}} \div \frac{\text{U.K. imports}}{\text{World exports}}$$

In this case we could have obtained exactly the same ratio simply by dividing British exports by her imports.

Were we actually to try to find directly the ratio described in the text (2), instead of the one we have actually obtained (1), we would have fallen into error, because both U.K. and most world imports are valued c.i.f. This would have made ratio (2) unduly low. Using ratio (1) we avoid this pitfall, as the c.i.f. valuations cancel their effects in the second fraction. The result is the true picture of (2) with the error eliminated, for, if total imports do equal total exports (or the effect of higher import valuation is canceled out, as here), (1) and (2) are precisely the same.

[14] The effects of differences in relative levels of purchasing power which caused both South African and British imports to exceed their exports are eliminated in this comparison between the ratios of Table A and the ratio for Britain's share in world trade (0.705). On the South African side this is done by the use of percentages of her total imports and exports, thus eliminating the effect of absolute differences between the two. In the case of Britain it is done by comparing her shares in South African trade with her shares in world trade, the general purchasing power influences, tending to give her a passive balance in both cases, thus canceling out.

TABLE 27

RELATIVE SHARES OF THE EMPIRE AND THE UNITED KINGDOM IN THE TOTAL
FOREIGN TRADE OF EACH OTHER [a]

A. *Percentage of Total Empire Countries' Trade*

	(1) IMPORTS FROM UNITED KINGDOM		(2) EXPORTS TO UNITED KINGDOM [b]		(3) RATIOS: (1) ÷ (2)	
Country	*1928*	*1929*	*1928*	*1929*	*1928*	*1929*
India	45.84	43.84	20.88	21.39	2.20	2.05
British Malaya	16.00	16.11	11.55	14.31	1.39	1.13
Australia	42.67	39.79	38.64	38.09	1.10	1.04
Union of South Africa	44.29	43.78	49.90	49.50	0.89	0.88
Total empire	35.24	34.05	35.17	34.10	1.00	1.00
Irish Free State	77.94	78.11	96.17	92.78	0.81	0.84
New Zealand	47.38	46.17	74.46	75.03	0.64	0.62
Canada	15.34	15.16	31.68	25.32	0.48	0.60
Ceylon	22.37	22.22	40.54	42.47	0.55	0.52

B. *Percentage of Total British Trade* [c]

	(1) EXPORTS TO EMPIRE		(2) IMPORTS FROM EMPIRE		(3) RATIO: (1) ÷ (2)	
Country	*1928*	*1929*	*1928*	*1929*	*1928*	*1929*
Union of South Africa	4.36	4.46	2.02	1.99	2.16	2.24
India	11.60	10.73	5.39	5.15	2.15	2.08
Australia	7.69	7.44	4.55	4.56	1.69	1.63
Malaya	2.09	2.13	1.04	1.45	2.01	1.47
Total empire	45.28	44.49	30.41	29.41	1.49	1.51
Irish Free State	4.85	5.95	3.78	3.69	1.28	1.34
Canada	4.76	4.80	4.78	3.80	1.00	1.26
New Zealand	2.67	2.93	3.95	3.91	0.68	0.75
Ceylon	0.83	0.81	1.15	1.24	0.72	0.65

[a] Source: *Statistical Abstract for the British Empire; Board of Trade Journal; Annual Statements of Trade of the United Kingdom.*
[b] Includes only goods of domestic origin, but covers, of course, all empire exports to Britain, whether or not goods are subsequently re-exported.
[c] Imports include goods subsequently re-exported; exports are of British goods only.

been active in 1929 instead of passive. Similarly, of course, it would have been much more active than it was with the areas with higher ratios than Ireland in Table A: South Africa, the empire as a whole, Australia, Malaya, and India. Only with Canada, New Zealand, and Ceylon did reciprocal supply-demand dispositions not favor Britain, on balance.[15]

The relative influence of the purchasing power factor alone may be demonstrated by the use of the two tables A and B, in conjunction. Gold sales and capital inflows into South Africa entailed a heavy passive trade balance. England was less well situated in reciprocal supply-demand dispositions in respect to this empire country than the others with whom her trade balance was active (see Table A); but she shared in South Africa's general passive trade balance, with the result that that country's ratio in Table B is the highest of the four countries. This factor is also of vital importance in the case of India, in the opposite direction. The Indian total trade balance was normally strongly active, her balance of payments being dominated by heavy outpayments for precious metals, debt service, and political obligations. Thus, although Indian-British reciprocal demand and supply dispositions were relatively most favorable to Britain of all empire countries (Table A), this benefit was offset somewhat by the above purchasing power factors, so that the ratio in Table B was by no means so high relative to the others as these dispositions alone would have dictated.

Finally, there were the purchasing power factors already discussed, making for a passive total British trade balance. These factors offset the favorable demand-supply position with respect to the empire; as we have seen, in the case of Ireland they alone were responsible for a negative bilateral balance.

Because of the complete inadequacy of her domestic food supply, Britain alone among the leading industrial countries of the world imported considerably more food than raw materials in 1929. The empire, on the contrary, was primarily a raw material producer. In this basic situation lies much of the explanation for the configuration of supply-demand dispositions under study.

[15] The relatively disadvantageous empire position in its trade with Britain may be illustrated similarly. The empire supplied 26.9 percent of Britain's retained imports in 1929, while taking 44.5 percent of her domestic exports. On the other hand, the empire (excluding Britain) supplied 15.06 percent of the world's total retained imports while taking for home consumption only 13.44 percent of the world's total exports. The first ratio is 0.60, the second 1.12 (1.155 if intra-empire trade be excluded), and their discrepancy is a measure of the relative unfavorableness of the empire situation vis-à-vis Britain. World percentages from Board of Trade, *Statistical Tables*, I, 164–65.

In 1929 the empire supplied a relatively small portion (¼ or less) of Britain's major food imports, except for a share of ⅓ (and usually more) of grains and flour, roughly ⅖ of the less important butter and sugar, and ⁶⁄₇ of the tea. Because of the head start of other producers, their greater propinquity to England in some cases, their more favorable climate in others, and the mere fact that as world suppliers of foods non-empire countries simply bulked larger than empire countries, beef from Argentina, pork products from Denmark, dairy products from Denmark and the Netherlands, fruits and wines from across the Channel and from Mediterranean Europe, fruits, too, from the United States, fish from northern Europe, tobacco from the United States, and grains from the United States and Argentina dominated the British market. In raw materials also, except for wool and the much less important rubber, the empire's share was equally small, largely because of the greater distance from the British market or because Britain's industries required raw materials other than those which the empire was especially capable of producing. These factors seem to explain Britain's heavy imports from non-empire sources of cotton, petroleum, wood, and nonferrous metals. Finally, the empire, being relatively unindustrialized, supplied but 9 percent of Britain's purchases of manufactures and semi-manufactures.

Whereas customs, tastes, and the head start of older producers tended to incline the British consumer to non-empire products, all these factors, as well as others already mentioned, created in empire markets a preference for British goods. The empire countries were importers mainly of staple manufactures—textiles, apparel, iron and steel, machinery—and in 1929 Britain was still the world's leading exporter of manufactured goods, and particularly of these very staples.

Canada, New Zealand, and Ceylon were exceptions to this pattern of United Kingdom empire trade relationships. The latter two were not particularly striking. The trade of Ceylon was relatively small. And New Zealand took a large share of her imports from Britain, her exceptional position resulting from the very high percentage of her sales (mainly of foods and wool) taken by that country (see Table 27). In the more important case, Canada, a stronger policy of protection, more advanced industrialization than in any other empire country, and the predominance of the United States competitors, cut her purchases of British manufactures, whereas Britain remained a good market for Canadian foods and raw materials.

THE EMPIRE–"FOREIGN" SIDE

The United Kingdom was in 1929 incapable of absorbing more than one-fourth of the enormous empire raw-material exports, as Table 28 indicates. She obtained 80 to 93 percent of her rubber, wool, jute, tin (and cocoa) from these countries, but the major empire production was left to find other markets. No system of tariff preference could alter this. In contrast with the small British share, the United States alone took 64 percent of the rubber and 56.6 percent of the tin exports listed in Table 28.

There were evidently other causes for this situation. The greater distance of the empire supplier from the British market would seem to explain why so important an exporter as Canada supplied so small a part of British requirements of wood products and metals, while 86.6 percent and 68 percent of her exports of these goods, respectively, went to the United States. Settled connections and the peculiar needs of British industry were perhaps also significant. These factors plus transport costs might explain the negligible British purchases of Indian raw cotton, 56 percent of which went to Japan and China.[16]

In their major food products, except for the intermediate case of grains, quite the contrary situation prevailed. Of empire meats, dairy products, sugar, and tea the huge British market took almost all; [17] but, as we have seen, except for tea, this satisfied far less than half of her vast needs. Here inadequacy of empire ability to supply, rather than of Britain's power to absorb, was the crucial factor.[18] The bulk of empire exports were of the first group, the raw materials (and cocoa), for which it had to find its major outlets in industrial America, Japan, and the continent of Europe.

Among its other staple products, the British Empire was in 1929 responsible for about three-fourths of total world gold production.[19] The exports of South Africa, Canada, and Australia, out of normal produc-

---

[16] Britain took only slightly more than one-fifth of her oil seeds and nuts from India, but, except in the case of linseed, India filled the major part of Britain's demand for those varieties in which India's supply was great (notably ground nuts and castor seeds), and was still left with a great surplus to sell elsewhere.

[17] See Table 28, and p. 47n, above.

[18] Cocoa is the sole exception among the foods (see Table 28), Britain's inadequate demand being the main factor, as with the raw materials.

[19] B.I.S., *Tenth Annual Report*, p. 66 (1940).

TABLE 28

LEADING EXPORTS OF BRITISH EMPIRE COUNTRIES IN 1929 [a]

Product	Exports from Leading Exporting Countries [b] (£000)	Percentage to Non-empire Countries
Tin [c]	21,248	95.7 [d]
Raw cotton	49,184	93.2
Wood, timber, and products [e]	56,395	92.7
Rubber [c]	57,282	88.8 [d]
Jute and jute manufactures	57,357	86.5
Raw and waste wool	91,273	83.3 [d]
Oil seeds and nuts	19,238	83.0
Raw cocoa	13,812	79.2
Metals: ores, concentrates, scrap, and manufactures	40,306	77.3
Total	406,095	
Grain (incl. pulse)	124,300	45.2
Tea	30,065	13.0
Meat, live animals for food	36,207	5.0
Butter, cheese, eggs	36,105	4.2
Raw sugar	8,172	0.1
Total	110,549	

[a] Sources: *Statistical Abstract for the British Empire; Annual Statement of the Sea-Borne Trade of British India; Economic Survey of the Colonial Empire.* Unless otherwise noted, Australian figures are for the year July, 1929, to June, 1930, Indian for April, 1929, to March, 1930.

[b] Tin and rubber, Malaya; cotton, jute, oil seeds, and nuts, India (jute exports for April, 1928, to March, 1929); wood, Canada; wool, Australia (July, 1928, to June, 1929), New Zealand, and South Africa; cocoa, the colonies; metals, Canada, Australia, India; grain, Canada (1928), India, Australia (July, 1928, to June, 1929); tea, India, Ceylon; meat, Eire, New Zealand, Australia; butter, New Zealand, Eire, Australia, Canada; sugar, the colonies, Australia, South Africa. Except for tin and rubber, exports to empire countries other than Britain are excluded, i.e., the totals and the foreign share thereof refer only to the total of exports to the United Kingdom and non-empire countries.

[c] Exports to empire countries other than Britain are included both in the total and in the non-empire share thereof, the latter being derived by deducting from the total the specified exports to England. The resultant overstatement of the foreign percentage is probably small.

[d] The original percentages (portions exported directly to foreign countries)—tin 84.9, rubber 81.1, and wool 59.2—are adjusted upward by the following estimates of that portion of the exports listed as going directly to Britain which was subsequently re-exported to foreign countries (net of re-exports to the empire): tin £2,300,000, rubber £4,000,000, and wool £22,000,000.

[e] Including wood pulp, paper, and newsprint, etc.

tion, amounted to £55 million in 1929.[20] Although the major part or all was sold to foreigners, empire gold was a sure source of sterling, at a fixed price. It went to the highest bidder, whose currency was strongest and whose fixed demand to buy was, accordingly, made effective. If there had been any difficulty in turning those proceeds into sterling, the latter would *ipso facto* have been the strong currency. Therefore the export of gold by empire producers, to whomever sold, may be regarded as having diminished the necessity for multilateral settlement. South Africa's sales of £45 million were more than adequate to equate her London balance in 1929.

England was an entrepôt not only for gold but also for many other empire products going ultimately to non-empire markets. In 1929, of total British imports from the empire, fully 16⅔ percent were subsequently re-exported, as against 5½ percent of those from non-empire countries. On the other hand, 79 percent of Britain's re-exports in that year went to foreign and only 21 percent to empire countries. The result was a net credit of £37 million for the empire as a whole, composed primarily of sales of wool, and, to a smaller extent, hides and skins, rubber, tea, tin, and cotton. Although these goods were for the most part sold for sterling in England, and hence used to meet various sterling obligations, this cannot be characterized bilateral empire-British transfer. The goods were not absorbed by the British market, but by foreigners. The fact that the sellers could be paid in sterling, as indeed they were often paid for goods which never went through England, was an indication of the ease of multilateral transfer, enhanced by the use of England as entrepôt and the pound as medium of payment; but it remained multilateral transfer nevertheless.

The Great Britain–"Foreign" Aspect

In the heavy British demand for non-empire foods and raw materials, already discussed, we have part of the explanation of heavy passive balances of trade and payments with Argentina (grains, meats), Scandinavia (meat, dairy products, wood products), Egypt (cotton), Persia, Java, and the Dutch West Indies (oil, rubber, tea), Russia (timber, petroleum, fish), and very largely also of the United States (cotton,

[20] From respective official trade statistics. Canadian data for year April, 1929, to March, 1930; Australia July, 1928, to June, 1929. Australia's gold exports were about seven times higher in the year July, 1929, to June, 1930, but this was the result of monetary difficulties, and represented a loss of monetary stock.

oil, grains, tobacco, meat), and the Netherlands (meat, dairy products).

The relatively slight competitive power of British industry in non-empire markets supplies the remainder of the explanation. England was once the workshop of the world. Yet the balance of her trade in manufactured goods alone with the entire non-empire world was active only by £26,000,000 in 1929, whereas with the empire it was active by no less than £242,000,000. And with the world's other leading manufacturing countries the balance was in 1929 distinctly negative.[21] Aside from the purchasing-power factors contributing to this anomalous situation (Britain's heavy net receipts, *in toto*, and from the empire in particular), probably the major cause was heavy foreign protection of local industries.

Thus, Britain had substantial passive balances in 1929 in her trade in iron and steel and manufactures thereof with Germany and Belgium, in machinery with the United States and Germany, in motor vehicles with the United States, in electrical goods and apparatus with Germany, the Netherlands, and the United States, in rayon yarns and manufactures with France, Germany, Switzerland and Italy. She purchased heavily of foreign luxury textiles, with resultant adverse balances in silk yarns and manufactures with France, Switzerland, and Italy, in various kinds of textile apparel with Germany and France, and in woolens with France. Even in her cottons and woolens, in which alone Britain attained an appreciable active balance of trade with the world's leading manufacturing countries, her exports were preponderantly yarns and other semi-manufactures, serving as raw materials for the importing countries. In fact, Britain actually bought more cotton manufactures, beyond the yarn stage, from Belgium, France, and Germany than she sold to them.[22] Thus, England, traditionally the industrial nation par excellence, was to a large extent a supplier of raw material for the manufacturing countries of Europe.[23]

[21] Britain's exports of wholly or partly manufactured goods (domestic products) to Germany, Belgium, France, Switzerland, the U.S.A., Czechoslovakia, Italy, and the Netherlands were £118,700,000 in 1929, as against similar retained imports from them of £226,100,000. Omitting manufactured oils (mainly petroleum products), the balance was still adverse, by £78 million. This trade classification is not entirely satisfactory, since, for example, it excludes processed foods, and includes only partly manufactured nonferrous metals.

[22] While the countries listed in note 21, above, provided fully 87 percent of Britain's retained imports of both woolen and worsted, and cotton yarns and manufactures, they took only 32 percent of her total exports of the woolens and 16 percent of the cottons. But they took fully 60 percent of her much smaller exports of the semi-manufacture, cotton yarns.

[23] One of her heaviest exports to the continent was coal.

The countries of the empire obtained the £190 million which they were able to transmit to Britain, in excess of receipts, primarily by sale of raw materials to the United States, Japan, and industrial Europe. In general the latter countries, in turn, directly or again multilaterally, were reimbursed not only for their balance of purchases from the empire but also for their own invisible obligations to Britain by a surplus of sales to that country and, to a smaller extent, by an inflow of British capital. Britain's adverse trade balance with 14 leading European countries [24] was £207 million in 1929. She also took up perhaps £20 million of European securities in that year. Income from her European investments, and income derived from shipping services rendered these countries, of the order of £65 million, clearly fell far short of this total, by perhaps £125 to £150 million, even with income from reparations and from other services. Thus, in great part, was the major triangle closed.[25]

FILLING IN THE PATTERN

Lying within and cutting through and across this great triangle was a vast complex of other patterns of international transactions, which can only be suggested here.

Part of India's enormous transfers to England were effected via a net active trade balance with other empire countries. To Ceylon, Malaya, and South Africa India sold rice, cotton manufactures, and jute gunny bags, which she produced in abundance but for which Britain had little use. Since Ceylon's tea and South Africa's gold gave those countries a more than sufficient sterling income, here were minor partial triangles. For Malaya, on the other hand, whose trade balance with the mother country was passive, empire trade increased the burden of multilateral transfer, which was effected by heavy rubber and tin exports to foreign countries.

Canada's strong position in relation to Britain gave her an active bilateral trade balance, amounting to fully £48 million in 1928–29. This balance was usually large enough to meet returns on British capital, to finance small net capital repayments and, indeed, still (in 1927 and

[24] U.S.S.R., Finland, Sweden, Norway, Denmark, Poland, Germany, Netherlands, Belgium, France, Switzerland, Spain, Italy, Czechoslovakia. These 14 countries are alluded to several times below.
[25] Folke Hilgerdt has graphically described the world-wide transfer mechanism centering on Britain, in "The Approach to Bilateralism," *Index*, August, 1935, pp. 177–80, and "The Case for Multilateral Trade," *Amer. Econ. Rev.*, Suppl., March, 1943, pp. 393–407; see also League of Nations, *Europe's Trade* (Publications II A, 1941, No. 1), and *The Network of World Trade* (Publications II A, 1942, No. 3).

1928) to leave a bilateral credit of some £15 to £20 million.[26] Moreover, Canada had a heavy active trade balance of £30 to £35 million in 1928 and 1929 with the entire world except England and the United States —especially with Holland, Germany, and Japan. All these sums were transferred to her via a very heavy passive balance of payments with the United States, to whom Canada paid heavy interest and dividends on past investments and with whom her trade balance was passive by no less than £75 million in 1928–29. The United States had relatively little need for Canada's exports, whereas Canada imported heavily of American foods, raw materials, machinery, and other manufactures, which gained preference over the British because they were generally cheaper, because of similarities of United States and Canadian tastes and styles, fostered by American advertising, and because of the close business relations between the two countries.

The United States was, patently, a crucial link in many of the empire's multilateral chains. There were Malaya and British India, for whose raw materials there was a great demand in America, while the consumers of these empire countries purchased most heavily of British goods. Their credit trade balances with the United States in 1929, £46 million and £19 million, respectively, were a major factor (in the case of Malaya, a more than sufficient factor) [27] in covering their sterling obligations.[28] On the other hand, the United States had a huge active trade balance with Canada, and smaller ones with Australia, South Africa, and New Zealand, giving her an active balance with the empire, outside of Great Britain, of $297,000,000 in 1929. The Canadian and New Zealand balances [29] matched the active balances which those countries enjoyed with Great Britain. For South Africa heavy gold sales were the main offset. For Australia, who bought more heavily of both British and American goods

[26] Trade data from Canada, Dept. of Trade and Commerce, *Trade of Canada*. Balance of payments data from *The Canadian Balance of International Payments*, pp. 241–43.

[27] Malaya used her income obtained from this source and from smaller net sales to Europe to buy rice, copra, sugar, and cotton manufactures from other Asiatic countries. In large measure, however, this triangularity was only apparent, a large portion of Malayan total imports from the Dutch East Indies and Siam consisting of rubber, tin, and petroleum for transshipment, mostly to America.

[28] In addition, India's active trade balance with Japan, amounting to £12.5 million in 1928–29, largely because of heavy sales of raw cotton, was supported by the United States' adverse balance with that country, about £36 million in 1929, resulting from heavy American purchases of raw silk.

[29] In contrast with India and Malaya, New Zealand had little to sell to the United States, whereas American machinery, petroleum, motor vehicles and miscellaneous manufactures supplied a fair share of the high levels of consumption of her population.

than she sold, the major offsets were heavy imports of British capital, and large sales of wool to the manufacturing countries of Europe and to Japan.

There remains the very important United States balance of payments with Britain herself, an estimate of which appears in Table 30 (p. 252). Britain's passive bilateral balance on current account of £100 million in 1928 contrasts with her credit balance of £222 million with the rest of the world in that year. The tariff and manufacturing strength of the United States effectively forestalled imports of British goods, on the one hand, whereas Britain purchased American primary products in immense quantities. The inadequacy of the invisible offsets is largely attributable to the war, when the United States built a large competing merchant marine, when the greater part of Britain's American investments were liquidated, and when, finally, Britain was saddled with heavy war debt obligations to this country.

This balance, or a large part of it, may be regarded as a necessary link in many of the transfer chains—including the major triangle described above—completion of which constituted equilibrium. To the extent to which the passive bilateral balance was a relatively irreducible datum, Britain found offsets elsewhere in her strong net position toward the empire, China, Japan, and Brazil,[30] in her reparations from Germany, and in her invisible income from non-empire countries. To the extent that it was determined by purchasing power factors stemming from these other bilateral balances, it was their result and necessary counterpart.

However, the balance was too large. Some of its relatively unyielding causal determinants, such as American protection and the war debts, required greater adjustments elsewhere than Britain proved capable of making. It was therefore in part a persistent obstacle to enduring equilibrium, one of the constant sources of strain upon Britain's total balance of payments in the 1920's.[31] These strains were intensified by the great and rapid flows of capital between the two countries and by America's widely fluctuating foreign lending; the catastrophic reduction of all imports from the United States after 1929 helped supply the *coup de grâce* to

[30] With the last three, the United States trade balance was passive and Britain's active, largely because of the former's greater taste for coffee and heavier requirements of raw silk.
[31] Such weakness need not have shown in a flow of gold to the United States or an inflow of short-term capital therefrom. It was in fact temporarily relieved, instead, by short-term capital inflows from empire countries, gold exchange standard countries, and France, inflows in part made possible by American lending to, and purchases from, these countries.

the existent pattern of international relationships. This balance and the great European balance with Britain were an evidence both of the great amount of multilateral transfer consistent with equilibrium in the world economy of the 1920's and of the great strains posing what proved eventually to be insuperable problems of equilibration.

XIII. THE PATTERN IN TRANSITION

IT IS EVIDENT that the world economy of 1929 was characterized by an essential interdependence of all its segments. Every transaction was a link in the chain of an economic process, and each link was dependent upon the consummation of all others. As a result the whole pattern, and the real incomes dependent at every turn upon the continuance of trading and borrowing connections, were subject to alteration by the cutting of any one of the links, by the blocking of any of the channels through which purchasing power flowed. These conditions by no means precluded adjustment to change. However, the system was not infinitely flexible, and successful adaptation was by no means inevitable.

In the peculiarly rapid and basic changes of the period 1919 to 1939 the abrupt cutting of many cords brought breakdowns of the mechanism and the shattering of its operational unity. And when the wheels began at length to turn again in more or less synchronized fashion after the post-1929 breakdown, it was a fundamentally altered British and world system, not merely modified patterns, which emerged.

GRADUAL CHANGE, 1900–1929

In respect to the geographical pattern of Britain's international transactions there was no great difference between 1913, or even 1900, and 1929. In 1900 Britain's trade balance (gross trade) with the empire was negative by only £7.6 million, with non-empire countries by £161 million. In 1913 the two balances were + 17.4 and − 151.3 and in 1929 both were again negative, by £11.3 and £370.4 million, respectively.[1] The discrepancies between the two balances were evidently the product of enduring supply and demand dispositions.[2]

The changes that occurred between 1900 and 1913 resulted primarily from the long intervening cyclical upswing. Heavy British capital exports to India, Canada, and the United States show in an improvement

[1] The considerable difference from net trade figures results from the heavy British entrepôt trade in empire goods. In net trade, the respective 1913 balances were +£60,000,000 and −£194,000,000, and in 1929 +£26,000,000 and −£407,000,000. Comparable figures are not available for 1900.

[2] It is true that changes occurred in the flows of capital and interest and dividends between Britain, the empire, and the rest of the world, but explanation can hardly be found therein for the stability of this transfer pattern.

of the British trade balance with those countries; the balance with Argentina failed to react only because of the rapid growth in British purchases from the emergent Argentine farmer and meat packer. America's balance, nevertheless, remained heavily negative; Canada spent the enormous quantities of British capital in the United States, while India spent them largely for British goods.[3] New Zealand, Ceylon, and the countries of Europe on Britain's debit side, Australia, South Africa, Straits Settlements, India, China, Japan, Italy on the credit, all had by 1913 found more or less their 1929 positions in relation to England and each other.[4]

However, there were signs of secular transformation by 1929. Britain's relatively favorable position with respect to the empire was partly the result of a secular time lag; her large share in empire imports and the smaller empire share of British imports may thus have been expected gradually to converge,[5] with continued development of empire supply capacities and increased foreign competition in empire markets. These developments were sped by the war. As we have seen in Chapter XI, above, the ratios did converge between 1900 and 1929. The reduction in Britain's active balance of trade with the empire from £60,000,000 in 1913 to only £26,000,000 in 1929, despite rising prices and improved terms of trade, and despite the more rapid ascent of total empire than of total British imports, may be attributed in part to this secular shift in demand-supply dispositions.

Britain's greatly increased debit balance with New Zealand, £19.3 million in 1929 as compared with only £5.4 million in 1913, was an in-

[3] See T. H. Boggs, "Capital Investments and Trade Balances within the British Empire," Q.J.E., XXIX (1914–15), 776, 780–92; Viner, Canada's Balance, pp. 280–94; Hobson, Export of Capital, pp. 9–10, 13–14; J. W. Root, The Trade Relations of the British Empire, Liverpool, Root, 1903, pp. 286–88.

[4] An interesting confirmation in an individual case is found in the study of "Trade with France before and after the War," by Paul Mantoux, J.R.S.S., LXXX (1917), 383–407. For a long time before 1913 France had an active trade balance with England, her sales of specialties exceeding her purchases of staple British manufactures and coal, and a heavy passive balance with the rest of the empire, from whom she imported heavily of raw materials. Even the trade of rice and cottons from Burma and Bombay to Ceylon, of tea from Ceylon to England, and of cotton piece goods from Lancashire to India, all offsetting in a triangular circuit, was inveterate. See Root, The Trade Relations of the British Empire, p. 293.

[5] Indeed, the respective shares of each in the total consumption of the other would show an even more rapid convergence, with the rise of the domestic empire producer. That is, Britain might retain a fairly stable share in a declining total of empire imports, and empire countries an only slowly rising share of a rising total of British imports.

teresting example of the operation of these long run forces. That country was just emerging as a supplier of Britain's foods, especially of dairy products. Her share of gross British imports rose from 2.64 percent to 4.06 percent, her butter and cheese sales alone increasing from £1.8 million to £19.1 million between 1913 and 1929. Meanwhile Britain's earlier predominance in her market was fast declining, although British sales were sustained by the rapid rise in the national income of New Zealand, whose imports increased considerably more than the rest of the empire in these years.

The trade balances in the 1920's also show the effects of the weakness in international competition of British industry in general, and of the staple trades in particular. Between 1913 and 1925 British sales to Italy rose only from £14.6 to £18.8 million, and the normally active trade balance disappeared, largely because coal exports declined from 10 to 6.8 million tons. A diminished British active balance with India in these years was in major part the reflection of a decline in her sales of cotton piece goods to that country, from £35.0 million in 1913 to £26.1 in 1929, despite the intervening price rise. Exports of new ships and cotton piece goods to China and Japan, similarly, declined from £13.5 to £5.5 million, between 1913 and 1929, offsetting a rise by £6.2 million in the remainder of Britain's exports to these countries.

Partly as a result of this and despite increased European borrowing in the twenties, Britain's trade balance with the Continent became even more adverse than it had been in 1913.[6] Although the rise in British imports from Europe was in large part a specific rise in Scandinavian and Dutch foods, it also encompassed greatly increased purchases of iron and steel, machinery, rayon, electrical goods, from Belgium, Germany, France, Switzerland, and Holland. Meanwhile British exports did not respond particularly to the flow of capital, except perhaps indirectly because of the increased buying power of empire and other producers, who supplied the continent with the food and raw materials which it was enabled by British loans to purchase.

On the other hand, the reciprocal demand and supply of Britain and the United States showed some signs of change to the former's benefit. Britain's exports to that country actually grew considerably faster than her imports from there between 1913 and 1929, despite new American tariffs and heavily increased British purchases of American petroleum,

---

[6] The balance with the 14 countries listed on p. 232n, above, increased from £111,000,000 in 1913 to £207,000,000 in 1929.

tobacco, fruits, machinery, and automobiles. Britain's exports to the United States were relatively strong only because of the much more accelerated rise of American than of world imports. But her purchases of American goods lagged because of the feebleness of the British cotton industry, and, probably even more crucial, because of the relative decline of the American supplier in many important lines such as wheat, cotton, pork products, leather, in which he had once reigned supreme, and in which Argentina, Denmark, New Zealand and others were now playing a secularly increasing part.[7] The latter developments augured a continued secular diminution of this large bilateral balance of trade—amounting to £101,000,000 in 1913 and £138,000,000 in 1929—a counterpart of the increased passive balance with these younger suppliers and of the decreased active balances with the major markets for British cottons. Purchasing-power factors, notably America's shifting role from great payer to great receiver of foreign dividends and debt service, also contributed to this development.

Rapid Change, 1929–38

The already weakly integrated world economy and the interdependent patterns of international transactions which composed it were subjected to abrupt strains at all points by the great world depression. These strains set up re-equilibrating tendencies, and in fact such enormous adjustments of balances of payments were made that there was reason to believe that had the changes been less abrupt, the declines less precipitous, and the willingness to play the game greater, the world economy might still have possessed sufficient flexibility to have righted the situation eventually and avoided the complete and perhaps permanent disintegration which followed. Whether the results would have justified the costs is another question.

The pressures of the period 1929–31, intensified by protection and restriction, were rapidly transmitted to Britain because of her direct dependence upon debtor areas for a large part of her income. Deflation, cur-

---

[7] The United States supplied 67 percent of Britain's gross imports of raw cotton (by value) in 1913, 50 percent in 1929, and 38 percent in 1931. This was largely because Britain's greatest export losses were in the coarser grades of cotton goods, sold to the Far East, and American raw cotton consisted almost entirely of the short and medium staples used for such goods. In wheat the United States supplied 47–58 percent of Britain's gross imports by volume in the years 1899 to 1902, and 20–23 percent in 1928–29; however, the share was already this low and lower in the period 1906–12. The United States supplied 43 percent of Britain's gross imports of bacon and hams in 1913 and 15 percent in 1929, and 35 percent of her leather in the former year, 16 percent in the latter.

rency depreciation, and high crisis duties resulted in a dwindling of Australia's purchases of British goods from £54.2 million in 1929 to £14.5 in 1931. British sales to India, similarly, declined from £78 to £32 million, largely also because of the boycott. Other leading debtors, British exports to which declined particularly heavily for similar reasons, were Germany, Argentina, and the other countries of Latin America.

On the other hand, as a result of the strength of Britain's imports of consumption goods, Australia, New Zealand, and the Irish Free State, leading suppliers of meat, grain, and dairy products, supplied a rising share of British purchases in the period 1929–31.[8] Europe's portion turned upward even more sharply in this period, from 36.2 percent in 1929 to 43.1 percent in 1931; the greatest rises were of German manufactures, dumped heavily upon the unprotected British market, Danish butter and bacon, and Russian grain, this last the result of erratic bountiful harvests. The United States continued to decline, from 16.1 percent to 12.1 percent in these two years, her cotton and other raw material exports severely cut by British industrial depression, the price of her manufactures being well maintained, and her farmers continuing to lose ground in the British market as they had done throughout the 1920's.

By these changes in trade alone the balances of payments of the three leading debtors, Australia, India, and Germany were eased in the years 1929–31 by no less than £35, £25, and £15 million, respectively [9]— India's entirely by the reduction in her imports. Likewise, Britain's large passive balance of trade with the fourteen leading continental European countries mentioned above actually rose from £207 to £214 million. This substantial rise in real terms was attributable to heavy imports; British exports to these countries, who were not preponderantly debtors or primary producers, were considerably better sustained than her exports to the rest of the world.

Some of the changes in bilateral balances were the result of continued long-run changes in supply and demand dispositions, whose development would not under ordinary conditions have been inconsistent with equilibrium. Many were the result of recurrent cyclical phenomena, which, however harsh in the short run, by no means precluded a return

---

[8] Their combined share of Britain's gross imports increased from 12.2 percent to 13.9 percent in this period. British purchases of Australian grains and meats actually rose in value terms, despite—indeed, partly because of—the fall of prices.

[9] Britain's imports from Germany declined only by 6.1 percent, while her exports to that country fell by 50.2 percent.

to the old patterns in recovery: e.g., the decreased relative importance among Britain's imports of raw materials, the increased importance of consumption goods, the decline in international investment, and the great change in terms of trade.

Other changes were in a sense equilibrative adjustments. Britain's heavy imports were a fulfillment of her historic function as a source of exchange for the world's distressed debtors. Incomes of these countries were severely reduced by loss of markets in the United States, Europe and Japan, as a result of depression and resurgent economic nationalism. European debtors were oppressed by capital flight in 1931. These purchasing power factors, supplemented by debtor countries' tariffs, aimed at conserving limited exchange, helped to adjust their bilateral balances with Britain.

Many of these changes involved adjustments to the blocking off of the more vulnerable channels of triangular transfer. The £60 million shift in Britain's trade balance with Australia and India, whose non-empire markets had been reduced by industrial depression, meant that she was now taking more of her income from them bilaterally.[10] Such a trend to direct bilateral transfer of invisibles was less essential for the other empire countries, whose balances thus changed less: New Zealand and Canada had always had sufficient credit balances with Britain, South Africa had her gold sales, which were slightly higher in 1931 than in 1929, and Malaya's burden was doubtless reduced in part by a great decline in income on British investments there.[11] In keeping with the same trend were substantial declines of the heavy adverse British trade balances with the United States, Argentina, and Egypt, which had been in 1929 far in excess of invisible inpayments from these countries.[12]

[10] There could have been no equivalent offsetting shift in invisibles. Britain's lending to India was greater in 1930 and 1931 than in 1929, and invisible receipts from these countries were undoubtedly considerably smaller.

[11] If the markets of raw material producers were contracting, their outpayments for shipping services and the income earned by foreign investments therein also declined sharply. Whether the latter meant commercial bankruptcies or a reduction of equity earnings, it involved an automatic offsetting reduction of transfer burdens. The significance of this adjustability of equity earnings has been discussed by Erich Schiff, "Direct Investments, Terms of Trade, and Balance of Payments," Q.J.E., Feb., 1942, pp. 307–20. The shifts in the trade balances of India and Australia alone constitute almost the entire change of £71 million in Britain's balance with the empire as a whole. The rest of the empire, indeed, took a notably larger share of Britain's exports in 1931 than in 1929 (31.7 percent and 26.3 percent, respectively), while supplying approximately the same proportion of her gross imports.

[12] In all these cases, the decline of prices and of total trade was the major factor, Britain's

However, the stability of the European balance, in the face of a heavy decline in invisible receipts therefrom, would seem to indicate the opposite tendency, except perhaps in the case of the increased direct transfers from Germany to Britain.

Despite these equilibrative tendencies in individual parts, and the "normality" of many of the changes, this violent upsetting of international patterns was, from the point of view of the world economy, a breakdown. Since each country's difficulties were in large measure the result of autonomous and conscious "adjustments" of others, and since its own adjustments in turn created stresses elsewhere, taken as a whole there was mutual frustration and progressive deterioration.

Britain's position was growing rapidly worse in 1930 and 1931; unemployment was spreading, and she was threatened with the necessity of living on her foreign capital, as other countries cut themselves off from her goods and services. The reduction in her active balance on current account with the empire, a reduction certainly greater than in her net capital exports thereto, and her increased passive balance with Europe, far outweighed the improvements vis-à-vis the United States and Argentina. The balances of payments of the empire and Europe may have been eased, but the British balance was weakened thereby. With settled policies and systems disintegrating all around, with each country, finding its old paths blocked, consciously seeking new paths, it was not surprising that Britain should also succumb to the desire actively to seek a way out. Her distress was too great to permit her further to countenance those actions by which other countries, hard pressed, were trying to attain equilibrium by forcing disequilibrium and unemployment on her.

Not all the changes after 1933 were the result of these conscious British governmental policies. The pattern was altering before 1929, and would inevitably have continued to alter after 1929 under the impact of such secular causes of growth and decline as the deteriorating competitive position of British industry and the related rise of younger suppliers. The extreme depression and the foreign tariffs which it engendered would certainly have strengthened these forces, apart from changes in British trade policy. Thus the trade balances with the empire and with such growing non-empire oil and rubber producers as Persia and the Dutch East and West Indies might have been expected to become more

imports from the United States and Argentina, in fact, declining considerably less than did her exports to them.

adverse and the balance with the United States to continue to improve, in any case. The disappearance of the active trade balances with China and Japan after 1929 must be attributed in major part to the rise of industry in the Far East, which seemed effectively on the road to eliminate those balances before that date. The same was true in the case of India, Britain's most important market, her exports to which were in 1937, despite preference, exactly half of their 1929 level. In this case preference was a contributory factor; because of it, British imports of Indian raw cotton, wheat, and leather were higher in 1937 than 1929.

These factors alone tended to revise the geographical pattern in the direction of greater bilateral transfer. The most striking positive British balances of payments, those with the Far East, were doomed. Those with the empire as a whole and with the United States would probably have veered toward the same end. Only the European balance may not have tended in this direction, had it not been for British trade policy, in view of Britain's growing demand for continental manufactures and foods.

However, such extrapolations cannot be made with complete confidence. The stimulus given to European industry by reconstruction might have been approaching its limits, and the adjustments of British industry to post-war difficulties may, on the other hand, have helped sustain her share in world exports thereafter. A continued increasing tendency of Britain to import manufactured goods would have operated against the empire, as would also the continued rise of the food suppliers of Denmark and Argentina. And many of these changes would have increased rather than decreased the relative importance of triangular transfer.

Purchasing-power factors would have contributed to these changes. The apogee of British foreign lending for imperial development was reached before 1914; Australia, which borrowed heavily during the twenties, was overborrowed by the end of that decade. Inevitably, relatively increased interest and dividend receipts and debt repayments would have contributed to a disappearance of the anomalous active British current balance with the empire, especially with India and Australia, without, however, thereby increasing or decreasing the triangularity of transfer.[13] Shorter-run purchasing-power factors likewise had their effects,

---

[13] A diminution of Britain's credit balance with an empire country as a result of the substitution of a capital repayment therefrom for a previous equal capital export thereto, by the same amount as the credit balance was previously increased by that capital export,

with little relation to British trade policy. Increased South African incomes, resulting more from expanded gold sales than from increased British lending, help explain why that country became Britain's major market after 1936 and almost alone continued to provide Britain with an active bilateral trade balance in 1937. The capital flows from Britain to Wall Street from 1935 to 1937 could have had little effect on actual expenditures, because of the easy money policies in Britain and the United States and offsetting operations by the British authorities. However, the continuous flows in the years 1932–37 from sterling area and gold bloc to Britain contributed to easy money there, intensified gold-bloc deflation, and hence must have had considerable effect on bilateral current balances.

Finally, there were cyclical factors which would have been effective in any event: increased purchasing power (after 1933) of primary producing areas, greatly increased British purchases of raw materials, and, at the peak of the boom, of European and American iron, steel, and machinery.

The empire clearly obtained greater absolute, demonstrable benefits from imperial preference than did Britain.[14] Empire countries (excluding Eire) increased their share of Britain's gross imports from 25.7 percent in 1929 to 37.9 percent in 1938, while Britain was not able to hold permanently a larger percentage of total empire imports than she held in 1929. Thus, the greater share which the empire took of Britain's exports, 39.5 percent in 1929 and 45.6 percent in 1938, was the result entirely of a more rapid rise of their total imports than of British exports. The approximately equivalent increase in the portion of total empire exports going to Britain, from 34.1 percent to 40.6 percent in the same period, is on the contrary attributable entirely to the increased participation of these countries in the British market, since Britain's total retained imports and the empire's total exports fell about equally. When we realize, in addition, that these roughly equal rises in the proportion of exports of each taken by the other relate to totals which behaved quite differently, British exports declining by 28.5 percent and empire exports by only 13.7 percent between 1929 and 1937, the discrepancy in absolute benefits becomes even clearer. In this period Britain's exports to the

demand and supply dispositions being unaltered, represents no change whatsoever in the relative importance of triangular transfer.

[14] See Heaton, *The British Way to Recovery*, pp. 73–75, and above, p. 212.

empire declined by 22 percent, while her retained imports therefrom rose by the same percentage.[15]

Britain, extending imperial preference generally for the first time, experienced a much more marked diversion of her import trade than did the Dominions, who had long discriminated in favor of her goods. Moreover, Britain's tariff, being of necessity aimed primarily at manufactures, did not particularly injure the empire's primary producers directly; the rather meager successes of agricultural protection were, as we have seen, almost entirely at the expense of other producers. On the other hand, the greatly increased tariffs of Canada, Australia, and India, who were thoroughly committed to a policy of high protection, were a serious blow to Britain. The concessions which she obtained at Ottawa did not fundamentally alter those policies.

Thus, Britain's trade balance with the empire shifted by fully £138 million between 1929 and 1937, and by £128 million between 1929 and 1938. Of the £63 million rise between 1935 and 1937 (in an adverse balance), Canada accounted for 25 and India 20 millions. In the case of Canada, the cause was the great rise in Britain's imports of her primary products, notably nonferrous metals, wood products, and bacon and hams, partly because of boom demands and rising prices, partly because of the longer-run diversion to Canada of much that would without preference have been purchased from foreign suppliers. British exports to that highly protectionist country meanwhile did no better than those to the rest of the empire.[16] In the case of India, the situation was exactly the reverse, Britain's imports from there increasing between 1929 and 1937 only approximately as much as from the empire as a whole, but her exports failing almost completely to recover from their depression low. The expanded British passive balance with the other empire countries was primarily a price change, but part of the remaining shift in comparison with 1929 mirrored also her increased imports of colonial raw materials, and the secular development of these younger regions as suppliers.[17]

[15] The respective changes between 1929 and 1938 were −27.7 percent and +13.0 percent. Of course, it is impossible to say how rapidly the British share of the empire market would have declined had it not been for preference.

[16] British imports from Canada rose by 91 percent between 1929 and 1937 and 67 percent between 1929 and 1938, as against rises of only 22 percent and 13 percent for the entire empire in these respective periods. The year 1929 was apparently abnormally bad for Canada; the rise from 1928 to 1937 was 54 percent.

[17] The outstanding example is Northern Rhodesia, Britain's balance with which was posi-

British imports of manufactures from Belgium, Germany, France, the Netherlands, Italy, Switzerland, Czechoslovakia, and the United States were in 1933 one-third to one-half of their 1931 levels, as a result of the tariff. Since the major damage to her exports to these countries had already been done, these adverse balances fell headlong. After 1933, however, Britain's demand for their products recovered strongly. As recovery turned into boom, there came in over the tariff machinery, chemicals, iron and steel products (duties on some of the latter being temporarily reduced because of domestic shortages), and motor vehicles, as well as nonferrous metals and refined oils, with the result that these adverse balances recovered some of the ground lost in 1932. There were considerable gains also by producers of certain raw materials, in which the empire (and British) supplier bulked relatively small, and where, hence, neither tariff nor preference had much effect: notably by Iran, Java, and the Dutch West Indies, because of their oil. Especially striking was the great increase in Britain's imports of Swedish and Finnish timber after 1931, because of the heavy demands created by her building boom.

On the other hand, pressure on non-empire food producers continued after 1933. Consequently, while Britain's negative balances with the manufacturing countries recovered after 1933, and more rapidly after 1935, those of the food producers, Argentina, Denmark, and Poland, continued to decline between 1933 and 1935.[18]

As we have already stated, it was an avowed purpose of Britain's trade agreement program, explicitly set forth in many of the treaties, to reduce her passive trade balances with the contracting non-empire countries.[19] Her exports were favored by special concessions; only on wood products did England offer these countries important tariff reductions. This was simple bilateralism. Thus, the high shares which these countries enjoyed of Britain's imports and the relatively low shares which they took of

---

tive by about £150,000 in 1929 and negative by some £1.5 and £5.2 million in 1935 and 1937. Rhodesian copper supplies the explanation.

[18] See pp. 216–17, above. British imports from the Netherlands, Sweden, and Finland recovered from 1933 to 1935, but this recovery was confined to goods other than food, and a decline of the German balance was due primarily to decreased British food purchases. Only from the United States, among the non-empire countries, did Britain's Class I imports rise strongly, and that expansion was mainly of products in which the empire did not compete strongly—tobacco, and, to a less extent, fish and tinned fruits. United States sales of lard, bacon, and hams, preferred empire foods, declined in these years.

[19] See Tasca, *World Trading Systems*, p. 54. The Russian agreement stipulated a reduction of the ratio between British imports from Russia and her exports thereto, by stages, from 1.7 in 1934 to 1.1 in 1938 and thereafter.

her exports began to converge during the years 1933–35—movements inverse to those of the comparable United Kingdom–Empire trade ratios.[20] The high British debit trade balances with the agreement countries, far above any net invisible receipts from them, were reduced as a direct consequence.

THE PATTERN IN 1937

In a period of such swift and basic economic change, when the old was being destroyed and the outlines of the new were still vague, when some policies looked backward and others forward, and the spread of nationalism paved the way to war—there was no "normal" year. The following survey of the situation in 1937 is undertaken only as a convenient means of showing how radically the pattern of Great Britain's trade had changed in the mere eight years following 1929.

Britain's invisible receipts from the countries of the empire, as from the entire world, were undoubtedly smaller in 1937 than in 1929, with the possible exception of shipping earnings inflated by suddenly soaring freight rates. Her return on investments of perhaps £120 million was some £30 million less, because of lower earnings, conversions, and repayments. Reduced home charges from India reflected diminished Indian government capital expenditures in England for railroad construction. Including an estimated £50 million of shipping earnings, here was a total of transfers on the order of £200 million as against perhaps £240 in 1929.[21] On the other hand, net inflows of British capital seem to have fallen from perhaps £25 million in 1929 to zero in 1937.[22] Thus, in the whole invisible account there seems to have been, if anything, some net reduction between 1929 and 1937 in the amount to be transferred from the empire to England.

The merchandise trade balance, however, showed a fundamental change. In 1929 there had been a balance in favor of Britain by £25 million, raising the multilateral transfer burden from £215 (including capital movements) to £240 million. In 1937 a balance in favor of the empire by £113 million sharply cut this net burden to but £85 million.

[20] The ratio between the shares of Britain's domestic exports and gross imports, respectively, purchased and supplied by Finland, the Baltic States, U.S.S.R., Norway, Sweden, Denmark, and Argentina, rose from 0.51 in 1929 and 0.59–0.61 in 1931–32, to 0.73–0.74 in 1936–37 and 0.87 in 1938.

[21] See p. 221n, above.

[22] According to Kindersley, in 1937 all new issues in London were almost exactly offset by repayments, and this seems to have been roughly true of empire issues as well.

The residual gap was more than amply filled by greatly expanded empire gold sales. In 1929 gold exports from empire producing countries were £59 million. In 1937, stimulated by the great rise in the price of gold in terms of their currencies, such exports amounted to no less than £126 million, and the disgorging from India's hoards, a flow already much reduced, brought the total to £139 million.[23] In 1937, accordingly, the empire could obtain directly from England more sterling than it needed to meet its direct bilateral obligations.[24]

The demand and supply situation of the empire with respect to Britain had clearly shifted to a position less adverse. In 1929 the ratio between the respective shares of empire imports and exports which Britain supplied and took was 1.00, whereas Britain's comparable ratio in relation to the entire world was 0.705. In 1937, the ratios were 0.77 and 0.58, respectively.

The divergencies between the various empire countries had also diminished, mainly by individual changes in the direction indicated for the empire as a whole. South Africa's increased merchandise trade balance with Britain (£18,000,000 in 1929, and £28,000,000 in 1938) was not an exception; it was on the contrary merely an equilibrative adjustment to her rising purchasing power, from gold sales and capital imports. The situations of New Zealand and Ceylon, who in 1929 apparently had no problem of multilateral transfer of their obligations to England, were also generally unchanged, in relation to both the mother country and the rest of the world. New Zealand continued to gain notably as a supplier of Britain's food, but, her industry being as yet young, she also was comparatively generous in her tariff concessions; her purchases were thus relatively well sustained. In the case of Ceylon, a quota discriminating against Japanese goods preserved a large part of her market for Lancashire.

Malaya was the one real exception, retaining roughly her 1929 position. Britain supplied 15.44 percent of her imports in 1937 and took only 10.95 percent of her exports. The ratio of 1.41 between these two figures contrasts with the much lower ratios of Britain in relation to the empire and the world, and their discrepancy shows the persistent tend-

[23] Sources, respective official trade statistics. Canadian and Indian data for years beginning April 1, Australian July 1, 1937. Other producing countries—South Africa, Rhodesia, Gold Coast, New Zealand.

[24] Gold could always buy sterling, to whomever it was actually sold. Sterling may no longer have been regarded as good as gold; except in the gold scare of early 1937, however, gold was certainly still as good as sterling.

ency of reciprocal demand-supply dispositions, reinforced by preference, to favor Britain. The United States and continental Europe still provided Malaya with a trade balance more than sufficiently active to settle her accounts with the mother country.

The really great changes between 1929 and 1937 were made by India, Australia, and Canada. Of the £138 million shift of the empire's trade balance with Britain from 1929 to 1937, these three countries alone accounted for £131 million. They had made the greatest strides in dispensing with British goods and, given current expectations as to yields from investment there, with British capital as well. While the portion of British exports going to the rest of the empire, excluding Eire, rose from 16.6 percent to 24.9 percent between 1929 and 1938, the Indian share declined from 10.7 percent to 7.7 percent, and the Canadian and Australian combined rose only from 12.2 percent to 12.9 percent. Meanwhile the share of these three countries in Britain's imports rose from 15.95 percent in 1924 and 13.5 percent in 1929 to 22.45 percent in 1938. Canada's resultant bilateral credit was increased also by the reduction of her interest and dividend and other invisible obligations, although this was offset in part by increased capital repayments. Here apparently was more, rather than less, multilateral transfer for Britain, although in Canada's position taken as a whole, there was a definite trend to bilateralism.[25]

The change in Australia's economic relations with England clearly reduced the importance of triangular transfer. Her interest and dividend and shipping service obligations to that country, perhaps £35 million in 1937, were now mainly covered by a £27.5 million active bilateral trade balance and by increased gold exports. This change in trade could not have been caused entirely by the great decline in her foreign borrowing, the effect of which was offset somewhat by heavy conversion operations, which reduced the burden of her debt service. The concomitant disappearance of Australia's £30 million passive trade balance of 1928–29 with the United States, and the reduction of her large active balance with the heavy wool buyers, France, Belgium, Japan, Germany, and Italy, from

[25] Her tariff and industrial growth, increased gold sales, and the change from heavy imports to heavy repayments of America's capital, effected a very great reduction in her huge adverse current balance with the United States, including gold, from an annual debit of $170 to $300 million in 1926–30 almost to zero from 1935 to 1937. Similarly her heavy active trade and current balance with the world outside England and the United States also declined very greatly. See *The Canadian Balance of International Payments*, pp. 241–43.

£34.9 million in that year to £19.6 in 1936–37, show an unmistakable trend to bilateralism.[26]

The Indian case is at once the simplest and the most striking. India's invisible obligations were almost exclusively obligations to England. Yet normally England was the only major country with whom her balance of trade was passive; and India was one of the few leading countries with whom England's balance was active—an extreme case of multilateral transfer. Table 29 shows the elimination of India's great offsetting triangular trade balances with Britain and the rest of the world, under influence of depression, economic nationalism, and secular growth and change.[27]

TABLE 29

INDIAN BALANCES OF PRIVATE, SEA-BORNE MERCHANDISE TRADE [a]

(Rs 000,000)

Year Beginning April 1	Total	With U.K.	With Rest of World
1928	+768	−442	+1,210
1931	+295	− 19	+ 315
1932	− 3	−120	+ 117
1935	+261	− 17	+ 278
1936	+708	+154	+ 555

[a] Source, *Annual Statement of the Sea-Borne Trade of British India*. Exports are of Indian produce alone, imports are gross.

As Britain took an increased share of her invisible empire incomes directly from these countries, she took a decreased portion indirectly through foreign countries. Her debit trade balance with the non-empire world was in 1937 £90 million less than in 1929. Net invisible receipts therefrom could not possibly have fallen so far, in view, among other things, of the decline of new European and South American issues floated

[26] The greater decline in adverse than in active merchandise trade balances mirrors, of course, the adjustment of Australia's total balance to her diminished foreign borrowing.
[27] The stability of the total balance of trade indicates that this readjustment was not simply the result of a net change in the flow of invisibles (nor could there have occurred any important alteration in their direction or geographical distribution), but instead entailed a real movement toward the eradication of multilateral transfer.

Application of the method of measuring bilateral trade mentioned in p. 220n, above, shows a decline in the proportion of India's triangular trade from 22 percent in 1929–30 to 8 percent in 1935–36. B. K. Madan, "Bilateralism and Indian Trade and Bilateral Treaties," *Indian Journal of Economics*, XIX, Part 1 (1938), 52–53. This method is less open to the objections which we cited above when applied to India, because of the almost exclusive concentration of all India's invisible transactions in its balance with Britain.

in London. This change was in major part the result of a conscious redirection, through British protection and preference. It was also in large measure an equilibrating adjustment, which would have had to come, whether by British tariff or otherwise. The decline of American and European purchases of empire raw materials, for example, resulted indirectly in a relative decline of British purchasing power, which tended automatically to bring a compensatory reduction of her balances with these countries. There is, however, no proof that such automatic tendencies would alone have been adequate to forestall such a serious weakening of Britain's total position as in fact occurred from 1929 to 1931, when the adverse balance with Europe increased, despite the considerable deterioration of Britain's balance of payments with the empire.

With British policy changes as the major factor, the share of imports coming from the three leading areas, continental Europe, the United States, and Argentina, declined from 59.0 percent to 48.3 percent between 1929 and 1938, while the portion of her exports to them rose from 40.1 percent to 41.3 percent. As an inevitable counterpart, attributable in part to a resultant relative decline of European purchasing power relative to the empire, and the many trade controls which European countries were thereby forced to adopt, the share of its total exports which the empire (outside the British Isles) sent to the Continent (excluding Russia and the Baltic States) declined from 25.1 percent to 18.8 percent between 1929 and 1937, the share of its imports from there only from 12.1 percent to 11.9 percent.[28] In this manner, multilateral transfer was forced out.

Germany was one of the most dramatic cases. In the increase of her active balance of trade with Britain from RM 286,000,000 in 1928 to RM 680,000,000 in 1931, and the concurrent reduction of her passive balance with the remainder of the empire from RM 1,369,000,000 to RM 442,000,000, we see the remarkable success of the great German program utilizing trade restriction, deflation, and exploitation of the unprotected British market, in order to remain solvent, in the face of heavy debt and reparations obligations, sharply reduced capital inflows, capital flight, and shrinking markets. The pressure of deflation and unemployment was thus transferred in part to Britain and to empire exporters. The British tariff negated Germany's efforts, reducing the bilateral balance below the 1928 level, and the latter's trade balance with the empire as a whole became once more strongly passive as a result. Germany's only re-

[28] Cleona Lewis, *Nazi Europe and World Trade*, Washington, Brookings, 1941, p. 162.

sort now was to strict exchange control, bilateralism, and a program of self-sufficiency. By cutting her imports from the empire outside of Britain almost to zero,[29] she attained again an active trade balance with the entire empire. The result, as in the period 1929–31, was mutual impoverishment.

The position of the important United States link in Britain's transfer patterns was also radically altered in the period 1929–37. As Table 30 indicates, the huge bilateral current balance between the two countries was greatly reduced by British trade policy and by her default on war debts, which more than offset declines in her invisible incomes from the United States.[30]

TABLE 30

ANGLO-AMERICAN BALANCE OF PAYMENTS, 1928, 1936, AND 1937 [a]

($000,000)

	1928	1936	1937
Merchandise, adjusted (excluding silver) [b]	+551	+285	+381
Freight and shipping	−120[c]	− 20	− 34
Interest and dividends	− 63	− 32	− 50
Tourist and immigrant remittances	− 33	− 12	− 41
Other invisibles [d]	...	− 28	− 28
War debts	+161	...	...
Balance on current account	+496	+193	+228

[a] Sources: 1928 from "The Anglo-American Balance of Payments in 1928," *Statist*, CXIV (1929), 374–75; 1936 adapted from "America's Balance of Payments," *Economist*, CXXVIII (1937), 617; 1937, adapted from "British-American Trade Agreement," Suppl., *Economist*, Nov. 26, 1938, p. 1. The debits and credits are from the American point of view. The 1928 estimates are probably only roughly comparable with those for 1936 and 1937.

[b] Silver (a one-way trade from U.K. to the U.S.A.) is excluded because Britain produces none, her heavy purchases and sales representing simple transit trade. Estimated non-British products imported into the United States from Britain in 1936 and 1937 likewise excluded by the author.

[c] Includes ship chandling and repairs, insurance, royalties, etc.

[d] Insurance payments and premia alone.

[29] German imports from Canada declined from RM 386 million in 1927 to 99 in 1931 and 12 in 1935, from Australia from 264 in 1928 to 100 in 1931 and 10 in 1935. All from Schlie, *Die britische Handelspolitik*, pp. 212–19.

[30] Inclusion of gold and the rather heavy inflows of British capital into the United States in the latter years might seem necessary to give the true equilibrium picture. However, the gold was mainly metal belonging to other countries, passing through London. And the capital flow was mainly speculative, and distorts rather than clarifies the equilibrium bilateral situation, particularly since neither gold nor capital flows could have particularly influenced relative levels of purchasing power, and hence the current balance.

The United States' balance of trade with the remainder of the British empire, it will be recalled, customarily completed some triangles, and left others even wider open. These situations were greatly altered after 1929. India's increasing direct transfer to Britain was both forced upon her by and itself helped cause a decline in her active trade balance with America, from $94 million in 1929 to $60 million in 1937. Australia was forced by the loss of foreign markets and British capital to restrict her American purchases, and her heavy adverse trade balance of 1929 with the United States actually turned slightly positive in 1937. Canada's heavy adverse balance with the United States declined drastically. Only the balances of South Africa and Malaya showed little change, the one remaining heavily negative, the other heavily positive; the complete transfer systems of both, as we have seen, were little altered in these years.

For all but South Africa and Malaya, however, and for the empire as a whole, the heavy bilateral current balances with the United States, whether active or passive, tended to disappear. The result is that by 1936 the large current balance of 1929 of the United States with the British Empire in favor of the former was gone.[31] As we have seen, these changes were not the simple result of the decline in international lending. The disappearance of large bilateral balances definitely involved a disappearance of multilateral transfer.

In 1929 the United States and the fourteen European countries listed above, while accounting for only about 13.5 percent of Britain's total foreign investments, at the same time made up fully 90 percent of Britain's net adverse commodity trade balance, the vehicle for the importation of income therefrom. In 1937 they contained 14.2 percent of the investment total, but now accounted for only 48 percent of that net trade balance. This is a fair indication of the headlong disruption of the old system, with its relatively high degree of triangularity.[32]

Perhaps the crucial distinction between commercial policies of the 1930's and the older protectionism lies in the former's conscious discrimination between countries as well as goods. The distinction is not hard and fast; ordinary tariffs inevitably hit certain countries more than others, and these newer policies fell with different weight upon different goods.

[31] *Economist:* "America's Balance of Payments," CXXVIII (1937), 617–18, "British-American Trade Agreement," Suppl., Nov. 26, 1938, p. 1.
[32] Hirschmann's index of bilateralism, for England, in which 100 represents the complete absence of bilateral tendencies, shows a decline from 25.8 in 1929 to 17.5 in 1937. Cited by Condliffe, *The Reconstruction of World Trade*, pp. 282–83.

Bilateralism is, after all, merely an extreme and narrow protectionism. Nevertheless, the newer developments awaited, and themselves necessitated, far greater governmental intervention in economic life than the old. Bilateralism resulted when governments undertook actively to push exports by demanding preferential treatment, something they could best exact only from those from whom they bought more than sold. It resulted also from extreme efforts to maintain balance of payments "equilibrium" by conscious detailed controls, which led rather naturally to a narrow barter psychology. And it intensified the breakdown of the world economy.

British policy after 1931 exhibited these bilateral characteristics. Nevertheless, this represented no consistent and conscious purpose. A government, subject to the usual pressures, was, like other governments, trying to combat the depression by cutting imports, by forcing debtor countries to pay, and by fostering exports—the last, by encouraging industrial reorganization and by bargaining with other countries. There was no single motivation, no single policy.[33] The reduction of multilateral transfer consequent upon the tariff was only an incidental effect, although doubtless protection was motivated in part by a desire to stop buying from those who would not buy British goods. Britain's major motive in extending empire preference was a desire to expand exports rather than to obtain more of her net invisible incomes bilaterally. Thus, there was disillusionment at the failure of empire purchases to recover as greatly as British imports from the empire, even though this involved stricter bilateral balancing. However, it was inevitable that these desertions from laissez faire entail strong bilateral tendencies, conscious or unconscious. Pragmatic government negotiation is the essence of economic control, and *ad hoc* negotiations are usually bilateral.

There is no doubt that by arbitrarily diverting trade, by helping disrupt the settled interdependent connections of an operating mechanism, these new policies contributed toward frustration of optimum international specialization and reduction of the British incomes particularly dependent upon her specialized position. Britain could not offer an adequate demand for the surplus products of the world's primary producers, upon the maintenance of whose purchasing power much of her income depended. If she refused to take the manufactures of the continent of Europe, she inevitably reduced their demand for those surplus primary

[33] See Tasca, *World Trading Systems*, p. 146 and chap. xii.

products, and thus indirectly cut down the ability of primary producers to meet their obligations to her and to buy her goods.[34]

Nevertheless, it must be remembered that the old order was being disrupted without the aid of British policy and that Britain adhered longest to free trade while her unemployment grew and tariffs multiplied against her goods. It was inevitable for her finally to fall into line and seek to shield herself from the strains imposed by strict adherence to the rules. It is not surprising that in time of stress she abandoned the potential maximization of income offered by free multilateralism for the more tangible goal of preserving or increasing what she could, while the world did the same. Nor were these efforts fruitless. Empire preference retarded the rise of protection within the empire, and trade treaties brought real concessions to British exporters.

With the advent of a measure of internal recovery the time may have come in Britain for halting these restrictive defensive policies; a concerted international effort at reconstruction of the older patterns may once again have been a real possibility. Opportunism may have been the only possibility in the years 1931–35; 1936–37 may on the other hand have called for a bolder stand. England might have tried to lead the way to a restoration of world trade along controlled lines,[35] or joined wholeheartedly in totalitarian economic warfare. Or she might have given substance to her verbal espousal of the most-favored-nation cause by supporting Mr. Hull in his devout pursuit of free trade.[36]

There was mounting pressure for the latter course. The fundamental supply and demand factors which gave rise to the international pattern of 1913 and 1929 had by no means been destroyed. The artificial severance of established connections had created prolonged maladjustments and complaints. The dominions were coming to realize that a slowly expanding British market could never take all their great and growing primary production. British agricultural protection increased their discontent with preference, which hampered their ability to grant reciprocal concessions to foreigners who might take more of their goods. Countries

---

[34] See, for example, P.E.P., *Report on International Trade,* pp. 44–45, 69; Robertson, "The Future of International Trade," *Econ. Jour.,* LXVIII (1938), 13; and League of Nations, *World Economic Survey,* 1935–36, pp. 179–84.

[35] See the persuasive argument of Paul Einzig, *Exchange Control,* New York, Macmillan, 1934, chap. xiii, and *The Exchange Clearing System,* New York, Macmillan, 1935.

[36] P.E.P., *Report on International Trade,* pp. 71–75; "The Empire and the World," *Economist,* CXXVII (1937), 250.

of Europe starved for raw materials complained that they could not buy empire products if neither Britain nor the empire would take their manufactures. The persistence of depressed British export areas led to complaints, on the British side, of inadequate tariff concessions by dominions committed to protection, and British farmers resented the preferential treatment to empire agricultural products.[37] The British diplomacy of conciliation reinforced arguments that peace was impossible while economic warfare raged. The colonies resented the exclusion of cheap foreign goods, and dissatisfied countries justifiably used empire discrimination to press their "have" and "have-not" propaganda.[38]

The policies which culminated in the trade agreement with the United States were an attempt to abandon some of these temporary controls. Dominion trade policies became increasingly liberal after 1934. Britain's participation in the Tripartite Currency Agreement of 1936 was an attempt to restore currency unity to the world beyond the sterling area. And in the American trade agreement of 1939, empire preference was relaxed, with the consent of Canada, and the most favored nation clause, with its corollary policy of undiscriminating universal tariff reductions, was extended.[39] However, political *rapprochement* was also an important factor in the agreement, and in fact in this immediate prelude to war there was no longer any strictly economic policy. After Munich Britain reluctantly entered into totalitarian economic warfare, with fighting funds, and political "lending."

The British situation in the years just before the war was a hybrid situation, its policy a hybrid policy. Great changes had been wrought, but the trends had by no means been brought to their logical conclusion. Triangularity was greatly diminished but persisted, and it had a basis in actual unchanged supply and demand conditions. And increasing dissatisfaction with the changes of the thirties augured a possible reversal rather than a continuation of the recent trends.

[37] See Benham, *Great Britain under Protection*, pp. 80–86, 108–9, and the predictions by Beveridge, *Tariffs: the Case Examined*, pp. 137–46, and Angell, *If Britain Is to Live*, pp. 84–87.
[38] Robertson, "The Future of International Trade," *Econ. Jour.*, XLVIII (1938), 14.
[39] See Norman Crump, "The Anglo-American Trade Agreement," *Lloyd's Bank Ltd. Mo. Rev.*, n.s., IX (1938), 601–6; Kreider, *The Anglo-American Trade Agreement, passim*.

Conclusion

—————◆—————

XIV. THE BRITISH ECONOMY
IN TRANSITION

THE MOST VITAL changes in the international economic position of
Great Britain in the years 1919–39 were the improvement in
her barter terms of international exchange, the decrease in her
exports of capital, and the deterioration in the competitive power of her
industry.[1] The first was a windfall addition to real income, to the extent
that the economy was able to take full advantage of it. The second offered
an increased potentiality for consumption or domestic investment, without involving a change in income, strictly defined. The third meant a
real decline in income, the extent of which depended mainly upon the
elasticity of Britain's demand for foreign goods, services, and securities.
All imposed upon the British economy a need for enormous readjustments, which were in continuous process during the entire period.

As we have seen, these three changes joined in causing a decline of
income and severe unemployment in Britain's export industries (and
reduced incomes of her investing classes), with a tendency for both to be
spread over the entire economy by the multiplier effect. There were other
causes of a British unemployment in the period 1919–39 which was inordinate by pre-war standards.[2] However, its heavy concentration in the

---

[1] See Chapter VIII, particularly pp. 152–57, above.

[2] See Liberal Industrial Inquiry, *Britain's Industrial Future*, pp. 21–24; MacM. Comm.,
Report, pp. 48–49, *Evidence*, II, 253; Clay, *The Post-War Unemployment Problem*,
passim; Beveridge, "An Analysis of Unemployment," *Economica*, n.s., III (1936), 357–86,
IV (1937), 1–17, 168–83. Overexpansion of the engineering and metal industries during
the World War, of shipbuilding, textiles, and coal in the years immediately following, and
fluctuations in government subsidies to the building industry, were also largely responsible
for this heavy unemployment. See also Colin Clark, "Statistical Studies," *Econ. Jour.*,
XLI (1931), 347–49.

Wages in export industries declined considerably, indicating that, rather than high wages
explaining unemployment, falling wages and employment were both caused by outside
factors. Nevertheless, a greater flexibility in real hourly wage rates, which had increased
very considerably, would undoubtedly have prevented so great an increase in unemploy-

staple export trades indicates that it was primarily a result of Britain's altered international economic position and, in particular, of her waning competitive power in world markets.[3]

ment as actually occurred. And the stability of wages in industries serving the domestic market (the "sheltered trades") may well have impeded the very necessary reabsorption of the unemployed into the supply of the home market. For the most naïve statements of the relation of high wages to unemployment, see Jacques Rueff, "Les Variations du chômage en Angleterre," *Revue politique et parlementaire*, CXXV (1925), 425–36, and Loveday, *Britain and World Trade*, pp. 172–77. See the more sophisticated discussions of Pigou, "Wage Policy and Unemployment," *Econ. Jour.*, XXXVII (1927), 355–68, especially, p. 357n; Clay, "Unemployment and Wage Rates," *Econ. Jour.*, XXXVIII (1928), 3, 5, and *passim* (1928); Cole, *British Trade and Industry*, pp. 305–14; MacM. Comm., *Evidence*, I, 247, 313, II, 48–49, 78, 254.

The immobility and conservatism of British labor also prevented adaptations which might have mitigated unemployment. See Balfour Comm., *Final Report*, pp. 236–42. Colin Clark offers the suggestion that the meager distribution of the benefits of education in Britain helped to account for the failure of labor to move more rapidly from old to new, and particularly from unskilled to skilled, occupations. *The Conditions of Economic Progress*, pp. 224, 231, 237–39. Additional "transitional" unemployment was created by technological renovation of British industry, mechanization of coal mines, modernization of iron and steel mills, with the result that stable or declining output meant declining or rapidly declining employment. See Gregory, "Rationalisation and Technological Unemployment," *Econ. Jour.*, XL (1930), 558–65; (D. H. Robertson), MacM. Comm., *Evidence*, I, 324.

[3] This situation can be expressed in savings-investment terminology. Despite their decline in comparison with 1913, there is evidence that savings were in the 1920's still excessive in relation to available investment outlets. For this the weakness of the balance of payments position was partly to blame, since, while Britain remained on gold, interest rates had to be so high that they impeded the absorption of savings in domestic industry. And the real level of foreign investment (as measured by the positive current balance) was greatly reduced in comparison with 1913. The result may be said to have been a considerable excess of savings over investment. See MacM. Comm., *Evidence*, I, 267–68, 331–32, 335, 341 (Keynes and Robertson), II, 89–90 (Pigou), *Report*, pp. 192 ff.; Keynes, *A Treatise on Money*, II, 188–89; Witt Bowden, "Surplus Labor and the Social Wage in Great Britain," *Amer. Econ. Rev.*, XXVII (1937), 31–44.

Nevertheless it seems a little ridiculous to blame "oversaving" or "underconsumption" for the British difficulties of the 1920's. If they had been the causes, the most depressed industries would have been those serving the domestic market. The contrary was the case. Or imports of foreign consumption goods might have been weak; as a matter of fact they were strong, and the balance of payments was weakened, because of the *decline* in savings. If insufficiency of foreign "investment" had been the cause, presumably increased subscription to foreign issues would have eased the situation. In actual fact, it would not. It would have been accompanied mainly by an equilibrating inflow of short-term capital— i.e., net foreign investment would not have been appreciably increased thereby, and domestic investment would have had to be further discouraged by high interest rates. The situation of the 1920's may be said to have been tantamount to an excess of savings over investment; a decrease of savings or an increase of investment might have served to remove the deflation. However, these words lose all precise meaning when made to cover a situation where decreased savings (with resultant disequilibrating effects upon the balance of pay-

Whatever the causes of unemployment, what was required was the quickest and greatest possible absorption of the labor displaced from export industries into production for the home market.[4] Of course, it was desirable that costs be reduced and labor be re-employed in old and new export trades as well. For the most part, however, this was not possible, and the home market had to be the chief outlet.[5] Although there remained a hard core of British unemployment throughout the period 1919–39, as the volume of exports declined secularly, these adjustments were being made.

The declining importance of exports in relation to domestic production was thus a mirror of the absolute increase of the latter as well as of the absolute decline of the former. While the volume index of British exports declined from 100 in 1924 to 89.5 in 1937 (after having recovered only to 108.3 in 1929), industrial production rose from 100 in 1924 to 111.8 in 1929 and 137.0 in 1937.[6] It would appear from the censuses of production that exports accounted for approximately 30 percent of industrial output in 1907, 27 percent in 1924, 22 percent in 1930, and, very roughly, 16 percent in 1935.[7] The decline of exports was even greater in relation to national income, in view of the disproportionately great rise in the period 1919–39 of distributive, service, and other such industries, which by their nature are unproductive of exports.

The rise of industries supplying the domestic market in far greater degree than had the staple trades was an important evidence, as well as a means, of adjustment. There was a real shift of workers from old to new industries. While between July, 1924, and July, 1938, the insured workers attached to the coal mining industry declined from 1,259,000 to 858,000, cotton textiles from 572,000 to 393,000, wool textiles from

ments) and a deteriorated competitive position of British industry were two major causes of the existent unemployment. This is the result of attempting to straight-jacket economic phenomena into a prescribed narrow theoretical dogma.

[4] In so far as the British people, fully employed, would continue to demand more foreign goods and securities than they could secure by similar exports, some labor would perforce remain unemployed, if this were the only remaining means of holding down British purchasing power and thus maintaining equilibrium of the balance of payments. See pp. 154–55, above.

[5] See the arguments of the Liberal Industrial Inquiry, *Britain's Industrial Future*, p. 46; Snow, "The Relative Importance of the Export Trade," J.R.S.S., CXIV (1931), 390–95.

[6] The figures are only roughly comparable, being computed by linking separate official series.

[7] Based on official census estimates. See also Daniels and Campion, "The Relative Importance of British Export Trade," London and Cambridge Econ. Service, Special Memorandum No. 41, Aug., 1935.

262,000 to 216,000, shipbuilding from 254,000 to 175,000, and iron and steel from 318,000 to 286,000, those in building rose from 726,000 to 1,050,000, in the various electrical trades [8] from 330,000 to 563,000, motor vehicles, cycles, and aircraft from 204,000 to 388,000, road transport from 270,000 to 416,000, and silk and artificial silk from 41,000 to 77,000. Even greater increments were recorded by the distributive trades (from 1,355,000 to 2,096,000 workers in the same period), and the various service industries [9] (1,103,000 to 1,881,000).[10]

Inordinate geographical concentration of the staple trades created an ineradicable British problem of great depressed areas, regions suffering deep impoverishment and a disproportionately high degree of unemployment from at least 1924 through 1939. The newer industries, which cater mainly to consumer demands, were attracted to these areas only with difficulty, because of their relative poverty. However, in a sense this phenomenon had its bright side, taking the national view. Other areas, notably in the South and the Midlands, in which were concentrated the rising trades, were enjoying great prosperity. The growth of industries catering primarily to the home market, entailing a marked change in the geographical distribution of domestic investment activity, was as a result accompanied by a very marked corresponding shift of Britain's industrial population.[11]

[8] Gas, water, and electricity; electric cable, lamps, apparatus; electrical wiring and contracting; electrical engineering.

[9] Government, professional, hotel, other services, miscellaneous.

[10] The relative changes in the net output of the leading British industrial groups sharply limns these changes. The depression of the staple trades of the 1920's is shown by the fall in the rank of cotton spinning and weaving (by this criterion) from fourth in 1907 to fifth in 1924 and thirteenth in 1930, iron and steel from second to fifth, shipbuilding from thirteenth to seventeenth, wool and worsted from twelfth to eighteenth, all between 1907 and 1930. However, while cotton and shipbuilding continued to decline in rank thereafter, the recovery and adjustments of the other staples (aided by the tariff) is indicated by the rise between 1930 and 1935 of iron and steel (rank 5 to 2), mechanical engineering (6 to 5), and wool (18 to 15). Most prominent among the rising industrial groups were the new industries, and those, old and new, supplying the home market for consumer goods. Over the period 1907 to 1935, the elevations in rank were as follows: electrical engineering 20 to 11, electricity supply 23 to 13, chemicals 10 to 6, motor vehicles 21 to 8. Prominent among the older industries of the second group were paper and publishing (7 to 3), brewing and malting (6 to 4), clay and building materials (15 to 12), as well as the manufacture of hosiery, preserved foods, and cocoa and sugar confectionery.

[11] See P.E.P., *Report on the Location of Industry;* Dennison, *The Location of Industry;* Gr. Brit., Royal Commission on the Distribution of the Industrial Population, *Report,* Cmd. 6153, 1940; Champernowne, "The Uneven Distribution of Unemployment in the U.K., 1929–36," *Rev. Econ. Studies,* V (1937–38), 93–106, VI (1938–39), 111–24. The Board of Trade's figures show that of the 1,300 openings of new factories in

Much more important than the changed geographical distribution of Britain's investment in domestic industry was the considerable increase of the total. The decline of British savings entailed an increased expenditure for domestically produced consumption goods and services. The great improvement in terms of trade likewise released British purchasing power in this direction. With the shift in world demand to newer consumption goods went a heightened British demand for these goods— goods produced at home as well as those produced abroad. Finally, the great decrease of foreign lending, for lack of adequate foreign investment opportunities, released large quantities of capital for absorption into domestic industry. In each case the factor bringing a deterioration of Britain's current balance of payments, with consequent deflationary effect on British incomes, was at the same time tending automatically to effect an adjustment in a recovery of the domestic economy, thus providing the means as well as the necessity for a shift of productive factors from the supply of foreign needs to the supply of domestic needs.

If the staple export trades were relatively unprofitable in the late 1920's, the rate of return in new and old home-market industries was highly satisfactory.[12] Thus, despite unemployment and high short-term money rates, Britain was in general moderately prosperous in the late 1920's. Security prices rose considerably and there was a flood of new domestic issues in 1928–29, many highly speculative, many exploiting new products and processes—issues by investment trusts, manufacturers of rayon, phonographs, radios, and cinema producers and exhibitors.[13]

The most dramatic evidence of these adjustments of the British econ-

---

excess of closings, in the five years 1932–36, no less than 1,100 were in the South of England. *Surveys of Industrial Development.* See the very interesting article "The Disposal of Britain's New Capital," *Midland Bk. Mo. Rev.*, Oct.–Nov., 1937, pp. 1–4.

[12] See "Boom in Steel," *Economist*, CXXVI (1937), 105. In the year beginning Oct. 1, 1929, profits of iron, coal and steel companies were 4.5 percent of capital, shipping 6.9 percent, and textiles 8.3 percent, as against an all-industry average of 10.3 percent. On the other hand, in the following year, when the average return for all industry had fallen to 8.0 percent, electric light and power still earned 11.0 percent motor, cycle, and aviation companies 11.4 percent. In the year of recovery beginning Oct. 1, 1934, the average return was 8.2 percent; the staple trades, iron, steel, and coal earned 5.6 percent shipping 4.0 percent, textiles 5.2 percent. On the other hand, earnings in electric power and light were 11.5 percent, motors, cycles, and aviation 14.2 percent, breweries and distilleries 13.4 percent, tobacco 15.7 percent, building materials 13.9 percent, and shops and stores 12.8 percent. Bank of England, *Statistical Summaries.*

[13] See Grant, *The Capital Market in Post-War Britain*, pp. 141–46; *Statist*, CXIII (1929), 14. Table 21 (p. 139) shows how well maintained were domestic issues in this period.

omy was its great recovery from the 1929–32 depression, while most other countries floundered in a morass of gold deflation or succeeded only in slow painful reflation at the cost of heavy budgetary deficits or totalitarian regimentation.[14] The free upsurge of long-suffering British capitalism was the envy of the world.

This enormous recovery was, like the longer-run adjustments, made possible in very large measure by the disappearance of saving, the great amelioration of terms of trade, and a consequent marked improvement of the real incomes and living standards of the employed population (largely the upper working classes), whose wages remained relatively rigid.[15] There resulted a great increase in demand for new houses, motor cars, electricity and electrical consumption goods.[16] These rising industries, especially building, accounted for a disproportionate share of the increased employment and investment in the years 1932–35, when recovery began and matured into prosperity. In 1936 and 1937, as the business revival became general and the additional rearmament demand created boom conditions, investment and employment in the heavy staple

---

[14] See B. of T.J., CXXXII (1934), 551; British Assoc., *Britain in Recovery*, pp. x–xii, 46–52; Grant, *The Capital Market in Post-War Britain*, pp. 147–50.

[15] Indeed, taking the dole into account, P. Sargant Florence has arrived at astonishing estimates which show the real purchasing power of the entire wage-earning population, employed and unemployed together, to have risen after 1929. "An Index of Working Class Purchasing Power for Great Britain, 1929–35," J.P.E., XLIV (1936), 687–90. The opposite income effect of the deterioration of the current balance of payments was to a large extent minimized by the low income elasticity of expenditure of the investing classes, who suffered heavy reductions in income from oversea investments, but maintained consumption out of saving.

[16] See Clark, *National Income and Outlay*, p. 193. There have been many interesting discussions concerning the ultimate causes of the building boom. The thesis expounded above is similar to the one discussed, and apparently originated, by the *Economist*, which pointed out that total wages and salary payments decreased far less in Britain during the depression than total public expenditure on food, clothing, liquor, and tobacco. The discrepancy represented a great amount of free buying power in the hands of the middle and lower middle classes, buying power which went primarily into new housing, new motor vehicles, etc. See "The Housing Boom, I," CXXI (1935), 795–96; also Stolper, "British Monetary Policy and the Housing Boom," Q.J.E., Nov., 1941, Part 2, pp. 39–42, and chap. v; and Radice, *Savings in Great Britain*, p. 61.

Grant, *The Capital Market in Post-War Britain*, pp. 244–47, argues that, although this large body of disposable income was a *sine qua non*, the major initial impulse in 1932 was a speculative development by builders, the result of lower interest rates and a quest for new investment opportunities. See also Benham, *Great Britain under Protection*, pp. 225–26, 236–37. Any apparent controversy here arises simply from the futile practice of seeking original and ultimate causes. The initial speculative efforts of builders would not have continued had not the conditions of demand been propitious. On the other hand, the mere existence of favorable demand dispositions seldom in itself initiates booms.

trades also recovered considerably. Here also, however, the increase went almost entirely into meeting the greatly expanded requirements of the home market.

British government policy contributed to recovery. The depreciation of the pound adjusted sterling costs to gold prices and, in conjunction with empire preference and the trade agreements, halted the decline of British exports. It released British bank policy from the gold chains by which it had been bound and permitted a bold cheap-money policy. Although cheap money is in itself incapable of inducing recovery, it proved a highly important contributory influence in England, where interest rates had long been too high and other conditions were propitious.[17] The tariff helped restore a measure of prosperity to some industries—including such staple trades as wool and iron and steel. The heavy investment in iron and steel which occurred thereafter, most observers agree, was partly attributable to the guarantee of its home market.[18] Little of the initial recovery of investment or employment occurred in the newly protected industries, it is true.[19] However, the tariff (in conjunction with the fall of sterling) effected an immediate readjustment of the balance of payments, the inflationary effect of which was undoubtedly felt throughout the entire British economy. By diminishing British demand for foreign goods, at given income levels, it reduced the extent to which British incomes had to decline by virtue of the decline in exports.[20] It can well be argued, thus, that the tariff was partially responsible even for the boom of the unprotected building industry, because it confined to domestic products (houses) purchasing power which might otherwise have been dissipated (as it was to a large extent from 1929 to 1931) in purchases of foreign consumption goods.[21]

There is nothing inherently desirable in an active current balance of

[17] See Conolly, "Reflections on the Cheap-Money Policy," *Index,* Suppl., Oct., 1939, pp. 1–20; H. D. Henderson, "The Case against Returning to Gold," *Lloyds Bk. Ltd. Mo. Rev.,* n.s., VI (1935), 338–45; Benham, *Great Britain under Protection,* pp. 229–32; Harris, *Exchange Depreciation,* pp. 389–400; Jean Marchal, "L'Abandon de l'étalon-or," *Rev. Econ. Int.,* 1937, Part 3, pp. 264–76; Brown, *The Int. Gold Stand.,* II, 1147–58; R. J. Truptil, *The British Banks and the London Money Market,* London, Cape, 1936, pp. 294–309.

[18] See Benham, *Great Britain under Protection,* p. 193. New capital issues in the coal, iron and steel group soared from £4.1 million in 1932 and 1933 combined to £26.6 million in the two years 1934 and 1935. Bank of England, *Statistical Summaries.*

[19] Benham, *op. cit.,* p. 220; Allan W. Rather, *Is Britain Decadent?,* pp. 252–53.

[20] See pp. 56–57, 154–56, above.

[21] For a judicious discussion of the relation of British policy to recovery see Heaton, *The British Way to Recovery,* pp. 9–18, and chap. iv.

payments, in heavy foreign investment. If a creditor country finds it possible to sustain almost full employment by a choice on the part of its people to consume the fruits of their present and past labors, to build themselves more efficient tools and more commodious cities and homes—there is nothing less desirable in such a situation. The benefits of foreign investment are not uniformly great at all times or for all countries. The maximization of national income made possible by the freedom of savers to invest wherever the marginal efficiency of capital is, or appears to be, highest may not materialize, if hopes prove to have been over-sanguine.[22] Britain's investments abroad might result in cheaper food for her people and raw materials for her factories, or they might create foreign industries directly competitive with her own, with the net effect of a deterioration of her real income. In view of the considerable use of British capital by foreigners in the 1920's to equip competitive industries; in view also of the fact that much of the capital was in any case lost, it would appear that the British people might better have consumed their capital than permit the countries of Latin America to do so, cleaned out London slums rather than rehouse the working classes of Berlin and Vienna, and equipped depressed domestic industries rather than contribute to the superiority of the German.[23]

Even in helping to solve the problems of full employment, capital exports had been decreasingly successful. The attempt to transfer British capital abroad during the 1920's was largely responsible for balance of payments weakness and monetary stringency, which depressed domestic industry. In the changed world economy, heavy free British capital exports were an anomaly. By the great revival of domestic investment, England was made a better place in which to live, and unemployment was considerably offset.

Moreover, British industry was partially refitted thereby for its new place in the world, with the result that the productivity of British labor increased considerably in the period 1919–39. This advance was doubtless slower than the American and German, and there remained much to

---

[22] Domestic investment may also reap a harvest of defaults, but the capital equipment remains within the country. A bankrupt railroad may continue to offer employment and services as long as it can cover marginal expenses, and municipal parks may still beautify a city even though the loans by which they were laid out are in default. See Keynes, "Foreign Investment and National Advantage," *The Nation and the Athenaeum*, Aug. 9, 1924, p. 586.

[23] See Loftus, *A Main Cause of Unemployment*, p. 55; also Gregory, in *Foreign Investments*, p. 116; Liberal Industrial Inquiry, *Britain's Industrial Future*, pp. 110, 300, 307 ff.

be done, but absolute progress was impressive even during the twenties.[24] It was even more so thereafter, this time largely because of the recovery and rationalization of the leading staple trades.[25]

The period 1919–39 witnessed, then, a concurrence of two powerful factors tending to increase British incomes: a rising productivity of her labor and an improvement in her terms of international trade. The decline of savings entailed rising standards of consumption out of existing incomes, as well. On the other hand, partly as a result of these very factors, Britain suffered severe unemployment. The mature British economy was incapable of sufficient expansion of consumption and domestic investment to fill the gap created by decreased foreign demand, and as a result most of this great potential increase of income was dissipated. Of course, as we have seen, to a large extent this dissipation was inevitable, the failure of demand resulting from the fact that foreigners were learning more and more to dispense with British goods and services, while the demand of British people for foreign products remained strong.

The net effect was nevertheless a marked improvement in the real income, and even more in the living standards, of the British people.[26]

---

[24] See MacM. Comm., *Report*, pp. 53–54, *Evidence*, II, 237 (Bowley); Clark, "Statistical Studies," *Econ. Jour.*, XLI (1931), 360.

[25] The following indexes of output per employee in major industry groups, for 1924, 1930, and 1935, respectively, were computed by E. Devons, "Production Trends in the U.K.," *Transactions of the Manchester Statistical Society*, Dec. 16, 1938, pp. 9–15. The base is 1930. The mechanization of the coal mines and lengthened work day after the 1926 strike resulted in a considerable increase of per capita productivity in coal between 1924 and 1930 as well as thereafter: the index for mines and quarries rose from 85.4 in 1924 to 100 in 1930, while that for British industry as a whole rose only from 90.6 to 100. The lag in the other staple trades in this period was both cause and result of their competitive difficulties: textiles actually declined from 103.4 to 100 (mirroring a policy of spreading work by short-time), iron and steel rose only from 98.9, and engineering, shipbuilding and vehicles from 97.7, to 100. By 1935, however, the indexes of per capita productivity of the staple trades show a satisfying increase. From 100 in 1930, iron and steel's index was 115.8 in 1935, that of engineering, etc. 127.8 and textiles no less than 134.3. See also Witt Bowden, "The Productivity of Labor in Great Britain," J.P.E., XLV (1937), 347–69.

[26] Clark, *National Income and Outlay*, pp. 208–10, 267–70; Pigou and Clark, *The Economic Position of Great Britain*, pp. 31–34, 37–40. As we have just seen, even in the short period 1928–31, the rapid improvement of terms of trade and virtual disappearance of savings very greatly mitigated the adverse effects of a rapid cyclical downswing. The increase in average per capita consumption of foreign foods attested to a very substantial benefit to the living standards of the employed worker. See A. E. Feaveryear, "The National Expenditure, 1932," *Econ. Jour.*, XLIV (1934), 33–47; Villeneuve, *La Préférence impériale*, pp. 166–67, 171; Sir George Schuster, "British Economic and Financial Policy,"

This was no fortuitous concurrence. Almost exactly the same things happened to Britain during the "great depression" of the last quarter of the nineteenth century: a slower rise of exports of goods and capital, heavier unemployment, income deflation—but rising productivity, improving terms of trade, and rapidly improving real incomes. On the contrary, in the decade before 1913 great British "prosperity"—rising prices and money incomes, increasing foreign lending and exports, and low unemployment—were accompanied by a much slower rise in the productivity and real wages of British labor.[27]

The causes of this strange phenomenon—of real progress in time of apparently long-run depression, of real stagnation in a period of apparent prosperity—can only be suggested tentatively and hesitantly. The reader will recall our outline of the "purchasing power" cycle.[28] In the upswing, British investment (mainly in other countries) rose rapidly, causing expansion of money prices, incomes, and employment. Why did the productivity of labor, and incomes (except for the relatively small class of profits and income from foreign investments) tend to increase much less rapidly? For one thing, in such a period efficiency in production became secondary to speed; less efficient labor was probably hired, less efficient methods used, and labor turnover increased by the plethora of jobs. Perhaps more fundamentally, for Britain such a period was one of abstinence, of increased saving and lending. Domestic investment in the mature lender was more likely than in the younger debtors to be depressd by the rise of interest rates.[29] The rise in marginal productivity and money wages of British labor was therefore retarded, with slackening of expansion or renovation of domestic capital equipment. The tendency for barter terms of trade to deteriorate in these long cyclical upswings, finally, retarded the rise of real wages as well.

After foreign investment fell off, and interest rates declined, the bulk of investment was in domestic industry. A revival of house construction also seems to have been encouraged by the plethora of capital and by rising real incomes of labor. The revival of domestic investment tended to raise the marginal productivity of domestic labor. The profit deflation which resulted from the diminution of investment activity probably caused laying off of less efficient labor and decrease of labor turnover.

Nineteenth Century and After, CXVIII (1935), 516; Cole, British Trade and Industry, pp. 196–98.

[27] See Taussig, International Trade, p. 257; John G. Newlove, "The Unrest among Workpeople," Econ. Jour., XXI (1911), 470; Clapham, An Economic History of Modern Britain, III, 466–77.

[28] See above, pp. 145–48.   [29] See p. 169, above.

More efficient methods of production were sought, encouraged by lower interest rates and also, possibly, by rigid money wages. While money incomes, especially those of the investing and profit-earning classes, declined, expenditures tended to be maintained at the expense of savings. The period of abstinence was over; the fruits of the previous international investment and foreign development were being enjoyed.[30] The only major drawback was the familiar inability of a mature capitalist economy to maintain full employment in a period of declining foreign investments, technological progress, and falling prices.[31]

The loss through unemployment in the years 1919–39 was great,[32] and it bore particularly heavily on the lower working classes. Great and satisfying as was the recovery after 1932 and despite the successful adjustments of the British economy, unemployment was greater in absolute terms in the peak year 1937 than it had been even in the period 1924–29 (excluding 1926), and the problem of the depressed areas was just about as serious as ever.[33] Around 1935–37 the internal market for

[30] Without the abstinence of the upswings during the nineteenth century, the increase of real incomes during the downswings would have been the less, of course.

[31] See Clark, *National Income and Outlay*, p. 264. Sir Robert Giffen in 1887 pointed out the indications of continued progress in Britain during the "Great Depression": increased construction of houses, growth of new domestic industries, and expanded employment in service industries. "The Recent Rate of Material Progress in England," in *Economic Inquiries and Studies*, London, Bell, 1904, II, 99–144, especially, 134–40. See W. W. Rostow, "Investment and the Great Depression," *Economic History Review*, VIII (1938), 136–58, and "Investment and Real Wages, 1873–86," *Economic History Review*, IX (1939), 144–59; Cole, *British Trade and Industry*, pp. 84–86, 99–102, 112–14; Clapham, *An Economic History of Modern Britain*, III, 24, 28, 52–53, 464–68, 474–76; Sir George Schuster, "British Economic and Financial Policy," *Nineteenth Century and After*, CXVIII (1935), 517; Feis, *Europe, the World's Banker*, pp. 29–31; W. H. Beveridge, "Population and Unemployment," *Econ. Jour.*, XXXIII (1923), 462–67.

It is interesting to note that there were during the world-wide depression following 1873 much the same predictions of continuing world stagnation as have been heard since 1929. In both cases the concurrence of the ends of a short and a long cycle of very heavy world investment made the resulting decline very long and very difficult, especially for business classes and the unemployed. See A. J. Mundella, "Conditions on which the Commercial and Manufacturing Supremacy of Great Britain Depend," J.R.S.S., XLI (1878), 88–89; Ohlin, *The World Economic Depression*, pp. 290–93, 298. There were, however, important differences between the two periods, which must qualify any optimistic expectations that a similar recovery will occur after the later one. Such differences are suggested by the slackened rate of increase of the world's population and the unprecedented unemployment, the failure of the volume of world trade to recover, and the greater economic nationalism and more devastating wars of recent years.

[32] "Employed and unemployed taken together, we have during the last few years been producing per head only a little more than in 1913, the increase of 15 to 20 percent in productivity per worker being almost exactly balanced by the increase in unemployment." Clark, *National Income and Outlay*, p. 269.

[33] See Donald Tyerman, "Recovery and the Distressed Areas," *Lloyds Bk. Ltd. Mo. Rev.*,

houses and automobiles reached the point of saturation at existing prices. The 1937–38 recession, caused largely by a heavy decline of staple exports, exposed again the narrowness of the base on which recovery had been constructed and the enduring weakness of the British position. Some of these weaknesses could never be obliterated unless the world economy could again function more or less as a unit, instead of an agglomeration of warring states. To this end a reorientation of British policy may have been required.

The pendulum had swung too far. The old world economy could not possibly be restored intact, but its destruction had been in large measure the result of conscious government policies, and these were coming increasingly into question. The inadequacy of empire preference was becoming more and more apparent. There was evidence that the cheap-money policy had become dangerous, once recovery turned into a boom based almost entirely upon the domestic market.[34] There was little economic excuse for agricultural protection, from a short- or long-run point of view. A government policy which intensified the rigidities could not obliterate the necessity for economic flexibility and easy adaptation in a country as inevitably subject to the vagaries of the international competitive struggle as was Great Britain.[35] The tariff and the governmentally encouraged combination movement in industry created entrenched vested interests who were content to exploit the protected domestic market and, as the price for being undisturbed at home, to leave to foreign producers the exploitation of foreign markets urgently required by the British economy as a whole. Trade policy and the restrictions on foreign lending likewise thwarted a very necessary recovery of British exports.

This necessity for foreign markets would increase if, as it appeared, private domestic investment was reaching a point of rapidly diminishing returns. Only technological advance and lower prices could have prolonged the absorption by the domestic market of more automobiles, houses, and even electricity. The problem of investment outlets promised to become a pressing one for the British economy, and undoubtedly threatened to result in heavy unemployment, when the war opened up more than enough opportunities and postponed its resolution.

n.s., VIII (1937), 619–30. Only during a few months in 1937 did the percentage of unemployment among insured workers reach down around the 1929 level of 10 percent. British Assoc., *Britain in Recovery*, pp. xii, 6–8, 38.

[34] See Conolly, "Reflections on the Cheap-Money Policy," *Index*, Suppl., Oct., 1939, pp. 10–19.

[35] See testimony of O. M. W. Sprague, MacM. Comm., *Evidence*, II, 308–9.

XV. THE POSITION OF BRITAIN IN THE POST-WAR WORLD

Hﬤ ISTORY is a continuous process. Even wars seldom by themselves
cause fundamental alterations of secular economic trends. There
is little reason to suppose that "victory" in a defensive war will
make for any greater improvement in Great Britain's international economic position than it did in 1918. On the contrary, the war will add
difficulties of its own. The serious problems which the British people
faced in the years 1919 to 1939 and the merely partial and temporary
solutions which they were able to find, justify considerable anxiety concerning their economic welfare when the second World War comes to a
close.[1]

The major changes of the period 1919–39 all joined in causing a continuous reduction of Britain's balance of payments on current account, a
measure of both the regular increments from abroad to her money incomes and her customarily large exports of capital. Thus, the most useful frame of reference for a comparison of post-war prospects with pre-
war experience is the current balance of international payments.[2]

Britain's greatest invisible income, interest and dividend returns from
past investment will be much smaller in the future. Her debtors had
clearly become increasingly self-sufficient with respect to financial requirements even before the war, while Britain found it impossible to add
to her foreign investments. Still, the experience of the 1930's does not
in itself permit us to predict a continuation of these trends: it is by no
means clear to what extent this represented a secular development, to
what extent a severe and protracted cyclical phenomenon. As a result of
the war, however, a reduction in these payments by as much as 40–50
percent can confidently be predicted. The British government has been
forced to requisition and sell for precious foreign exchange roughly

---

[1] We can scarcely discuss here the various conceivable outcomes which will depend upon
the kind of victory won, the destructiveness of the war, and the decisions of the peace
conference. However, such discussions are not entirely necessary if there is foundation for
our thesis that neither a victorious outcome nor the conscious choices of government policy
per se will substantially alter the position of Britain.

[2] We are interested in the long-run determinants of British real incomes, rather than in
the immediate effects of the war. Hence our considerations apply to the prospective position
over a period of ten to twenty years after the war.

£1,000,000,000 of the country's foreign investments. At the same time, it has to an even greater extent incurred liabilities to foreign countries, who have exported heavily to meet Britain's war needs, while being able to purchase little from her. According to an official estimate, total net disinvestment in the four years 1940–43 amounted to £2,843,000,000—including sales of gold, foreign assets, and the growth of these foreign liabilities. This figure may be compared with an estimated market value of Britain's total overseas assets (including gold) at the outbreak of war of "possibly more than £5,000,000,000." [3] The loss of income may not be proportional, since the assets liquidated gave a relatively low yield, and the liabilities incurred bear little or no interest.

Canada, India, and South Africa, in particular, have been using their accumulating London balances regularly to redeem their sterling debt. For example, by the end of 1943 India repatriated in this manner no less than £363,750,000 of her pre-war (March, 1936) sterling debt (government and railroad) of £376,000,000. And still these balances have grown apace. India's holdings of sterling cash and securities were £721,000,000 on April, 1944, as against only £58,000,000 at the outbreak of the war. [4]

Britain's heavy accumulation of short-term liabilities (including Lend-Lease), the concurrent reduction almost to zero of her short-term international assets, and heavy sales of the most marketable long-term investments, have left the country in a financial position technically far weaker than that of 1931 and 1938. Some sort of co-operative international arrangement for the settlement and orderly liquidation of these obligations will clearly be necessary, or continued unilateral British exchange controls are inevitable. In any case, real British income will have to be reduced to pay off all or part of these heavy foreign claims; this is part of the cost of war.

The other "service" incomes, it may be presumed, will also be considerably reduced after the war. The gradual disappearance of Britain's financial and shipping supremacy seems bound to continue: witness, for example, the continued growth in prestige of the dollar and the huge American war shipbuilding program. However, one major cause of the

[3] N. Kaldor and T. Barna, "The 1943 White Paper on National Income and Expenditure," *Econ. Jour.*, June–Sept., 1943, p. 261; see pp. 260–62; also "The Budget Speech," *Economist*, CXLVI (1944), 563, and the estimate of Lord Kindersley, reported in New York *Times*, Nov. 30, 1942, p. 31.

[4] *Economist*, CXLVI (1944), 688. "India has completed the transition from a debtor to a creditor country," according to the British Finance Minister. "India's War Gains," *Economist*, March 6, 1943, p. 302. See also "India's Sterling Accumulation," *Economist*, Sept. 26, 1942, p. 393.

weakness of these invisible earnings during the years 1919 to 1939, as of the income from foreign investments, was the stagnation of total international economic intercourse. A revival of world trade and investment and of primary prices after the present war, which is by no means inconceivable, may well lead to a considerably stronger showing of these inpayments than a simple extrapolation of past trends would indicate, despite continued decline of Britain's relative share in the world totals.

Any estimate of the absolute totals of merchandise exports and imports in the future must also, obviously, be based upon some assumptions as to the condition of total international trade and investment. Nevertheless, it seems desirable first to evaluate the probable relative competitive position of Britain's export industries in the post-war world, before attempting to translate qualitative judgments into predictions of absolute growth or decline.

The causes for the decline of British industrial supremacy, we have maintained, are deeply rooted in impersonal historical processes. There is little reason to expect any appreciable alteration or reversal thereof. The staple trades continue to constitute the bulk of exports, and their outlook is, if anything, less encouraging than ever. Nationalist aspirations in the Far East and elsewhere definitely include industrialization, and the displacement of what is left there of the demand for British textiles may be expected to continue, with iron and steel and various clothing industries to follow. There seems little possibility of a reversal of the fate of coal in general or of British coal in particular. The present war, it may be presumed, will have the same contributory influence as the last in hastening this decline. Customary markets have been closed to the British exporter and have been spurred to find alternative sources of supply. Although world-wide wartime shortages have likewise hampered these efforts, many markets have become more self-sufficient.[5] Moreover, further programs for domestic industrial development will be sped after the war, probably financed in some measure out of the blocked sterling and dollars which these countries are steadily accumulating.

Whether or not international trade declines absolutely as a result, it will certainly experience a considerable change in content and pattern,

[5] Steel capacity in the dominions is said to have been increased from 3.5 million tons annually in 1938 to 6 million in 1941, and the output of empire machine shops to have tripled or quadrupled. Canada, India, and Australia are building their own ships and have developed new chemical industries; and in such industries as textiles and clothing they are now practically self-sufficient. See National Planning Association, "Britain's Trade in the Post-War World," Planning Pamphlet No. 9, Dec. 1941, p. 11.

notably a rise in the relative importance of newer and higher-income consumer goods and of the machinery necessary for the industrial development of former markets. The extent to which British industry can maintain a large export trade will depend, clearly, upon its ability to take or retain the lead in these latterly more important lines, while at the same time recovering and sustaining as much as possible of the old staple trades, upon which it must continue to rely heavily.

The opportunities are considerable, if the British prove sufficiently enterprising. The skill of British labor has been a positive disadvantage where foreign mass production has duplicated British quality at lower labor costs. However, the shifting of world demand, as incomes rise, to those quality lines, new as well as old, in which British skill remains an advantage, may yet support her exports, even though this promise was not fulfilled in the years 1919 to 1939. The performance of the Spitfire planes in 1940 gave testimony to the world that British craftsmanship was not confined to woolens and whiskey. If the airplane will be in the next few decades what the automobile was in the last few, British producers may find a wide market.

However, any appreciable results will require radical changes and vigorous efforts to eliminate those individual and social frailties which have so handicapped British industry in the past. Certainly the removal of competitive incentives (by tariffs and schemes of industrial "reorganization," involving the freezing of relative market positions of all producers, efficient and inefficient alike), no other incentives being substituted, was not the way to assure adjustment to an altered technology or to a shift of consumer demand. Certainly the single-minded exploitation of the protected domestic market, behind cartel agreements with foreign producers, involving reciprocal undertakings not to export in competition, was no way to restore an export trade of which the country as a whole stood in sore need. Yet British industry did these things and the British government condoned, encouraged, or actively initiated them in the inter-war years. Because of their co-operation, there evolved in Britain a regime of industrial self-government under which business interests found temporary security, while the interests of the consumer and the economy as a whole were neglected. As long as these developments are not undone, it is difficult to see how British industry can make the adjustments necessary to preserve an adequate export trade after the war.

The present war may bring about considerable changes in this regard. On the one hand, war is the mother of monopoly. National industrial mobilization calls for industry-wide planning and co-operation and for centralized control of the national economy by powerful government agencies, customarily staffed by leaders drawn from large private businesses. Usually the result is a permanent injury to the competitive regime.[6] On the other hand, total war demands maximum efficiency, and British industry may have benefited by this fact. The programs for concentrating the production of civilian goods in a minimum number of "nucleus" factories, and related programs limiting output to a few prescribed standard models and eliminating frills and gadgets may help to remove some of the most persistent weaknesses of the staple trades: the welter of small, inefficient firms, all competing for a shrunken market, working short hours, and producing an excessive variety of brands. However, there are manifest dangers. The plans were formulated largely by the industries themselves, and the selected firms appear to have been the biggest, most powerful ones. The various provisions for post-war aid to plants closed down in these programs, however necessary, may err in providing excessive protection for the less efficient, giving them a vested interest in their former share of the market which must be bought out at the expense of the remaining producers. Finally, the choice of nucleus firms was not necessarily made on the basis of lowest costs; the current local labor supply, for example, was one important consideration, relevant in wartime but possibly misleading for purposes of maximum peacetime efficiency.[7]

A second significant wartime development has been the increased participation of organized labor in management. The spread of joint labor-management committees has in many cases contributed, it is asserted, to a more ready co-operation of labor in maximizing production. It is possible that British industry will benefit permanently by this development. There is little doubt that labor is capable of making a considerable contribution; industrial labor organization, for example, may well contribute to genuine industry-wide reorganization. Whether, however, these committees will make the same contributions in time of peace and can be expected to induce a more co-operative attitude of labor unions toward cost-reducing measures even at the expense of their members, may well be open to question.[8]

---

[6] See Robert A. Brady, *Business as a System of Power*, New York, Columbia Univ., 1943, pp. 181–88.

[7] See *Financial News*, London, April 28, 1942, p. 2.

[8] Nevertheless, the new situation will probably represent an improvement over the present one, where organized labor possesses a great power without corresponding responsibility.

Finally, destruction by enemy action may prove the greatest war-time boon to post-war industrial efficiency. Perhaps only enemy bombs can wipe out inefficient plants, as well as London slums, and thus clear the slate for the building of modern factories and houses. Obsolescence of unutilized plants, e.g., those closed down for lack of materials or in concentration programs may have the same ultimately beneficial results.

Most encouraging of all is the growing consciousness among English-men of the gravity of their industrial position and their growing disposition to do something about it. It is to be hoped that one of the effects of the war will be unwillingness to leave the settlement of these problems, as of other problems, to the mercy of vested interests within the framework of outmoded institutions and slogans.

Nevertheless, there is little reason to expect Britain to make any better showing in this regard than she made in the years 1919 to 1939. Re-adjustments in old industries and growth of new industries both failed to sustain her share in a diminished world trade, for reasons essentially impersonal and unavoidable. On this account, accordingly, the prospects are that exports and national income will continue to fall.

On the import side, too, there is little basis for a prediction of important change. The fundamental conditions of Britain's demand for foreign primary products are facts of nature. This is not to say that imports need bear an inflexible relation to national income.[9] It is to say, however, that the costs of greater self-sufficiency, in terms of real income sacrificed, would be too great to justify governmental control of imports with that end in view.

To the extent that the increase of Britain's imports in the interwar period, or the need for a tariff to prevent their increase, was a result of the weakness of her industry in international competition, the prospects for the future may be qualified by the same considerations as were applied above to the discussion of exports. British industry can go far toward catching up or going ahead, if it will, and thus either decrease imports in free competition or reduce the real sacrifices imposed by governmental control of imports in the interest of balance-of-payments stability. Modern chemistry, for example, is already helping to curb the tyranny of natural disadvantage, from which Britain suffers particularly. There is a broad range of new materials which she may now be able to

---

If only to protect wage levels, union leaders are often the most ardent advocates of the introduction of cost-reducing expedients other than wage cuts.

[9] See Clay, "The Place of Exports in British Industry after the War," *Econ. Jour.*, June–Sept., 1942, p. 151.

make as well as any other country from her coal, air, and sea water, notably synthetic fertilizers,[10] plastics,[11] rubber,[12] and magnesium.[13] However, as in the discussion of exports, it must be concluded that these interesting possibilities hardly seem likely to upset Britain's heavy dependence upon imports or to make possible appreciable relaxation of the tariff unless exports expand greatly.

For these many reasons it is frequently stated that after the war there will be a "gap" or "deficit" in Great Britain's current balance of payments, variously estimated at from £200 to £500 million sterling. Of course, if Britain is able regularly to borrow (or withdraw capital) from abroad to this extent, then there will be no deficit at all, in any usual sense of the term. A true "gap" in the balance of payments of such a size could never exist, much less persist; Britain could not possibly draw down her greatly depleted short-term international assets, or accumulate such liabilities, to this extent, for any appreciable length of time.

This is the meaning of the "gap": that at full employment, with only such controls on imports as existed in 1938, and at assumed levels of world incomes and trade barriers against her goods, Britain would tend to purchase several hundreds of millions sterling more of foreign goods and services than foreigners would be willing to purchase from and otherwise remit to her. Consequently, unless other countries are willing to provide her a more or less permanent subsidy of this order of mag-

[10] Germany was the predominant supplier before the war. It is possible that economic disarmament may involve the elimination of many German synthetic industries (nitrogen, rubber), not to mention her airplane industry, which are as important for war as for peace. Britain may well fill the resultant gap in world markets.

[11] Plastics may increasingly be substituted for wood, an enormously increased demand for which may be expected in connection with a post-war building program. The government has appointed a special committee to inquire into this possibility. *Statist*, Sept. 12, 1942, pp. 666–67.

[12] Polychloroprene (American Neoprene), which comes ultimately from coal, is understood to have fully as great technical and economic potentialities as the butadiene rubbers. The failure of the American program to include greater provision for Neoprene resulted from a shortage of chlorine, which is also required. Britain can derive chlorine easily and cheaply from sea brine in peacetime. However, the political power of those with heavy financial interests in Malayan rubber will undoubtedly forestall any government aid for such a program. This may explain the fact that during the war Britain has acquired her synthetic rubber from the United States rather than manufacture her own.

[13] Britain's small production before 1939 is understood to have been under license from the German I. G. Farbenindustrie, but a large, and possibly the major, part of her requirements were imported from Germany. Whether or not the I. G. contracts involved definite restriction of British production, there does not seem to be any reason why Britain could not produce magnesium as cheaply at home as she could import it.

nitude,[14] British money incomes and their purchasing power in terms of foreign goods and services will have to decline, relative to those of other countries, sufficiently to keep her net remittances abroad lower by an equivalent amount.

Whether Britain's deteriorated relative position will necessitate an absolute decline in her real income will depend largely on the trend of world income. The very factors causing a decline in the demand for pounds (i.e., the development of foreign industries, reduced foreign burdens of indebtedness), imply rising foreign incomes, which will thus be available to demand sterling for other purposes. Since, moreover, the increment to world incomes thus implied is bound to be much greater than the amount of demand for sterling initially displaced, the result on balance may be an increased demand for pounds, that is, a net increase in British income. The extent to which Britain benefits clearly depends upon the way in which this increment to world income is expended, e.g., as between domestic goods and services and those which Britain is more or less capable of supplying. Much depends, thus, upon the future of international economic intercourse.[15]

One strong determinant of the rate of increase of world income and international trade will be the rate of international investment. The belief is fairly widespread that, even apart from immediate post-war "political" loans and gifts for relief and reconstruction,[16] international investment will for some time after the present war exceed the shrunken levels of the 1930's. It can scarcely be smaller. The time is riper than ever, politically and economically, for continued and intensified industrialization of large sections of the world: China, India, Russia, the British Dominions, and sections of Latin America. Primary producers who suffered because of their extreme specialization before the war will not be satisfied without introducing industry into their territories. If profit motives fail to induce lenders to meet this need, the governments

[14] It seems clear that it would have to be a subsidy, rather than a normal private investment dictated by considerations of maximum return, in view of the probably low marginal efficiency of capital in Britain.

[15] See pp. 55–58, above.

[16] The distinction between these and more "normal" loans will probably not be very clear. It may be doubted whether such customary economic considerations as the prospect of higher returns abroad will ever again become the major determinants of international investment. "Political" and "economic" motives, "reconstruction" and "developmental" purposes, will not be easily separated, and doubtless all lending will be more closely supervised by governments than in the past.

of the financially stronger of the United Nations may be subjected to increasing pressure to do so themselves.

However, the developments of the years 1919 to 1939 will not be simply reversed or obliterated. However short the memories of investors have been in the past, neither they nor their governments will completely forget the experience of the 1920's. Neither the overzealous promotion and lending of the United States nor the practically equal treatment of competing domestic and foreign demand for limited supplies of capital in Great Britain is likely to be repeated. On the demand side: the dominions, Russia, India, and Argentina have already become far more self-sufficient than they were in 1913. They may not be eager once again to impose fixed external obligations upon unresilient balances of payments or to contract further to pay "tribute" to foreigners. Their eagerness to pay off external obligations and their present plans to utilize accumulating sterling and dollar balances to finance their own future requirements would seem to be evidences of their distrust of international debt.

As we have already argued, the basic conditions of international investment have been changing secularly. The development of competitive manufacturing industries in former markets for industrial products, even if financed internationally, cannot be as conducive to a steady growth of world trade as the development of complementary primary production, once the initial flow of materials and machinery associated with the investment is over. The result of such investment is, on the contrary, a narrowing of the margins of comparative advantage on which international trade is based. Far less will the receipt of capital by debtor countries equip them to produce commodities which will be readily accepted abroad in repayment. Creditor countries will scarcely be anxious to sacrifice domestic industry in order to take in repayment a flood of competitive products from industrialized debtor areas. On the contrary, this is the field in which economic nationalism has thrived and will thrive. To most Indians, for example, independence, industrialization, and protection are as one. And in the creditor United States imports, the only possible means of collecting on past debts, are considered a threat to accustomed standards of living.[17]

True, foreign industrialization will mean an increasing demand for higher grade manufactures, consumption goods, and machinery. Great

[17] See Royal Institute, *The Problem of International Investment*, pp. 34–52.

Britain can maintain a substantial trade by thus adjusting her production. But this was not the bulk trade of the nineteenth century, based upon climatic and other natural differences, upon the head start in industrialization enjoyed by western Europe, and upon the existence of undeveloped areas offering huge potential markets, investment outlets, and sources of materials. The remaining possibilities of today—cultivation at intensive margins, maintenance and development of specialized types of industrial leadership—all of which were present in the nineteenth century as well, cannot be expected alone to provide as secure a basis for international trade, particularly in an atmosphere of economic nationalism. The British experience of the inter-war years is not encouraging in these regards.

This is not to say that there will be no revival of investment in primary production, such as may provide the basis for enduring complementary trade. The diets of all but a very small fraction of the world's population have been utterly inadequate, and the social upheavals resulting from the present war may involve concerted governmental efforts to satisfy minimum nutritional standards, with a consequent increase in the demand for foods. Industrialization of younger countries and a more even distribution of income in richer countries may provide the income which will translate these vast potential demands into reality. Thus, international investment in primary production in large sections of Africa, Asia, and Latin America may well become profitable once more. In India and China, likewise, peasants make up the bulk of the enormous populations and will continue to do so for many years. The greatest boon to these undernourished peoples would consist in agricultural development: irrigation, the use of fertilizers and modern farm machinery, the control of famines and disease. And their governments, in borrowing, can scarcely ignore these crying needs.

Nevertheless, the prospects for a revival of international investment and complementary trade along the nineteenth-century pattern are not bright. The relative overproduction of primary products in the years 1919 to 1939 will probably be accentuated by wartime expansion. And on the demand side there must be reckoned the widespread adoption of substitutes—synthetic rubber, fertilizers, fibers (rayon, nylon, glass, casein, etc.), plastics, and light metals such as aluminum and magnesium, which are less dependent upon highly localized raw materials. Any appreciable increase in the effective demand for foods by the great undernourished classes and areas of the world awaits an increase in productivity.

The problem remains as to how and where this will occur. And even if there is a revival of investment in primary production in China and India, the resultant investment will be mainly, and the resultant increased reciprocal trade almost entirely, domestic. Here, too, economic nationalism will prove an extremely great obstacle. Not British exporters, but Chinese and Indian manufacturers will benefit by the increased farm incomes of those countries.

Colin Clark predicts that long after the war Britain will still be the main source of an appreciable flow of international capital, because of her high saving propensities relative to domestic capital requirements.[18] Although this seems a valid explanation of why Britain must invest abroad in order to sustain full employment, it is difficult to reconcile the prediction that she will do so with an anticipated great "gap" in her balance of payments. If the latter expectations are justified, a constant tendency toward leakage of income through a high propensity to import will inevitably depress British incomes relative to world incomes to a point where balance-of-payments equilibrium is possible, and a diminished flow of savings will no longer necessitate such a great flow of domestic and foreign investment as Clark predicts.

A considerable rise of world incomes, leading to an increased demand for British (among other) goods would relieve the pressure and perhaps even make some international lending possible. But the initial stimulus can scarcely come from large-scale British lending. Her exporters would not experience an equivalent increase in commodity orders. Only, therefore, if they can share also in increased orders for machinery, and so forth, arising from American loans (or from capital raised within the expanding economies), will Britain be able to continue to lend. Real net international investment is an outlet for domestic savings, on a par with domestic investment. But a flotation of foreign issues is an initial strain on a balance of payments and by no means assures that the current balance (which is the measure of real net investment) will in fact adjust sufficiently to permit continued flotations.

The trends of the period 1919 to 1939 were in part merely aspects of long cyclical movements, as Clark suggests, and are hence subject to reversal. Nevertheless, in many ways they represent a secular alteration in the structure of the world economy, and particularly of Britain's place therein. It is doubtful that a revival of international investment in general is possible on the scale of 1900–1913 or even of 1922–29. And it is espe-

[18] *The Economics of 1960*, pp. 79, 83.

cially doubtful whether the demand for British goods would be such or would respond sufficiently to make possible a restoration of British investment on the scale of these earlier periods.

The conclusion seems justified, therefore, that while a considerable revival of international economic activity is likely after the war, with a corresponding rise in the purchasing power of debtor areas, and while British industry will benefit thereby to some extent, such a revival will not solve Great Britain's basic difficulties. Her exporters will share in rising foreign investment demands only by displaying far greater resiliency and adaptability than they did in the inter-war years. Moreover, once the initial construction orders are placed, the difficulties of the export trades will be greater than ever, as they meet more and more effective competition from newly erected foreign industries.

Colin Clark also predicts a sharp reversal in the years 1945–60 of the favorable trend in Britain's barter terms of trade, which has persisted more or less steadily since 1880. This, he argues, will result from a rapid industrialization of Japan, China, Russia, and India, who will as a result become exporters of manufactures and importers of primary products, and from a continued rapid rise of productivity in the United States— events which "within themselves constitute a world industrial revolution." [19] The evidence indicates, it will be recalled, that there was a great steady deterioration of Britain's terms of trade between 1700 and 1860, as a result of the first "Industrial Revolution."

There will be factors mitigating this trend. First of all, countries like China and India will undoubtedly put into effect broad programs for raising the meager productivity of their great agricultural populations as well. Second, there is the probability of a further application of modern biology and chemistry to the manufacture of synthetics and substitutes for primary products, already greatly stimulated by the war. High primary prices will encourage further developments along these lines. Nevertheless, the latter developments will probably not have an appreciable effect for the next decade or two, and even the former, however significant, probably will not by 1950 or 1960 have price effects comparable to those consequent upon the application to huge new areas of established industrial processes. [20]

Clark's predictions are based on a scheme of long cycles, of alternat-

[19] Ibid., p. 52; see also pp. 53–54. He predicts a rise by 1960 of as much as 90 percent in the ratio of world primary to industrial prices.

[20] Clark does not ignore these qualifications, although it may be questioned whether he accords them adequate weight. Ibid., pp. 65–69.

ing "capital-hungry" and "capital-sated" periods. During the former (1850–75 and 1900–1930), primary prices tend to gain relative to industrial prices, because labor tends to be rapidly drained away from primary into secondary (industrial) production. Conversely, in the "capital-sated" periods (1875–1900, 1930–40) labor is less rapidly absorbed into secondary production, and the relative prices of primary products fall correspondingly, the extremity of these price fluctuations being enhanced by the relative inelasticity of the demand for these goods.[21]

This is hardly an adequate statement of the process. Clark's explanation ignores the fact that in these long cycles international lending has fluctuated much more widely than domestic (i.e., within the creditor countries), where, indeed, the two have not moved in opposite directions.[22] Since international investment has involved mainly the development of primary producing areas, and domestic mainly the development of industrial productivity, the divergent behavior of the two surely requires some place in the theory of cyclical primary and secondary price movements. In fact, if our argument is correct, it supplies the basic explanation. The major reason for relatively high and low primary prices in "capital-hungry" and "capital-sated" periods, respectively, must have been the alternating under- and over-development of the productive capacities of primary-producing countries in the respective "capital-sated" and "capital-hungry" periods which preceded them. Certainly, here is to be found the major reason for the heavy fall of primary prices after 1873 and again after 1920 and their recovery in the late 1890's. Neither the increase of such investment in the upswings nor the subsequent declines prevented the respective strength and weakness of primary prices within each period, for two reasons. First of all, primary production did not respond quickly, either in the upturns, when most of the investment was in such developments as railroads, which increased primary capacity only indirectly and tardily, or in the downturns, when producers had little choice except to produce their utmost, in order to pay their swollen debts. Secondly, there were the effects upon primary prices of the fluctuations in relative levels of purchasing power, within the framework of the "purchasing-power cycle."

[21] *Ibid.*, p. 90.
[22] A table compiled by Clark, covering five periods, 1870–76, 1877–85, 1886–93, 1894–1903, and 1904–10, shows divergent movements of Britain's domestic and foreign investment (each expressed as a percentage of national income) in three of the four intervals, and virtually divergent movement in the fourth if the behavior of prices is taken into account.

Thus, in the immediate post-war years there may occur a considerable improvement, rather than a deterioration, of Britain's barter terms of trade, as a result of the rapid extensions of agricultural and raw-material production induced by the war and of the release of pent-up consumer demands for manufactures. Since, however, the years 1930–40 witnessed no such international investment as occurred before the first World War, the relative decline of primary prices should not be as protracted this time as it was after 1920. In the longer run Clark's prediction of a relative improvement of these prices seems justified—but not only because of a cyclical shift of productive factors into secondary and tertiary production. It will occur partly because the bulk of international investment will continue to be directed toward primary producing countries, with the usual purchasing power effects upon their prices. But the most important reason will become effective only after a while, and the experience, instead of duplicating that of previous cycles, should be just the opposite.

For when capital flows level off, there will occur an outpouring upon world markets, not of food and raw materials, but, instead, of industrial products, because of the altered character of post-war investments. Thus the next "capital-sated" period, instead of bringing a reversal of the previous trend in favor of primary prices, should bring an intensification of that trend. To this there will be two offsets: first, the greater elasticity in the world's demand for industrial products, and second, the purchasing power effects upon all prices in debtor countries (upon primary as well as secondary prices) of the change from net capital imports to net outpayments of interest and dividends. Despite these offsets, it would appear that the prospective decline of Britain's terms of trade, like the previous rise, will continue for a considerable length of time.

Thus, we have returned to a restatement of our basic thesis. In the past, Great Britain was greatly benefited by international investment not only because it provided an outlet for and a greater return on her savings, sustaining employment, and maximizing income during its outflow, but even more because of the cheaper food and raw materials which it eventually helped make possible. Increasingly in the future international investment will develop competitive rather than complementary production, so that at the end of periods of heavy investment, instead of deriving the benefit of an improvement of her terms of trade, Britain will be faced with stronger competition in world markets and consequently deteriorated barter terms of trade. In the decade or two after the war, a revival of international investment will entail an increased demand for British goods, thus mitigating the effects on real British incomes of these secular changes. But thereafter, in the downswing, this deterioration in terms of trade will continue, thus intensifying, instead of, as in the past, allaying the evils of declining exports, invisible incomes, and relative underemployment. The resultant strains upon the British balance of payments and real incomes should be considerably more severe than in the period 1919 to 1939.

These are certainly gloomy prospects for what was until the turn of the century the workshop, middleman, shipper, creditor, and banker for the world. The picture is, however, not yet complete. Britain is a rich country; she retains a large, skilled working population, and, as the war experience itself proves, she is capable of a considerable production and accumulation of wealth. By proper use of but a small portion of the capital and labor power which are now wasted in each year of the war, she can effect a great reconstruction, reorganization, and re-equipment in time of peace. At the worst, it is inconceivable that the British people should not be able thereafter to acquire from abroad merely by current earnings the minimum essentials which they are physically incapable of supplying at home. For the rest, they can to a large extent, if necessary, live within themselves and enjoy at home the fruits of their own skills and saving. Nor can it be believed that this would prove so terribly meager a diet, *providing* Britain succeeds in mobilizing her resources without the wastage in idle men and capital which the decline of foreign markets entailed in the years 1919 to 1939.

The decline in Britain's current balance of payments after the war will not entail an equivalent decline in her income. Just as in the period from 1919 to 1939, it will result also from a considerable domestic investment program, as well as from a releasing of consumer demand for domestic consumption goods. Britain obviously cannot expect to consume all her exportable goods and still procure the heavy imports essential for reconstruction. Nevertheless, a decline of exports because of the insatiability of home demand, for reconstruction and consumption, clearly does not have the same significance as one caused by an unwillingness of foreigners to buy British goods.

In an era of capital scarcity such as may be expected after the war, domestic and foreign investment will be competitive. A balance will have to be struck between them. It may well be questioned whether, with the experience of the 1920's and the war behind them, the British people will choose relatively as much foreign investment as they did then. Certainly they are not so likely to be deceived by the higher income promised by foreign borrowers: nor may the prospective rate of return be the sole determinant. There is much to be done at home, and if the reports concerning the present mood of the British people are correct, and the mood persists, more of it will be done after this war than after the last.

Indeed, Britain's greatest problem immediately after the war will probably be to restrain domestic investment and consumption demands. Pent-up consumer needs, postponed industrial repairs, replacements, and extensions, house-building, "social" rehabilitation—reconstruction of destroyed areas, slum clearance, construction of roads, bridges, harbors—at home and abroad, will all press against limited resources. The great danger will be that domestic spending and investment will be too high for balance of payments equilibrium. The problem for perhaps a decade after the war may be, therefore, to hold back the expenditure of war savings, air-raid damage insurance, and high earnings and so to prevent serious inflation, in order, on the one hand, to sustain full employment for a longer period and, on the other, to permit some international investment (or debt repayment), while assuring essential imports.

Thus, while there may be considerable unemployment in localities most heavily expanded during the war and in those where the staple export trades are concentrated, widespread general unemployment will probably not be a major concern except perhaps immediately after the war. This prediction would seem to conflict with those made for the period 1945–60 by Colin Clark:

Great Britain and France . . . will have become, in the economic sense, fully mature countries. By this is meant that, largely owing to the stagnancy of their population, there will be very little scope for investment within their own economies, and virtually the whole of their savings will have to be invested abroad . . . any interruption to the outward flow of these savings would, with its secondary effects, produce unemployment in Britain and France on a gigantic scale.[23]

As we have stated, it is difficult to see how Britain can become the world's leading exporter of capital after the war. In any case, it is doubtful whether the British people will permit lending on a vast scale when as

[23] *Ibid.*, pp. 109–10; see also p. 113. By permission of the Macmillan Company, publishers.

much remains to be done at home as will remain in 1950 or even in 1955. If private investment proves incapable of doing what can be done to make Britain a better place in which to live, it is doubtful that the government can remain aloof. And if, because of inability or unwillingness of capitalists to lend abroad, unemployment threatens on a large scale, it is again doubtful whether the government will be permitted to remain aloof. Clark may be wise to ignore "political" changes in his predictions; nevertheless, if he envisages the possibility of heavy unemployment consequent upon a failure of heavy foreign lending, he cannot ignore the possibility also of politico-economic changes which may radically alter the savings-investment dilemma of capitalist economy.

The world's most striking economic problem in the years 1919 to 1939 was its inability to employ its resources fully. But unemployment need not be the most serious economic problem at all times. It was not in Germany or the U.S.S.R. before 1939, or in England thereafter. A deteriorated competitive position of British industry may not cause or be permitted to cause heavy unemployment; but relatively full employment will not forestall a tendency toward serious loss of income as a result of this change.[24]

In the face of these and other problems it seems inevitable that government participation in the basic economic decisions will be far greater after than before the war. There will be need for pervasive controls to prevent immediate post-war inflation, to mitigate the evils of a weak balance of payments, to introduce inescapable political considerations into the decisions concerning the allocation of total savings. The government will probably be forced to take an increasingly active role in investment, partly in order to maintain the flow of income, partly to meet great needs the satisfaction of which private capital does not find economically remunerative. There will be a pressing need for slum clearance and better housing for the "lower third" of the population, a need which private building, on the basis of its 1919–39 record, seems incapable of meeting. Electrification will continue, but the necessary rationalization of distribu-

---

[24] One specific illustration of this newer situation may be given. Britain's former debtors have accumulated huge sterling assets, as we have mentioned. Liquidation of these assets will undoubtedly involve considerable orders for British machinery and other goods, partly, perhaps, because Britain will not be able to permit liquidation except in the form of commodity exports. The result will be a great stimulus to employment and money incomes. The fact will remain that these goods will go as gifts; Britain's real ability to import foreign goods will be not one whit increased by such exports. See, for example, "India's War Gains," *Economist*, March 6, 1943, pp. 302–3.

tion will undoubtedly require, as did that of production before it, some form of government co-ordination. The persistence of distressed areas, the intensified post-war demand for town and regional planning—all will call forth extension of the realms of government activity.

Even if some measure of unity is restored to the world economy, it will be fruitless to expect restoration of the world order of 1928 or 1913. The hope of universal free trade is a vain one. Perhaps nondiscrimination in commercial policy is the most that can be hoped for. Perhaps, on the contrary, ways will have to be devised to expand world trade, in controlled fashion, on bilateral or simple triangular lines. Perhaps the increasing intrusion of the government into economic life will permit such an expansion, as general national interests supersede vested interests of protected classes in the determination of trade policy. The old international gold standard likewise cannot possibly be restored in its earlier form. Countries will simply not be willing to leave their domestic monetary policies entirely to the play of autonomous external forces. Free international investment is for the same reason a thing of the past. Governments will control their foreign lending, in order to maintain domestic stability and to meet first the requirements of the domestic economy. Of such foreign investments as may continue to be permitted, there may be expected an increased use of loans specifically contracted for the purchase of exports and of direct investments, which avoid the dangers of balance-of-payments disequilibria entailed by free lending. Government or government-guaranteed loans will probably increase in importance as a means of financing international reconstruction and of overcoming or compensating for the reluctance of private investors or of controlling the flows according to broader conceptions of national interest.[25] So, even in the event of an expansion of international activity, increased government participation in economic life may be expected.

The manifest dangers of such tendencies must be recognized. Pervasive economic planning may entail increasing rigidity, inadaptability, and discrimination at home and in international trade. The solution to this dilemma hardly lies, however, in denouncing the inevitable. What is required is a serious continual effort to safeguard against the dangers, while yet meeting the problems which call forth such expedients.

Space does not permit, and our frame of reference does not require, extended discussion of the possible adjustments which the British may consciously make to their altered position. Our major interest has been

[25] See Royal Institute, *The Problem of International Investment*, pp. 61–65, 95–96.

in the basic determinants, and it has not seemed to us that decisions of policy can be so characterized. Nevertheless, these decisions will be of increasing consequence in the future, and some brief discussion of the general range of possible choices is desirable.

Great Britain has an obvious and particularly great stake in the development of the world economy and in the maximization of international economic intercourse. She has scarcely any choice, in the long run, but to strive continually for the removal of international economic and political instability, as well as of all the formal barriers to such intercourse. These are not simple ends, the accomplishment of which merely requires courageous adherence to certain fixed courses of action. Domestic economic stability and stable exchange rates may at times be incompatible, yet both are essential to the long-run maximum development of the world economy. All that can be prescribed a priori is that the policy chosen shall strike a fair balance between temporary necessities and the long-run goal.

For example, Britain may well find it necessary to retain some form of exchange control immediately following the war. Nevertheless, in view of her clear long-run interests, it would seem foolish for her not to provide strong safeguards against its use as an instrument of discrimination, bilateralism, and the creation and protection of vested interests and against its perpetuation, except, perhaps, to prevent erratic flows of short-term capital. Moreover, such policies can no longer be adopted unilaterally: their disruptive influence in the past has resulted more often from their competitive and retaliatory use than from the lack of justification in individual instances. Britain simply cannot afford to enter again into such a competitive struggle.[26] The introduction or retention of any policies which may tend to injure international economic order can be justified on defensive grounds only, and the major powers must in each case be consulted and convinced of its necessity and of Britain's reso-

[26] This is the fatal objection to the much-discussed proposals of the Federation of British Industries, which in a recent report advocates strict British protection, exchange control, and bilateralism after the war. See "The Post-War Exchange Regime," *The Banker*, July, 1942, p. 8; A.J.B., "Aspects of U.S.–British Post-War Economic Problems," *Bulletin of International News*, April 4, 1942, p. 280; National Planning Ass'n., "Britain's Trade in the Post-War World," pp. 26–31. In a world of competing economic nationalisms, Britain may indeed be forced to such expedients. But they must be considered an unfortunate last resort if other policies more truly to her advantage fail, rather than long goals. One may well suspect that, on the contrary, the authors of these proposals feel no particular repugnance to them, seeing in them, rather, protection and security in the home market and the suppression of competition.

lution to safeguard against its abuse or retention beyond the period of necessity.

Successful international economic collaboration requires serious national sacrifice. Britain and the co-operating powers may well have to surrender a portion of their sovereign right to unilateral determination of international economic policies. Short of the institution of some world plan for co-operative scrutiny, veto, or even active determination of such policies, Britain must at least be prepared to surrender exchange controls, empire preference, and agricultural protection, if bilateral or multilateral negotiations with other countries offer an immediate *quid pro quo*, or a promise of attaining the broader goals. Britain cannot afford permanently to overlook the fact that such restrictions on her imports do mean dearer food and raw materials and decreased ability and willingness of many countries to purchase her goods.

To this end, a sincere intention to deal in co-operative fashion with all problems as they arise is more important than single-minded adherence to slogans or prefabricated plans. The most-favored-nation clause, for example, while often a useful instrument for lowering trade barriers, proved the crucial obstacle to sincere efforts by the Scandinavian and Danubian countries to lower trade barriers by the establishment of customs unions in the thirties, because of Britain's pious assertion of her claims to such treatment, without offering additional *quid pro quo*. The same considerations apply to "the" international gold standard. Because of Britain's interest in the maintenance of international stability, she cannot countenance a regime of freely fluctuating currencies. On the other hand, not even she can be expected to permit her level of domestic employment to fluctuate with the fortunes of the balance of payments. Here, obviously, some workable compromise is essential, involving international co-operation and agreement, combining the optimum proportions at any given time of currency stability and flexibility, perhaps by the operation of some such institution as the proposed International Monetary Fund.[27]

Returning to Britain's immediate post-war balance-of-payments problem: it will certainly be necessary to fix the value of sterling considerably below $4.86, in order to eliminate gross handicaps to British exporters and to measure more accurately the true purchasing power of British money incomes consistent with equilibrium. However, in view of the

[27] This combination, in co-operation, of stability and flexibility, was, at least at the outset, the goal of the monetary discussions held during the summer of 1944, although it seems doubtful that the plan finally evolved is capable of attaining this goal.

anticipated magnitude of the gap, a decline of sterling sufficient in itself
to equilibrate the balance of payments would probably involve undesir-
ably great hardships for both the British people and other countries
thereby subjected to increased competition.[28] The alternative of active
deflation is even less possible than in the 1920's, in view of the greater
problem and the far greater resistances. However, a policy of inflation
control successfully combating a spiraling of wage rates and other money
costs, of new financing and overcapitalization, would make an important
long-run contribution in this direction. Temporary government controls
over investment and over nonessential imports would seem to be inevitable, at least until it is seen how far exports can be expanded and the
restraints dispensed with.[29] A combination of a lower pound, nondiscriminating import controls, and other restraints upon inflation thus would
seem to be the least painful solution to Britain's major immediate post-
war problems.

In the long run, however, the benefits to Britain of an overvalued
pound sustained by exchange controls are likely to be far outweighed by
the drawbacks. To countries whose economies are increasingly planned
along national lines and who have succeeded in solving the problem of
full employment, a high purchasing power of domestic currencies in
terms of foreign goods should appear far more attractive than a lower
purchasing power. Competitive overvaluations, combined with the necessary import controls and export subsidies, therefore becomes a distinct
possibility. The devastating effects upon the world economy of such competition, which is after all the totalitarian method of international economic aggression, is amply attested by the experience of the 1930's.[30] As
an instrument of long-run policy British exchange controls can be justified only in order to prevent speculative attacks against a managed
sterling or as a last defensive means, if the world refuses to abandon the
policies of economic nationalism.[31]

Within the framework of whatever new world order and British

---

[28] Two reasons for this are the relative inelasticity of Britain's demand for imports, on
the one hand, and the fact that the sterling area countries at least, and probably others,
would follow the pound, thus removing the competitive advantages of depreciation. See
C. J. Hitch, "The Controls in Post-War Reconstruction," *Oxford Economic Papers*, April
1942, p. 47; National Planning Ass'n., "Britain's Trade in the Post-War World," pp.
24–25; A.J.B., "Aspects of U.S.–British Post-War Economic Problems," *ibid.*, pp. 276–78.
[29] See the proposals of C. J. Hitch, *ibid.*
[30] A.J.B., "Aspects of U.S.–British Post-War Economic Problems," *ibid.*, p. 279.
[31] The reader is referred to the weekly articles on "The Principles of Trade" in the *Economist*, Jan. 1–Feb. 19, 1944, for an extremely valuable discussion of these problems of
post-war policy.

policies emerge after the war, the real incomes of the British people will depend upon their own productivity and adaptability. What can be accomplished in this direction by public policy? A few suggestions may be in order. Heavy subsidization of industrial research and of education for modern business management would seem to be obviously desirable first steps in a country which appears to have been relatively backward in these respects. But the progressive ossification of British business organization under the control of vested interests must also be attacked more directly. It must be the function of public policy to restore freedom of opportunity for superior men and methods and thus to see that the unfit, however strong in a business sense, are weeded out.[32] Where free competition provides a suitable method of industrial organization, the government must assume the responsibility for recognizing, fostering, and protecting certain defined rights of actual and potential competitors. Where it does not, the government must see to it that whatever alternative schemes are adopted meet certain standards of social performance—among other ways, possibly, by insuring that control be exercised by managers responsible to consumer and public as well as to producer and labor interests.[33] Thus, the government must assert the public interest by supervising and controlling international cartel agreements, which divide markets, protect domestic business interests, and often seriously retard technological progress. For the same reason it must take definite steps to prevent the use of patents as instruments of business aggression instead of as means for fostering invention. And for precisely the same reasons it must assert and exercise jurisdiction over certain aspects of employer-employee contracts, in so far as they also may impair business efficiency or hinder the introduction of superior technological expedients.

The British people have a vital stake in their industry. They have a

[32] These, it would appear, are strange proposals to make in an age whose major preoccupation is with "social security." Is a continual ferment in British industry, a ruthless weeding out of the inefficient, an acceptable goal of public policy? It is perfectly legitimate for society to attempt by legislation to provide security for the individual against external adversities over which he has no control and for which he is not capable of making provision. But true social security, security for society as a whole, cannot be provided simply by legislating financial protection for every individual or by assuring every producer a fixed income. This is particularly true of a country as inevitably exposed as is Britain to the play of international economic competition. It cannot find security except by constant adaptation, progressiveness, resiliency; it will never find security, except at far lower standards of living (if, for example, it attempts to dispense with imports) in stratification.
[33] See, for example, the interesting suggestion made by Myron W. Watkins, "Present Position and Prospects for Antitrust Policy," Amer. Econ. Rev., Suppl., June, 1942, pp. 108–18.

basic right, superior to the rights of property or of collective bargaining, to demand that it meet certain basic standards of performance. This right may, perhaps, be effectuated partly by a rigorously enforced "antitrust" law or by appropriate stipulations in charters granting the privilege of incorporation. In the case of the nucleus firms chosen in wartime plans for concentration of industry, the public may be in an especially favorable position to demand corresponding reciprocal benefits.

However the British people decide to exercise their "rights in industry," they must be exercised. Effectuation of even the few inadequate recommendations suggested above will involve the flouting of powerful interests, who have behind them not merely their own power but also the dead weight of social acquiescence in their inveterate practices and prerogatives. But Britain is faced also with difficult problems. Neither the people nor their leaders do themselves any service by refusing to recognize that serious problems often require drastic remedies.

Appendix

———— ◆ ————

THE BRITISH BALANCE OF PAYMENTS; METHODOLOGY AND DEFINITIONS

THE ONLY available British balance-of-payments estimates are the Board of Trade statistics, issued annually in the *Board of Trade Journal*. Except for the trade figures, they are composed of the roughest of guesses. Moreover, they take no account whatsoever of capital movements. To use the residuum of so imperfectly compiled a current balance as a measure of net capital movements is, of course, extremely unsatisfactory.

The *merchandise trade* figures include silver exports and imports. Since Britain produces no silver and consumes little, this is almost entirely entrepôt trade. Although for the period as a whole inflows and outflows were almost exactly equal, American silver purchases after 1933 sometimes gave rise to large annual balances.

Imports are valued c.i.f.; exports f.o.b. Thus, debits are overstated by the amount of British payments to British shippers and underwriters of British imports. The error is compensated in the shipping (and insurance) estimate. Imports and exports are gross values, both including a large amount of imported goods subsequently re-exported.

Net *income from overseas investments* seeks to show, in the case of British companies operating abroad, all earned income, including undistributed earnings directly reinvested. It differs, thus, from the well-known figures of Sir Robert Kindersley, who attempts to estimate only actual gross distributions to the United Kingdom.[1]

Shipping income has as its basis (on the credit side) the gross earnings of British shipping wherever gained, thereby including receipts from British importers. This offsets the inclusion of the latter in the c.i.f. valuation of imports. Receipts from British passengers seem to be deducted, although this is not stated explicitly. The figure also includes all disbursements of foreign ships in British ports and British ships in foreign ports, for wages, fuel, stores, dues, commissions, etc.

The major *government transactions* are war-debt payments, reparations re-

[1] Kindersley, in *Econ. Jour.*, XLII (1932), 191–92.

ceipts, and the Indian "home charges" (also receipts), the latter exclusive of the service of the Indian government and railway debt, which is included under "income from oversea investments." The Board of Trade excludes from the 1938 figure a receipt of £10 million from Eire, pursuant to the financial agreement of April, 1938, because it was "in the nature of a capital payment." Since, however, this heading includes so many other capital transactions, we have put the credit back into the balance.

Earnings from *short interest*, etc., include receipts on acceptance credits, discounts of foreign bills, bank interest, commissions on new issues, insurance company receipts and remittances, etc. Net *other receipts* is a catch-all category, including sales of second-hand ships (a net credit), expenditures by foreign diplomats in Britain, emigrant remittances, tourist expenditures (net debit), film royalties (net debit), etc.

GOLD COIN AND BULLION

The balance of payments is a balance of actual transactions. Mere physical movements of commodities or bullion without change of ownership do not belong in it. Conversely, actual international transactions, even though they do not lead to such physical movements, do belong. In the case of gold, particularly in recent years, there is a wide discrepancy between import-export figures of physical movements and balance-of-payments "movements," and the former figures therefore cannot be used. This discrepancy results from considerable accumulations in London of foreign-owned gold which might be increased or decreased by balance-of-payments transfers of title between foreigners and Englishmen without physical movement, or by nonbalance-of-payments changes in location without such transfers of ownership.

At least since 1932 private British ownership of gold (i.e., outside the Bank of England and the Treasury) has been very small. The Bank of England has had the right, under the Currency and Bank Notes Act of 1928, to buy up all such holdings above £10,000 at the statutory price; in view of the much higher market price since 1931, this threatens a prohibitive penalty for hoarding. These powers have not been used, evidently because hoarding has been negligible.[2] Hence, practically all gold actually bought or sold by Englishmen since then, whether physically passing through Customs or added to or subtracted from foreign hoards already in England, will show itself in a change in the total gold holdings of the Bank of England and the Exchange Equalisation Account.[3] We may, therefore, use changes in these official holdings as our balance-of-

[2] *Midland Bk. Mo. Rev.*, Dec., 1933–Jan., 1934, p. 1, July–Aug., 1934, p. 3; Einzig, *International Gold Movements*, p. 7.

[3] Since June, 1932, the Bank of England has obtained and sold its gold only through the Exchange Account. Double counting is easily avoided merely by taking the net changes in the total holdings of the two together.

payments gold "movements," treating an increase as a gold import, a decrease as an export.[4]

The Bank of England's gold figures are available and need only be converted at the market rate. For the holdings of the Exchange Account we have before 1937 only the rough estimates by F. W. Paish [5] of its foreign exchange purchases and sales, converted into sterling at the average monthly exchange rates (or gold prices). For 1937 and 1938 we have the periodic returns of the Fund itself. Since these returns show holdings as of March 31 and September 30, the intervening changes are estimated, with, it is believed, relatively little error.[6] These figures are far from infallible. Mr. Paish's clever indirect guesses are open to serious question.[7] Furthermore, there were some private and industrial users and holders of gold; nonbalance-of-payments transactions between them and the British authorities caused changes in official holdings, and true balance-of-payments transactions between them and foreigners were not recorded in official holdings. The *Economist* thus estimates that in 1932 gold coins and ornaments worth about 14 millions came out of circulation, attracted by the increased market price of gold.[8] The rise of official holdings of £29 million, a balance-of-payments debit, must thus be corrected by a credit of £14 million, whether the gold was actually bought by the Bank of England, or the Fund, or by foreigners. Such errors are, however, undoubtedly much smaller than those arising from use of customs statistics. Dishoardings had by late 1932

[4] See Imre de Vegh, *The Pound Sterling*, pp. 17–23. For these figures, 1932–38, we have used Mr. de Vegh's work sheets, for which thanks are due.

[5] "The British Equalisation Fund," *Economica*, n.s., II (1935), 61–74, III (1936), 78–83, IV (1937), 343–49.

[6] These are De Vegh's estimates.

[7] The Fund's assets at any time consist mainly of treasury bills acquired "through the tap" (in contrast with "tender" bills, offered to the open market), or of foreign exchange (customarily turned promptly into gold). In acquiring foreign exchange it customarily sells the tap bills for sterling, which it uses to make the purchases; in selling exchange it acquires sterling deposits, which it customarily turns back into tap bills. Hence, changes in the Fund's tap bill holdings would indicate (on these assumptions) changes in its holdings of gold and foreign exchange. Paish makes this estimate by deducting from total treasury bills outstanding weekly figures of successful tenders; the changes in the difference, a rough measure of tap bills outstanding, he attributes to the Fund alone, on the assumption that other government departments' tap holdings do not change substantially.

This makes several very broad and more or less unjustified assumptions. The *Economist* argues that the tap holdings of other government departments have varied substantially. Further, the procedure of the Fund is much more flexible than outlined above, particularly in view of its desire to keep its operations secret and also because of the exigencies of credit management. Paish is aware of these serious deficiencies, but argues that over a period of time his results are reasonably valid, and accord with actual market experience and whatever other evidence is available. See his articles, cited above, and "Twenty Years of the Floating Debt," *Economica*, n.s., VI (1939), 256–58; *Economist*, CXX (1935), 368, 420.

[8] "Commercial History and Review of 1932," Feb. 18, 1933, p. 10.

already dwindled to a low level and seem to have been roughly offset there-after by industrial consumption.[9]

It is more doubtful which were larger before 1931, private domestic holdings and circulation or foreign purchases and sales not actually resulting in physical movement. The common belief is that little gold circulated even before the 1928 law; England was on a gold bullion standard. A comparison of export-import figures with those of the Bank shows that from 1925 through 1928 more gold was entering the country than the Bank gained.[10] Although part of this discrepancy may have represented private British gold accumulations, especially by the joint stock banks, most of it was apparently gold purchased and earmarked in London by foreign central banks (the "unknown buyer"), usu-ally preparatory to returning to the gold standard.[11] In 1929, similarly, the smaller gold loss by the Bank than net physical exports seems mainly to have resulted from foreign withdrawals of such earmarked gold.[12] The Bank of England figures seem thus to be the pertinent ones, and they are used here.[13] In any case, the figures do not differ greatly in these years.

LONG-TERM CAPITAL MOVEMENTS

It is impossible to construct an adequate balance of capital transactions. We can only cast some light on certain major aspects, leaving a large portion in the catch-all residual.

The Midland Bank (in its *Monthly Review*) annually estimates foreign issues floated in London, one of the most important types of British capital movements. These figures, which we have used without alteration for the years 1924–28, exclude refundings and take no account of the portion of the issues taken up by foreigners. In his estimates for the years 1929–38, which we use, Sir Robert Kindersley has adjusted the Midland figures to exclude foreign

[9] "The Decline in Sterling," *Midland Bk. Mo. Rev.*, Nov.–Dec., 1932, p. 4; B.I.S., *Seventh Annual Report*, p. 41; B. of T.J., CXXXIV (1935), 277, CXXXVI (1936), 262. Waight estimates for the entire period 1932–38 an excess of dishoardings over industrial consump-tion of £24.5 million, £14 of which we have accounted for in 1932. This leaves an error of only £10 million over the remaining seven years. *The Exchange Equalisation Account*, p. 108.

[10] In 1925 the Bank lost more gold than did the country, which comes to the same thing. In making this comparison, it is necessary to exclude a gain of £27 million by the Bank, in 1925, the result of transfer from the Currency Note Reserve, with the return to the gold standard, and an export in 1928 of £18 million of gold, previously held in England as collateral for a loan to the Bank of France, and now returned. B. of T.J., CXXII (1929), 277.

[11] See, for example, "Commercial History and Review of 1927," *Economist*, Feb. 11, 1928, p. 11; *Midland Bk. Mo. Rev.*, Jan.–Feb., 1928, pp. 5–6.

[12] B. of T.J., CXXIV (1930), 322.

[13] The 1925 figure is adjusted to exclude the gold transfer from the currency reserve fund, mentioned in footnote 10, above.

subscriptions. In addition, he has added foreign refunding issues so as to obtain offsetting figures for his estimates of repayments by foreigners on past loans, many of which are made out of the proceeds of refunding issues.[14]

For 1929 throughout 1938 Kindersley has made annual estimates also of the nominal value of total British investments abroad. The year-to-year changes in this total result from (1) British subscriptions to new foreign issues in London, net of repayments, (2) British purchases and sales of existing securities, direct investments, and participation in new issues on foreign markets, and (3) adjustments of the nominal value: these adjustments always lag considerably behind market values. Since we have the figures for the first factor, we can readily ascertain the combined values of (2) and (3). The former reflects a most important balance-of-payments item, the general order of magnitude of which can be obtained, very roughly, by estimating and excluding the influence of (3) and then allowing for the probable discrepancy between nominal value and the actual market value of the (2) transactions remaining. We have attempted these adjustments, as shown in Table 31 and described in Chapters IX and X, above, guided throughout by Kindersley's own discussion.

SHORT-TERM CAPITAL MOVEMENTS

For short-term movements [15] a consistent year-to-year series is even less possible, comparable limited data being available only for a few years at a time. Despite their restricted coverage and frequent lack of comparability, however, it is believed that the figures given are useful.

The MacMillan Committee report of 1931 gives figures from 1927 through March, 1931, of foreign deposits at the Bank of England, the Clearing and Scottish Banks, and the Acceptance Houses and other short-term foreign liabilities of Great Britain. There are major omissions; the total of £415 million for 1930 may be less than the real total short-term liabilities of the London market by as much as £300 million.[16] On the asset side, the MacMillan Committee gives data as to the holdings of acceptances on foreign account by the same British and Scottish institutions. This is also highly incomplete, major omissions being the foreign bill holdings and deposits of British banks. The

---

[14] *Loc. cit.*, annual articles, 1929–39. The 1926–28 repayment figures are also from Kindersley; the 1928 figure is apparently an estimate of net repayments, i.e., omitting those made out of the proceeds of refunding issues, and also seems to include an allowance for foreign subscriptions to the new issues in London.

[15] The distinction between long and short capital movements is not clear. Dealings in existing securities may for example be either erratic, speculative short-term movements, or real long-term investments. The flow of foreign funds into and out of London, which we treat correctly as essentially short-term, went to a large extent into purchases and sales of long-term British securities. There would be no point, however, in making a clear definition for present purposes, in view of the impossibility of applying it statistically.

[16] Royal Institute, *The Problem of International Investment*, p. 339.

TABLE 31

ESTIMATED BRITISH DEALINGS IN EXISTING SECURITIES, SUBSCRIPTION TO ISSUES
ON FOREIGN MARKETS, AND DIRECT INVESTMENTS

(£000,000)

Year	Kindersley: Nominal British Capital Abroad (1)	Change During Year (2)	New Issues (+) Net of Repayments (−) (3)	Amount of Change Due to Remaining Factors 2−3 (4)	Estimated Market Value Effect of Factor 2; i.e., Actual British Receipts (−) or Payments (+) (5)
1929	3,738	...	...	...	...
1930	3,724	−14	+59	−73	−40
1931	3,700	−24	+14	−38	−15
1932	3,640	−60	−11	−49	−10
1933	3,666	+26	+16	+10	−10
1934	3,714	+48	+21	+27	+15
1935	3,788	+74	−30	+104	+70
1936	3,764	−24	−46	+22	+20
1937	3,753	−11	−1	−10	−10
1938	3,692	−61	−10	−51	−30

year-to-year changes in these totals are presented separately in our balance of payments. For the behavior of liabilities some later estimates are available. The figures for the years 1931–34 are given by the Royal Institute [17] and are in general accord with contemporary financial opinion.[18] However, the 15 million increase estimated in 1934 is rather dubious, since 1934 was a year of pressure on sterling. The figures for 1934–37 and 1937–38 are taken roughly from the B.I.S. chart of "certain holdings of sterling assets" for those periods.[19] The total covered is not quite so large as in the previous studies, being restricted mainly to the sterling area, and the United States and Canada; the 1937–38 change also omits the sterling holdings of the four empire currency boards. In contrast with the 1927–34 series, these totals are net figures, i.e., sterling assets of these countries net of sterling liabilities; the changes are therefore net changes.

The remaining short-term capital item covers the special transactions of 1931 and 1932. In the former year New York and Paris advanced £50 mil-

[17] *Ibid.*, pp. 339–41. They are also responsible for the asset figure for 1931, obtained by extrapolating from the MacMillan Committee's first quarter (and previous) figures.
[18] See "Commercial History and Review of 1931," *Economist*, Feb. 13, 1932, p. 8; B.I.S., *Fourth Annual Report*, p. 29.
[19] *Ninth Annual Report*, p. 82.

lion to the Bank of England, and then £80 million to the British Treasury, in their respective currencies, to protect sterling. The precise distribution of the repayments between 1931 and 1932 and their real costs at fluctuating sterling rates are not entirely clear. Royal Institute figures are used; they estimate that about 30 percent was repaid by the end of 1931, at a cost of £56 million, and the remainder, repaid in 1932, cost £123 million.[20]

We are left, finally, with the very large residual item. There is no reason to expect it to be small, even if our data were not inaccurate, because they are also far from complete. This item contains the many long- and short-term capital movements which are lacking from the meager estimates we are able to give, and it contains the net effects of all errors and other omissions, which are probably very large.

[20] *The Problem of International Investment,* pp. 341–42. The available evidence seems to be that in fact only £20 million of the Bank of England debt and none of the Treasury's was officially repaid by the end of 1931. However, the Bank of England was evidently already acquiring additional foreign exchange in 1931, made available by returning short-term capital, and although it may not have used this exchange to extinguish the rest of the debts until 1932, the balance of payments debit for these purchases belongs in 1931. See *Banker,* XXI (Jan., 1932), 18; *Economist,* CXIII (1931), 851, CXIV (1932), 229; W. A. Brown, *The Int. Gold Stand.,* II, 1101–5.

Selected Bibliography[1]

Aftalion, Albert. L'Equilibre dans les relations économiques internationales. Paris, Loviton, 1937.

Allen, George C. British Industries and Their Organization. 2d ed. London, Longmans, Green, 1935.

Angell, James W. The Theory of International Prices; History, Criticism and Restatement. Cambridge, Harvard Univ. Press, 1926. Harvard Economic Studies, Vol. 28.

Angell, Norman. If Britain Is to Live. New York, Putnam, 1923.

Beach, W. Edwards. British International Gold Movements and Banking Policy, 1881–1913. Cambridge, Harvard Univ. Press, 1935. Harvard Economic Studies, Vol. 48.

Benham, Frederick C. British Monetary Policy. London, King, 1932.

—— Great Britain under Protection. New York, Macmillan, 1941.

Beveridge, Sir William. "An Analysis of Unemployment," *Economica*, new series, III (1936), 357–86; IV (1937), 1–17, 168–83.

—— "Mr. Keynes' Evidence for Overpopulation," *Economica*, IV (1924), 1–20.

—— editor. Tariffs: the Case Examined by Economists. London, Longmans, Green, 1932.

Bidwell, Percy. Our Trade with Britain. New York, Council on Foreign Relations, 1938.

Bourne, Stephen. Trade, Population and Food. London, Bell, 1880.

Bowley, Arthur L. Some Economic Consequences of the Great War. London, Home University Library, 1930.

—— Wages and Income in the United Kingdom since 1860. Cambridge (England), Cambridge University Press, 1937.

Britain without Capitalists; by a group of economists, scientists and technicians. London, Lawrence and Wishart, 1936.

British Association for the Advancement of Science, Research Committee of Economic Science and Statistics Section. Britain in Depression. London, Pitman, 1935.

[1] The selection involved in compiling the following bibliography has necessitated exclusion of several types of publications alluded to at one time or another in the text. In general, there are omitted the many specific studies and monographs which are not of general interest, specialized industry studies, statistical sources, world economic surveys such as those published by the League of Nations, and indispensable periodicals such as the London *Economist* (except for a few articles of general interest), *Statist*, and the *Board of Trade Journal*.

British Association for the Advancement of Science, Research Committee of Economic Science and Statistics Section. Britain in Recovery. London, Pitman, 1938.

"British Capital Abroad," *Economist*, CXI (1930), 699–700, 799–801, 895–96; CXXIX (1937), 359–66.

Brown, Jonathan A. "The 1937 Recession in England," *Harvard Business Review*, XVIII (winter, 1940), 248–60.

Brown, William Adams, Jr. England and the New Gold Standard, 1919–26. London, King, 1929.

—— The International Gold Standard Reinterpreted, 1914–34. 2 vols. New York, National Bureau of Economic Research, 1940.

Bryce, R. B. "A Note on Banking Policy and the Exchanges," *Review of Economic Studies*, IV (June, 1937), 240–43.

Butterworth, G. N., and H. Campion. "Changes in British Import Trade, 1924–36," *Manchester School*, VIII (1937), 48–55.

Cairncross, A. K. "Did Foreign Investment Pay?" Review of Economic Studies, III (Oct., 1935), 67–78.

Canada, Dominion Bureau of Statistics, Internal Trade Branch, Department of Trade and Commerce. The Canadian Balance of International Payments. Ottawa, J. O. Patenaude, 1939.

Carr, Robert M. "The Role of Price in the International Trade Mechanism," *Quarterly Journal of Economics*, XLV (1931), 710–19.

Cassel, Gustav. "The International Movements of Capital," in *Foreign Investments*. Harris Foundation Lectures. Chicago, University of Chicago, 1928.

Champernowne, D. G. "The Uneven Distribution of Unemployment in the U.K., 1929–36," *Review of Economic Studies*, V (1937–38), 93–106; VI (1938–39), 111–24.

Clapham, John H. An Economic History of Modern Britain. 3 vols. Cambridge (England), Cambridge University Press, 1926, 1932, 1938.

Clark, Colin. The Conditions of Economic Progress. London, Macmillan, 1940.

—— "Determination of the Multiplier from National Income Statistics," *Economic Journal*, XLVIII (1938), 435–48.

—— The Economics of 1960. London, Macmillan, 1942.

—— National Income and Outlay. London, Macmillan, 1937.

—— "Statistical Studies Relating to the Present Economic Condition of Great Britain," *Economic Journal*, XLI (1931), 343–69.

Clay, Henry. The Post-War Unemployment Problem. London, Macmillan, 1929.

Cole, George D. H. British Trade and Industry, Past and Future. London, Macmillan, 1932.

Condliffe, John B. The Reconstruction of World Trade. New York, Norton, 1940.

Conolly, Frederick George. "Reflections on the Cheap-Money Policy Particularly in England," Index (Svenska Handelsbanken), Supplement, October, 1939, pp. 1–20.

Damade, Pierre. Le Mouvement de réorganisation industrielle en Grande-Bretagne (1929–37). Paris, Recueil Sirey, 1938.

Daniels, G. W. "Overseas Trade of the United Kingdom in Recent Years as Compared with 1913," The Manchester School, II (1931), 1–9.

Davies, Ernest. "National" Capitalism. London, Gollancz, 1939.

Dennison, Stanley R. The Location of Industry and the Depressed Areas. London, Oxford University Press, 1939.

Einzig, Paul. The Fight for Financial Supremacy. London, Macmillan, 1931.

—— International Gold Movements. London, Macmillan, 1929.

—— The Tragedy of the Pound. London, Paul, 1932.

Explorations in Economics; notes and essays contributed in honor of F. W. Taussig. New York, McGraw-Hill, 1936.

Fanno, Marco. Normal and Abnormal International Capital Transfers. Minneapolis, University of Minnesota, 1939. University of Minnesota, Studies in Economic Dynamics, No. 1.

Feis, Herbert. Europe the World's Banker, 1870–1914. Council on Foreign Relations. New Haven, Yale University Press, 1930.

Findlay, Ranald M. Britain under Protection. London, Allen and Unwin, 1934.

Francis, Eric V. Britain's Economic Strategy. London, Cape, 1939.

Gayer, Arthur D. Monetary Policy and Economic Stabilization. London, Black, 1935.

Gilbert, J. C. "The Mechanism of Interregional Redistributions of Money," Review of Economic Studies, V (1937–38), 187–94.

Gilbert, Milton. Currency Depreciation and Monetary Policy. Philadelphia, University of Pennsylvania, 1939.

Glenday, Roy. "The Future of Export Trade," International Affairs, XVIII (1939), 641–60.

Gommès, Jean. La Baisse de la livre et les exportations Anglaises. Paris, Tolmer, 1936.

Gordon, A. P. L. Capital in Sterling. London, Hartley, 1931.

Grant, Alexander T. K. A Study of the Capital Market in Post-War Britain. London, Macmillan, 1937.

Great Britain, Committee on Finance and Industry (Macmillan Committee). Minutes of Evidence. 2 vols. London, 1931.

—— Report. London, 1931. Parliament. Papers by Command. Cmd. 3897.

—— Committee on Industry and Trade (Balfour Committee). Final Report.

London, 1929. Parliament. Papers by Command. Cmd. 3282.

—— Royal Commission on the Distribution of the Industrial Population. Report. London, 1940. Parliament. Papers by Command. Cmd. 6153.

Gregory, Theodor E. The First Year of the Gold Standard. London, Benn, 1926.

—— The Gold Standard and Its Future. London, Methuen, 1932.

—— "Great Britain and Foreign Investments," in Foreign Investments. Harris Foundation Lectures. Chicago, University of Chicago, 1928.

—— "The Causes of Gold Movements into and out of Great Britain," Selected Documents on the Distribution of Gold. Geneva. 1931. Gold Delegation of the Financial Committee, League of Nations.

Haberler, Gottfried von. The Theory of International Trade. London, Hodge, 1936.

Hall, Noel F. The Exchange Equalisation Account. London, Macmillan, 1935.

Hall, Ray O. International Transactions of the United States. New York, National Industrial Conference Board, 1936.

Harris, Seymour E. Exchange Depreciation. Cambridge, Harvard University Press, 1936.

Harrod, Roy. International Economics. London, Longmans, Green, 1933.

Hawtrey, Ralph G. Currency and Credit. 3d ed., London, Longmans, Green, 1928.

—— "The Gold Standard and the Balance of Payments," *Economic Journal,* XXXVI (1926), 50–68.

Heaton, Herbert. The British Way to Recovery. Minneapolis, University of Minnesota, 1934.

Heilperin, Michael A. International Monetary Economics. New York, Longmans, Green, 1939.

Hérisson, Charles. Le Contrôle du crédit à court terme par la Banque d'Angleterre. Paris, Recueil Sirey, 1932.

Hilgerdt, Folke. "The Approach to Bilateralism; a Change in the Structure of World Trade," *Index (Svenska Handelsbanken),* X (1935), 175–88.

Hobson, Charles K. The Export of Capital. New York, Macmillan, 1914.

Hobson, John A. International Trade. London, Methuen, 1903.

"The Housing Boom," *Economist,* CXXI (1935), 795–96, 844.

Hubbard, Gilbert E. Eastern Industrialization and Its Effect on the West, with Special Reference to Great Britain and Japan. London, Oxford University Press, 1935.

Inman, John. "The Terms of Trade," *The Manchester School,* VI (1935), 37–50.

Iversen, Carl. Aspects of the Theory of International Capital Movements. London, Oxford University Press, 1935.

Jenks, Leland H. The Migration of British Capital to 1875. New York, Knopf, 1927.

Jevons, W. S. The Coal Question. 2d ed., London, Macmillan, 1866.

Keynes, John M. "The British Balance of Trade, 1925–27," *Economic Journal*, XXXVII (1927), 551–65.

—— "The Economic Consequences of Mr. Churchill." London, Hogarth, 1925.

—— "The German Transfer Problem," *Economic Journal*, XXXIX (1929), 1–7.

—— "Discussion with Ohlin," *Economic Journal*, XXXIX (1929), 172–82, 400–408.

—— "A Reply to Sir William Beveridge," *Economic Journal*, XXXIII (1923), 476–86.

—— A Treatise on Money. 2 vols. New York, Harcourt Brace, 1930.

Kindersley, Sir Robert. "A New Study of British Foreign Investments," *Economic Journal*, XXXIX (1929), 8–24, and subsequent annual studies through 1939.

Kindleberger, Charles P. International Short-Term Capital Movements. New York, Columbia University Press, 1937.

Kreider, Carl. The Anglo-American Trade Agreement; a study of British and American commercial policies 1934–1939. Princeton, Princeton University Press. 1943.

Lewis, Ben W. Price and Production Control in British Industry. Chicago, University of Chicago Press, 1937. Public Policy Pamphlet, No. 25.

Lewis, Cleona. The International Accounts. New York, Macmillan, 1927.

Liberal Industrial Inquiry. Britain's Industrial Future. London, Benn, 1928.

Loftus, P. C. A Main Cause of Unemployment; an Indictment of Foreign Investment. London, Pitman, 1932.

Loveday, Alexander. Britain and World Trade, Quo Vadimus, and Other Economic Essays. London, Longmans, Green, 1931.

Lucas, Arthur F. Industrial Reconstruction and the Control of Competition; the British Experiments. London, Longmans, Green, 1937.

McGuire, E. B. The British Tariff System. London, Methuen, 1939.

Machlup, Fritz. International Trade and the National Income Multiplier. Philadelphia, Blakiston, 1943.

Macrosty, Henry W. "The Overseas Trade of the United Kingdom, 1924–31," *Journal of the Royal Statistical Society*, XCV (1932), 607–57.

—— "Trade and the Gold Standard," *Journal of the Royal Statistical Society*, XCI (1928), 303–36.

Marchal, Jean. "L'Abandon de l'étalon-or en Grande-Bretagne et ses conséquences," *Revue économique internationale*, 1937, Part 3, pp. 229–90.

Midland Bank. "The Disposal of Britain's New Capital," *Monthly Review*, Oct.–Nov., 1937, pp. 1–4.

—— "The Dollar Exchange, Commodity Prices, and Money Rates," *Monthly Review*, Dec., 1929–Jan., 1930, pp. 1–4.

—— "The Pound and the Dollar," *Monthly Review*, Dec., 1938–Jan., 1939, pp. 1–3.

Mlynarski, Feliks. The Functioning of the Gold Standard. Geneva, 1931. League of Nations. Publications II A, 1931, No. 25.

Morgan-Webb, Sir Charles. The Rise and Fall of the Gold Standard. New York, Macmillan, 1934.

National Planning Association. Britain's Trade in the Post-War World. Planning Pamphlet No. 9. December, 1941.

Ohlin, Berthil. The Course and Phases of the World Economic Depression. Geneva, 1931. League of Nations. Publications II A, 1931, No. 21.

—— Interregional and International Trade. Cambridge, Harvard University Press, 1935. Harvard Economic Studies, Vol. 39.

——, and J. M. Keynes. "The Reparation Problem; a Discussion," *Economic Journal*, XXXIX (1929), 172–82, 400–408.

—— "The Reparations Problem," *Index* (*Svenska Handelsbanken*), March, 1928, pp. 2–13; April, 1928, pp. 2–33.

"Ottawa Section," *Economist*, CXXVII (1937), 262–71.

Paish, F. W. "Banking Policy and the Balance of International Payments," *Economica*, new series, III (1936), 404–22.

—— "The British Exchange Equalisation Fund," *Economica*, new series, II (1935), 61–74; III (1936), 78–83; IV (1937), 343–49.

—— "Twenty Years of the Floating Debt," *Economica*, new series, VI (1939), 243–69.

Paish, Sir George. "The Export of Capital and the Cost of Living," *Statist Supplement*, Feb. 14, 1914, pp. i–viii.

Pigou, A. C. "Wage Policy and Unemployment," *Economic Journal*, XXXVII (1927), 355–68.

Pigou, Arthur C., and Dennis H. Robertson. Economic Essays and Addresses. London, King, 1931.

Pigou, Arthur C., and Colin Clark. The Economic Position of Great Britain. London, 1936. London and Cambridge Economic Service, Special Memorandum No. 43.

Plummer, Alfred. New British Industries in the Twentieth Century. London, Pitman, 1937.

Political and Economic Planning (P.E.P.). Report on International Trade. London, PEP, 1937.

—— Report on the Location of Industry. London, PEP, 1939.

"The Principles of Trade," *Economist*, CXLVI (1944), 4–5, 32–34, 64–65, 94–96, 136–37, 169–70, 204–5, 232–33.

Richardson, John H. British Economic Foreign Policy. London, Allen and Unwin, 1936.

Robertson, D. H. "The Future of International Trade," *Economic Journal*, XLVIII (1938), 1–14.

—— "Note on the Real Ratio of International Interchange," *Economic Journal*, XXXIV (1924), 286–91.

Royal Institute of International Affairs. The Problem of International Investment. Report by a Study Group of Members. London, Oxford University Press, 1937.

Salter, Sir Arthur. World Trade and Its Future. The William J. Cooper Foundation Lectures, 1936, Swarthmore College. Philadelphia, University of Pennsylvania, 1936.

Sayers, R. S. Bank of England Operations, 1890–1914. London, King, 1936.

Schlie, Hans. Die britische Handelspolitik seit Ottawa und ihre Weltwirtschaftlichen Auswirkungen. Jena, Fischer, 1937. Probleme der Weltwirtschaft, Vol. 59.

Schlote, Werner. Entwicklung und Strukturwandlungen des englischen Aussenhandels von 1700 bis zur Gegenwart. Jena, Fischer, 1938. Probleme der Weltwirtschaft, Vol. 62.

Siegfried, André. England's Crisis. New York, Harcourt Brace, 1931.

Silverman, A. G. "Monthly Index Numbers of British Import and Export Prices, 1880–1913," *Review of Economic Statistics*, XII (1930), 139–48.

—— "Some International Trade Factors for Great Britain, 1880–1913," *Review of Economic Statistics*, XIII (1931), 114–24.

Snow, E. C. "The Balance of Trade," *Journal of the Royal Statistical Society*, XCV (1932), 76–104.

Stewart, Robert B. "Great Britain's Foreign Loan Policy," *Economica*, new series, V (1938), 45–60.

—— "Instruments of British Policy in the Sterling Area," *Political Science Quarterly*, LII (1937), 174–207.

Stolper, Wolfgang F. "British Monetary Policy and the Housing Boom," *Quarterly Journal of Economics*, Vol. 56 (Nov., 1941), Part II.

Tasca, Henry J. World Trading Systems; a Study of American and British Commercial Policies. Paris, International Institute of Intellectual Co-operation, 1939.

Taussig, Frank W. "The Change in Great Britain's Foreign Trade Terms after 1900," *Economic Journal*, XXXV (1925), 1–10.

—— International Trade. New York, Macmillan, 1927.

Thomas, Samuel E. British Banks and the Finance of Industry. London, King, 1931.

Vaneetvelde, Alphonse. La Depréciation de la livre sterling et les exportations Britanniques. Paris, Recueil Sirey, 1935.

Vegh, Imre de. The Pound Sterling. New York, Scudder, Stevens and Clark, 1939.

Vicose, Gilbert Courtois de. Le Commerce extérieur de la Grande Bretagne depuis la guerre. Toulouse, Imprimerie Parisienne, 1932.

Villeneuve, Jacques. La Préférence impériale et le commerce des pays Britanniques depuis la crise. Paris, Librairie Technique et Economique, 1936.

Viner, Jacob. Canada's Balance of International Indebtedness. Cambridge, Harvard University Press, 1924.

—— Studies in the Theory of International Trade. New York, Harper, 1937.

Waight, Leonard. The History and Mechanism of the Exchange Equalisation Account. Cambridge (England), Cambridge University Press, 1939.

Walker, Charles H. "The Working of the Pre-war Gold Standard," *Review of Economic Studies*, I (1933–34), 196–209.

Whale, P. Barrett. "International Short-Term Capital Movements," *Economica*, new series, VI (1939), 30–39.

—— International Trade. London, Home University Library, 1932.

—— "The Working of the Pre-war Gold Standard," *Economica*, new series, IV (1937), 18–32.

White, Harry D. The French International Accounts, 1880–1913. Cambridge, Harvard University Press, 1933. Harvard Economic Studies, Vol. 40.

Whittlesey, Charles R. "Foreign Investment and the Terms of Trade," *Quarterly Journal of Economics*, XLVI (1932), 444–64.

Winston, A. P. "Does Trade Follow the Dollar?" *American Economic Review*, XVII (1927), 458–77.

Index

Aftalion, Albert, 10*n*, 25*n*

Aircraft industry, 260

American Monetary Commission, 20*n*

Angell, Sir Norman, 3*n*

Argentina, 74*n*, 102 f., 215 ff., 227, 230, 246, 247*n*, 251, 277; British imports from (1900–29), 237, 239; British exports to (1929–31), 240; trade balance of, with Britain (1929–31), 241

Australia, 74*n*, 99*n*, 102 f., 169, 186, 190, 209 ff., 215 f., 222*n*, 225 f., 228, 229*n*, 233, 252*n*; British trade balance with (1913, 1929), 237; (1937), 249-50; trade of, with Britain (1929–31), 240; balance of payments of (1929–31), 240; industries of, 271*n*

Automobile industry, 110-13, 260, 262, 268; protection of, 108, 111-12, 113; growth of, 110; exports of, 110-12; and foreign competition, 110 ff.; conditions affecting, 111, 112-13

Balance of payments, 1-8; defined, 2-3; inevitability of, 3-4, 9; current and capital balances, distinction between, 4-5; causal relationship between, 5-8; cyclical fluctuations of, 7-8; equilibrium in, defined, 9; theory of international equilibrium in, discussed, 9-16; *see also* International equilibrium

Balances of payments, British, trends in, 125-57; (1924–38), 126; current account (1907, 1910, 1913), 127; annual averages of (1870–1913), 128; annual averages (1907–38), 132; equilibrium of, as influenced by gold and short-term capital flows, 164-78, 195-207; bilateral (1929), 221-35; Great Britain and empire, 221-27; the empire and foreign countries, 228-30; Great Britain and foreign countries, 230-32; other transactions, 232-35; effect on, of depression, 239; Great Britain, empire, and continent (1930, 1931), 242; factors influencing, in 1920's and 1930's, 243-44; effect of tariff on, 263; effect on, of foreign

loans in 1920's, 264; after second world war, discussed, 269 ff., 275, 279, 283, 288; methodology and definitions, 293-99

Balance of trade, *see* Trade balances

Baltic States, 213, 215, 247*n*, 251

Banking system, British, inadequacy of, 77-78

Belgium, 74*n*, 76, 98, 189, 209, 216, 231 f., 238, 246, 249

Benham, Frederick C., 182*n*

Beveridge, Sir William, 148*n*

Bilateralism, effects of, 254-55

Bourne, Stephen, 127*n*

Brazil, 74*n*, 98, 234

Brewing industry, 260*n*

British Empire, *see* Empire

British industry, *see* Industry, British

British Iron and Steel Federation, *see* Iron and Steel Federation, British

British Malaya, *see* Malaya

Building boom, British, 262*n*, 263

Building industry, 121-24, 136, 260, 262, 266, 268

Burns, E. M., 76*n*

Business, British, inadaptability of, 78-83

Canada, 6, 34 ff., 74*n*, 99*n*, 102 f., 112, 140, 209 ff., 215 ff., 225 ff., 229*n*, 232 f., 252*n*, 253, 270; borrowings of (1900–1913), as case study of theory of international equilibrium, 34-37, 39; British trade balance with (1900–13), 236-37; (1937), 249; (1929–38), 245; industries of, 271*n*

Capital, effect on industry of scarcity of, 76-77

Capital exports, 6, 127, 129, 160, 236-37

Capital flows, (1924–31), 164 ff.

Capital imports, German, 6-7

Capital movements, short-term (1932–39), 195 ff.

Carr, Robert, 34-35

Cartel, international steel, 91

Catiforis, S. J., 173*n*

Central Electricity Board, 115

Ceylon, 99*n*, 225 ff., 229*n*, 232; British trade balance with (1913, 1929), 237; (1937), 248

Chemical industry, 260*n*, protection of, 108

China, 94, 98, 215*n*, 228, 234, 276, 278 ff.; British trade balances with (1913–29), 237 f., 243

Clark, Colin, 138, 279 ff., 284 f.

Clay, Henry, 76

Coal, 65 ff., 71, 75 f., 80, 84-88, 158-59, 259, 265*n*; production and exports of, 84-85; and foreign competition, 85-86; conditions affecting industry, 86-88; reorganization and controls applied to industry, 87-88

Coal Mines Act (1930), 87

Coal Mines Act (1938), 88

Coal Mines Reorganization Commission, 87, 99

Coal strike (1926), 159, 171

Colonial Stock Act (1900), 162

Combinations, business, 61, 80-82

Commodity trade, and capital balance, 6-7

Competition, control of, 80 f.

Confectionery industry, 260*n*

Continent, 116*n*, 129, 210, 213, 216, 227, 232, 251, 253; British trade balances with (1913–29), 237 f.; (1929–31), 240

Co-operation, in British industry, 80 f.

Cotton textiles, 67 f., 71, 73 ff., 80 f., 92-100, 259; production and exports of, 92-98, 99 f.; and foreign competition, 94-98, 99; conditions affecting industry, 94, 98-99; reorganization and controls applied to, 99; exports of (1913-37), 134

Credit system, British, and British industry, 77-78

Current balances, *see* Balance of payments

Czechoslovakia, 74*n*, 231*n*, 232, 246

Denmark, 189, 210, 215 ff., 227, 232, 246, 247*n*; British imports from (1913–29), 239; (1929–31), 240

Depression, 1929 and after, 44, 161, 163, 177, 182, 205, 239-40, 241 f., 262

Distributive trades, 260

Domestic market, British, 259 ff.

Dominions, British, 276 f.

Dutch East Indies, 215*n*, 233*n*; trade balance of, with Britain, 242

Dutch West Indies, 230, 246; trade balance of, with Britain, 242

East Africa, 94, 99*n*

Economic nationalism, *see* Nationalism, economic

Economic system, traditional, causes of disappearance of, 41, 44

Egypt, 74*n*, 96; British trade balance with (1929–31), 241

Eire, *see* Irish Free State

Electrical industries, 113-20, 260, 262; growth of electrical power, 113-15; growth of electrical manufacturing industries, 115 ff.; foreign competition in, 115 f., 118; exports of, 115 ff.; imports of, 116 f., 119; protection of, 116; conditions affecting, 118 ff.

Electrification, post-war, 285

Empire, as investment field, 139f.; its trade with Great Britain (1928, 1929), 223-27; (1929-38), 244-45; (1937), 247-51; with other countries (1929), 228-30; its balance of trade with Great Britain (1900-29), 236-38; (1929-38), 241 ff., 245; post-war industry in, 271

Empire preference, 183 f., 244-45, 246; effect of, on British-Indian trade, 243; on economic recovery, 263; *see also* Tariff

Employment, after 1929–32 depression, 262-63

Engineering products, 65 ff., 75, 102-104, 260*n*, 265*n*; conditions affecting industry, 103; and foreign competition, 103; exports of, 103

Equilibrium, pattern in (1929), 219-35

Equilibrium, international, *see* International equilibrium

Europe, *see* Continent

Exchange Equalisation Account, 199-205

Exchange rates, 14-19

Exports, British, 129 ff., 143; decline of, 63 f., 210-11, 263; and staple industries, 66-70, 71-72, 79-80, 82 f., 85-86, 88, 91, 92-98, 99, 100-101, 102 f., 107 f.; and new industries, 107-109, 110-12, 115 ff., 120 f.; average annual rate of growth of (1700-1929), 131; and world exports (1913-37), 132; indexes of export volume (1924-37), 133; (1924-

31), 158 ff.; (1932–39), 179 ff., 184 f.; indexes of average value and volume of (1929–38), 180; shifting geographical pattern of, 1815–1939, 208-14; relation of, to investment abroad, 209 f.; empire's share of, (1913–38), 210; percentages of, to other regions (1913–38), 210; after 1931, 213; effect on, of empire preference, 211-12; effect on, of economic recovery after 1933, 212-13; effect on, of depreciation of sterling, 213; rise of, to sterling bloc, 213-14; to empire, in 1928 and 1929, 223-27; to non-empire countries (1929), 231; compared with industrial production, 259; in post-war world, discussed, 271 ff., 278 ff., 288

Fanno, Marco, 10n, 22n
Finland, 232, 246, 247n
Florence, P. Sargant, 262n
Flour milling, 81
Foods, foreign, imports of, 134
Foreign investments, *see* Investments
Foreign loans, *see* Investments
Foreign trade, British, *see* Exports; Imports
France, 46, 48 f., 72, 74n, 76, 95, 103n, 112, 120, 162, 167, 209, 215 f., 231 f., 234 n, 246, 249, 284; effect of increased financial power of, 48-49; trade balances of, with England and British Empire, 237n; British imports from, 238
Franco-Prussian War indemnity, 6
Free trade, 49, 59; relative (1929), pattern in equilibrium under, 219-35

General Electric, 79
Germany, 21n, 34, 37 ff., 73, 75 ff., 86, 95, 103, 112, 114, 116n, 118, 120 f., 162, 167, 169, 209 f., 215 f., 231 ff., 246, 249, 275n; British imports from (1913–29), 238; (1929–31), 240; British exports to (1929–31), 240; balance of payments of (1929–31), 240; British trade balances with (1928-37), 251-52
Gold Coast, 248n
Gold exchange standard, 45, 167
Gold flows, 16-21, 45 f.; (1924–31), 164 f., 167, 175; (1932–39), 195 ff.
Gold standard, old, exchange rates under, 16-19; effect of war and inflation on, 44; Great Britain abandons, 49

Gold standard, international, in post-war world, 286, 288
Grant, Alexander T. K., 262n
Great Britain, threat to financial supremacy of, 46-49; abandons free trade and uncontrolled foreign lending, 49; adopts policy of trade and lending controls, 50; changing real position of, 51-64; real income of, 53-54; industrial position of, 65-124; bilateral balances of payments of (1929), 221-35; percentages of trade with empire in 1928 and 1929, 223-27; its trade with non-empire countries, 230-32; its trade balances (1900–29), 236-39; (1929–38), 241 ff., 245; (1937), 247-52; transition in economy of (1919–39), 257-68; its post-war international economic position, discussed, 269-91

Hall, Noel, 205
Hilgerdt, Folke, 232n
Hobson, Charles K., 150n
Holland, *see* Netherlands
Hong Kong, 94
Hosiery industry, 260n
Hot money, *see* Money, hot
Housing, post-war, 285
Hull, Cordell, 255

Imperial Chemicals, 79
Imperial preference, *see* Empire preference
Imports, British, 130 ff.; and products of new industries, 108 f., 116 f., 119 f.; average annual rate of growth of (1700–1929), 131; and world imports (1913–37), 132; after 1932, 135-36; indexes of volume of (1924–36), 136; (1929–31), 160; retained, indexes of average value and volume of (1929–38), 180; (1932–39), 180 ff., 184 f.; shifting geographical pattern of, 1815–1939, 214-18; tendencies affecting (1900–13), 214; after 1913, 214-15; proportion from empire (1913–39), 215 ff.; effect on, of empire preference, 216-17; from empire, 223-27; from non-empire countries, 230 ff.; in post-war world, discussed, 274, 279
Income, British, in post-war period, discussed, 276, 283
Income, real, British, 265-67

India, 73n, 86, 94 ff., 191, 209 ff., 215, 217, 225 f., 228n, 229n, 232 f., 243, 270, 276 ff.; British trade balances with (1900–13), 236–37; (1913–29), 237 f.; (1931), 241; (1929–38), 245; (1937), 249 f.; balance of payments of (1929–31), 240; industries of, 271n

Industry, American, 74 f.

Industry, Belgian, 76

Industry, British, 65–124; deteriorating position of, 65–72; reasons for relative decline of, 72–83; reorganization of, 80–82, 87; backwardness of, 134; expansion of, after 1932, 135–36; in transition (1919–39), 257–68; effect on, of domestic investment, 264–65; in post-war world, discussed, 271–75, 277–78, 283; see also Aircraft industry; Automobile industry; Brewing industry; Building industry; Chemical industry; Coal; Confectionery industry; Cotton textiles; Electrical industries; Engineering products; Hosiery Industry; Iron and steel industry; Malting industry; New industries; Paper industry; Preserved food industry; Printing industry; Rayon industry; Service industries; Shipbuilding industry; Shipping industry; Silk industry; Staple industries; Synthetic industries; Textiles; War industries; Woolen trade

Industry, French, 76

Industry, German, 76

Internal transactions, 1

International equilibrium, theory of, 9–26; and causal relationship between current and capital balances, 5; and theory of transfers, 7; need for organic theory of, discussed, 27–40; case studies of, 34–40

International transactions, distinguished from internal transactions, 1–3

Investments, domestic, effect of, on British industry, 264–65, 266, 268; and foreign loans, 283–5

Investments, overseas, 128 ff., 136–37, 160–61, 172, 186–87, 189, 266; changes in, after first World War, 43; causes of relative lag in, 61–62; decline of, after first World War, 138–44; long-term lending, 161–64, 188–95; short-term lending, 166, 173–74; income from (1929–38), 187; government controls of, 188 ff.; after

1929–32 depression, 262–63; and competitive industries, 264; post-war world, discussed, 269, 276 ff.; in competition with domestic investment, 283–5; and governmental participation, 285 ff.; see also Capital exports

Iran, see Persia

Irish Free State, 73n, 132n, 210, 212, 224 ff., 229n; exports of, to Britain (1929–31), 240

Iron and Steel Federation, British, 91–92

Iron and steel industry, 65 ff., 71, 73, 75 f., 80, 86, 88–92, 158, 260, 263, 265n; exports of, 88, 90; production of, 88–89, 92; and foreign competition, 89–90; conditions affecting industry, 89, 90; reorganization and controls applied to industry, 90–92

Italy, 96n, 97, 112, 120, 210, 231 f., 246, 249; British trade balances with (1913–29), 237 f.

Iversen, Carl, 7

Japan, 71, 74n, 86, 94 ff., 102 f., 120 f., 215n, 228, 232 ff., 249, 280; British trade balances with (1913–29), 237 f., 243

Java, 230, 246

Jevons, W. S., 73n

Keynes, John M., 7n, 14n, 21n, 23n, 58, 149n, 155n, 163, 165

Kindersley, Sir Robert, 161 f., 163n, 164, 190, 193n, 194n, 221n, 222, 247n

Labor, demands of, 78; conservatism of, 82, 258n; productivity of, 83; participation of, in management, 273

Latin America, 97, 187, 210, 276; effect of British loans to, 264

Lithuania, 213

Loans, foreign, see Investments

Luxuries, demand for, and British industry, 74

Machinery, exports of, 133–34

Machlup, Fritz, 14n

Malaya, 99n, 225 f., 229n, 232 f., 253; trade balance of (1937), 248–49

Malting industry, 260n

Mantoux, Paul. 237n

Manufactured goods, imports of, 135 f.

Market control, of iron and steel, 91

Metropolitan-Vickers, 79

Money, cheap, effect of new British policy of, 263, 268

Money, hot, effect of, 44-46

Munich crisis, 198

Nationalism, economic, 60-62, 241

Netherlands, 74n, 98, 217, 227, 231 ff., 246; British imports from, 238

New industries, 69-70, 77, 81, 105-21, 133, 139, 259-60, 261 f.; growth of, 105-107; and foreign competition, 107-109; in post-war period, discussed, 272; see also Automobile industry; Electrical industries; Rayon industry

New materials, post-war utilization of, discussed, 274-75, 278

New Zealand, 74n, 99n, 209 ff., 215, 225 ff., 229n, 233; British trade balance with (1913, 1929), 237-38; (1937), 248; exports of, to Britain (1929-31), 240

Northern Rhodesia, British trade balance with (1929-37), 245n

Norway, 210, 232, 247n

Ohlin, Berthil, 7, 21n, 23n

Ottawa agreements, 183, 212, 216n

Output control, 80 f.; of coal, 87-88; of iron and steel, 91

Overseas investments, see Investments

Paish, Sir George, 221n

Paper industry, 260n

Persia, 230, 246; trade balance of, with Britain, 242

Poland, 74n, 86, 232, 246

Pound, depreciation of, see Sterling

Preserved food industry, 260n

Price control, 81; of coal, 88

Price decline (1919-39), 43

Prices, British and American (1924-25), 170-71

Printing industry, 135 f., 260n

Radice, E. A., 137n

Raw materials, imports of, 135

Rayon industry, growth of, 120-21; and foreign competition, 121

Recession (1937-38), 268

Recovery, after 1929-32 depression, 262-68

Re-exports, British, average annual rate of growth of (1800-1929), 131

Reparations, German, 21n, 160; as case study of theory of international equilibrium, 34, 36-40

Research, industrial, 79

Rhodesia, 190, 248n

Robinson, Joan, 17n

Russia, see U.S.S.R.

Sales methods, British, in foreign trade, 79-80

Scandinavia, 211, 213, 215, 230; British imports from, 238

Schlote, Werner, 149

Self-government of industry, 91n

Service industries, 260

Shipbuilding industry, 65, 68, 75 f., 80 f., 86, 100-102, 260, 265n; and foreign competition, 100-101; conditions affecting industry, 101-102

Shipping industry, British, 101

Siam, 233n

Silk industry, 260; protection of, 108

Silverman, A. G., 150 f.

Slum clearance, 123 f.; post-war, 285

South Africa, 74n, 86, 94, 99n, 190, 197, 209 ff., 215, 224 ff., 228, 229n, 232 f., 248n, 253, 270; British trade balance with (1913, 1919), 237; (1929, 1938), 248

Soviet Russia, see U.S.S.R

Spain, 232

Stamp, Sir Josiah, 169

Standard of living, British, 83, 265-67

Staple industries, 65-72, 84-104, 133, 135, 259-60; effect of overproduction of (1919-39), 42-43; importance of, 65-66, 84; effect of war on, 71, 75; and foreign competition, 73 ff., 85-86, 91, 94-98, 99, 100-101, 102 f.; and depression, 73-74

Steel cartel, see Cartel, international steel

Sterling, in period 1924-31, 159, 165 ff., 170 ff., 174-78; fall of, 179, 263; effect of depreciation of, 181-83, 185; fluctuations in (1932-39), 195 ff.; value of, in post-war world, 288-89

Sterling bloc, 213-14

Straits Settlements, 74n; British trade balance with (1913, 1919), 237

Sweden, 74n, 210, 232, 246, 247n

Switzerland, 74n, 103n, 216n, 231 f., 246; British imports from, 238

Synthetic industries, in post-war period, 274-75, 278

Tariff, Australian, 245

Tariff, British, 61, 81, 107 f., 111-12, 113, 116, 120, 134 f., 136, 141, 179, 209, 211 f., 216, 245; effect of, on imports, 246; on economic recovery, 263, 268

Tariff, Canadian, 245

Tariff, Indian, 245

Tariffs, foreign, 242

Taussig, Frank W., 7, 23n

Taxes, effect of, on British industry, 76

Technology, new, and British industry, 72-73

Terms of trade, see Trade, terms of

Textiles, 265n; see also Cotton; Woolen trade

Trade, international, causes of relative lag in, 61-63

Trade, terms of, British, 144-57; indexes of, 144, 153; after second World War, 280-2

Trade agreement program, 246-47

Trade balance, and capital movements, 6-8

Trade balances, British, 127, 129, 158 ff., 170; (1932-35), 184; (1900-29), 236-39; (1929-38), 241 ff., 245; (1937), 247-52

Trade Facilities Act (1921), 162

Trade treaties of 1930's, British, 183 f.

Transfers, theory of, 7

Transportation, 260

Unemployment (1930-31), 242; (1919-39), 257-9, 260 ff., 265 ff.; in post-war period, 284 f.

Unemployment insurance, 83

United States, 29n, 46, 48 f., 71, 73 ff., 77, 95 ff., 99n, 102 f., 110 ff., 116n, 118, 121, 129, 133, 162, 167, 196 ff., 209, 213 ff., 217, 220n, 227 f., 230 ff., 246, 249n, 251, 275n, 277, 280; effect of increased financial power of, 48-49; and new industries, 74; as creditor, 139, 239; foreign investments of, 163, 166, 172; British trade balances with (1900-29), 236-39; (1929-31), 241; (after 1933) 242; British imports from, 240; balances of payments of, with Britain (1928, 1936, 1937), 252; trade balances of, with empire (1929-37), 253

U.S.S.R., 63, 86, 95, 210, 213 f., 216n, 230, 232, 247n, 251, 276 f., 280; British imports from (1929-31), 240

Viner, Jacob, 7, 10n, 34 f.

Wages, 82 f.; money and real, in post-war years, 138

Walker, Charles H., 20n

War debts, 196

War industries, 71

War loans, of U.S., 6

West Africa, 94, 99n

West Indies, 211

Western Europe, 209

White, Harry D., 7

Woolen trade, 67 f., 74, 102, 259; and foreign competition, 102; and home market, 102